Pitt Series in Policy and Institutional Studies

Pitt Series in Policy and Institutional Studies
Bert A. Rockman, Editor

Selected Titles

The Atlantic Alliance and the Middle East

Edited by
Joseph I. Coffey
Distinguished Service Professor Emeritus
of Public and International Affairs
University of Pittsburgh

and
Gianni Bonvicini
Director
Istituto Affari Internazionali
Rome

University of Pittsburgh Press

Published in Great Britain by The Macmillan Press Ltd

Published in the U.S.A. by the University of Pittsburgh Press, Pittsburgh, Pa. 15260

Printed in China

Library of Congress Cataloging-in-Publication Data
The Atlantic Alliance and the Middle East.

  (Pitt series in policy and institutional studies)
  Includes index.
  1. Middle East—Foreign relations—Europe.
2. Europe—Foreign relations—Middle East.   3. North
Atlantic Treaty Organization—Middle East.   I. Coffey,
Joseph I.   II. Bonvicini, Gianni.   III. Series.
DS63.2.E8A86   1989   327.4056   88-20605
ISBN 0–8229–1154–X

Contents

MAY 3 1991

Notes on the Contributors

Gianni Bonvicini is Director of the Istituto Affari Internazionali, Rome, and heads the European Studies Section of the Institute. He is also Editor of IAI's quarterly English language journal, *The International Spectator*, and is Visiting Professor of International Relations at the Johns Hopkins University, Bologna Centre. Dr Bonvicini has written and contributed to many books on European integration, including *The Prospects for European Integration* (with J. Sassoon, 1977), *Governing the Economy of Europe: Divergence and the Integrative Process* (editor, 1978), *The Foreign Policy of Europe: Autonomy or Dependency?* (editor, 1980) and *The Economy of the Common Market* (editor, 1980). He has also served as consultant on European affairs to the regional authority of Trento, Italy.

Joseph I. Coffey is Distinguished Service Professor Emeritus of Public and International Affairs and Senior Research Fellow in the Centre for International Studies at the University of Pittsburgh, and also holds the post of Visiting Professor of International Peace and Security Studies at Carnegie Mellon University. Prior to these appointments, he served as Chief, Office of National Security Studies, Bendix Aerospace Systems Division and as a Research Analyst in the Institute for Defense Analysis. As an officer in the United States Army, he held various command and staff assignments in Army Intelligence, Army Plans, in the Office of the Assistant Secretary of Defense and on the White House Staff. He has also served as consultant to a number of Federal Agencies on security related issues. Dr Coffey has authored or co-authored six books (including *Strategic Power and National Security* and *Arms Control and European Security*) and has published more than forty monographs or articles on strategy, deterrence, arms control and defence policy.

Anthony Cordesman has served in various capacities in the Office of the Secretary of Defense, the State Department, and the Department of Energy, analysing the military balance and strategic situations in both the Gulf region and the Near East. He has served as a US government official in Iran and has made numerous visits to the region, most recently as a Woodrow Wilson Fellow and as international policy editor of the *Armed Forces Journal International*. In that capacity, he also made extensive assessments of the military situation in Western Europe. His most recent book, *The Gulf and the Search for Strategic Stability* (1984), provides a comprehensive military and strategic analysis of the Persian Gulf and the Arabian Peninsula, assessing the internal security and stability of the Gulf nations and the impact of defence spending and Western and Soviet bloc arms sales in the region.

Richard W. Cottam is University Professor of Political Science at the University of Pittsburgh. He holds a BA from the University of Utah and an MA and PhD from Harvard University. Dr Cottam has written extensively on Middle Eastern topics, including *Nationalism in Iran* (1964, revised 1978), *Foreign Policy Motivation: A General Theory and Case Study of the British in Egypt* (1977), 'Nationalism in the Middle East' in *From Nationalism to Revolutionary Islam* (Said Amir Arjomand (ed.) (1984), and 'Iran in the American World View' in *The Middle East and Western Alliance*, ed. Steven Spiegel (1982). Dr Cottam has also held positions in the US Foreign Service and served as a consultant to the Department of State.

Maurizio Cremasco is Senior Researcher at the Istituto Affari Internazionali, Rome, and Professor at the Institute for Advanced International Studies in Florence. He holds a degree in Political Science from the University of Padova. Prior to assuming his current positions, Professor Cremasco served in the Chief Nuclear War Planning Office (NATO Command), as Commander, and on the Italian air force staff as the Chief Operational Intelligence Division. He retired as Brigadier General in 1978. Professor Cremasco has written several books, including *The Standardization of Armaments in NATO* (1978), *NATO's Southern Flank* (with S. Silvestri, 1980), and *Peace from Terror to Disarmament* (1983), as well as numerous publications concerning security in the Mediterranean; among them, 'East–West Relations and Security in the Mediterranean' and 'The Mediterranean, the Atlantic and the Indian Ocean: A Difficult Strategic Equation'.

Geoffrey Edwards is presently Assistant Director of Studies at the University of Southern California's School of International Relations, United Kingdom Program. Previously, he was with the Federal Trust for Education and Research, London. His publications on the subject include *The Defence of Western Europe* (co-authored with Ambassador Sir Bernard Burrows). Dr Edwards has also contributed to the Texas Study on *European Official Cooperation in the Arab-Israeli Conflict*, edited by David Allan. He is the co-author (with Hugh Arbuthnott) of *A Common Man's Guide to the Common Market*.

Reinhardt Rummel has been at the Stiftung Wissenschaft und Politik since 1972. He has been a visiting scholar at Harvard and has served as an officer to the EC in Brussels. His publications include: *European Political Cooperation*, which he co-edited. His latest work is *European–US Cooperation in the Third World*.

Preface

This book, like most, is the work of many hands. Along with the authors of the several chapters, who obviously had a major influence on the scope and direction of the study, those who helped to give it the shape it now has include Mme Francoise Paublant, currently Director of Information for the French Red Cross but at that time Assistant to the Director, International Security Studies Programme, University of Pittsburgh; Ms Mari Seaman, presently in charge of the Department of Agriculture's exchange programme with the USSR but then an intern in the Programme; and Mr James McGann, Programme Officer, the J. Howard Pew Freedom Trust. Additionally, Sir Bernard Burrows, erstwhile British Ambassador to the North Atlantic Treaty Organisation, made valuable suggestions, as did Professor Jacques Vandamme, University of Louvaine, President of the Trans European Policy Studies Association (TEPSA) and Dr Wolfgang Wessels, Director of the Institut fur Europaische Politik, Bonn. Though their contributions were of a different nature, credit must also be given to Mr Kenneth Ruby and Mr Brian Sahd, Research Assistants, to Ms Marion Recktenwald, of the University of Bonn, also an Intern, and to Ms Rosemary Anderson, Senior Secretary of the Programme, as well as to Ms Myriam van der Geyt, Administrative Assistant to the President of TEPSA.

But as we know, the hand can accomplish nothing unless the heart sustains it. Support in the form of encouragement came not only from Professor Vandamme but also from Dr Burkart Holzner, Director of the University Center for International Studies, University of Pittsburgh. Moreover, not only TEPSA and UCIS but also the J. Howard Pew Freedom Trust (through Mr McGann), the Rockefeller Foundation (via Dr John Stremlau, Acting Director of International Relations) and the NATO Information Service (in the person of Ms Elaine McDevitt, US Liaison Officer) gave more tangible aid.

For all this assistance we are grateful, because it made possible what we deem an important study. As indicated in the introductory chapter, the question whether, and if so, when and how, to respond to threats to Western interests arising outside the North Atlantic Treaty area is an old issue which has recently taken on new importance and greater urgency. As indicated in the final chapter, the answers given by members of the Atlantic Alliance, individually and collectively, will determine not only whether these interests can be safeguarded but also the consequences for NATO of different choices with respect to the means employed to do so. We hope that the conclusions we have reached and the recommendations we have made will be of assistance to those responsible for advising on, or making decisions with respect to, the maintenance of security outside NATO. If so, then both our purposes and those of our supporters will have been served.

JOSEPH I. COFFEY
University of Pittsburgh
GIANNI BONVICINI
Istituto Affari Internazionali

1 Out-of-Area Issues: A New Challenge to the Atlantic Alliance

Gianni Bonvicini

In recent years, crisis management outside the province of the Atlantic Alliance has ceased to be a theoretical and prospective problem. On the contrary, it is very real and topical, with much more complex implications than expected in its political, military and institutional aspects.

The concept of collective security acknowledged and applied within the NATO area has had little bearing on management of peripheral crises. In the absence of a clear institutional context within which to work out political and military responses to threats, protection of common interests has been left to chance or to the good will (and contingent interests) of the parties concerned.

The various forms taken by external threats (*coups d'état*, territorial fighting, civil wars, terrorism, economic boycotts, etc.) have called for modulated responses and *ad hoc* measures, and have made it even more difficult to extend the Western concept of collective security to the new situations that have emerged in areas other than those of traditional East–West confrontation. Accordingly, each government has given the response that it felt able to give, by means of political, economic and in some cases, military pressures, according to the circumstances. It is the last, and certainly most controversial aspect, that is of particular interest to us.

On the practical side, an outcome of that troubled period of huge crises is that some countries have had instruments for military intervention in the Middle East and, more generally, in crisis areas, for some years now. The most obvious aspect of these initiatives has been the formation of rapid deployment forces as the *longa manus* of a national will to deal directly with threats to the periphery of the Atlantic Alliance.

The presence of these structures and rapid intervention forces has

1

raised some very specific questions: how to define relations between these instruments and the Atlantic Alliance; when and in what situations to resort to their use; how to coordinate, with partners directly or indirectly involved, the use of these instruments. These are the basic problems to be dealt with by all countries involved in the out-of-area problem, but the Europeans are faced with the additional problem of defining the relation between out-of-area initiatives and pre-existent or *in fieri* European institutions: in particular, the EPC (European Political Cooperation) and the WEU (Western European Union), even if these are only partially competent in dealing with this kind of problem.

I   OUT-OF-AREA: A HISTORY WHICH STARTS WITH THE SIGNING OF THE NORTH ATLANTIC TREATY

The history of the interrelations between NATO and out-of-area issues is pretty well known. Under Article 6 of the North Atlantic Treaty, the Alliance boundaries are drawn at 'the Islands under the jurisdiction of any Party in the North Atlantic area north of the Tropic of Cancer'.

This geographical limitation was the result of strong United States pressure; the US did not want to be involved in European colonial conflicts. Furthermore, Americans were the 'champions' of democracy, freedom and human rights, since they had helped Europe to fight against Nazism and fascism. Finally, at the end of the Second World War America's most evident concern was to confront the emerging power and the threat of the Soviet Union. As Herrero de Minon points out in a recent NATO report, 'the line was established, therefore, to mark a distinction between Alliance territory on the one hand, and, on the other, national interests that did not fall automatically within the protection of the Alliance'.[1]

The intervening years brought many declarations about the interrelationship between Alliance interests and happenings 'out-of-area', the real impetus to change came with the Afghanistan crisis at the end of 1979. The Soviet invasion, moreover, followed the downfall of the Shah of Iran and the subsequent Islamic Revolution, and therefore contributed towards accelerating destabilisation in the area. The West was already concerned with its energy dependence on the Middle East and the Gulf by the repeated oil shocks; the increasing closeness of the Soviet Union to the sources of oil supply provided additional elements of trouble. Regional instability was then further intensified with the start of the Iran–Iraq war and the threats of a closure of the Strait of Hormuz. This combination of events forced the Alliance to devote more attention to the Middle East and to consider what kind of action the Allies might be obliged to take in order to protect their own interests.

The situation which emerged in the Middle East during the 1980s was a perfect example of the complexity of the new kinds of threats and challenges that Europeans and Americans had to face. These, in fact, included: a large and unmanagable number of local conflicts; the overlapping of political, economic and military factors in every crisis; the actual risk of reproducing the East–West confrontation in a less controllable context; the intermingling of East–West and North–South interests in a single region.

The Western allies, in addition, were particularly concerned with the possible repercussions on the NATO area of the deployment of US forces in the Gulf region. As a result, the Defense Planning Committee (DPC) in May 1981, took the initiative in attempting to define how out-of-area issues should be treated by members of the Alliance.

The first element was a clear recognition that national actions could serve Alliance purposes: 'Although the policies which nations adopt outside the NATO area are matters for national decision, the Allies have recognized that situations outside NATO's boundaries may . . . threaten the vital interests of the West and therefore have implications for the security of members of the Alliance'.[2]

The second concept was that of enlarging NATO consultations on out-of-area issues, with the aim of starting a process of coordination in the assessment of a threat and its implications and, if possible, in identifying common objectives for the West. These consultations are considered particularly important for those nations which are in practice able to deploy forces out-of-area and are willing to do so, in order to deter aggression and respond to other nations' requests for help. This last recommendation reflects the concept of the 'principal nations approach', which became famous in the Four Institutes 1981 Study on NATO.[3]

A final, important double concept was the need to consider the effect of such deployments on Alliance security and defence capabilities. Allies must consult in the appropriate NATO bodies both to maintain out of area deployments in support of the vital interests of all *and* to maintain the levels and standards of forces necessary for defence and deterrence in the NATO area.

The same communiqué recognised the prevalent role of the United States in bearing the military responsibility out-of-area, in that it favours a certain already emerging tendency towards what has been called American global unilateralism.

The above-mentioned points have been reconfirmed on several occasions, both at NATO's Committee and Ministerial Council level, but the most important elaboration was carried out by the NATO International Military Staff with a South–West Asia Impact Study in 1983. This study was based on four major considerations: events outside the treaty area can affect the common interests of the Allies as members of the Alliance; the importance of timely consultations on such events; the maintenance of sufficient military capabilities in the Treaty area to guarantee a credible defence posture; and finally, the need for Allies to facilitate the deployment of forces outside the Treaty area when they are in a position to do so.

II OUT-OF-AREA EXPERIENCES

In the extreme case in which Europeans and Americans decide to manage a peripheral crisis together, this leads to problems of coordination different from those wherein the Europeans limit themselves to playing the role of spectator. In fact, in the case of a multilateral initiative out-of-area, the directives of the various governments will have to coincide, as well as their general political aims – and all this under the pressure of a situation of international emergency.

Crisis handling calls for the ability to evaluate the threat, the possibility of foreseeing it to some extent and access to the greatest possible number of sources of information. Generally, there is not enough time during a crisis for complete information – a necessary condition for correct action. In fact, the crisis alters response times to an event and increases the difficulty of straightening out errors. Lastly, it causes shifts in the aims that a government or a group of states initially had in the area.

Coordination in crisis management, therefore, requires a series of preconditions making possible a positive conclusion:

1. The mandate given to a group of states must be clear and sufficiently broad, both in terms of means provided and implementation time.

2. *In loco* operations require very strong political support. Furthermore, this support must be continuous and must prevent rapid erosion of consensus.
3. An operation must have the support of the government of the host country involved or threatened.
4. The financial burden of the operation must be well distributed among the allied countries and generous enough to allow for freedom of action and a massive initial action.
5. The size of the military force must be commensurate with the type and foreseeable length of the threat.
6. The tasks of the (integrated) military commands must be clearly defined and must respond to unambiguous political objectives.

These are only a few of the guiding criteria which would allow for a reasonable response both to unexpected events and, above all, to crisis situations of a certain importance that seriously jeopardise Western interests in the peripheral area.

The difficulty of applying even the minimum criteria mentioned above must be understood in the light of the out-of-area experiences up to now in the Middle East. If we take into consideration some of the rare cases of multilateral cooperation in recent years (for example, the multinational operation in Lebanon), limiting ourselves to the purely operational aspects, it is easy to realise that the major drawbacks to lasting success derive from:

1. insufficient forces in the field for the tasks assigned them;
2. gradual changes in the political reasons for intervention and the relative tasks assigned;
3. paucity of coordination among military commands;
4. insufficient exchange of information;
5. collapse of the support of the host country;
6. lack of clear political instructions.

Almost none of the criteria listed earlier as being necessary for success has been respected. The same kind of reasoning can be extended to more recent cases, such as management of the *Achille Lauro* affair. The most evident deficiency is the practical impossibility of effectively coordinating out-of-area operations (the only exception being the multinational peace-keeping force in the Sinai). Despite attempts made up until now, coordination has escaped any precise regulation and has been almost exclusively left up to the goodwill and interests of the parties in question. Each country personally manages its own special intervention forces on the basis of different criteria, thus making operational integration difficult. On the other hand, in common out-of-area action, there is a vital need to create a unified command structure able to function as an integrated and efficient military unit. Efficiency of operation also calls for a considerable degree of harmony among the various parts, constant and reliable communication and the operational compatibility of the military forces in the field.

Possible Threats and Military Responses

One of the main difficulties encountered in the management of crises in the Middle East is the virtual impossibility of defining the nature of the threat. In fact, both with regard to extension (global, regional or local) and with regard to implications (economic, political or military), the critical criteria and perceptions of Western governments are profoundly different. The web of political, religious, nationalistic, *irredentist* and economic factors relating to the Middle Eastern situation is such as to render problematic both identification of the threat and, naturally, formulation of an appropriate response (see Chapter 2).

Application of labels such as 'high intensity threat' or 'low intensity threat' is rather risky and responses to crises may well depend on other circumstances such as the urgency of the problem to be solved, the national perception of it or the concrete possibility of reaching a positive result. In other words, the decision to resort to a military solution does not necessarily depend on the possible extension of the problem (for example, to other parts of the globe) nor on its meaning (for example, military), but rather to the national perception of a vital interest to be defended or the conviction of being in possession of the means to rapidly solve the problem unilaterally. Therefore, analysis of concrete intervention possibilities in the Middle East is complicated by various factors and circumstances that are difficult to classify in a very rigid manner.

Furthermore, it must also be observed that, even if threat perception was homogeneous on several occasions, choice of instruments for intervention was not. It does not follow therefore that similar perceptions result in the same kind of reaction on the part of the countries in question.

Finally, one of the reasons that can lead to the decision to resort to the use of the military instrument seems closely linked to the interrelationship between the scope of the military instrument available and foreseeable political effects. In other words, the use of force is closely tied to predictions of the possible success of the operation. The use of limited forces may thus be eschewed unless both the objective itself and the time of intervention are limited, as otherwise these may not achieve significant political results.

This means that, first of all, one must have a rather precise idea of the military forces being fielded and the concrete possibilities of their integration (see Chapter 3). Of all Western countries, only the United States, France, Great Britain, Italy and Turkey have set up rapid intervention forces or have used the military instrument for actions in the Middle East. Other countries have at best supported them or engaged in indirect intervention in the area.

This military capacity has been used in different ways in recent history depending on the kind of conflict situation:[4]

1. law and order enforcement operations;
2. dissuasion operations;
3. multilateral and multinational buffer operations;
4. coercive operations;
5. anti-terrorist operations.

There is nothing to rule out the possibility that the range of actions may increase and diversify in extent and roles in the future. But it is clear that intervention forces must be of appropriate dimensions. Factors such as rapidity, mobility and surprise may not be sufficient to cope with extensive crises.

It may be said, moreover, on the basis of the peace-keeping experience accumulated up until now, that the use of force can – within the bounds and in the forms employed to date – give negative results in the long run. The fundamental problem is that actions of that kind have strong political motivations and since the political reasons behind the use of force are liable to change with time and with the development of the situation, the military instrument can at a certain point prove inadequate or even counter-productive in solving the crisis.

The Role of Western Governments and Political Factors in Out-of-Area Actions

Naturally, the problem of organisational coordination cannot be explained without referring to the political context which made it possible. Behind the practical problems implicit in an out-of-area action, there is the question of the political factors conditioning it. These factors work at three levels: national, multilateral, and institutionalised international.

1. The National Context

It is obvious that the will of a nation to take on a problem outside of the NATO area is required to give rise to an action. In the Four Institutes' report on Western security, mention is made of a 'principal nation's approach', meaning that only those nations in a position to take on the political and military risk of a specific action can be taken into consideration.[5] Past experience indicates that, at least for the Middle East, the main actors are the USA, the UK, France, Italy and to a lesser extent Turkey. (It would be interesting to study what kind of role neighbouring countries such as Greece and Spain can play and to explore the limits of the 'rearguard' role assumed by the German Federal Republic which has sometimes, in the fight against terrorism, stepped into the forefront.)

However, the fact that decisions concerning out-of-area matters are taken mainly in the national sphere points to the difficulties that coordination of an action of this kind may encounter. Each government bases its policy on strictly national strategic and military security considerations and its reactions to external threats are dictated by defence of individual rather than common interests. This makes both the means and the modalities of out-of-area intervention hardly comparable (see Chapter 4).

2. The MultiLateral Factor

Despite objective difficulties in surpassing the national level, there is a kind of conditioned reflex in favour of and some political convenience in undertaking certain actions in a multilateral context (see Chapter 4). This is true, above all, for operations with strong popular backing such as buffer forces or peace-keeping forces in crisis areas. Cooperation becomes more difficult in strictly military actions or in the case of incidents due to terrorist acts.

Nevertheless, even in the event of political consensus to pursue a common end, cooperation among countries can deteriorate. The principal factors determining the survival (or break-up) of consensus are the following:

1. length in time of the operation. The longer it is, the more difficult cooperation becomes;
2. stability of the causes requiring the action. If they change, the interest in collaboration vanishes;
3. a constant cost/benefit ratio for each party concerned;
4. achievement of a few concrete successes in terms of field operations.

Obviously, calculations relative to multilateral cooperation also depend on the sharing of some fundamental ideological values and the concrete possibility of agreeing on political strategies with regard to specific problems. But these factors generally play a role in the initial phases and are later overcome by the concrete effects of the action being carried out.

3. The Institutionalised International Factor

The role in decision-making of international institutions and agencies to which countries interested in the out-of-area action belong is much more ambiguous. NATO, lacking authority in the area, European Political Cooperation (EPC), lacking authority in the matter (politico-military and security) and the Western European Union (WEU), lacking any real power and means, are essentially additional political covers for out-of-area intervention (see Chapter 6).

Nevertheless, they can, at least indirectly, be operationally involved in actions:

1. for NATO, the main problem is use of its bases for operations. Secondarily it could hypothetically also offer information and communications support:
2. for the EPC, the main supportive instrument is constituted by common declarations. Nevertheless, in the past, economic instruments have sometimes been resorted to (sanctions, for example) in support of actions independently carried out by an EEC member state.

In general, therefore, the problem of political coordination of these three factors represents a conditioning element for all out-of-area actions. Without it, integrated action at a political-operational level among responsible nations is inconceivable.

Public Opinion and Out-of-Area Military Actions

Besides the role of the government and, more generally, that of common interest among nations, there is another all-important element and that is public opinion. In Western democratic societies, public opinion often plays a decisive role in sectors such as foreign policy which traditionally escaped its control. Governments can deal with crisis situations even without widespread consensus, but that is true only in very exceptional cases of extreme danger.

Political, parliamentary and party elites are actually much more sensitive to the mood of public opinion. In justifying the decision to take actions outside of national territory, government explanations must be particularly convincing. From experience acquired in the past, some motivations which can create initial consensus become evident:

1. defence of a violated national interest;
2. risk of serious negative effects on the national economy and society;
3. the desire to foster a pacification process;
4. assistance to a friendly government in a very dangerous situation;
5. defence of a fundamental ideological value such as liberty and democracy.

Naturally, and above all, when defence of concrete national interests is invoked, the political motivations of each country involved may diverge radically and not find many points of intersection allowing for actual coordination among partners, either at a political or at an operational level. Common action is easier when it comes to defending a more abstract interest such as pacification, defence of the weak or the restoration of democracy and liberty.

But in the latter case, much more so than in the former, the factors of time, danger and financial burden of the operation take on importance. A positive initial attitude in public opinion can rapdily turn into open hostility to actions which cause death in the family or give the perception of failure. Even if governments can influence public opinion with new arguments, resistance to strong pressures exerted by citizens and the mass media diminishes with time.

Finally, perceptions of interests and risks out-of-area vary greatly from country to country, depending on the culture, the ties with the Third World and other factors peculiar to each society. Especially between Europeans and Americans, there is the risk that perceptions are almost never the same (see Chapter 5).

Divergent American and European Interests

In the process of the definition of an updated concept of collective security out-of-area, one of the basic elements is clearly constituted by the convergence of Western interests. The Middle East particularly has proven to be a hard point for combining American and European interests in a homogeneous way. In this respect, the history of the Alliance in the Middle East is not a successful history. The many episodes of these last years have stressed the differences more than the agreements between the two sides of the Atlantic, in fact, the common concept of European security which has started to emerge is largely based on a growing divergence of interests with the US.[7]

The Middle East is particularly relevant for the US because of the complex nature of its interests. The first element of this complexity is due to the growing closeness of the Soviet Union, after the invasion of Afghanistan, to the vital Western strategic energy sources. But apart from this aspect of the East–West confrontation in the region, other elements are relevant to the US presence: for example, the strategic linkage with Israel; the variety of economic interests; the importance of some channels and straits; the need to maintain some stability in key countries (such as Egypt and Saudi Arabia); the challenge to Western values of Islamic fundamentalism.

Most of these concerns are shared by the European allies. Nevertheless, they increasingly feel the need for a more autonomous presence, based on a different political and strategic perception of the threat and on a more frequent use of economic and diplomatic means for stabilising the region.

More generally, the difficulty of cooperation between Europeans and Americans in the Middle East is just one aspect of the widening gap between the two sides of the Atlantic. The main reason lies in the European attempt to introduce a more independent concept of security.

It is in itself evident that security concerns have increasingly become, among other issues, one of the top priorities for European governments. What is far less clear is the European willingness and capability both to transform that issue into a homogeneous and actual security policy and to set up a credible common mechanism to deal with it.

As far as growing European interest in security issues is concerned, some of the major reasons have already been pointed out several times: long-lasting divergences with the US affecting the whole range of common policies (economic, monetary, military, international, etc.) and a parallel, subsequent and growing perception of a European 'specificity' in the solution to be given to international crises and problems (for instance, *detente* policy, Central America and the Strategic Defense Initiative (SDI).

It is mainly in the Mediterranean and in the Middle East that Europeans and Americans have come up against the greatest obstacle to coordinating a common action. The very first signs of the reluctance go back to 1973, to the time of the oil crisis and the start of the difficult but meaningful Euro–Arab dialogue.

Distances between the Allies have grown with the Venice Declaration and subsequent initiatives in the Middle East. The same four European countries' participation in the Sinai peace-keeping force, in support of the American presence, has been publicly kept separated from the Camp David peace process.[8] More generally, Europeans have tried to underline their own desire for an autonomous role in the area and to avoid any overlapping between the concept of East–West confrontation, in which NATO has strict competence, and other issues, both global or regional, having at least an open chance for alternative interpretation in terms of threats and possible responses to be given.

From a strategic viewpoint, Europeans have therefore enlarged their concerns from the Soviet threat to Western Europe to other kinds of threats in neighbouring areas such as the Middle East and the Persian Gulf. Under the pressure of the growing number of crises arising in those regions, some European countries have adapted both their military doctrines and structures of force. But the real questions still remain the availability of national military forces for operations in the Middle East; their effectiveness and the credibility of policies calling for their employment; and it is those questions that we will attempt to answer in this study.

III THE MIDDLE EAST AND THE OUT-OF-AREA ISSUE

Experience in recent years in the Middle East, the area in which most crisis situations have cropped up, damaging Western interests and sometimes requiring military (as well as political and economic) responses, has underlined the fact that the West lacks conceptual and practical instruments with which to deal with emergency circumstances with an acceptable degree of cohesion. In fact, the trend that seems to be emerging from this experience is that the more serious the crisis, and the more experience in cooperation grows, the less cooperation there is; from the MFO (Multinational Force and Observers) in the Sinai, the MNF (Multinational Force) in Lebanon, the Task Force for the neutralisation of mines in the Red Sea, to the *Achille Lauro* hijacking (not to speak of the American strike on Libya), the capacity for joint military intervention and application of a homogeneous security concept has rapidly diminished.

This factor requires a deep reconsideration of the ways in which the Western Allies deal with regional security issues. As past experience has taught us, the major focus in the debate among Allies for the forthcoming years will remain the strategic situation in the Middle East and the use of force to match the threats arising there. Our analysis, therefore, will limit itself to these aspects, the Middle East and the recourse to military means, with the objective of describing not only their availability and credibility, but also the limits on, and alternatives to, their use.

In carrying out this analysis, we have decided to touch in turn on various points directly or indirectly linked to it, then to see how our findings might apply in future contingencies and finally to make some suggestions for improving the situation.

The first task is that of attempting, by means of a fresh analysis of the Middle Eastern environment, to draw a picture of the level of conflicts in the region, with particular reference to political interactions and the factors underlying them; the ways in which they threaten Western interests; the interplay of changing alliances on the stability of the area, the effects of manoeuvres by external actors, notably the US and the USSR, and the types of threats more likely to arise in the future (see Chapter 2).

A second task is that of reviewing the incentives and constraints on the use of force, adapted to the circumstances in the Middle East. But more importantly, our study also points out the Western military capabilities and the forces available for deployment to the Middle East. Particular attention is paid to the forces of the United States, Italy, France, Great Britain and Turkey and to their balance both in that area and in Western Europe (see Chapter 3).

Chapter 4 deals with the national positions on the out-of-area question, describing the attitudes of the principal governments concerned, their views with respect to the circumstances under which force should be used, and the types of responses which seem appropriate to the various types of threats. This chapter also describes, as do those subsequent to it, national responses to past crises and the ways in which these responses were (or were not) congruent, consistent and continuing.

Public perspectives on threats to security arising from the Middle East is another important factor. It is, in fact, essential that Western governments know how public opinion and political elites would react to the use of force, both before and during its application and incorporate this element in their decision processes (see Chapter 5).

Finally, any Western out-of-area initiative needs a certain level of coordination between Europeans and Americans at the various possible levels, military, political and economic. This implies an overview of the direct or indirect role played by existing organisations such as NATO, the Western European Union, European Political Cooperation and the EC in the formulation of responses to threats from the Middle East and of the utility of *ad hoc* instruments for coordinating policy and directing operations in the area (see Chapter 6).

All this effort is meant to help us try to define the Western interests in the Middle East, the possible ways of combining them together for common actions and the prescriptions for the future drawn by the lessons from the past. More particularly, what is relevant to us (and this is reflected in Chapter 7) is to be able to judge the effects of Western military actions in the Middle East both on the Atlantic Alliance and, more generally, on Western cohesion. (In fact, one of the less clear points concerning out-of-area crises is the role, direct or indirect, that NATO can play and the ways in which Europeans and Americans perceive that role.)

Such a judgement must, however, be based on specific assessments of Western interests and Western responses, as well as on broad conclusions about their nature; it is for this reason that we examined past cases where force was used, including two where naval units were used to protect access to oil, the deployment of the MNF in Lebanon and the bombing of Libya. However, the past is not a perfect guide to the future, which is, as Heraclitus pointed out more than two thousand years ago, necessarily different; thus we planned to refine our judgements by an inquiry into contingencies which might arise.

Even if the cases envisaged are limited to those likely to require the employment of the military instrument, 'their name is legion'. After a careful examination of both past experiences and current trends, we developed a number of criteria for choosing the 'instances' to be examined: their (admittedly subjective) probability, the kinds of demands they would place upon Western military forces, the extent to which they could give rise to differences arming the Allies, the lessons that could be learned concerning cooperation and coordination, and the degree to which they would impact upon the security of the Alliance. After constructing a number of 'scenarios' which satisfied to some degree all of these criteria we selected three: internal strife in a Middle Eastern country of crucial importance to the West, a local conflict having a major impact on the regional balance and, finally, an Israeli–Syrian clash with the direct involvement of the superpowers. (At the beginning of our research project there were four, including an American strike on a Middle East country in retaliation for some terroristic activity but events progressed too quickly, so that we were obliged to change that scenario into a case study, the bombing of Libya.)

We hope that these will remain theoretical scenarios and that the Libyan affair will remain an isolated one. Our general aim is, in fact, that of underlining the high risk and unpredictable consequences of military intervention, in the light of the many difficulties encountered in the past and the necessity for determining a clear rationale for the use of force. If that can be done, the military instrument can take its place alongside the diplomatic, political and economic ones; if it cannot, then we may misuse that instrument, to the detriment both of Western interests and of the cohesion and security of the Atlantic Alliance.

Notes

1. North Atlantic Assembly, Political Committee, *Interim Report of the Sub-Committee on Out-of-Area Security Challenges to the Alliance*. Rapporteur, Herrero de Minon, October 1985, p. 2.
2. *NATO Communiqué, 1981* (Brussels: NATO Information Service, 1981), p. 17.
3. Karl Kaiser, Winston Lord, Thierry de Montbrial, David Watt, *Western Security: What Has Changed, What Should be Done?* (London: Royal Institute of International Affairs, 1981).
4. Richard W. Nelson, 'Multinational Peacekeeping in the Middle East and the United Nations Model', *International Affairs*, Vol. 61, No. 1, Winter, 1984/85.
5. Kaiser, Lord, de Montbrial, Watt, *Western Security: What Has Changed, What Should be Done?*, op. cit. (see note 2).
6. Nelson, 'Multinational Peacekeeping in the Middle East and the United National Model', op. cit. (see note 3).

7. R. Dahrendorf and T. Sorenson, *A Widening Atlantic? Domestic Change and Foreign Policy* (New York: Council on Foreign Relations, 1986).
8. A. Pijpers, 'European Entry into the Multinational Sinai Force and Observers', *The International Spectator*, No. 1, 1984, pp. 34–41.

2 Levels of Conflict in the Middle East
Richard W. Cottam

Conflict in the Middle East is best viewed as a web of intersecting conflicts linking the international system, state systems and a plethora of intra-state systems. As such, it is typical of conflict in any extended area. The tendency of both observers and participants is to view conflict at the level of primary national interest concern. Thus the American or European observer is likely to see conflict in the Middle East primarily as it affects political and economic questions at the international system level and as it affects the security of the Jewish people in the area. Questions concerning the cold war, oil flow and the Arab–Israeli conflict will, for them, give definition to conflict in the area. Critical socio-political movements such as that of resurgent Islam typically will be viewed in terms of their impact on the primary foci of concern. When resurgent Islam is useful for the achievement of a major objective, as for example containing the Soviets in Afghanistan, it will be supported. But when it is seen as damaging to objectives, as for example in threatening to destabilise friendly regimes, it will be opposed. For many Iranians and Arabs, in contrast, the fortunes of resurgent Islam will be of consuming concern and for them will give definition to conflict in the area.

The purpose of this chapter is to tease out the primary patterns of conflict at each of the levels of conflict and to describe the interactions of these patterns with those developing at each of the other levels of conflict. It is important to begin with conflict at the social level in order to place the interactions in a perspective that is fundamental and too often missing in American and European analyses.

I THE INTRA-STATE LEVEL OF CONFLICT

The Middle East is an area that has been undergoing change for the past century at an accelerating tempo. Even the most basic social norms have been challenged as has the authority structure in every section of the region. Intense conflict inevitably has been a characteristic feature as traditional ruling groups struggle to survive and various competing groups seek to replace them. The resulting instability and uncertainty, in turn affects the relations of regional regimes with one another and the relations of external powers both with regional regimes and with each other. No factor is more important in giving form to the conflict patterns in the area than that of the force of rapid change, and no factor is less well understood.

In this chapter only two politically significant aspects of revolutionary change will be considered: (1) the growth in the percentage of the population that is or is predisposed to become politically participant and (2) a shift in the politically relevant community to which individuals granted a primary intensity loyalty. A century ago, the vast majority of Middle Easterners were politically acquiescent. The thought that they should play a role, however indirect, in the decision-making process simply did not occur. Their primary community identity focus tended to be the extended family or clan. Today in many parts of the Middle East the level of political participation is approaching that of the Western democracies. And primary community identification tends to be with an ethnic, a national or sectarian community. Change at this rate and in these dimensions, in turn, has compelled radical adjustments in terms of composition of the governing elite, governmental and social institutions and prevailing norms. It follows that the primary patterns of conflict at the intra-state level reflect differing strategies of competing elites, for adjusting to change in these two dimensions.

Historical Development

Political leaders who looked with favour on the change process and whose various strategies were all designed to advance the rate of change appeared in the first stages of change. They tended at this time to be attracted to Western political norms including both an attachment to enlightenment values and to the goals of independence and dignity for their national communities. Since the commercial and political impact of the West was a major catalytic force for change, it is not surprising that the West was looked to as a model to be emulated. The institutions they favoured were, therefore, those of a parliamentary democracy. In these early days, the pro-change leaders assumed that the Western democracies would give them sympathetic support in both their aspirations for broad participation in the form of liberal democracy and for real, not simply formal, independence for the national community. Movements associated with these goals appeared in the nineteenth and early twentieth centuries in Turkey, Egypt, Iran and the Arabs of West Asia.[1]

The task of gaining real control over societies in which the vast majority of peoples had yet to be touched by the change process, and who were therefore part of the traditional system, was a formidable one. Not surprisingly none of the movements in the early stage of change was successful for long in achieving and maintaining control. The modernising elites had expected a difficult struggle with the traditional governing elites they sought to displace. What they had not expected, however, was that the representatives of the Western democracies in the Middle East would side with their traditional foes. But the change process, by definition a highly destabilising one, led to the kind of chaos that representatives of the imperial powers feared would lead to loss of control and to confrontation with their imperial rivals. A pattern took form in this first stage that has persisted for several generations and that is one of the major factors affecting the current situation: even though contact with the West was catalytic in inaugurating the change process in the Middle East, and even though pro-change elites accepted Western European societies as a developmental model, the representatives of European powers tended to align with traditional elites in social conflict. This led to disillusion, bitterness and also to the weakening of liberal nationalists within the pro-change elite.

The truly lasting effect of this early experience in determining patterns of conflict, however, is best seen in terms of its meaning for nationalist legitimacy of Middle Eastern leaders. Those early leaders, advancing the causes of the dignity and independence of their national communities, came to be seen as the truly legitimate spokesmen for national aspirations. Their losing struggle with Western imperialism was viewed as heroic. The imperialists came to be seen as devious, cynical and little interested in supporting abroad the liberal nationalism they seemed to value at home. The imperial response, in other words, was seen as essentially contemptuous. Arabs or Iranians, usually drawn from the traditional elite, who agreed to a cooperative relationship with imperial powers were viewed by those seeking change as at best unprincipled stooges, at worst as traitors. The tendency thus to judge Arab or Iranian leaders who have close, friendly and cooperative relationships with the West persists to this day and is an essential key for understanding conflict patterns in the area.

Representatives of the Western democracies in the Arab and Iranian Middle East rarely recognised this anti-imperial world view and the intensity with which it was held by the nationalists in the area and in particular by the nationalistic intelligentsia. In contrast, they tended to see their own role as civilising and tutorial, helping the local populations to 'develop' and to 'modernise'. In this view, the cooperating elites were 'moderate' and 'responsible' gentlemen who shared with the Westerners a dedication to orderly development. Their opponents were not dedicated nationalists, as they claimed to be, but rather self-serving, opportunistic agitators who played on the fears and desires of untutored and uncomprehending masses.[2] Whether directly and consciously or not, these agitating leaders served the imperial interests of the great external rival powers, either German, Imperial or Nazi, or Russian, Tsarist or Bolshevik.

The competing world views are presented purposefully in their stereotypical form because they are to this day responsible for much mutual misunderstanding. Qaddafi, Assad and Khomeini are viewed by many in the West in the same agitating mould as were their early and mid-twentieth-century predecessors. But for many nationalistic or religious Arabs and Iranians they are the leaders with the greatest claims to legitimacy. King Hossein, Anwar Sadat and King Hassan are clear examples of 'moderate' and 'responsible' leaders for these same Westerners. But for nationalistic Arabs and Iranians, they are to one degree or another stooges of Western imperialism.

However, these world views are better seen as ideal typical referrents than as models of functioning world views. As the change process continued the relevance of early dichotomies, such as those between modernising or traditional societies, began to fade. Conflict at the intra-state level increasingly occurred between groups which in earlier years had jointly supported great nationalist leaders. This conflict did not usually have an ideological focus. Early nationalist leaders did tend to favour secularism, liberalism and a social democratic model. But their pre-eminence apexed in the middle stage. Names such as Zaghlul, Musaddiq, Aflaq, Suleiman Nabulsi, Rashid Ali al-Gaylani typify this period. Their successors were more inclined to be secular nationalist authoritarians who favoured a statist model much as did Ataturk in Turkey at a similar stage in the change process there. Nasser and the authoritarian Baathist leaders of Syria and Iraq typify this period. But this change was as much a consequence of the defeat of the liberal element by external powers and their local allies as of any purely domestic factor.

Conflict between more doctrinaire Marxists, especially those allied with the Soviet Union, and change oriented nationalist leaders is somewhat more serious. In South Yemen and in Iraq it has been of major importance as it was following the failed CIA sponsored coup in Syria in 1957 and also briefly in the Sudan in 1971. But generally in the area Marxists have not been sufficiently successful in gaining a popular foothold to pose a serious challenge. Soviet policy has reflected this situation closely and has tended to ally with more broadly based leaders than to rely on local pro-Soviet Marxists.[3]

Conflict and Alliance Patterns

A conflict among change-oriented leaders that is sufficiently serious to offer regional opportunities to external competitors is primarily that between leaders who identify with competing national communities. There are two major variants in this category, one being the conflict between pan-Arab nationalism and 'state nationalism' and the other that between state nationalism and ethnic communities that are minorities in established states. The first variant was a direct consequence of European intervention in Arab affairs following the First World War. Proponents of the Arab nation envisioned a great Arab nation state that would embrace all or most of the Arabic speaking world. There were strong parochial identities even among sections of the population that were pro-change and participant. Arab nationalists therefore had many internal obstacles to overcome before achieving their objective. European policy added enormously to their difficulties. Following the First World War much of the Arabic speaking population was divided into arbitrarily-constructed political communities by the Europeans and centrifugal, parochial tendencies were encouraged, most explicitly so by the French. Over time, as vested interests developed within these artificial entities, identity with the community embraced by the state began to develop. For some this identity became sufficiently intense to lead to what is commonly referred to as 'state nationalism', which was co-equal with or even more intense than the identity with a pan-Arab nation. Since most state nationalists continued to identify as well with the broader Arab community they and pan-Arab nationalists tended to view many external threats to the Arab world similarly. But conflicts inevitably developed among rival state interests that could become serious enough to persuade competing leaders to seek alliances with external powers. Rivalry for influence in Arab affairs also followed inevitably, with competing leaders able to draw on their state based communities for support. When this occurred each of the competitors would claim to be the repository of true Arab nationalist legitimacy. Much of the mystery of inter-Arab political rivalry can be explained by this factor.

The case of Egypt is somewhat different. Early nationalism in Egypt from the time of Arabi Pasha in the 1870s through Saad Zaghlul's leadership in the 1920s was unambiguously Egyptian. But in the 1930s the sense of some identity also as Arab became more evident as did an identity with the broader Islamic community.[4] It is doubtful that identity as Arab approached in intensity identity as Egyptian for more than a small percentage of the population. But identity as Arab was sufficiently intense to sustain the bid Gamal Abdul Nasser was to make for pre-eminence among Arab leaders. Egyptian leaders in the Nasser era behaved very much as did other state nationalists who had a deep attraction to the pan-Arab dream. But the support Sadat was to receive when he broke ranks with other Arab regimes, even those thought of as 'moderate' and 'responsible', in making peace with Israel suggests a modal Egyptian attachment to the Arab community that is lower in intensity than that of most other Arabic speaking populations. There were Egyptians who shared the view of pan-Arab nationalists that Sadat had followed a treasonous path. But clearly they were a minority.[5]

A second variant in competing national communities arises from the demand of minority ethnic and sectarian groups for independence or at least for substantial autonomy. There are two major patterns to this type of conflict. The first occurs when the majority group is generally a good deal farther along the change process than is the minority community. Examples of such minorites in the Middle East are the Kurds, the Baluchi, the Turkoman, the Druze, the Alawis and the Shia of Lebanon. In the early stages of change, nationalist leaders of the majority attempt to coopt progressive leaders of the minority community and are often successful in doing so. The minority leader is susceptible to the appeal of influence exercised at the national level. However, as the change process continues a counter elite will appear in the minority community arguing a case of economic, social and political deprivation and calling for either autonomy or independence from the majority community dominated state.

When this point is reached advocates of autonomy/independence for the smaller community will be opportunistic in their choice of allies – external and internal. The external alliance preference will be dictated by the exigencies of the international environment and is unlikely to be instructed seriously by ideological preference. Internally the alliance is likely to be with opposition elements within the larger community who wish to overturn the government and are willing to make major concessions to the minority leaders in return for their support. A classic example of this pattern was the alliance of Kurds with competing factions of the Ba'athist military of Iraq from 1963–8. At the end of the period the Kurds had achieved, at least on paper, a most liberal autonomy agreement from the victorious so-calld Takriti faction of the Ba'ath.[6] But this did not inhibit them from making an alliance with an Iranian-American-Israeli coalition five years later which appeared to offer some prospect for real independence.

When the smaller community is farther along in the change process than the majority community, a sharply different pattern from the above is likely to develop. In this situation, the leaders of the minority community tend to view the majority community as culturally inferior and will have little interest in integrating with it. Indeed they are likely to see the developing nationalism in the majority community as seriously threatening, possibly even with a genocidal potential. Alliance preferences for the minority community leaders therefore are likely to be with traditional or conservative elites which are less inclined to base their control on nationalistic appeals. The minority community may also seek to maintain some external control in the area and the preference among external allies is clearly for those whose policy favours stabilising the political situation in the area.

In the Middle East the only minority in this category that can aspire seriously to major autonomy/independence is the Maronite Christian community located largely in Lebanon. There are of course Maronites who occupy leadership positions in the camps of Arab nationalism and in Marxist movements. But the general pattern holds and both for the traditional zoama, or leaders, and such populist organisations as the Phalange.[7]

Other Middle Eastern minorities in this category are too small in number or too scattered to aspire seriously even to limited autonomy. At the turn of the century the Armenians and the Greeks in Anatolia fell into this category and their experience with the Turks illustrated fully the exceptional difficulty of integration for high achieving minorities. By the end of the first quarter of the century, any aspirations for autonomy/independence were eliminated through a genocidal struggle or population transfers. Other minorities that today fall into this category are Jews, Assyrians Copts, Baha'is and Zoroastrians. Even though these minorities cannot aspire to autonomy, the alliance patterns suggested above have held. In Iran Jews, Christians, Baha'is and Zoroastrians tended to be more comfortable in the non-nationalist government of Mohammad Reza Shah than they had been in the liberal, chaotic and intensely nationalistic regime of Mohammad Musaddiq. In Egypt, Copts tended to prefer Anwar Sadat to the populist Gamal Abdul Nasser and indeed Nasserism was perceived as threatening to members of the minorities mentioned in this category in the remainder of the Arab world.

With regard to their relationships with external powers, members of these communities tended to view those powers as potential protectors against the threat of majority nationalism. Individuals from those minorities sought and frequently found employment with external power-connected commercial firms and with foreign embassies. As a consequence they came to be seen, especially by rapid change elements of the majority, secular nationalists and even more radical Islamics, as predisposed to follow a treasonous course of action. Persecution of Baha'is in Iran rests as much on this as on religious attitudes.

The Jews are a special case within this category. In fact, if Israel is thought of as an independent Jewish island within a very large Arab community, it can be viewed in this category. For Jews living outside Israel in the Middle East, the creation of an independent Jewish state exacerbated conflict patterns. Relationships with nationalistic or radical religious elements in the majority community became exceedingly difficult and the perception of threat from them intensified.

An increasingly important basis of conflict developed as the change process continued: conflict between those with a primary identity attachment to national communities and those who looked primarily to religious communities. Like conflict between Marxists and non-Marxists and that among competing nationalisms, the religious-nationalist conflict could become serious enough to be a major complicating factor at all levels of conflict. Either or both sides of the conflict at times accepted or even solicited a working alliance with external powers that were engaged in a struggle for influence in the region. This aspect of the overall conflict in the area was already apparent in the middle stage of the change process and has become steadily more important since. In Iran, for example, Ayatollah Ruhollah Khomeini refused in the early 1950s to collaborate with the secular nationalist Mussaddiq though they shared many goals and many enemies. Musaddiq, as an Iranian nationalist, identified intensely with the Iranian national community. Khomeini, on the other hand, identified with the ummah, the broad community of believers in Islam. Musaddiq's goals were defined in terms of the independence, dignity and welfare of the Iranian nation, Khomeini's in terms of bringing Islamic justice to the ummah. Khomeini's friend and like-thinker, Ayatollah Abol Qasem Kashani, did collaborate for a time with Musaddiq. In fact he was second only to Musaddiq in the Iranian regime. But their conflicting goals led to a break and Kashani ultimately may have played a decisive role in bringing success to a failing Anglo-American coup against Musaddiq.[8] The collaboration of other Iranian clerics with the externally-sponsored coup was virtually overt. So convinced were they of the treason of the clerics that many Iranian secular nationalists concluded when Khomeini became the leader of Iran that the Anglo-Americans had cunningly orchestrated this outcome of the Iranian revolution.

Seen in terms of a movement toward mass participation in politics, the change process in core areas in the Middle East is approaching its end. In place of an acquiescent, politically inert mass of a few decades ago there is a population, as Iran illustrates, capable of being fully mobilised for political purposes. As this point is approached, the old traditional/modern elite dichotomy has less and less relevance in explaining conflict in the Middle East. Along with the growth in political participation has appeared a complex socio-economic system. A highly trained and competent technocratic element in government and industry is absolutely essential if such systems are to be managed successfully. Whether a regime has evolved from a traditional governing elite, as for example in Jordan, or from a nationalistic and self-consciously modernising elite, as for example in Syria, there is a great deal of resemblance in terms of domestic managerial practices.

In terms of the other major dimension of change advanced in this paper however, identity alteration, the change process is far from complete. Indeed it is at a critical point in generating conflict. A generation ago secular nationalist leaders in the Arab and Iranian worlds appeared likely to consolidate control just as their Turkish counterparts had a generation earlier. But those leaders suffered

severe reverses at the hands of the Western powers and in the case
of the Arabs by the Israelis. Their publics lost both respect for these
leaders and any confidence in their ability to stand up to the forces
of Western imperialism. This lack of confidence in turn led many of
these people to accommodate to leaders with whom the external forces
were cooperating. But despite this accommodation such leaders
lacked any real legitimacy in the eyes of their publics and hence their
position of authority was always vulnerable. The challenge to this
authority, however, was to come less from secular nationalists, badly
discredited as they were, than from individuals representing other
identity communities, usually sectarian or ethnic. Is is far too early
to conclude that these new identity patterns will replace the old
attachments to the Arab and Iranian national communities. But
conflict among a diversity of identity communities is the most apparent
of facts and is certain to be a primary determinant of overall conflict
patterns in the region for some years to come.

The fact that when viewed in socio-economic managerial terms
Middle Eastern regimes today resemble each other a great deal does
not obviate another fact, and that is that what primarily underlies
conflict at the intra-state level is the old conflict between elites
favouring change and those seeking to maintain their traditional
vested interests. The explanation for this persistence thus is not
structural; it is psychological and very much a consequence of the
old pattern of Western external support for traditional elements in
their struggle with pro-change elements.

In the early stage of the change process, the policy preference of
British and French representatives in the area for dealing with
traditional leaders was clear. The Europeans and the traditional
elements shared an interest in maintaining internal stability and hence
emerged as natural allies. The Americans in this period had few
important interests to maintain in the area. American representatives
as disinterested observers in this stage therefore were often inclined
to express sympathy for the aspirations of those Middle Easterners
seeking to achieve full control of their affairs. But by the middle
stage of change, US interests in containing perceived Soviet expansionism and in Middle Eastern oil were important enough to dictate a
new direction to US policy. Not surprisingly that new direction was
one of favouring stability and looking to alliances with conservative
elites in the area to achieve it. This led inevitably to the perceptual
pattern described earlier among Middle Eastern elites favouring
rapid change: traditional elements were agents of the policies and

aspirations of Western imperialism, now very much including US imperialism.

At a fairly early point in the change process a section of the old governing elite did adopt a strategy that had the potential for preserving for them much of their influence and privilege. This adaptation was one that accepted the inevitability of change but sought to control both its tempo and its direction. It involved a working alliance of four elite elements: a progressive section of the traditional governing elite; merchants, entrepeneurs and industrialists who feared uncontrolled and accelerating change would lead to state socialism; technocrats who had the skills necessary to construct and man increasingly complex commercial and governmental institutions; and trained, modern armed forces and police. This pattern proved to be naturally attractive to Americans and Europeans, and those governments following this path generally had Western support. Since they were able to satisfy the material interests of much of their populations they were reasonably stable. Furthermore, as time passed the 'traditional' aspect of the ruling element became less apparent and as it did the structural resemblance to, for example, the Ba'athist regimes of Syria and Iraq, became close.

Nevertheless the negative judgement regarding those regimes persisted even as they evolved into thoroughly modern-appearing entities. The question raised was that of nationalist legitimacy and, as the experience of the Shah of Iran illustrates so well, that it is the source of serious vulnerability. It also provides, as will be seen in the following section, some explanation for the deep suspicion regimes hold regarding one another, despite their resemblances.

II THE INTER-REGIME LEVEL OF CONFLICT

The Early Pattern

The basic alliance/conflict pattern in the Arab–Iranian Middle East in the post-Second World War period reflected closely the response of the regional regimes to revolutionary change. Those regimes that were based primarily on traditional leaders looked to each other and to the Western powers outside the region in their efforts to slow down and to control the force of change. Their internal and regional governmental opponents tended to be highly nationalistic and looked on traditional-based regimes as they did on traditional elites internally – as effectively puppets of the imperial West. However, the major nationalist leaders in Iran and the Arab world sustained serious set backs just at the moment they were making their bid to furnish leadership for the next generation. Either they were defeated and suppressed as in Iran or contained and seriously discredited as in the Arab world. By the 1980s when mass political participation characterised the Iranian and Arab worlds, they were at a serious competitive disadvantage in their struggle with religio-political leaders for the political affections of the newly participant mass. Those leaders speaking for pan-Arabism in particular had lost much of their appeal.

A second consequence is more subtle but nevertheless of major importance in contemporary conflict in the Middle East. Those Iranian and Arab leaders, most of them either traditional or heavily dependent on traditional support, who had allied with what many of their countrymen saw as Western imperialism suffered de-legitimisation. It was the Nassers and Musaddiqs who were accepted as having full nationalist legitimacy. Their opponents, especially those who collaborated actively with external forces, were, it follows, of questionable patriotism and hence fundamentally vulnerable. They would have difficulty, as was to be true of the Shah of Iran, in surviving a serious economic crisis. As the following pages will illustrate, legitimacy lines today have been blurred to the point that very few leaders in the area are now accepted as fully legitimate on nationalist grounds. But there is a persistingly strong tendency to see the friends of the United States and Western Europe among Middle Eastern leaders as suspect on nationalist grounds.

The case of Sadat[9]

The most shocking breakdown of the early alliance patterns came with what was widely described in the Arab world as Anwar Sadat's 'defection'. As Nasser's successor, Sadat inherited legitimacy both as defender of the broad Arab community and of the Egyptian national community. But, in marked contrast to Nasser, Sadat's personal identity balance appears to have been strongly tilted in favour of the Egyptian community. Sadat emerged from the 1973 war with great prestige and a bargaining position far stronger than that of any contemporary Arab leader. That position was sufficiently strong, in fact, that a pressure strategy directed against Israel to achieve Palestinian self-determination was now easily conceivable. But his

leverage rested largely on his ability to play the Americans and
Soviets against each other and on his ability to direct the use made
of the so called 'oil weapon'. Within two years, at the time of the
1975 Sinai II agreement, Sadat had discarded all the bargaining
advantage of having the two superpowers compete for his friendship.
He had moved Egypt to the US side and had so offended the Soviets
as to be unable to make the military purchases necessary to maintain
in good condition his Soviet-based weapons system. Furthermore, he
had exacted no price from the Americans for his shift in alliances.
Then, by beginning the process of moving toward a separate peace
with Israel, implicit in the Sinai II negotiations, he lost influence with
other Arab regimes including the oil producers. Sadat willingly paid
the price of loss of leverage in the hope that his actions would
ingratiate him with the United States – the one power that all Arabs
agreed could apply great pressure on Israel. For a time Sadat, in his
weakened position, maintained close relations with Saudi Arabia and
other Arab states that followers of Nasser saw as, to one degree or
another, American or Anglo-American clients. But when Sadat
signed the Camp David agreement with Israel, he lost the formal
friendship of all but the most marginal of Arab regimes.

The basic premise of the step-by-step diplomatic model of Henry
Kissinger was that Arab regimes can be viewed in terms of degree of
moderateness.[10] Since the most 'moderate' are most willing to make
formal peace with Israel, it follows that the effort to move toward
peace should focus diplomatic attention first on those most moderate
regimes. Then, having established a major precedent and having
crossed a psychological barrier, it should be possible to bring the
next most moderate to the bargaining table. But the fallacy in this
approach lies with the assumption. Nationalist legitimacy is an
absolute, not a scalar concept. An Egyptian nationalist such as Sadat
could make peace with Israel without having achieved Palestinian
self-determination and with the support of those of his countrymen
whose identity with Egypt far outweighed any identity with the Arab
community. Arabic speakers who identified intensely with the large
Arab community, including many Egyptians, were inclined to see
Sadat as having embarked on a path of at best questionable patriotism,
at worst of treason. No other Arab regimes were willing to follow
the Sadat path even though some of their leaders must have identified
with the Arab community at a low intensity level, comparable to that
of Sadat. This behaviour may be negative but even so strong evidence
exists that the people of other Arab states identify more strongly

with being Arab than does a major section of the Egyptian people. It follows that Western strategists cannot afford to ignore, as Henry Kissinger and Jimmy Carter did, Arab nationalism as a significant determinant of Arab behaviour.

The Case of Saddam Hossein

Sadat's foreign policy shift that began in 1973 and culminated in the Camp David agreement constituted a major systemic disturbance in the Arab world and in the Middle East generally. It badly weakened those Arabs who continued to cling to pan-Arab aspirations and those Arabs as well as other Middle Easterners who saw Western imperialism as seeking to rule the region indirectly through client regimes. Since these peoples looked sometimes with favour on the Soviet Union as a counter weight to the Americans, it damaged the Soviet influence position as well.

At this point Saddam Hossein, long Iraq's strong man and soon to be its president, moved to mitigate the damaging effects of Sadat's 'defection'. In the months that followed, Saddam Hossein's diplomacy appeared at first a major effort to restore and reinvigorate the early alliance pattern outlined above. But then in a sudden shift Saddam Hossein appeared to be engaged in changing sides much as Sadat had done at the time of Sinai II. In so doing Saddam Hossein both demonstrated the degree to which the early pattern had atrophied and hastened the process of its disintegration.

As Anwar Sadat moved toward formalising his peace treaty with Israel, Saddam Hossein moved to assert his position of pre-eminence among Arab leaders in the nationalistic camp. Given Sadat's departure, it was not at all unreasonable that Nasser's heir as symbolic if not real lader of the Arab nation should emerge in the important Arab state of Iraq. Saddam Hossein's diplomacy was highly creative and followed two parallel policies. The first was his sponsorship of a meeting of Arab kings and presidents in Baghdad that effectively sanctioned Sadat's (not Egypt's) excommunication as a member of the Arab community. Effectively, Saddam Hossein had achieved the objective of becoming the Arab leader who best articulated the Arab sense of indignation, even outrage, at Sadat's act.[11]

Simultaneously Saddam Hossein and Hafez Assad of Syria engaged in what appeared to be a serious effort toward phased unification of Iraq and Syria. Had a union of these two states, surely the second and third powers after Egypt in the Arab world, occurred there would have been a major balance of power rectification offsetting to a considerable extent the loss of Egypt in the Arab power equation. No one underestimated the obstacles facing such a union. Both Syria and Iraq were pluralist societies. The only significant minority in each without some Arab identity were the Kurds, but attachments to a variety of sectarian communities was strong. State nationalism was developing in each and was reinforced by the strong vested interests focused on the individual state governments and related institutions. Not the least of these was the strong desire of Assad and Syria's top leaders and Saddam Hossein and Iraq's top leaders to retain at least the influence level they had exercised in the two separate states. Outside observers were, on the other hand, inclined to underestimate the centripetal force exercised by Arab nationalist sensibilities in the two societies. Arab identity was and is of high intensity among critical elements of both populations and is at least of medium intensity for broad sections of the population. Were this not the case the effort to unify would not have been made. Success for the endeavour was not out of the question.

Not long after he acceded to the presidency of Iraq in 1978, Saddam Hossein suddenly abandoned the strategy that appeared to be working so well for him. Largely thanks to his initiatives, the bloc of progressive Arab states was setting the course for post-Camp David Arab diplomacy. Real progress was being made toward overcoming the terrible psychological blow to Arab nationalist aspirations resulting from Sadat's diplomacy. Then Saddam Hossein announced that he had uncovered and destroyed a plot against him which had major external connections. The alleged external involvement, it was quickly apparent, was Syrian. Among the victims of Saddam's furious response, and surely the most important victim, was the move toward Iraqi-Syrian union.

It soon became obvious, however, that Saddam Hossein's move involved far more than an impulsive response to a perceived plot against him. In the next few months he abandoned his campaign for leadership of the progressive bloc of Arab states and moved toward rapprochement with the very conservative regimes he had described as vassals and lackeys of the western imperial-Zionist alliance. He moved as well to distance himself from the Soviet Union, with which Iraq had a friendship agreement, and to reduce the distance separating him from Western Europe and the United States. In making these moves he demonstrated a willingness to risk an association with regimes, the conservative Arabs, whose legitimacy was widely questioned by Arab nationalists, and to move toward the United

States which they and he had described as the major enemy of the Arab nation. The proposition is a strong one, however, that Saddam Hossein made these moves with entirely different objectives in mind than those that led Anwar Sadat to break with the progressive Arab bloc and the Soviet Union and to ally with the United States. Far from being willing, as Sadat was, to risk separating from the Arab world, Saddam Hossein was continuing to make his bid, albeit with a radically altered strategy, to gain unchallenged leadership of the Arab national movement. For achieving this purpose events in Iran were of critical importance and it is necessary at this point to look briefly at what was happening in Iran.[12]

The Shah, Khomeini and the Iran–Iraq War

Without question the most important systemic disturbance in the contemporary Middle East was the overthrow of the monarchical dictatorship in Iran and its replacement by the Islamic Republic.[13] The Shah of Iran had repeatedly advanced his claim that in influence terms Iran was approximating second level state actors such as the Federal Republic of Germany. Because of his economic leverage; the size, equipment and training of his armed forces; and the competition among world powers for his friendship, the Shah had indeed become a major world figure. As a charter member of the conservative regime *de facto* alliance in the region, he was well and again its most important member. He took the lead in welcoming Sadat's move away from Nasser's old allies and fully embraced Sadat's decision to make formal peace with Israel. As early as 1975 he had sensed the willingness of Saddam Hossein to follow his own diplomatic course and as of that year moved toward *rapprochement* with this one time bitter enemy. Since these moves by the Shah had the effect of strengthening not only his Arab friends and allies but Israel's position in the region and the competitive position of the United States and the People's Republic of China *vis-à-vis* the Soviet Union, the balance of power impact in the region was extraordinary. Furthermore, the response of the Soviet Union and even more Eastern Europe was to establish and maintain close economic relations and friendly political relations with the Shah. The only external assistance the Shah's opponents received, and it was minor, was from Syria, Libya and sections of the Palestine Liberation Organisation.

The unparalleled internal political stability in Iran from 1963 to

1977 reflected the fact of a rapidly developing oil-based economy. Before inflation developed in 1974 the real income of most Iranians improved each year. The economic crisis that began to develop in 1974 was serious and did expose major structural and policy weaknesses.[14] But it could not have brought down the Shah were he not so fundamentally vulnerable on nationalist legitimacy grounds. In retrospect the case is easily made that the Shah could have survived had he dealt with his opposition with the same degree of brutality that has characterised Saddam Hossein's regime. Even so the collapse of the Shah in the face of his foreign policy and economic achievements should underline for any observer the exceptional importance of nationalist legitimacy for any regime. The point is important to make because virtually all of the Shah's Arab allies share to some degree a similar vulnerability.[15]

Ayatollah Ruhollah Khomeini made clear even before achieving power in Iran that his God-ordained leadership had two goals in world affairs. The first was to furnish leadership to the oppressed peoples of the world (read the 'south') to throw off the control of the oppressors (read the 'north'). This task was in large part a psychological one: to develop a sense of efficacy among the oppressed and to demonstrate to them and to the oppressors that the latter no longer had the capability to maintain their overwhelming control. Translated, he was saying that the United States, the Soviet Union and the lesser allies of each were functionally overextended and could maintain control only so long as neither they nor their victims recognised that a fundamental shift in the balance of power had occurred. Khomeini sanctioned alliances with those oppressed regimes that were sincerely attempting to destroy the influence position of the oppressors. The regional regimes so identified were essentially the nationalistic, pro-change regimes referred to above. The fact that these regimes had close ties with one of the great oppressors, the Soviet Union, was indeed a source of tension. But Khomeini clearly considered the United States the pre-eminent oppressor and was willing to close his eyes to this error on the part of his allies.[16]

Khomeini's second goal was to bring a true expression of the Islamic ideology, in effect his own interpretation, to the Islamic and ultimately to all the world. Only with a full and true acceptance of the holistic view of society abstracted from the Qoran and fleshed out by interpretation could the individual achieve self-realisation. Khomeini has never explicated a strategy for achieving this goal, seen by those who fear him as one of exporting the revolution. On the contrary he seems serene in the belief that since this is God's, not his, plan such a strategy will unfold and he and other guides need only have the wit, the faith and the understanding to recognise its manifestations when they appear. Since Khomeini's goals are expressed in such vague abstractions, his lieutenants have wide latitude in formulating tactical plans. There is a great deal of difficulty in reconciling Khomeini's two objectives and the strategy adopted by his lieutenants is sometimes messianic, sometimes pragmatic and often contradictory.

Iran's primary allies in the region were strongly secular and as such resembled closely Khomeini's one time revolutionary allies in Iran whom he had purged from any position of influence. Because of this experience of the Iranian secular elements, there was a wariness among Iran's allies and a sense that the alliance was likely to be a temporary one. This conclusion was quickly drawn in Iraq, Iran's next-door neighbour and a country in which Shia Moslems were a somewhat deprived, politically, socially and economically, majority. As the course of the Iranian revolution followed a path of erasing all traces of secularism, the very secular Iraqi Ba'athist regime became increasingly nervous. Radio Teheran openly encouraged religious Moslems (it was careful not to appeal to Shia only) to carry the Islamic revolution into Iraq. Saddam Hossein responded with a brutal suppression of pro-Khomeini leaders and the enmity of the two regimes deepened.

However the Iraqi response differed sharply from that of its sometime allies in the progressive nationalist camp. Syria, Libya and the PLO in particular argued that the Iranian revolution had altered the Middle East balance of power sharply in their favour and against the interests of what they called the 'imperialist-Zionist' camp. The Iraqi leadership challenged that view and countered that the Khomeini regime was so weak that it was more a liability than an asset to the cause of the Arab nation.[17] Given this expression of contempt for Iranian capability, it is most difficult to make a short-term case for a defensively motivated Iraqi strategy when Iraq invaded Iran in September 1980. The initial nervousness at the possibility of Iran's being able to appeal to the religious sensibilities of the mass public appeared to have evaporated. Indeed the Iraqi government seemed to have agreed with secular Iranian exiles that the Khomeini regime was too weak to withstand an external attack and would collapse under its impact.

The Iranian revolution was in high gear when Saddam Hossein broke with Syria and its allies and turned toward the conservative Arab regimes. There is nothing to suggest, however, that the Iranian revolution was a factor of any significance in that decision. But as Khomeini became increasingly isolated during the hostage crisis and in the view of many Iranians near collapse politically, the situation became one that Saddam Hossein could believe he could exploit to his personal political advantage. He heralded his invasion as a struggle of Arab versus Iranian nationalism and in so doing made untenable the position of Iranian nationalist exiles who had encouraged him to move against Khomeini. The Iraqi media described Saddam Hossein as the great leader of the entire Arab nation who would rectify the past humiliations at the hands of Iran.[18] Had the invasion fulfilled Saddam Hossein's expectations of a quick victory that would give the Arab nation a renewed sense of grandeur, he may well have achieved the goal of being accepted as Nasser's successor. In that event the Iraqi regime would have gained pre-eminence in the Arab world and could have expected to be supported by both the progressive and conservative blocs of Arab regimes. But as the course of events made clear the fact of Saddam Hossein's historic miscalculation, he became seriously dependent on his conservative allies for financial support. They, not he, had their leverage position greatly strengthened.

Whatever expectations Saddam Hossein had held regarding his former progressive allies, his lack of success in the battle with Iran destroyed his leverage with that bloc as well. Despite the fact that a war of terrible proportion was being waged between an Arab state, Iraq, and Iran, the three core regimes of the bloc that regarded itself the repository of Arab nationalist legitimacy sided with Iran. Algeria whose regime also claimed Arab nationalist legitimacy sought to retain good relations with both sides. The Iraqis of course depicted the behaviour of these self-proclaimed leaders of Arab nationalism as in fact a betrayal of the Arab nation.

There is little question that Arab nationalists everywhere felt a good deal of ambivalence on this issue. Saddam Hossein had in effect taken the gamble of associating with regimes of questionable nationalist legitimacy in the hope that he could, with their cooperation, take action so dramatic as to advance the Arab cause and to capture the imagination of the Arab mass. In that event all Arab regimes would have had no option but to support him. But he lost his gamble and was reduced instead to a desperate struggle for political survival in Iraq. However, the consequences of Iraq's defeat on the battlefield may prove far more profound than simply the destruction of individual ambitions. Saddam Hossein's depiction of the war as Arab vs. Iranian nationalism reflected his contempt for the military capability of his Islamic opponents. As the war progressed, it was depicted in Iran as combat between the forces of Islam and a godless secular nationalist Ba'athist regime in Iraq in association with the great oppressors. Thus far the persistence of the Iranian-Syrian alliance has prevented the polarisation of the conflict in the Arab world. But the possibility is serious that a major pattern may develop throughout the region in which secular nationalists are pitted against self-proclaimed defenders of Islam. In that event the basis for establishing effective regime legitimacy will be even more complicated than it is at present.

Arafat and Assad

The contemporary case that is most revealing of the point the previous cases have illustrated, that is the erosion of the early conflict pattern at the regime level, is the conflict between PLO chairman Yasir Arafat and Syrian president Hafez Assad. On the surface what has occurred is the defection of the Arafat PLO from the progressive, Arab nationalist-Islamic Republic alliance and a movement toward an alliance with the conservative Arab regimes. In so doing Arafat has followed the path of Anwar Sadat and Saddam Hosssein and the risk he takes is the risk they took: the tarnishing of their Arab nationalist legitimacy. Sadat, it will be recalled, ultimately went even further and following Camp David was expelled from both alliances. His successor, Husni Mubarak, has been returning gradually to the Arab world, not simply one faction of it, and there is movement in that direction.[19] Saddam Hossein, the previous case suggested, probably saw his alliance shift as a temporary manoeuvre in a strategy designed to place him in the role of unquestioned leader of the Arab world. His catastrophic set backs in the war with Iran have left him a prisoner in the conservative camp and seriously dependent on its members' financial assistance. The case is far from clear that these are examples a wise political leader would seek to emulate. And indeed the near collapse of the peace process and the efforts being made today to produce an Arafat–Assad *rapprochement* underline the great dangers to his leadership implicit in Arafat's actions.

There is a strong tendency among outside analysts to conclude that the constant twisting and turning of alliances in the Middle East is essentially a product of personality conflicts. Implicit in this attitude is a low estimation of the force of public attitudes in setting the boundaries within which a Middle Eastern leader can act. In effect it amounts to a denial of a base assumption in this chapter: that the Middle East is now characterised by mass politics and the corollary assumption that Middle Eastern citizens play a comparable boundary-setting role in the foreign policy decision-making process to that played by Western citizens. Personality conflicts and deep personal enmity are aspects of explanation of foreign policy choices anywhere, and the personal enmity between Arafat and Assad has reached the point of being close to unbridgeable. However the explanation for Syrian-PLO conflict is far more complex than that.

The Arafat–Assad conflict is a major manifestation of the kind of disagreements that appear when individual identities reflect both a pan-Arab nationalism and a state nationalism. Both Assad and Arafat identify and at high intensity with the broad Arab nation. But Assad also identifies at an increasingly intense degree with the community of individuals who live within the confines of that artifical, Anglo-French imperial creation called Syria. Arafat on the other hand identifies first with the Palestinian community. As a consequence Assad and Arafat will be inclined to define the general situation in the Arab world similarly, reflecting their shared Arab identity. But their separate Syrian and Palestinian identities lead to sharp variations in definitions of the situation in the more concrete level. Since each man sees himself as sincerely devoted to Arab interests, each will be inclined to judge the other as betraying Arab interests when their disagreements are, as at present, profound.

The basis for a serious state nationalist conflict between the PLO and Syria developed when the Palestinians began to institutionalise their political presence in Lebanon. Following the month of Black September 1970 when King Hossein attacked and destroyed the infrastructure of an informal Palestinian government in Jordan, the PLO began the process of reconstructing that infrastructure in Lebanon. This particularly affected adversely the position of the Maronite community in the fragile balance of intersts on which the Lebanese government was based. Then when Palestinian cross-border operations into Israel expanded, the Israelis responded with punishing raids that resulted in many Lebanese casualties and terrible property damage. A reaction toward Palestinians developed among many in the Maronite community that can be described as a loathing capable of producing genocidal responses. Reactions in the Shia community of south Lebanon, the most frequent Israeli target, were more diverse but among many residents resentment was only slightly less intense than that of the Maronites. This is reflected in current battles between the Shia organisation, Amal, and Palestinians in Beirut. The Palestinians found support from the left and from Lebanese, particularly in the Sunni and Orthodox communities, who continued to feel the tug of pan-Arab nationalism. But the Palestinians had learned early that reactions of their 'brother' Arabs among whom they lived as refugees was at best ambivalent. They therefore felt they had no alternative to providing for and defending themselves. As mutual resentment grew, so did the tendency to value state nationalism more highly than pan-Arab nationalism.

The first civil war in Lebanon in 1958 involved the complex interaction of each of the levels of conflict discussed thus far plus the international system level. But strangely unimportant in that conflict maze was the Arab-Israeli struggle focused on Palestine in spite of the fact that there were more than a quarter of a million Palestinian refugees in Lebanon at the time. At the intra-state level the conflict pitted traditional elites and the sectarian Maronite community against change-oriented elites many of whom identified strongly with the broad Arab national community. At the inter-regime level the familiar conservative versus progressive dichotomy was quickly manifest in internal Lebanese alliances, the former siding with traditional leaders, the latter with pro-change groups. The American intervention initially was in support of the conservative alliance and Soviet sympathies, at least, were with their opponents. This was a manifestation of the classic pattern interaction of area conflict. It is important to note because of the later tendency to see intra-state conflict in Lebanon as generated by the Palestinian presence. Clearly there was a major conflict potential independent of the Palestinian struggle.[20]

By the time of the second civil war in 1976, the PLO was an important organisation and the Palestinian governmental infrastructure was being constructed in Lebanon. The Palestinians and the Arab-Israeli conflict were now an essential aspect of the conflict maze embracing Lebanon. However, the claim of Arab nationalists that the active diplomacy of Henry Kissinger which was taking Anwar Sadat away from the progressive alliance toward the conservative alliance was the major precipitant of the second civil war deserves serious consideration.[21] The weakening of the progressive front by Sadat's departure; the strengthening of Israel by eliminating its foremost Arab opponent; the seeming willingness of the United States to associate itself actively with conservatives; and Soviet diplomatic passivity surely were grounds for encouragement of conservative and Maronite sectarian leaders. They could reasonably conclude there was a sharp shift of the balance of power in their favour. And with such a shift the options available to the conservatives had multiplied.

Arafat, who well understood the dangers of Palestinian involvement in a dispute that was adding to the depth of polarisation in the Arab world, attempted to stay out of the civil war. But Palestinians were too much the focus of conservative-Maronite enmity for that and the PLO was drawn into the conflict. In the succeeding weeks events made clear the fact that the conservative side had badly miscalculated. American concern for the outcome was far less intense than they had assumed. The conservative side began losing the civil war and it was clear it would receive insufficient external support to reverse this outcome. The PLO threw its not inconsiderable military weight on the side of an alliance of leftists, Arab nationalists and progressive Sunnis and Druze.

Conservative and Maronite leaders, bitterly disappointed in their lack of support, then made a strong appeal for help from Assad, a seemingly unnatural ally. But Assad was receptive to the appeal. Confronted with a probable victory by a force in which the PLO was clearly the dominant element, Assad had to face the prospects of what would amount to a Palestinian government in the south of Lebanon. That government could hardly resist taking action against the Israelis and these actions could well provoke an Israeli invasion and a high probability of war between Israel and Syria. This meant a loss of control for Syria that could lead to an unwanted and potentially disastrous war. Unable to persuade Arafat and his Lebanese allies to allow a restoration of a balance of forces in Lebanon similar to that at the start of the civil war, Assad ordered an attack in March 1976 on the Palestinian-Lebanese left alliance and shifted the balance in favour of the conservative-Maronite alliance. Bitterness toward Assad for this decision is hardly confined to Arafat and his entourage. It is felt by many, probably most, Palestinians, Druze and Lebanese who are leftist or Arab nationalist. Assad's decision amounted to a temporary shift in alliance patterns. His action was welcomed by conservative Arab regimes, Israel and the United States. It was viewed with consternation in Libya, Iraq and the Soviet Union. Inevitably questions were and still are raised regarding Assad's claim to Arab nationalist legitimacy. Within months he had returned to more familiar patterns of alliance. But the episode is a highly instructive one. Even though Assad and his supporters can easily make the case that in effect what is bad for Syria is bad for the Arab nation, the episode is clearly one of conflicting state nationalist interests by peoples both of whom identify strongly with the Arab nation and saw their actions as in harmony with the needs of that nation.[22]

When Israel invaded Lebanon in June 1982, the Syrian response added to Palestinian bitterness. Syrian support for the PLO did not materialise in any important way until Syrian forces were directly attacked. Then, when offered a cease fire, Syria accepted with an alacrity that was unseemly in Palestinian eyes since the Israelis continued moving against Palestinians. Then, after the Israeli victory over the Palestinians, Assad made clear his determination not to allow Arafat to re-establish a position of dominance in southern Lebanon.

This time it was Arafat who executed a major shift in alliance and in the direction of the conservatives. He violently condemned Assad who, although grudgingly, had given some support to the Palestinians and met with Husni Mubarak who had given only verbal support and who persisted in defending the Camp David agreement which Palestinians believed had made the invasion of Lebanon virtually an inevitability. Arafat's migration to the conservative side with its *de facto* alliance with the United States, Israel's ally, resembled in its consequences Sadat's move away from the Arabs altogether. Neither man was able to bring important elements of his community along with him. Arafat has been compelled to retreat from his active association with King Hossein and clearly has sustained serious blows to his claim to Arab nationalist legitimacy. The Assad–Arafat conflict thus illustrates both a degree of erosion of the early conflict pattern but also a still persisting vitality.[23]

The Turkish Variant

The Turkish government of Prime Minister Adnan Menderes, in power in the late 1950s, resembled in many particulars those of the Arab and Iranian worlds that found favour with Americans and became core members of a conservative alliance. It was supported by entrepreneurial elements and was opposed to radical, social or political change. And Turkey's alliance patterns in this period resembled closely those of similar regimes elsewhere in the Middle East. But this behaviour did not reflect so much an attitude toward change as it did an assessment of the most effective alliance for the purpose of containing perceived Soviet expansionism.[24]

After Menderes was overturned by a student-initiated revolution and following a brief military control, Turkish foreign policy in the Middle East followed a different pattern. The primary concern continued to be one of dealing with a perceived Soviet threat and close relations with the Shah of Iran and the Central Treaty Organization was a constant in Turkish policy. But there appears to have been a careful distancing of Turkish policy from disputes among Arab regimes and from the Arab-Israeli conflict. There was no apparent interest in influencing the internal conflicts in Middle Eastern states. The one exception has been with the Kurdish minorities in Iran, Iraq and Syria. Since the largest Kurdish population concentration is in eastern and southern Turkey, concern with the internal security implications of the policies of their neighbours towards the Kurds is intense. But the response appears always to be *ad hoc* and tailored to each situation.

Turkey's response to the Iranian revolution and the proclamation of an Islamic Republic in Teheran has been a complex one. The Iranian revolution coincided with a period of internal disruption in Turkey that reflected long-standing dissensus in that country. The military take-over and the crack down on the old political leadership included a policy of suppressing political leaders whose appeal was primarily to that of the religious community. Radical Islamic leaders are well represented in the Turkish political elite. But the change process which is just now reaching a climactic point in most of the Middle East is probably two generations beyond that point in Turkey. This means that although there is a large mass receptivity for a radical Islamic appeal in Turkey, that mass base is not growing as it is elsewhere in the Middle East.

The Turkish government therefore has far less to fear from Islamic resurgence and has adopted a relaxed policy toward Iran. Relations are good and trade between the two economies is large and growing. Iran's powerful speaker of the Majlis, Hashemi Rafsenjani, indicated that although Turkey had a government that was a tool of the great oppressor, the United States, pragmatism dictated good relations.[25] Turkey's regional concerns focus far more on Greece, Cyprus and the Aegean Sea.

The Arab-Israeli Conflict

The three primary sources of conflict in the Middle East are: (1) the challenge to established authority implicit in the rapid change process, (2) the struggle for a Jewish homeland, and (3) the intense struggle between the United States and the Soviet Union for influence in the area. The objectives of a free flow of oil to the markets of the United States, Europe and Japan and of petro-dollars to world financial and commercial centres are of top priority but have not as yet given strong definition to overall conflict. The other three have become part of a conflict compound that cannot be disaggregated easily. However some clear patterns do emerge that relate directly to the struggle of political Zionism to establish a strong and enduring Jewish state in the confines of the old Palestinian mandate.

The response to the effort to establish a Jewish homeland in the proximity of the territory of ancient Israel was almost universally negative among non-Jewish Middle Easterners. But viewed in terms of intensity of that negative response, the reaction was highly differentiated. At one end of a scale there was negative affect but no willingness to make any real sacrifice to oppose the creation of the Jewish state. At the other end of the scale the intensity was sufficiently high to produce a willingness to risk one's life in a persisting struggle with Israel.

A common wisdom often found in the popular literature on the Arab-Israeli conflict is that the negative reaction to Israel reflects the fear of traditional forces of Israel as an agent of change.[26] Implicit in this belief is the assumption that traditional elements would be most threatened by and hostile to the movement for the creation of a Jewish state. But behavioural evidence indicates the exact opposite is the case. Traditional elites outside the Palestinian area were little affected by and little concerned with the creation of Israel. Inside Palestine a strong pattern developed in terms of overt opposition with many Arab notables (the name given the traditional leaders) ready to reach accommodation with Jewish settlers and then with a Jewish state. But Palestinians who looked with favour on rapid change tended to be intransigent in their opposition. This pattern of rapid change elements tending to oppose the creation of Israel and to support the Palestinian cause after Israel's independence is, with some important exceptions, the common one throughout the area.

At the high intensity end of the scale of opposition to Israel are three groups: (1) Arab nationalists, (2) Palestinian state nationalists and (3) those who identify with the broad Islamic community or ummah. All three groups see Israel as a European enclave, imposed on the region for its own purposes by Western imperialism. The United States is perceived as Israel's primary source of support and strength and American policy is hence the primary target for all three. All agree that Israeli aggression and expansionism will continue so long as American support continues and will end only when that support is withdrawn. Strategies and tactics differ sharply, however. Those who are described as favouring the peace process follow an ingratiation strategy as did Anwar Sadat. They believe the American government can be persuaded of the utility of friendship with Arabs to the point that it will place serious pressure on Israel to cement that friendship. Their opponents believe internal Zionist influence in the United States is too strong for such a strategy to succeed and that, in any case, the American government has broad imperial goals in the Middle East for the achievement of which Israel is a major instrument. They prefer a strategy of demonstrating to the American government that the costs of unquestioning support of Israel are too high. Given Arab military weakness, preferred tactics for this group are acts of violence, described by the target as terrorism, or the application of economic leverage. The latter is difficult to accomplish, however, because the Arab leaders able to apply economic leverage tend not to be in one of these three groups.

Next on the scale near the high intensity end are state nationalists with a territorial dispute with Israel. Egypt is an excellent illustration of the complexity of this point. When led by Gamal Abdul Nasser with his strong attachment to the Arab nation, Egyptian behaviour fit easily in the first category. Then with Anwar Sadat, who wore his Arabism lightly, Egypt was willing to make peace with Israel when the territorial issue was largely resolved. But Egyptians who identify strongly as Arabs or with the ummah favour Egypt's return to a leadership role in opposition to Israel even at the risk of reoccupation of Sinai by Israel. Similarly, those Syrians who identify little as Arabs but can be classified as Syrian state nationalists feel intensely about the loss of Golan Heights. However, the sense of Arabism in Syria is strong and too often underestimated and hence the importance of Golan Heights as an issue is overestimated.

The preference for following a strategy of charging the United States a high price for its strong support of Israel correlates closely with an intense attachment to a broader Arab nation or to the ummah. Ayatollah Khomeini's negative concern with Israel and his preferred strategy for dealing with the Jewish state, for example, parallels fully the attitude of the Arab nationalist Moammar Qaddafi. The preference for a strategy of ingratiation with the United States correlates more with Arab state nationalists whose Arab national identity is below the primary level of intensity. But conservative Arabs, some of whom may be Arab nationalists, also tend to prefer that strategy. This is particularly true of Arab leaders whose position is traditional and hereditary in base. Such leaders are likely to fear the radical force of nationalism or of resurgent Islam and may well look to American assistance in preserving their authority position.

Much further down on the scale of hostility to Israel are the major non-Arab peoples of the Middle East, the Turks and the Iranians. Iranian nationalists more than Turkish nationalists empathise easily with the Arab position. The intensely nationalistic Musaddiq regime in Iran identified openly with the Arabs, and when the Shah appointed the nationalistic Shapur Bakhtiar prime minister in the final days of the royal regime, one of Bakhtiar's first acts was to halt the sale of oil to Israel and South Africa. The explanation for this attitude is the feeling among Iranian nationalists that they and the Arabs have a common heritage as victims of Western imperialism. The Turks, on the other hand, have not had in the post-Second World War years a comparable sense of being victims of Western imperialism. Such attitudes are to be found within the Turkish left and leftist sympathy for the Arab side and hostility toward Israel is fully comparable to that of Iranian nationalists. Iranians and Turks who identify intensely with the ummah can be classified, as Khomeini was, in the first category of extreme hostility toward Israel.

The Shah of Iran, it is important to note, owing much to the Anglo-Americans for his authority in Iran, turned naturally and enthusiastically if not quite formally to a *de facto* alliance with Israel. Both viewed Gamal Abdul Nasser and the Arab Ba'athists as threats. The Shah's closest friends in the area were Arab leaders who followed a strategy of ingratiation with the United States.

Two types of communities in the Middle East are at the low end of the hostility toward Israel scale. One type is non-Arabic speaking minorities who aspire to substantial autonomy or even independence. Most noteworthy here are various Christian and animist groups in the Sudan, Kurds, Turkoman and Baluchis. A second type are individuals identifying with minorities who are farther along in the change process or modally more achieving than the majority or core national communities. Most noteworthy of these are Armenians,

Coptic Christians, Maronites, Zoroastrians and Baha'is. At this end of the scale a willingness to ally with Israel if such an alliance serves their interests is easily conceivable. Indeed several of these groups, particularly the Maronites and Kurds, have made alliances with Israel.[27]

These are the most easily identifiable patterns of conflict involving Israel with regional actors in the Middle East. But the Israeli presence in the area is of sufficient importance that whenever intense conflict occurs in the region not involving Israel directly, one side or another may well consider the option of seeking some Israeli assistance. The result is seemingly unnatural, usually temporary, cooperation that adds considerably to overall bewilderment. Iranian purchases of arms from Israeli arms agents is a case in point.

III CONFLICT AT THE LEVEL OF THE INTERNATIONAL SYSTEM

Developing American Alliance Patterns

Foreign policy objectives of any government over time will be the outcome of a foreign policy process that involves a varity of interacting interests operating within a situational milieu defined by a prevailing world view. The foreign policy that emerges will reflect a balancing of interests and world view generated objectives (such as an intensely held perception of threat from another state). In this chapter the objectives of the United States and the Soviet Union in the Middle East will be inferred from the policies of the two governments in that region. The major objectives inferred for US foreign policy are three, one clearly more important than the other two: (1) most important, to contain perceived Soviet expansionism in the area, (2) to maintain the flow of oil and petro dollars to the United States and its industrial allies, (3) to preserve the security and well-being of the Israeli people. The shape of US policy in the area reflects the difficult task of reconciling these three primary objectives.

Given the dangers of Soviet-American confrontation in the nuclear era, the US expectation was that the path of Soviet expansionism in the Middle East and other such strategic areas would be via internal subversion. A major strategic aim of the US government, therefore, was to reduce the potential for subversion in Middle-Eastern states. To achieve this end, programmes were inaugurated for economic, technical and internal security assistance. But when these efforts were insufficient or too slow it seemed necessary to help more directly to achieve political stability in certain critical crisis areas. This came to involve interventions, occasionally direct and overt but more frequently clandestine. The policy involved in essence a struggle with the Soviet Union for pre-eminence in influencing the internal politics of the regional states.

How would United States policy respond to the appearance of a liberal nationalist movement in a strategically vital state? In the US view nationalist-based democratic populism, because of the lack of control, enhanced the subversive potential for Soviet expansionism and, because of its irrationality and fanaticism, threatened the free flow of oil to Western economies. Regimes so based should be deposed. No apparent thought was given to the de-legitimising consequences for a successor government perceived to have been imposed on a country by and in the interests of Western, mainly US, imperial forces.

US policy crystallised in early 1957. The formula that appeared to be most optimal for reconciling the three United States objectives was a close association with conservative or traditional Middle Eastern regimes and in opposition to a loose alliance of progressive, nationalistic regimes. These US allies were at least on a verbal plane strong anti-communists and unfriendly with the Soviets, anxious to establish a close cooperation in economic matters with the United States, and willing to limit their hostility to Israel to the verbal level.

The high point in success for this policy occurred in the mid-1970s when Anwar Sadat's willingness was made evident not only to shift away from Nasser's old allies but to separate from the Arab world altogether if occupied Egyptian territory were returned to him. But very shortly thereafter the situation began to deteriorate from the US point of view. As described above, the outbreak of the second civil war in Lebanon was based on expectations following from the logic of Kissinger's step-by-step diplomacy and of US support for anti-Palestinian and anti-Arab nationalist elements. The result was terrible carnage in Lebanon, the development of hatred at a genocidal level and the beginnings of lowered estimates of US capability and US determination

But the major blow to United States policy came with the shocking success of the Iranian revolution. The major lessons of that revolution were not learned at the time and still have not been understood. But they have much to tell about the external Western role in dealing with conflict in the Middle East. They are easily summarised. First, the revolution which overturned what had appeared to be the strongest and most stable regime in the conservative regional alliance was successful because of what proved to be a fatal vulnerability of the Shah. Because he had achieved absolute power as a consequence of a coup with major Anglo-American participation which had overturned a popular leader who symbolised for most politically attentive Iranians their country's quest for real independence and dignity, the Shah was denied nationalist legitimacy. When confronted with a serious economic crisis but one which should have been fairly easily surmounted, the Shah could not appeal to his people to stand by and to make sacrifices for his regime and to help it deal with the crisis. The result was this most stable of US regional allies became destabilised and collapsed. Since other conservative regimes, because of their close identification in the minds of their most attentive publics with Western policy, also were vulnerable on grounds of nationalist legitimacy, this lesson was a serious one and one that has not been internalised.

Second, among Iran's revolutionary leaders there were many who had, as the Shah did not, nationalist legitimacy. But these leaders were easily bested by radical religio-political leaders in the ensuing struggle for power. The nationalist elite, having been discredited by defeat in part administered by the Anglo-Americans, had lost the ability to furnish leadership for that very large number of Iranians who had become politically participant in the past two decades. These newly participant Iranians looked instead to religious leaders for political guidance as they and their fathers had looked to them earlier for personal guidance. Here too the lesson was generalisable. Throughout the region there had been an explosion in the extensiveness of a predisposition to political participation and large sections of the newly participant everywhere were looking to religio-political leaders rather than to the secular nationalist leaders who had been unable to stand up to the external powers and to Israel. Their new leaders called for the elimination of all vestiges of Western imperialism and indeed of all Western cultural influence.

Third, Iranians had long assumed that the United States would not allow its friend and ally, the Shah of Iran, to fall from power. Indeed, one of the bases for stable control in Iran was the belief that even if the Shah's own coercive apparatus failed, he would be saved by the CIA and the United States military might. In the presidential campaign of 1980 Jimmy Carter was charged by Ronald Reagan with having failed to preserve the Shah's regime. Reagan gave assurances that he as president would not permit the collapse of so true and important an ally. But neither Reagan nor others making the charge against Carter have specified how US capability could have been projected into an Iran undergoing one of the greatest popular revolutions of human history. The Shah's own large, well-trained and well-equipped military could not stand up to so massive a challenge and the United States could not conceivably have mustered and supplied a comparable security force. Nor is it conceivable that a half dozen United States intelligence officers in alliance with traditional leaders in Iran, the formula of the 1953 coup, could have executed a coup in an Iran that had entered the era of mass politics.[28] In the early years of the Cold War a major feature of the Soviet-American conflict was competing clandestine efforts to manipulate the internal politics of Middle Eastern states. This third lesson is that the era of such manipulation is over. The illusion persists both on the part of the American government and its conservative regional allies that this manipulative ability is still present. But the lesson of Iran is that it is not.[29]

American policy under the Reagan Administration persisted in following the same general patterns that crystallised in 1957. The alliances favoured continued to be with Turkey, Israel and conservative Arab states. But this formula which had seemed to serve well the three US objectives a generation earlier was no longer of such obvious instrumental utility. In the first place, the only conflict in the Middle East that was clearly a product of Soviet aggression was that in Afghanistan. Resurgent Islam had replaced radical nationalism as the basis for populist movements in the area and as the primary threat to established authority structures. The leaders of these movements were adamant in their opposition to Soviet-sponsored communism. Indeed, militant Islamic forces were in the forefront of opposition to the Soviet presence in Afghanistan. The case could not easily be made, as it had been in the 1950s, that the major populist movements in the area could serve the Soviet subversive purpose. On the contrary the case could far more easily be made that regimes based on resurgent Islam were the most resistant to Soviet moves to increase their influence. Furthermore, the experience of West Germany and Japan with the Islamic Republic of Iran suggested that that regime would be at least as forthcoming in its oil sales and commercial dealings with friendly external powers as the Shah had been. The one US objective that could quite conceivably be badly served by the Islamic movements was the security of Israel. But the Israelis seemed little concerned with a security threat from that direction and certainly there was no immediate threat.

United States policy toward the Iran–Iraq war has moved incrementally in the direction of a 'tilt' toward Iraq. A surface relating of that policy to the three US objectives in the region suggests that some redefinition of US policy is actually occurring; (1) Iraq, the initator of the war, has a friendship agreement with the Soviet Union and its arsenal is to a significant degree Soviet-supplied. Iraqi leaders frequently travel to Moscow and reaffirm their close relations with the Soviet Union; (2) Iraq has bombed oil shipping in the Persian Gulf and appears to be attempting to provoke Iran into taking action against oil shipments from Arab oil ports in the Gulf; (3) Israel continues to depict Iraq as a potentially dangerous enemy and has on several occasions sanctioned the sales of weapons and spare parts by its agents to Iran.

Why then is US policy tilting toward Iraq? The best answer appears to be that the tilt is in response to a concern for the threat to the conservative Arab regimes with which the United States developed allied relations for the instrumental purpose of advancing the three objectives a generation ago. In other words the instrument is becoming the end. The Arabian peninsula regimes clearly do feel seriously threatened by Iran's messianic policy and were these regimes to be replaced by regimes closer to the Iranian model there would be, for a time, the likelihood of some serious disruptions. But the case is far from self-evident that the new regimes would be any more susceptible to Soviet influence, any less willing to sell their oil to Western industrialists or any more able to threaten Israeli security. An American policy toward Islamic resurgence generally and toward the Islamic Republic of Iran specifically has yet to crystallise. In the conflict in Afghanistan there is a *de facto* alliance with both. But in the Iran–Iraq war and in the eastern Mediterranean region there is a developing hostility toward both.

As is true with the US alliance with conservative Arab regimes, the US relationship with Israel appears to have a momentum of its own – a momentum that is more instructed by the US domestic political process than by a perceived threat to Israel from either the Soviet Union or Israel's Arab neighbours. When Anwar Sadat took Egypt formally into peace with Israel and accepted as a price Egyptian ostracism from the Arab world, the regional balance of power made its sharpest shift in Israel's favour since 1967. The Israeli invasion of

Lebanon in 1982 was perceived by Arabs as an obvious reflection of that balance shift. Quite simply, there is no short-term threat to Israeli general security. Yet US assistance to and cooperation with Israel intensified in this period.

Arab responses followed the two opposed strategies identified earlier. The conservatives, friendly with the United States, pursued the ingratiation path. However, the pan-Arab sentiment within the Arab populations was too strong to grant them the kind of latitude Sadat, with his Egyptian state nationalism base, had had. A separate peace with Israel without first gaining minimal concessions to the demand for Palestinian self-determination was not for them an option. The Reagan Administration was attracted to the approach and the administration formula, called the Reagan Plan, resembled sufficiently the Fahd Plan put forward by the conservative Arabs that a reconciliation of their differences would have been manageable. But Israel rejected the Reagan Plan and never seriously considered the Fahd Plan. Very quickly the advocates of the ingratiation strategy had reached the familiar bottom line: a willingness of the US government to apply pressure on Israel to produce an agreement on minimally acceptable terms for the Arabs. The answer then, and again in 1986 when King Hossein, Husni Mubarak and Yasir Arafat tried once more, was that no significant pressure would be applied.

The alternate strategy, the one preferred by Arab nationalists and Islamic activists, was to charge the United States a price for its policy which would be higher than the American people would be willing to pay. Given the Arab capability disadvantage there were really only two options for such a strategy that could be considered and these have been outlined earlier. One, taking advantage of Arab oil wealth and the potential financial clout of petro-dollars, was to place heavy financial pressure on the United States. A denial of contracts to US based corporations would be an example of a possible tactic. The problem was, though, that those regimes that possessed such potential leverage were the very regimes that felt US support internally could be critical for regime survival. Saudi Arabia, for example, was willing to make major financial contributions to the PLO and nationalistic regimes such as Syria to avoid being pressed to follow a strategy such as this.

Effectively, therefore, those favouring this strategy had one option: to engage in acts of violence against US, Israeli and allied interests using institutions other than offical state institutions. This strategy has in fact had some remarkable successes of late. Most striking of these was in Lebanon. In a period of a few months the United States, which had begun to establish an ever increasing presence in Lebanon, withdrew its forces and acquiesced in a situation in which US citizens could no longer safely remain in Lebanon. The withdrawal in the face of costly acts of violence directed against the US embassy, US marines and private US citizens was a humiliation comparable to that the United States had suffered in Iran. But in fact no primary US interest was served by the large US presence in Lebanon. Soviet passivity made impossible the task of depicting the US role as one of containing the Soviets or their clients. Israel needed no help in defending the security of its northern borders. And there were no significant economic stakes involved. The Reagan Administration's decision to withdraw rather than to escalate in Lebanon was a significant success for the Arab strategy and as such confirmed the assumptions underlying that strategy. It had the effect as well of improving the Arab capability self-image and hence of a willingness to take additional risks in this strategic direction. However, success for terroristic tactics in an area of low interest would not predict success when the interest was of high intensity as is the US interest in Israeli security.

The rationale for the tactical scheme associated with the punishment strategy is easily spelled out. The acts of violence chosen must be sufficiently damaging to force the target, currently most frequently Americans and Europeans, to respond in policy terms. But those acts cannot be so repulsive to the Arab public as to lead to a revulsion that damages the perpetrators and those giving them financial support. The optimal outcome would be to generate overreaction on the part of the target. An out-of-proportion retaliatory attack on an Arab city, for example, would serve that purpose. The hoped for Arab response would be anger at a level that would compel supporters of an ingratiation strategy to retreat from their position. Ultimately, the hope would be to replace those leaders following a 'peace process' path with others who would support the punishment strategy. Even greater success would be to force the leaders of oil producing states to begin the process of applying economic pressure on the United States and unfriendly European states.

The US air strike against Libya served the hard line purpose moderately well. Leaders favouring pressure tactics saw their competitive position improve although only marginally. A parallel attack on Syria or on Iran would certainly produce a much stronger reaction and in the same direction. Should it produce as well a strong Soviet response the US price would be very high indeed.

There is one other course of action Arab nationalists could follow in an effort to reverse the dynamics of an Israeli absorption of all the territory of the Palestinian mandate. This is to take action designed explicitly to alter in their favour the capability image of the Arab states *vis-à-vis* Israel. The formula was developed by Gamal Abdul Nasser in 1970 and applied by Sadat in the October War of 1973. The objective was not to win a decisive military victory against Israel. Nasser then, and Arab nationalists in the mid-1980s, understood the impossibility of such a victory. The objective was to do far better than anyone, Arab, Israeli or outside observer, expected. This should lead to a greater sense of efficacy among Arabs and a substantial improvement in the Arab bargaining position. Such a course of action involved taking serious risks of loss of control but in 1986 it was apparently being considered by Syrian strategists.

The 1980s are a period in which a reformulation of US policy toward conflict in the Middle East must occur. In all likelihood that reformulation will occur, in fact is now occurring, incrementally. The major alterations will likely reflect the increasing perception of Soviet passivity, the challenge to established authority implicit in resurgent Islam and the declining leverage of conservative Arab regimes reflected in the persistent failure of their strategic approach as compared with that of their more radical challengers.[30]

Developing Soviet Alliance Patterns

The objectives of Soviet foreign policy in the post-Second World War Middle East are for the purposes of this essay inferred from Soviet foreign policy behaviour in the region. The list of Soviet objectives, is assumed to reflect, as did the list of US objectives, a balancing of interests and world view-generated objectives. The major objectives of the Soviet Union inferred from Soviet policy are three: (1) most important, to contain and to diminish perceived Western, primarily British and US, imperialist influence in the internal affairs of Middle Eastern regimes, (2) to advance the interests of pro-Soviet Marxist organisations in the area, and (3) to expand the economic ties of Middle Eastern economies with those of the Soviet Union and the Soviet bloc.

The pattern of Soviet policy prior to 1955 evinced little concern with the aspirations of either Arab or Iranian nationalists. The beginnings of a Soviet move toward the Arab nationalists appears opportunistic. Nasser, smarting under the humiliation of an Israeli raid on Egyptian occupied Gaza Strip in February 1955 and unable to wrench an unequivocal promise of arms sales from the Americans, his preferred source, turned to the Soviets and an arms purchase arrangement with Czechoslovakia. Then as US policy crystallised into what amounted to a *de facto* alliance with conservative Arab regimes, the Soviet Union moved in the direction of a similar association with rapid change, nationalistic regimes. Since these regimes were bitterly hostile toward Israel, Soviet policy became increasingly one of enmity toward Israel. But at no point has the Soviet government indicated any thought of a retreat from a position of supporting Israel's right to a secure and independent existence.[31]

The pattern of Soviet support for the so-called progressive Arabs has been one of military sales and technical assistance. But the case would be difficult to make that Soviet policy encouraged its Arab associates to move aggressively against Israel. Certainly the Arabs saw just the opposite policy, which they interpreted as one of undue restraint. They saw as typical of the Soviets the stand taken at the Glassboro Conference following the worst of Arab defeats in 1967. There they saw the Soviets as conciliatory to the point of being capitulatory.[32]

The relationship of the Soviet Union with progressive, nationalistic Arab regimes was comparable to that of the Americans with conservative, usually state nationalist Arab regimes. But for all the similarity in the type of relationship the judgements made about the relationships were entirely different. United States allies were widely seen as little more than puppets of Western imperialism but Soviet allies were seen as possessing nationalist legitimacy. The explanation for this asymmetry is historical. Traditional elites in the previous generations were most likely domestic allies of the British or French and frequently cooperated with the imperial mentor against their own countrymen who claimed to be struggling for real independence. The conservative regimes and elites that associated with the United States were the direct descendents of people who had had a long working relationship with the British. The associates of the Soviet Union on the other hand were seen as descendents of early nationalists and the Soviet Union as something of a disinterested protector of these aspiring nationalists. The association of the United States with its Arab allies thus created serious vulnerability. That of the Soviets with their allies did not.

Soviet and US involvement with the Arabs, though strikingly parallel, did differ in one dimension. US diplomacy in support of its

associates was far more vigorous than that of the Soviets for theirs.
An important case that illustrates the difference was that of the 1974
Kurdish rebellion against the government of Iraq. A report was
prepared summarising this case for the House of Representatives
Pike Committee on clandestine diplomacy. Later that report was
leaked to the press and published by the *Village Voice*.[33] The idea
for triggering a Kurdish rebellion in Iraq came from the Shah. Iraq
and Iran were respectively key members of the Soviet and American
blocs in the Middle East. Their mutual enmity was sufficiently intense
that each was pursuing a policy of interference in the internal affairs
of the other and occasionally one or the other turned to violence.
The Shah's proposal was that a Kurdish rebellion be triggered to
weaken and destabilise the Iraqi regime, a regime he knew the US
viewed as a Soviet client and an intransigent 'rejectionist' opponent
of Israel. The US government agreed and suggested that Israeli
cooperation be enlisted. The reason for this was to get captured
Soviet military equipment and secretly move that equipment across
the Iranian border into Iraqi Kurdistan. The manoeuvre would not only
provide an inexpensive source of arms but could mislead the Iraqis
into believing that the operation against them was in fact a Soviet
operation. There is no evidence indicating the Iraqis were deceived
by this too clever manoeuvre and presumably Soviet intelligence
concerning the Kurds, an ethnic group that is found in significant
numbers in the Soviet Union, was good enough to permit them to
read this operation. The operation in fact failed because the Iraqi
military was able to overcome the Kurds despite the external
assistance. The Shah's alternatives were direct military assistance or
the acceptance of an Algerian-mediated settlement. The Shah chose
the latter. But at no point in the Pike report is there a suggestion of
any Soviet role at all in support of their Iraqi ally. Apparently then
the Soviets simply observed a US-Iranian-Israeli manoeuvre using
an ethnic group with which the Soviets have a special relationship
and operating only a short distance from the Soviet border for the
purpose of destablising one of the Soviet Union's most important
friends in the Middle East!

The conclusion progressive Arabs have reached that the depth of
Soviet commitment to its friends in the area is far less than that of
US commitment to its friends is understandable. The Kurdish case is
particularly instructive because it occurred so close to the Soviet
borders. But it is in no way exceptional. It was part of a pattern that
suggests the conclusion that the Soviet perception of threat from the

United States and its allies in the region is of low intensity. If so, the objective suggested above of Soviet policy, to reduce US and allied influence in the area, is losing importance. The drift of Iraq away from the Soviet alliance became obvious shortly after this episode and it is difficult to resist the conclusion that the lack of support in so blatant a case may well explain in part that development.

Soviet support for pro-Marxist groups also falls into a pattern. The Soviets are willing on occasion to pay a large price to carry out a policy of protecting their ideological allies. The best example of course is Afghanistan where the price the Soviets have paid to preserve an unpopular Marxist regime is enormous in several dimensions.[34] Probably the next most important example involved support for Iraqi Marxists in the 1958–63 period, a policy that hurt the Soviets with both Nasserites and Ba'athists.[35] Ultimately the Soviets acquiesced in the Marxist defeat, although the acquiescence was not graceful. More typical was Soviet support for a Sudanese Marxist officer coup effort in 1971. The support was sufficiently open to annoy the Sudanese government but insufficient to help the coup succeed. The pattern seems to be an attraction to supporting local, friendly Marxists but primarily when they are strong enough to have some real hope of success, as in Iraq, or their replacement was seen as being a security problem for the Soviet Union, as may be the case in Afghanistan. The Soviets evinced little reluctance to be friendly with Nasser in Egypt and the Shah in Iran even though both dealt harshly with local Marxists. Soviet support for the Marxist regime in South Yemen has been generous. But this relationship is mutually beneficial and it is not self-evident, given the pattern of Soviet behaviour elsewhere, that the Soviets would take any serious risks to maintain that regime in power if indeed they have the capability to do so.

Soviet relations with minorities in the Middle East that aspire to national independence or considerable autonomy could serve as a litmus test of Soviet concern with the area. As mentioned above, the Soviets did make a serious effort to take advantage of Azerbaijan and Kurdish separatist sentiment at the close of the Second World War. But they have not done so on a major scale since, although the case of the Baluchis in Pakistan is an important exception on the margins of the region.[36] Should the Soviets decide on a more activist policy in the area, the minorities provide some obvious arenas in which they could play. Their support almost certainly would be solicited and an agreement to give support would be unlikely to produce a confrontation with the United States and Europe.

The Soviet response to the appearance of resurgent Islam as the primary radical force in the Middle East today closely parallels that of the United States. The Soviets do have a major advantage, however. The Iranian government, in its campaign to eliminate the overweening influence of the oppressor states, has essentially allied itself to the Soviet Union's closest allies in the Middle East. The progressive bloc of states is seen from Teheran as sincerely opposed to external control in the region. The conservative bloc, on the other hand and fitting the pattern described above, is depicted as composed of lackeys of the wounded and hence more dangerous of the two great powers, the United States.[37]

However Khomeini and his government view the United States and the Soviet Union alike as 'great oppressors'. In Khomeini's eyes, the rivalry between the two oppressors is real and possibly exploitable. But he believes both superpowers are ultimately dedicated to preserving oppressor hegemony over the oppressed world and will bury their antagonism if a threat to that hegemony develops. Thus when the Americans suffered two great shocks at the hands of the Islamic revolution, the fall of the Shah and the taking of hostages, the very basis of oppressor hegemony was challenged. The oppressed people were beginning to understand oppressor impotence in the face of a vast popular force. At this point, in the Iranian interpretation, the oppressors orchestrated an attack on Iran. The attack was spearheaded by a regime, that of Iraq, which had served faithfully one oppressor, the Soviet Union, but then moved closer to the other oppressor, the United States. The Iraqi attack, as expected, was supported by the entire camp of American vassals including Sadat whom the other vassals pretended to oppose. The 'usurper' state, Israel, it was clear to Khomeini, was involved as well. But the oppressor plot failed and the Iraqis were thrown back. At this point, completely as expected, the two superpowers dropped all pretence of discord and entered in an open 'tilt' toward Iraq.[38]

In Soviet eyes, this Iranian view, widely accepted by regime supporters, is apparently as other worldly as it is in US eyes and just as difficult to take seriously. The Soviet Union has made a far more determined effort to convince Iranians of its peaceful and non-hegemonic intent than have the Americans. But their success ratio is poor on the political front, somewhat better on the economic front. The Tudeh Party has been persecuted and Soviet diplomats summarily expelled from Iran. Soviet policy in Afghanistan is bitterly condemned and Iranian propaganda persists in equating the two great oppressors. However, even as the *Voice of Iran*, broadcasting for the Tudeh Party from Baku, calls for a popular front to overturn the Khomeini regime and arms shipments are resumed to Iraq, Soviet officials continue to visit Iran and argue the case for Soviet friendship with the regime.

In general Soviet policy toward resurgent Islam, like US policy, is situationally determined and implicitly contradictory. It follows patterns that reflect the meaning, favourable or unfavourable, of the impact of Islamic forces on the alliance patterns that have developed over the past generation. Thus in Afghanistan, where it is the primary destabilising force for a Soviet client regime, it is the enemy. In the eastern Mediterranean it is the at least temporary ally of Soviet allies, and there it is implicitly supported. In the Iran–Iraq war it is a serious threat to a sometime friendly regime and is opposed even though this policy makes the Soviets *de facto* allies in this one theatre of the United States. Each sees this support of Iraq as necessary to contain the other, however.

The picture that emerges here is of a Soviet policy in the Middle East that is far less activist and far more concerned with control than is US policy. The Soviet tilt toward Iraq is more equivocal than that of the United States, for example, and hence it is less likely that Soviet policy will be determined by the momentum of events in the area. In the Arab–Israeli conflict arena, the Soviets appear equally determined not to lose control of their policy to the vicissitudes of Arab fortunes on the battlefield or on the diplomatic front. The Soviets made clear their formula for a settlement of the Arab-Israeli conflict shortly after the 1967 June War. That formula called for an international conference jointly chaired by the United States and the Soviet Union, in which a comprehensive peace is negotiated.[39] The settlement would include Palestinian self-determination in some part of the old Palestinian mandate, mutual diplomatic recognition and suitable security guarantees. But the Soviets have not at any time pursued a vigorous diplomatic effort to achieve this formula. The Nixon and Carter administrations tentatively explored variations of it but in effect acquiesced in an Israeli veto of the approach. Kissinger's step-by-step approach and, its extension, the Camp David approach followed a very different formula – one that excluded Soviet participation and rejected the comprehensive approach in favour, as described above, of an effort to bring the most 'moderate' Arab regimes into an agreement with Israel as the first step. Soviet resistance to being excluded was surprisingly muted. There was no major Soviet diplomatic offensive on the subject even though the Soviet's Arab friends would have welcomed it. The pattern was one of an apparent general low intensity of concern.

There was, however, an important exception to this pattern and one that deserves far greater attention that it has received. The one truly vigorous Soviet military and diplomatic response was to the only major initiative taken by the Arabs since Israel's war for independence. That was during the 1973 October war in which the Arabs demonstrated a narrowing of the wide military technological gap.

The Soviet air-lift of weapons to Egypt and the negotiation of a cease-fire represented a sharp break with previous Soviet behaviour. Then when the cease-fire appeared to be breaking down the Soviets asked the United States to join them in enforcing it and warned that if the United States did not agree the Soviets would take unilateral action to do so. This Soviet note precipitated the crisis of 24–25 October 1973 – one of, if not the, most dangerous confrontations of the nuclear era. The crisis dissipated the following day when both the United States and the Soviet Union accepted a proposal that a United Nations force be sent to the area instead. But the episode demonstrated the potential for superpower confrontation in the Arab–Israeli conflict. The precipitant at the time appears to have been a possibly misinterpreted and certainly unexpected Soviet activisim in the area.[40] The pattern of Soviet diplomatic passivity was so well established that scenarios were not seriously considered which assumed a Soviet diplomatic activism. The episode argues that such scenarios should be taken seriously.

IV TRENDS IN THE BASES OF CONFLICT IN THE MIDDLE EAST

From the perspective of the political milieu of the Middle East, no trend is more important in giving definition to the situation than is that of the growth in an insistence on political participation on the part of the people themselves. That trend has developed to the point that only in marginal areas of the region can it still be said that much of the public remains politically inert. The huge mobs that appear on the streets of Teheran or Cairo with near spontaneity give testimony to the fact that the Middle East has entered the era of mass politics.

Every regime in the region has been placed on notice that the strategy of political control it must engage in has altered fundamentally. Those that fail to accommodate to this change are unlikely to survive. Similarly, the transition from traditional systems with acquiescent publics to modern systems with potentially assertive publics has led to a fundamental alteration in state power equations and in the regional balance of power. In the nineteenth century, European imperialism in the area was characterised by a relatively easy manipulation of traditional systems. Elements of the traditional elite were susceptible to purchase and when coercion was called for, the forces necessary to establish and preserve order were relatively small and inexpensive. Even in the 1940s and 1950s, years in which mass participation was already developing, coups could be executed by external powers operating largely through the still important traditional forces. Interventions occurred in this period in Iran, Iraq, Jordan, Syria, Lebanon, the Sudan and Egypt. Today interventions in these states on this order are surely impossible. However, even though this change represents a fundamental alteration in relative power, it has yet to be fully comprehended either in the region or in the international system. Recurring references such as that to the 'loss of Iran' or to Iran as the 'strategic prize' in the region implicitly reflect a view that external control of regional states remains a possibility.

The contest for external control of regional states throughout the modern era has been one involving competing interferences in the internal affairs of these states. The early post-Second World War period was one in which the remnants of the imperial rivalries of the British and French and Russians were still apparent. However, within a decade the Soviet-American struggle for pre-eminence in the region dominated the international system level of conflict involving the Middle East. British and French predominance persisted only in the periphery of the region and other European influence was manifest essentially through normal diplomatic channels. The US inability to influence the course of the Iranian revolution, Soviet difficulties in achieving military control in weak Afghanistan and the embarrassment of the Americans and Europeans in Lebanon in 1983 reflected accurately a radical capability alteration and a diminution in the ability of external forces to control events in the region. Nor was there any real likelihood that the Sino-Soviet conflict could be acted out in the form of competitive interference in the affairs of Middle Eastern regimes. During the rebellion in the Dhofar province of Oman, Soviet and Chinese officials competed for influence with the rebels and this competition seemed to forecast the entrance of China as an active external participant in regional affairs. But when the Shah of Iran, who was opposing the rebellion in Dhofar, urged the Chinese to cease their assistance to the rebels, they quietly acquiesced. Implicitly the Chinese had recognised the strength of regional actors and the difficulty in playing with their internal affairs.

The improvement in relative capability ratings produced by the development of participating mass publics in Iran and the Arab states has affected even more seriously the two Middle Eastern states that were already in the immediate post-Second World War period highly politically participant: Turkey and Israel. Turkey's focus from the Ataturk period had been self-consciously European and little concerned with its Middle Eastern neighbours whom it regarded as backward, undeveloped and highly vulnerable to external domination. Seriously concerned with a perceived threat from the Soviets, Turkish leaders looked for their defence to an alliance with the Americans and Western Europeans. Far from looking for assistance from regional states, they saw the vulnerability of their neighbours as a major defence liability. However, this attitude began changing as the development process accelerated in the Arab and Iranian worlds. Turkish policy increasingly reflected a greater concern with developments in the region and a concomitant willingness to follow a different path in the region from that of their Western allies. This was especially apparent in the October War of 1973 when the Turks refused to assist in any way US efforts to support Israel and instead permitted Soviet overflights of Turkish territory to air-lift supplies to Egypt and Syria. It is apparent today in Turkey's cooperative relationship with the Islamic Republic of Iran.

Israel effectively came into existence as a 'developed' state. The core population was European and by any standard of modernity was on a par with Western European states. The Oriental Jewish population passed through the development process with exceptional speed. It was the existence of a fully participant and technologically skilled population that was most responsible for the capability advantage of Israel over its Arab neighbours. However, the early Egyptian and Syrian successes in the October War in 1973 were dramatic evidence of a narrowing of the capability distance which separated Israel from her neighbours. The Israeli withdrawal from Lebanon following the 1982 invasion and the occupation of southern Lebanon was even more dramatic evidence of a continuing narrowing of the capability gap. Confronted with growing resistance from indigenous elements, previously seen as largely passive, Israel found herself seriously overextended. The capability distance measured in terms of military force remains a broad one in Israel's favour. But the appearance of assertive publics in the Arab world willing to accept major-sacrifices in opposing Israel has narrowed the capability distance measured in non-military terms.

The appearance of mass politics as a characteristic feature of Arab and Iranian behaviour is altering dramatically not only relative capability in Arab and Iranian favour but also the style of regional-external power interactions. The primary change in style, as mentioned, is the rapid decline in ability of external actors to interfere in the internal politics of regional actors. However, conflict in the middle East, far from diminishing as a consequence of the growth in political participation, is growing in scope and intensity. As such it presents external actors both with a threat to the stability of established relationships and an opportunity to improve relative influence in the region by taking advantage of new alliance prospects.

The trends that most clearly associate with the expansion of the scope and intensity of conflict in the region are trends in political community identity. Unlike the trend toward greater political participation, identity trends are complex, contradictory and uncertain in thrust. But there are among them some reasonably clear and identifiable patterns. Possibly the least ambiguous of these identity trend patterns is that of a growth in intensity of identity within minority ethnic communities that have sufficient capability to be able to think seriously in terms of establishing an independent nation state. The most significant examples of this are the Kurdish, the Baluchi and the Turkoman peoples. As discussed above, leaders of these communities tend to be opportunistic in terms of the alliances they are willing to consider. They can be counted on to respond enthusiastically to opportunities offered by the international political environment for alliances that have a serious prospect for helping them achieve their goal of independence or of significant autonomy. A long history of betrayals by past allies does not appear to have dampened the enthusiasm.

This developing identity trend offers to external actors the possibility for destablising or weakening regional allies of external competitors. Finding themselves with a declining ability to weaken or alter such regimes through involvement in internal domestic politics, external actor policy makers are likely to welcome the opportunity to exacerbate secularist tendencies. It is easily predictable that an intensifying Soviet-American rivalry in the region would lead to serious consideration of the relative merits of alliances with Kurds, Turkomans or Baluchis.

A related trend in the Arabic speaking world is a growth in the intensity of identity within minority sectarian communities. This trend is most apparent in Lebanon where it has produced a climate of hatred often at the genocidal level. The three sectarian communities in Lebanon that currently are the most serious aspirants for autonomy bordering on independence are the Maronites, the Druze and the Shia. The leaders of these communities, like the leaders of ethnic communities noted above, are opportunistic in their choice of allies. All three, for example, have been willing to deal with Israel, the enemy of the Arabs, to advance their prospects for some degree of independence. However, the capability potential of minority sectarian communities, is not sufficient to allow any of them a realistic, long-term hope for real independence. But in the short term, the political environment often appears to offer real hope of independence and, like the Kurds, they have been unable to resist the temptation to explore the opportunities. Because prospects for independence or serious autonomy are poor for these sectarian communities in the long run, current trends toward intensifying identity with small sectarian communities are unlikely to endure. Any peaceful solution to conflict in Lebanon almost certainly must involve establishing a *modus vivendi* which encourages reconciliation and a developing trend toward identification with a broader Lebanese community.

Also within the Arab world, strong trends have been developing toward identification with the communities embraced within the territories of the externally imposed boundaries of Arab states. These trends toward what has been called here 'state nationalism' have appeared to be at the expense of an identification with the broad Arab national community. Most external observers indeed have concluded that the predominant trend regarding identification with the Arab nation is one of declining intensity. However, the case studies concerning Sadat, Saddam Hossein, Arafat and Assad in this chapter suggest that this judgement is at best premature. Arab proponents of a broad Arab nationalism have suffered serious defeats, often at the hands of external forces, and have suffered a loss in credibility. But, as the case studies indicated, legitimacy for Arab political leaders still depends substantially on judgements regarding their loyalty to and support for the Arab nation. The real test for the relative importance of trends toward state nationalism as compared with a trend toward Arab nationalism would be made if, as a consequence of changing power relationships, a realistic possibility for establishing a large Arab nation state developed. In such an event the attachment to the Arab nation might well overwhelm competing attachments to, for example, Jordan, Iraq, and Syria.

A far more important source of regional conflict today, however involves competing attachments to national communities and to the ummah, the broad Islamic community. In this case the short-term trend picture is relatively clear. With the discrediting of and loss of faith in nationalist leaders, a strong trend has developed among those individuals who have recently become politically participant to turn to Islamic religious leaders for political direction. Since there is throughout the region a profound sense of economic, political and social deprivation among the newly awakened mass, the receptivity is great for religious leaders who can articulate both the grievances and aspirations of the mass. Without question, religio-political leaders have replaced nationalist leaders as the primary focus of populist attraction. Mass audiences are responding with far greater enthusiasm to the manipulation of religious as compared with national symbols. The Iran–Iraq War represents a serious challenge to both state nationalist and Arab nationalist forces. This challenge to secular leaders is at least as important as the Arab-Israeli conflict as the basis for major conflict in the region.

There is, however, a strong case to be made that the powerful trend toward an Islamic community identification and away from a national community identification is a short-term phenomenon. The trend toward secularism has gained strength throughout the period of rapid change. It reflects a conviction that modern societies must rest on advanced technology and technocratically competent bureaucracies that can administer the extraordinarily complex rules necessary for the functioning of advanced economies. In the secularist view, an Islamic ideology, like a Christian ideology, can offer little more than highly abstract normative guidance. Also society cannot continue to function well in the face of the extreme polarisation such as that in Iran in which those following and those opposing religio-political leadership seem to be part of different cultures cohabiting the same territory. Eventually reconciliation must occur and when it does is likely to reflect an identity with a community which is at once national and religious and in which a secular trend continues to develop.

Another basis of weakness of the Islamic trend is the great diversity within Islam. The most important problem here is that Ayatollah Khomeini is regarded by many Sunni Moslems as a leader of one section of the Shia sect, not of the ummah. This attitude has effectively blocked the spread of Khomeini's personal charismatic attraction to Sunni communities. But the diversity goes far beyond Sunni–Shia sectarian differences and includes many opposing schools of thought. To overcome it, a leader capable of appealing to a diversity of groups is almost a prerequisite for maintaining momentum. For the next decade, however, conflict between religious and nationalist leaders in the region is likely to be a primary source of conflict in the Middle East and will be a factor in conflict at every level.

The current so-called oil glut has reduced the importance of the objective of maintaining a flow of oil to world industries as a source of conflict. As mentioned above, despite the exceptional importance of the objective for many external and regional actors, it has not counted as one of the major sources of conflict in the Middle East. However, briefly in 1973 and 1974 there were serious indications that demands for access to oil at an affordable price could become the most important basis of conflict in the region and that as such it would lead to a fundamental reordering of alliances. Sadat's quick move to end the use of oil as a political weapon and easier than expected adjustments to the oil price rise obviated that crisis. But the oil glut is a temporary phenomenon. The long-term trend is toward oil scarcity and that trend carries with it a potential for generating serious conflict. Consumer competition for access to limited oil supplies and consumer efforts to prevent runaway oil prices from inflicting unacceptable damage to economies could lead to a consideration of interventionist strategies. Producer awareness of the enhanced bargaining force granted them could make almost irresistable the temptation to use oil as a political weapon, especially in the Arab and Islamic conflict with Israel.

Trends in the Arab-Israeli conflict are very much the product of capability and identity trends in the Arab world. But they reflect as well some basic patterns in Israel's own evolving political character. Foremost of the latter are two trends, one reflecting a growth in assertiveness of the most religious Jewish communities in Israel and the other the steadily increasing importance in Israeli political attitudes of the Oriental Jewish population. Both trends are pushing Israeli policy in a direction that makes difficult meaningful compromise with Palestinian Arabs whether living in Israel proper or the occupied territories. The point may already have been reached at which Israeli politicians can no longer consider a settlement with Palestinians that involves anything more substantial than some control over local affairs in Arab cities on the West Bank. If so, movement in the direction of serious compromise can occur only as a consequence of major environmental change either in the form of a substantial balance of power shift in the Arab favour or of the willingness of external states to apply serious pressure on Israel.

As indicated above, the case is easily made that a balance of power shift in the Arab favour is in fact occurring. This is largely a consequence of the growth in political participation in the Arab world. But it reflects also the overall results of identity change in the area. The expectation that other Arab regimes would follow the Sadat path and agree to bilateral settlements with Israel is not being realised. This behaviour indicates a continuing identity attachment to the Arab national community. Even more significant, evidence of a popular shift toward resurgent Islam is convincing. Since the leaders of this movement are even more adamant than Arab nationalists in their attitudes regarding the Palestinians, this important trend can only add to the Arab determination to reject the Sadat path. Legal opposition parties in Egypt which had initially endorsed the Camp David Agreement reversed their position in the spring of 1986. This reflected a growing strength of the Nasserite and Islamic movements, both of which are insisting that Egypt return to the forefront of the struggle against Israel.

Trends in the Soviet-American conflict in the Middle East are difficult to discern. There is some evidence of increased diplomatic activity by the Soviet Union since Gorbachev's accession to power, but both the Soviet Union and the United States have been reacting to rather than generating crises in the region. These reactions tend to fall into a pattern of protecting established alliances and have not in sum led to any significant exacerbation of relations between the two universal powers. Both governments express concern that the Iran–Iraq war will benefit the cause of the other and yet both governments are rather passively tilting toward Iraq in the conflict. The US preoccupation with terrorism has not led to a significant increase in suspicions of ultimate Soviet orchestration of terrorism and both governments appear determined to avoid confrontation in this matter. Both governments are on record with proposals for pushing the Arab-Israeli conflict toward resolution. But neither appears to be willing to place the kind of pressure on regional actors that would be necessary to give momentum to its proposal.

The conclusion is a clear one. The trends that are of vital importance in giving new definition to conflict in the region are those appearing from the intra-regime and inter-regime levels of conflict. At this point in time, therefore, the primary source of disturbance is emanating from the lowest conflict levels. The trends at this level, however, are of major importance and one of them, the trend of expanding Islamic influence, has the potential to produce major disruption even at the international system level of conflict. Despite its importance, however, the Islamic resurgence has yet to generate any consistent strategic and tactical response from external powers in their Middle East policies.

V   APPLICATIONS TO THE FUTURE

Even if one believes that 'all the past is but a prologue to the future', it is difficult to apply what has been learned, since the past has been marked by changes and contradictions. It is, however, possible, on the basis of an assessment of trends in the levels of conflict, to identify the types of crises that are most likely to occur and even to say something about the conditions and circumstances under which they may happen. The purpose is not prediction as such but the creation of a framework for analysis, which can then be used to determine whether and to what extent the lessons learned may be applicable to the future or whether we sail upon an uncharted sea. The scenarios that follow could be understood as being developed on that basis and as intended to serve that purpose.

Internal Strife

Regimes such as that of Saudi Arabia have been strikingly successful in controlling the direction and tempo of change.[41] They have been able to do so largely because of the extraordinary income from oil. This has given them the means to grant large subsidies to tribal leaders and religious leaders who represent the traditional structure of society. Through marriage virtually every traditional power group is related to the royal family, now vastly extended, and hence has a strong interest in its preservation. Middle-class and technocratic elements have seen their real incomes grow rapidly and a large percentage of the working force is composed of immigrants from other parts of the Arab world and South Asia. The Saudi leadership has purchased good relations from the PLO which they subsidise heavily, and from such regimes as that of Syria which is a self-appointed leader of the progressive and nationalistic bloc. Saudi foreign policy is carefully calibrated to reduce polarisation tendencies in the Arab world and to avoid appearing, as Anwar Sadat did, being too clearly tied to the Western powers and too accommodating of Israel. Saudi laws and institutions are in surface conformity with the Qoran and interpretations of it. In sum, Saudi policy overall has been skillful in its balancing of contending forces and has preserved largely intact the traditional governing elite.

However there are many Saudis who are dissatisfied with the slow pace of change, the lack of freedom and the lack of access to the centres of decision making. They lament the failure of the Saudi elite with its great oil wealth to play a leadership role in advancing the cause of Arab nationalism or of resurgent Islam. There is thus a considerable receptivity for revolutionary leadership. This presents to members of the royal family, particularly those who see little likelihood of their branch of the family gaining central power, the opportunity to mobilise popular forces to help them improve their competitive position in court politics. Some of the princes are themselves strong Arab nationalists and are aware of the potential for a great Arab leader emerging from the ranks of the royal family. The individual most frequently looked to as having exceptional potential in this regard is Prince Abdullah whose institutional base of support is the National Guard. Were he or another half brother to ally with either Islamic or Arab nationalist popular elements, the danger of the collapse of the carefully balanced and modulated control system would be a serious one. Since almost certainly this would unleash populist elements, the difficulties confronting an external power eager to help restore control would be serious. The analogy of Iran in which a large, well-trained and lavishly equipped security force could not hold back an essentially unarmed popular force would be close. Providing more conventional weapons to the loyalist forces would be of questionable utility in dealing with the situation and the West might have to consider direct intervention with all its costs and difficulties.

Local Conflict

President Saddam Hc sein of Iraq, much to the surprise and chagrin of the leaders of the Islamic Republic of Iran, remains in apparent firm control of Iraq even though he has suffered serious setbacks in his seven-year war with Iran.[42] But Saddam Hossein's survival is the consequence of a control system in which the instruments of terror are central. Thanks to the assistance of oil producing regimes of the Arabian peninsula, the Iraqi government has been able to meet the material needs of its citizens at an only slightly diminished level. However, the dreams of achieving the leadership of a revitalised Arab national movement have been destroyed and Saddam Hossein has lost personal legitimacy with much, probably, most, of his population. Fear among secular elements of a force in Iraq similar to that in Iran which would purge them from all positions of governmental or social influence, is a mainstay of the regime. But the picture in sum is one of fear and coerced acceptance.

This translates most seriously in the form of low morale for the Iraqi armed forces. A majority of those forces are drawn from the Shia community of Iraq which constitutes probably 60 per cent of the population of Iraq. An indeterminate percentage of that group is highly religious and basically sympathetic with the Islamic leadership of Iran. The danger therefore is omnipresent that Iranian successes in the battlefield could lead to desertions and an unwillingness to take the risks in combat that are essential for successful resistance. Because the Iraqi system is one of the most tightly closed in the world, the seriousness of this situation cannot be appraised with any confidence by outside observors. The possibility of sudden and rapid disintegration therefore cannot be ruled out.

The contrast with the Iranian armed forces could not be more sharp. Drawn largely from core support public elements, the Iranian military, especially the Revolutionary Guard component, manifests a willingness to risk sacrifices that is exceptional among military forces in history. But Iranian inferiority in terms of military equipment, particularly that of the air force, is sufficiently serious to preserve some balance of force with Iraq. However, the long-term prognosis, assuming Khomeini's personal survival in Iran, is poor for Iraq and good for Iran. Should a breakthrough occur, many new options will be available to the Iranian leadership. More serious still, the internal forces of resurgent Islam in every Arab state will be encouraged and the task of controlling them made more difficult. Should external forces seek to reverse the deterioration of the situation of Iraq the problem of restoring lost legitimacy to the Iraqi regime is one that would have to be addressed. Direct military intervention whatever its effectiveness in preventing an Iranian take-over could only add to that problem.

Superpower Confrontation

When Israeli forces entered Lebanon in June 1982, they did so apparently with three major expectations.[43] The first was that within forty-eight hours both the PLO and the Syrians would have sustained crippling defeats and would be on their way to leaving Lebanon. The second was that a strong government led by Bashir Gamyel as president would establish firm control in Lebanon and would make peace with, and ultimately ally with, Israel. The third expectation was implicit in the Israeli action but never explicated publicly. That was that the Soviet Union would give rhetorical support to its two local allies, the PLO and the Syrians, and later would replace Syria's lost equipment but would limit its opposition to the invasion to the rhetorical level. The first two expectations were not realised. Both the PLO and Syria did sustain serious defeats. But expelling the PLO required months and Syrian forces were not expelled. Bashir Gamyel was elected president. But he quickly demonstrated an awareness of the fact that controlling the various factions in Lebanon would be more the consequence of a deft balancing act than of the application of coercion. He simply lacked the decisional freedom to perform as Ariel Sharon had expected.

In the third area, however, Israeli expectations were fully realised. Even though the case was a strong one that the invasion was not the consequence of Palestinian provocation in the preceding twelve-month period, the Soviets did very little to help their two good friends who were under attack. This Soviet pattern of behaviour was familiar enough. But there is reason to believe that the activism of Soviet diplomacy in 1973 was not an anomaly. If there is any pattern to Soviet policy in the area that is really well established, it is the avoidance of losing tactical control in a critical theatre and allowing the dynamics to be determined by lesser and indigenous actors. The bewildering range of sectarian, ethnic and ideological conflicts in Lebanon virtually defy control and the Soviets appear to be well aware of that fact. But if caution in Lebanon is perceived as reflecting general Soviet diplomatic/military passivity, the possibility of miscalculation leading to superpower confrontation is very real. An Israeli attack on Syrian air bases inside Syria, if not the consequence of Syrian recklessness in Soviet eyes, could present the Soviets with a major dilemma. A failure now to give Syria the support needed to stave off another catastrophic defeat could cost the Soviets what regional credibility they still maintain. Soviet diplomacy in the Middle East in the Gorbachev era is reflecting an activism on a level not seen since the late 1950s except in times of outright warfare. So far this activism is in the form of personal diplomatic activity by a stable of major Soviet foreign policy figures, and may not signify a willingness to take risks. But the failure to respond militarily to an Israeli attack on Syrian air bases would result in very high diplomatic and imagery costs. On the other hand, an overt military response, such as introducing Soviet-manned fighter-interceptors into Syria, could both lead to direct clashes with the Israeli Air Force and induce counter-measures by the United States.

Indeed, a Syrian-Israeli clash could pose for the United States a dilemma similar to that posed for the Soviet Union. If Syria were the aggressor, the United States would find it hard to deny support to Israel, however much it might wish to dampen the conflict and to avoid an Israeli triumph, with all its unsettling implications. This denial would become virtually impossible were the Soviets to give material help to Syria, especially if that help were of a scale and nature sufficient to threaten an Israeli defeat or even to cause heavy Israeli losses. In such a case, the dynamics of the Soviet-American competition would reinforce the general US tendency to support Israel in time of crises and even if such a crisis had been precipitated by Israel, might well lead to US military involvement. At the very least, one might expect a crisis in Soviet-American relations and the pressures and counterpressures by the superpowers could conceivably affect Europe as well as the Middle East – a possibility of great concern to the European members of the Atlantic Alliance.

Notes

1. On Egypt see Afaf Lutfi al Sayyid, *Egypt and Cromer* (New York: Praeger, 1969). On Turkey see Niyazi Berkes, *The Development of Secularism in Turkey* (Montreal: McGill University Press, 1964). On the Arabs see George Antonius, *The Arab Awakening* (New York: Capricorn Books, 1965). On Iran see Richard Cottam, *Nationalism in Iran* (Pittsburgh: University of Pittsburgh Press, 1978).
2. For a seminal work outlining the stereotypical views see Archibald Thornton, *The Imperial Idea and Its Enemies* (New York: Praeger, 1978).
3. On Soviet policy in the area see Robert O. Freedman, *Soviet Policy Toward the Middle East Since 1970* (New York: Praeger, 1978).

4. On identity transformation in Egypt see Mahmud Ismail, 'Nationalism in Egypt Before the Revolution', unpublished PhD dissertation, University of Pittsburgh, 1966.

5. See Raymond A. Hinnebusch, *Egyptian Politics Under Sadat* (New York: Cambridge University Press, 1985).

6. On the Kurds in Iraq see Edgar O'Ballance, *The Kurdish Revolt, 1961–1970* (London: Faber & Faber, 1973).

7. On the Maronites see Jonathan C. Randal, *Going All the Way: Christian Warlords, Israeli Adventurers and the War in Lebanon* (New York: Vintage Books, 1984).

8. See Yann Richard, 'Ayatollah Kashani: Precursor of the Islamic Republic', in Nikki Keddie (ed.), *Religion and Politics in Iran* (New Haven: Yale University Press, 1983).

9. For critical views of Sadat's diplomacy see Salwa S. Gomaa, 'Egyptian Diplomacy in the Seventies', unpublished PhD dissertation, University of Pittsburgh, 1986; S. El Shazli, *The Crossing of the Suez* (London: Third World Centre for Research and Publishing, 1980); David Hirst and Irene Beeson, *Sadat* (London: Faber & Faber, 1981); M. H. Haikal, *Autumn of Fury: The Assassination of Sadat* (New York: Random House, 1983).

10. Henry Kissinger, *Years of Upheaval* (Boston: Little Brown, 1982), p. 639.

11. Foreign Broadcast Information Service, Middle East and Africa, 3 November 1978, A pp. 2–5. This is the president's address to the conference.

12. For a recent picture of Iraq see Christine Moss Helms, *Iraq: Eastern Flank of the Arab World* (Washington, DC: Brookings Institute, 1984).

13. See Barry Rubin, *Paved with Good Intentions: The American Experience in Iran* (New York: Oxford University Press, 1980), and Jerrold D. Green, *Revolution in Iran: The Politics of Counter Mobilization* (New York: Praeger, 1982).

14. For a good development of the Shah's economic difficulties see Robert Graham, *Iran: The Illusion of Power* (New York: St. Martins Press, 1979).

15. See Richard Cottam, 'Goodbye to America's Shah', *Foreign Policy*, No. 34, Spring 1975, pp. 3–20.

16. Foreign Broadcast Information Service, South Asia, 10 February 1983, I p. 14.

17. See the speech of Tariq Aziz in Tareq Y. Ismail, *Iraq and Iran: Roots of the Conflict* (Syracuse: Syracuse University Press, 1983) pp. 89–100.

18. See for example, Foreign Broadcast Information Service, Middle East and Africa, 21 September 1980.

19. In April 1986 two opposition parties, the Socialists and the Liberals, reversed earlier positions and have denounced the Camp David Agreement. See Foreign Broadcast Information Service, Middle East and Africa, 4 April 1986, D pp. 2–3, 9 April 1986, D pp. 1–2, 25 April 1986, D pp. 1–2.

20. For a good background of the milieu in Lebanon see Michael Suleiman, *Political Parties in Lebanon* (Ithaca: Cornell University Press, 1967).

21. A former aid of Kissinger's thinks there is a good reason to believe that

Kissinger played a direct role in inaugurating the civil war through the CIA and in cooperation with Israel. Roger Morris, *Uncertain Greatness* (New York: Harper & Row, 1977), p. 261.

22. Waled Khalidi, *Conflict and Violence in Lebanon: Confrontation in the Middle East* (Cambridge: Center for International Affairs, Harvard University, 1983).

23. For King Hossein's talk see Foreign Broadcast Information Service, Middle East and Africa, 20 February 1986, F pp. 1–16.

24. See George Harris, *Turkey: Coping with Crisis* (Boulder, Col.: Westview Press, 1985).

25. Foreign Broadcast Information Service, South Asia, 28 February 1983, I p. 11.

26. For a typical popular exposition see Frank Gervasi, *The Case for Israel* (New York: Viking Press, 1967).

27. Regarding the Maronites see, Randal, *Going All the Way*, op. cit. (see note 7).

28. A coup was seriously considered as late as January 1979. See Zbigniew Brezezinski, *Power and Principle: Memoirs of the National Security Adviser, 1977–1981* (New York: Farrar, Strauss, Giroux, 1983, p. 379).

29. For a full development of the case see Cottam, 'The Iranian Revolution', Juan R. I. Cole and Nikki R. Kiddie, (eds), *Shi'ism and Social Protest* (New Haven: Yale University Press, 1986).

30. For accounts of American diplomacy see Seth P. Tillman, *The United States in the Middle East: Interests and Obstacles* (Bloomington, Indiana: Indiana University Press, 1982), and William Quandt, *Decade of Decisions* (Berkeley: University of California Press, 1977).

31. The best account of this is Kettett Love, *Suez: The Twice Fought War* (New York: McGraw Hill, 1970).

32. *New York Times*, 24 June 1967, 5:1.

33. The *Village Voice*, 16 February 1976, p. 85.

34. Henry C. Bradsher, *Afghanistan and the Soviet Union* (Durham: Duke University Press, 1983). This is a good summary statement.

35. For an indication of the extent of pro-Soviet Marxist influence at least on the Iraqi government propaganda line see the FBIS reports from Iraq in 1962. The propaganda line clearly parallels that of the Soviet Union for the last year of Qasem's presidency.

36. See Selig Harrison, *In Afghanistan's Shadow: Baluch Nationalism and Soviet Temptations* (Washington, DC: Carnegie Endowment, 1981).

37. Foreign Broadcast Information Service, South Asia, 9 February 1983, I p. 11

38. Ibid.

39. See for this Brezhnev plan, *Pravda*, 16 September 1982.

40. Kissinger, *Years of Upheaval*, op. cit., p. 575 (see note 10).

41. For a full treatment of the royal family see David Holden and Richard Johns, *The House of Saud* (New York: Holt, Rinehart and Winston 1981).

42. See on Iraq, Christine Helms, *Iraq*, op. cit. (see note 12) and Shirin Tahir Kheli and Shaheen Ayubi (eds.), *The Iran-Iraq War: New Weapons and Old Conflicts* (New York: Praeger, 1983).

43. For an exposition of Israeli expectations see Zeev Schiff and Ehud Ya'ari, *Israel's Lebanon War* (New York: Simon and Schuster, 1984).

3 The Uses of Force in the Middle East

Anthony H. Cordesman

Any analysis of the West's ability to use force in the Middle East must carefully consider the match between the potential need for the use of force and the range of scenarios that may occur. This is not simply a matter of analysing the kind of high probability scenarios discussed in Chapter 2. The problem with the Middle East, as with most areas in the Third World where the West may have to use military force, is that real world cases tend to be the result of unexpected crises and not of predictable contingencies and long-term trends.

The practical problem is to determine how well the West can use military force in the face of the cumulative probability that one of many low probability scenarios will occur. In general, this means comparing the individual and collective military capabilities of Western military forces against both typical scenarios and the most demanding test cases for Western military intervention. For example, a direct US and Soviet military confrontation in Iran is now a low probability contingency. At the same time, it is the most demanding test the West may have to face, and the one which is now most threatening to the West's strategic interests.

Western military capabilities must, therefore, be evaluated in terms of capability analysis rather than probability analysis. It is easy to fix on a given case that seems to involve a broad range of Western interests, and make this the test case for evaluating the merit of NATO-wide action, or multilateral action by a number of NATO states. There are, however, many causes of violence in the region. Most do not justify any Western use of force, and many others will lead to contingencies where the West will not benefit from NATO-wide or multilateral action. Still others will tend to divide NATO rather than unite it, or to create unacceptable political and economic risks.

Even those contingencies which seem most likely to justify the

West's use of force generally involve strong pros and cons, particularly in the case of collective or multilateral action. The problem for the West is to identify those cases where there is the proper match between the need for force and the ability to use it effectively. Finding the match will never be easy, and the trends in regional military forces will steadily reduce the West's options for effective military action during the coming decade.

I FORCES IN, AND AVAILABLE FOR DEPLOYMENT TO, THE MIDDLE EAST

Both policy planners and international relations experts tend to be impatient with the details of military force. There is a natural tendency for many policy makers to see the use of force as a simple solution to the complexity of politics. In practice, however, military forces are inevitably limited in many critical ways. This is particularly true when they are asked to perform military tasks at long distances for which they have not been designed or tailored, and which involve new and unstable political and tactical conditions.

Only a few countries in NATO still preserve even a limited capability to perform such out-of-area missions, and budget pressures and the steadily rising Warsaw Pact threat have gradually reduced these capabilities over time. Britain, for example, had to use nearly 75 per cent of its major combat vessels to fight in the Falklands and had to rapidly convert RAF fighters to naval missions. Although Britain pioneered the global projection of military power, it was only able to fight with the help of US logistic support and stocks, emergency transfers of key US weapons like the AIM-9L air-to-air missile, US military communications satellites, and US fuel.

The West faces the practical problem that the US now provides so many of its power projection assets that the US is virtually the only Western nation that can fight more than very low level conflicts. The remaining European military forces in the Middle East, and European power projection capabilities in the region, are already severely limited and are likely to continue to decline at a time that regional forces continue to grow.

While the USSR also faces severe limitations on its force capabilities, the fact remains that the West has experienced steady reductions in its power projection capabilities since the end of the Second World War while the USSR is gradually building a 'blue water navy'.

Further, the fighting in the Iran–Iraq War has provided a very tangible demonstration that regional forces now have enough military assets and advanced enough technology to make even carrier task-force sized interventions increasingly hazardous.

Theoretical NATO Capabilities

NATO's theoretical military capabilities often disguise its practical limitations. There is no clear dividing point between the forces each Western nation provides to NATO and forces that might be deployed to the Middle East. This point is illustrated in Table 3.1. NATO has a large array of units that can theoretically play a role in Middle Eastern contingencies, and most NATO nations can draw down on their naval and air forces without crippling their ability to provide air and naval coverage of their own national territories. As a result, NATO seems to have great potential for out-of-area action.

Table 3.1   NATO allied forces available for out-of-area operations

Allied country	Land forces	Air forces	Naval forces	Mobility forces
Belgium	1 Paracommando regiment 2 Motorised infantry battalions	Misc. helicopters Up to 18 Mirage 5B fighters	None	12 C-130H 2 Boeing 727QC
Canada[a]	Elements of 2 light brigade groups Special service force of 1 armoured regiment, 1 infantry bn., & support units	20–40 CF-116 (F-5) fighters ? CP-140 & CP-121 MPA/SARs	Up to 10 Destroyers 1–2 replenishment support ships	26 CC-130E 5 CC-137 (707)
Denmark[b]	1 regimental combat team	None	None	3 C-130H
France[c]	1 Parachute division 1 Air-portable marine division 1 Light armoured overseas intervention brigade 1 Motorised infantry brigade 1 Infantry regiment	1–2 Combat helicopter regiments, Up to 100 Jaguar, Mirage III, and Mirage 5 plus 25–50 Alphajets	1 Carrier task force 1 Helicopter task force 80+ naval combat aircraft 8 Submarines 2–10 Atlantique and Neptune MPA 6 Assault ships 590 naval commandos	48 C-160 13 C-160NG 6 tankers 6 logistic ships

Allied country	Land forces	Air forces	Naval forces	Mobility forces
West Germany[d]	1 Airborne division 5–10 special security or commando battalions	1–2 F-4F FGA sqns, with 20–30 fighters	3–7 Frigates and/or destroyers 6 Type 206 submarines 5–10 Minecraft	2–4 Boeing 707-320C
Greece[e]	1 Paracommando regiment	1–2 F-5A/B or Mirage F-1CG sqns. with 36–40 fighters	3–5 Frigates and/or destroyers	3–4 C-130H 5–7 LSD, LST, LCT 5–10 LCU/LCM
Iceland	(No military forces of any kind)			
Italy[e]	1 Airborne brigade 1–2 Mechanised or motorised brigades 2 Amphibian battalions Misc. helicopter squadrons	2–6 Attack and light attack squadrons with up to 72 fighters 3–4 Atlantic MPA 1–2 Interceptor/recce sqns.	1–2 Helicopter carrier task forces with 5–8 surface ships each 1 Marine inf. grp. 4–8 Minecraft	8 G-222 3–5 C-130H 2 Tankers/logistic ships 4–9 LST/LCM/Hydrofoil
Luxembourg	(Token military forces only)			
Netherlands	1 Inf. brigade	18 NF-5B Misc. helicopters 1–2 MPAs	2–4 Destroyers/ frigates/corvettes 2 Amphib. combat groups	2 Fast combat support ships
Portugal[f]	1 Commando regiment 1 Special forces bn.	8–20 G-91 Lt. Attack fighters	3–6 Frigates 3 marine bns.	1–3 C-130H
Spain[f]	1 Paracommando brigade 1 Airportable brigade 3–5 Infantry battalions 1 Foreign Legion battalion Misc. command and other bns and cos	10–30 F-5A/B Fighters Misc. helicopters	1 VSTOL Carrier Task force with 6–8 surface ships 1 Marine regt. 5–10 Minecraft 5–10 Patrol craft	2–3 C-130H 2–4 KC-130H 4–7 Landing craft 2 Attack transports
Turkey[g]	1 Parachute brigade 1 Commando brigade ? Infantry brigades ? Other units	18–36 F-5/RF-5 Fighters ? F-100D OCUs Fighters Misc. helicopters	5–8 Destroyers/frigates 1 Marine brigade (5,000) 5–8 Patrol boats 6–12 Minecraft	2 Support ships 5 Tankers 2–5 C-130E 3–5 LST ? LCT/LCU/LCM
United Kingdom[h]	3 Parachute bns. 1 SAS regiment ? Inf. and armoured Recce bns.	45–72 Jaguar/Buccaneer/ Harrier Attack fighters 18–36 FGR-2	1–2 Heli-VSTOL carrier task forces with 8–16 surface ships each 1 Marine cdo bde.	11 VC10Cl 15 Victor K-2 & 14 CP-1 tankers 2 LPD assault 5 Landing ships

Allied country	Land forces	Air forces	Naval forces	Mobility forces
United Kingdom (continued)		(F-4)/Tornado AWX ? AEW/MPA aircraft Misc. helicopters 1–2 Rapier regiments	1 Special boat & 2 Marine raiding cos 3–6 SSNs 5–8 SS ? Other surface ships 7–20 Minecraft	2 Support ships ? Tanker ships

Notes:
  [a] Maximum practical out-of-area forces are likely to consist of peace-keeping infantry units totalling around 800 men. Canada now has 515 men in UNFICYP (Cyprus), 220 men in UNDOF (Syria/Israel), and 20 in UNTSO.
  [b] Maximum practical out-of-area forces likely to consist of 1–2 peace-keeping battalions of 326–400 men each.
  [c] There is no clear way of estimating the maximum practical forces France can deploy. It seems likely that two light divisions, one carrier task group, and something approaching 100 fighters would be a reasonable limit. France now deploys 16 500 men out of area in its overseas dependencies and 7720 in other overseas nations. It has four interservice overseas commands, and two naval commands.

  France already provides significant internal security support to Saudi Arabia, and has contingency plans to provide support to Saudi Arabia in the defense of its borders against the PDRY. There are 200 tanks and other equipment prepositioned near Sharurah. France also can provide extensive minewarfare support and other speciality vessel support which US Naval forces are not equipped to provide.
  [d] All forces listed fully committed to Central Region and Atlantic defense.
  [e] For Eastern Mediterranean or North African contingencies only.
  [f] For North African and South Atlantic contingencies only.
  [g] Can deploy significantly more forces for contingency involving Syria, Iraq, or Iran.
  [h] The UK has extensive contract, SAS, and RAF personnel in Oman and would play a critical advisory role. British and US ships have routinely cooperated in showing the flag and demonstrating Western willingness to defend transit through the Straits of Hormuz since the beginning of the Iran–Iraq War.

Source: Adapted from the IISS, *Military Balance, 1985–1986*.

Table 3.1, however, is largely a myth. In the real world, most of the forces shown in this table would have to be substantially re-equipped to meet the different conditions of combat in the Middle East. Most NATO countries are extremely specialised in terms of logistics and combat and service support. They draw heavily on fixed facilities, civilians, and reserve units to provide the tail they would need for fixed roles and missions in NATO.[1]

Most NATO squadrons cannot move most of their service and C³I/BM assets. Most NATO ships lack adequate naval replenishment and repair facilities to provide even limited endurance in the Middle East without access to local ports and key docks. Most NATO ground forces lack training in low level war, support capability for desert, mountain, or other special regional conditions, suitable long-range air- or sea-lift, mobile stocks, and specialised armaments.

Power projection assets are not cheap. While any generalisations are dangerous, the US probably spends about three times as much to be able to project a brigade, squadron, or major combat ship on a global basis as most European countries do to provide similar forces tailored to specific local missions in NATO. This cost estimate does not include strategic lift – which is virtually non-existent in NATO European forces, except for a limited capability in Britain, France, and Italy.

Further, the US itself is now, and will remain, severely limited in strategic lift. It lacks the lift to adequately deploy and support its power projection forces even over a 30–60 day period. It is a basic fact of military life that the US can only provide lift to a European state at the cost of diverting or delaying the build-up of its own forces.[2]

There are a wide range of NATO countries in which it makes little sense to seek contingency forces for the Middle East for political reasons, because of the weight of the Warsaw Pact threat, because of the lack of resources tailored for the job, or because of current manpower and equipment trends. Belgium, Canada, Norway, Denmark, the Netherlands, Portugal and Spain all face serious political problems in any out-of-area action other than the most popular peace-keeping missions. Greece faces both political and military problems. The FRG faces political and constitutional problems in out-of-area operations. It also faces a massive Warsaw Pact threat and must commit its resources to the defense of the Central Region.

This leaves the United States, Britain, France, Italy and Turkey. The United States now dominates NATO's power projection capabilities to the point where it would have to assume the major burden in anything other than a low-level conflict. Britain and France retain an important presence in key areas of the Middle East, and France is a Mediterranean power. Italy has comparatively large forces and is located where it can play a significant role in the Mediterranean. Turkey is thrust into 'out-of-area' operations by its geography: it has common borders with Iraq, Iran, Syria and the Southern USSR.

The Reality of US Dominance in Power Projection Capabilities

The size of the forces the US can commit to the region are determined more by the limitations on US strategic air- and sea-lift, forward basing and support facilities, and the risks inherent in redeploying US forces from other regions, than by the total combat forces available from the US order of battle. Since the fall of the Shah of Iran the US has steadily improved the forces it can commit to the Middle East which are tailored to regional needs and contingencies. This is particularly true in the Indian Ocean/Gulf area, where the US must rely heavily on prepositioned equipment and stocks to minimise the strain on its strategic lift, and must allocate lift resources to moving US forces, rather than equipment and ammunition.

Viewed from this perspective, the forces the US can commit to the Middle East can be divided into two main groups. The first is the forces available to a North African–Levant–Mediterranean contingency and the second is the forces it could deploy to the Gulf. There is no easy way to quantify the first set of forces because so much would depend on access to friendly bases and allied strategic lift facilities. The US could deploy two to three full carrier task groups and one to two Marine brigades with supporting tactical air forces anywhere in the Mediterranean area in seven to ten days.

The US could deploy most of the land elements of US Central Command forces to the Mediterranean area as quickly or more quickly than to the Gulf. It could deploy as many tactical aircraft and combat support aircraft as the main operating bases in any likely combination of friendly states could arm and support. This literally could involve hundreds of fighters, with the major limitation being supply lift and forward repair, service, sheltering and arming facilities.

The US forces already in the Mediterranean area normally include 470 army personnel in Greece, 3950 in Italy, and 1250 in Turkey. These are largely support personnel, but many could support out-of-area operations. The US air force has 5300 men in Spain, and a tactical wing with three squadrons of 72 F-16A/B. One tactical fighter wing with F-4E fighters is deployed in the US on an 'on call' rotational basis. The air force has 5800 men and two air base groups plus one GLCM unit in Italy; 2700 men and two air-base groups in Greece and 3800 men and two air base groups in Turkey.

The US Sixth (Mediterranean) Fleet has a nominal strength of 27 000 men. It typically has two SSNs, two full fleet carriers, twelve major surface combatants, eleven support ships, one Amphibious Ready Group (three to five ships and a battalion-sized landing team or marine amphibious unit), and three stores ships with prepositioned combat equipment. It has major base facilities at Rota, Spain (3600) and at Gaeta, Naples, Sigonella and La Maddalena in Italy (5250). The US Marine forces afloat normally total 1900 men or one Marine Amphibious Unit (MAU). (An MAU has a reinforced infantry

battalion group, including tank and artillery elements, a composite
air group with AV-8B fighters and helicopters, and an additional
logistics unit.[3]

What is especially important to note about such a force is that it is
not an assembly of ships but includes fully ready and functional
carrier task groups. It also involves far more air power than the much
smaller carriers deployed by other NATO countries. (The size of a
typical air wing in a carrier task group is shown in Table 3.2.)

This table merits close attention by anyone attempting to evaluate
Western power projection capabilities in the Middle East. The US
deployed two carrier task groups to deal with the forces of a relatively
small Middle Eastern power like Libya and still employed F-111s
striking from Britain to minimise its casualties. Yet, the detailed
distribution of aircraft types and numbers in Table 3.2 shows that
one US carrier holds enough airpower to provide about fifteen times

Table 3.2   Strength of typical US Navy and Marine air wings

Aircraft type	Function	Squadrons	Aircraft
A. Carrier air wing			
F-4, F-14 (TARPS)	Fighter (reconnaissance)	2	24
A-7, F/A-18	Light attack	2	24
A-6, KA-6D	Medium attack (tanker)	1	14
S-3A	ASW (fixed wing)	1	10
SH-SH	ASW (rotary wing)	1	6
EA-6B	Electronic warfare	1	4
E-2C	Airborne early warning	1	4
		9	86
B. Marine Corps air wing			
F-4, F-18	Fighter	4	48
A-4, A-18, AV-8A	Light attack	2–3	38–57
A-6	Medium attack	1–2	10–20
KC-130	Tanker/transport	1	12
EA-6B	Electronic warfare	1	4
RF-4	Reconnaissance	1	7
OV-10	Observation	1	12
AH-1	Attack helicopters	1	24
CH-53, CH-46	Transport/utility helicopters	6–7	131
UH-1	Helicopters	9	120
		27–30	403–432

Source: DOD, *Annual Report, FY 1984*, p. 163.

the attack payload delivery capability and air-to-air engagement capability of the two small carriers that Britain could send to the Falklands. Not only is one US carrier task group considerably stronger than the total naval forces of any other NATO nation, it is capable of self-defence, major air operations, and limited forced entry through amphibious or helicopter assault.

The non-US forces listed earlier in Table 3.1 – and which will be described shortly for Italy, Britain and France – do not meet this test. Although France does plan to build a modern carrier and may be able to equip it with a full complement of modern aircraft, no other NATO nation now has a single carrier task group capable of self-defence against a modern air force, and no allied carrier group is normally equipped to support land or air operations against an enemy possessing modern combat aircraft and tanks.

Table 3.3   USCENTCOM forces in FY 1986

Force element	Manpower
US Central Command Headquarters	1,100
US Army Central Forces Command	131,000
Headquarters US Army Central Command (Third US Army)	
XVIII Airborne Corps Headquarters	
82nd Airborne Division	
101st Airborne Division (Air assault)	
24th Infantry Division (Mechanised)	
6th Armored Cavalry Brigade (Air combat)	
1st Corps Support Command	
US Navy Forces Central Command	123,000
Headquarters, US Naval Forces Central Command	
3 Aircraft carrier battle groups[a]	
1 Surface action group	
3 Amphibious groups	
5 Maritime patrol squadrons	
US Middle East Task Force (Bahrain)	
US Marine Corps Forces	70,000
1 Marine Amphibious Force (MAF), including	
1 Marine Division	
1 Marine Aircraft Wing[b]	
1 Force Service Action Group	
(1 Marine Amphibious Brigade (MAB), including	(16,000[c])
1 Marine regiment (reinforced)	
1 Marine air group (composite)	
1 Brigade service support group	
US Air Force, Central Command Air Forces (9th Air Force)	33,000
7 Tactical fighter wings[d]	

Force element	Manpower
3 ⅓ Tactical fighter wings (available as attrition fillers) 2 Strategic bomber squadrons[e] 1 Airborne warning and control wing 1 Tactical reconnaissance group 1 Electronic combat group 1 Special operations wing	
Unconventional and special operations forces	3,500
Total	291,600

Notes: [a] A typical active navy carrier wing consists of nine squadrons (approximately 86 aircraft): two fighter squadrons, two light attack squadrons, one medium attack squadron, plus supporting elements for airborne warning, anti-submarine and electronic warfare, reconnaissance and aeriel refueling operations.

[b] An active marine corps air wing typically consists of 23–35 squadrons (338–370 aircraft) with: four fighter attack squadrons, two or three light attack squadrons, one or two medium attack squadrons, plus supporting elements for electronic warfare, reconnaissance, aeriel refueling, transport, airborne assault, observation, and tactical air control.

[c] The MAB is currently the only element of the MAF which has prepositioned equipment. By FY 1987–88, the full MAF will have prepositioned equipment on ships although the other two sets will be located for missions in NATO and Asia.

[d] Each air force wing typically contains three squadrons of 24 aircraft each. (Combat support units, such as those composed of EF-111 electronic warfare aircraft, are generally organised into squadrons of 18 to 24 aircraft). By the end of FY 1989, the US will have the equivalent of 40 tactical fighter wings – 27 active and 13 Air National Guard and Reserve.)

[e] There are a total of seven B-52G squadrons assigned to general purpose as well as nuclear missions. These have a strategic reconnaissance and anti-shipping mission as well as a conventional land bombing role.

Source: Data furnished by USCENTCOM, and in the Department of Defense, *Annual Report, FY 1986*, p. 212.

The second part of US regional contingency capabilities is easier to define: it includes the forces allocated to USCENTCOM. These forces are shown in Table 3.3, and once again it is important to contrast them with the other forces NATO can deploy. Britain, France and Turkey can all play an important role in Indian Ocean–Red Sea–Gulf scenarios, but all of these forces combined lack the muscle to sustain even moderate level military operations.

This does not, however, mean that USCENTCOM would find it easy to operate in the region or that its capability for force projection is without flaws. The US is still heavily re-equipping the forces shown in Table 3.3, is only now completing the prepositioning of equipment, and is still procuring sea- and air-lift. Even when all these steps are complete in the early 1990s, it will still take several weeks for the US to deploy the equivalent of a two-division force, and a month to six weeks to deploy three full divisions. These forces will still be light on armour compared to the major powers in the Northern Gulf.[4]

The US also faces the practical reality that carriers are vulnerable in Gulf waters, or anywhere else where they cannot operate a long-range air and missile defence screen and enemy operations can strike from nearby air bases or the terrain masking provided by land. The US air force will be almost totally dependent on access to friendly air bases. Its effectiveness will also be heavily dependent on having sheltered, defended, well-stocked and interoperable facilities with suitable C³I/BM capabilities. Such bases now exist only in Spain, Morocco, Italy, Greece, Israel, Egypt, Turkey, Oman and Saudi Arabia, and contingency access is uncertain and scenario dependent.

Major land force operations will be heavily dependent on friendly locals and good staging facilities. Strategic sea- and air-lift will be critical. This means free access to critical NATO and Middle Eastern staging facilities such as those in the Azores, Morocco, Egypt and Oman. The struggle to conduct successful operations half a world away from the US will be difficult at best.

The Four Key NATO European States: Italy, Turkey, France and Britain

Only four other NATO states can play any meaningful direct or indirect role in the Middle East: Italy, Turkey, France and Britain. The FRG has agreed to strengthen its role in NATO to help offset the growing burden of US power projection efforts. It will not contribute more than token naval deployments, and these only for demonstrative purposes.[5]

Italy
Italy has major contingency capabilities because it is a Mediterranean power. There is no clear difference between securing the Mediterranean and providing contingency capabilities along its coast, and Italy faces a less direct Warsaw Pact threat than any other major

NATO military power. This is reflected in the force totals in Table 3.4. Italy also has a number of ground force elements that could be adapted to out-of-area or rapid deployment force operations. These include the Centauro Mechanised Division, Cremona Mechanised Brigade, Folgore paratroop brigade, the Taurinense Alpine rear echelon brigade, and Lagunari and San Marco amphibious units.

At the same time, however, Italy also faces a number of severe practical problems. Italy does not have a deep water navy in the sense its forces are designed to project power in forced entries of other states or to conduct engagements with land based aircraft and missiles. Italy's new carrier, the *Giuseppe Garibaldi*, is a through deck light carrier designed solely for heliborne ASW operations. While it carries Otomat II missiles and has two Albaros point defence systems with Aspide missile launchers and 40 mm Breda Compact radar guided guns for terminal defence, it has no real AEW assets. The *Garibaldi* can take a total of twelve VSTOL and rotary wing aircraft. It now has only two SH-3D Sea King helicopters. Even if the *Garibaldi* is equipped with its maximum capacity of twelve AV-8Bs, or similar VSTOL aircraft – which would virtually deprive it of an ASW role – the British experience in the Falklands indicates that the *Garibaldi* will not be able to survive against determined air attacks by even a power like Libya. This will be particularly true if Italy cannot fund some form of AEW aircraft.[6]

While the Italian navy has talked about forming a small task force with the *Garibaldi*, two air defence destroyers and eight frigates, supported by a replenishment ship, this would be suitable only for ASW and anti-surface ship operations in waters near Italian air bases. Such a task force would have such limited air and missile defence that it would require either land based air cover or direct support by a US carrier task force to deal with a modern air or missile threat. Italy would also need naval platforms with considerably more EH-101 medium helicopters for amphibious operations, and would need ships with more troops and land weapons lift than is now available. Italy also lacks the strategic air-lift to support independent operations or to substitute for vertical assault from naval platforms. It would need to upgrade and expand its G-222 force or buy a significant amount of new air-lift.[7]

Italy's helicopter cruisers have no guns suitable for shore support, are not suitable for moving amphibious forces, and have limited air defences which are not suitable for dealing with the advanced anti-ship missiles being deployed into the region. Italy's smaller ships

Table 3.4   Italian contingency capabilities in the Middle East: 1985–95

Forces normally deployed in the area:
Mediterranean Fleet:
  10 Submarines
  2 Helicopter carriers: each with 9 AB-212, 4 Otomat 2 SSM, Terrier SAM
  2 Andrea Doria cruisers with 4 AB-212 and 1X2 Terrier SAM
  4 GW destroyers: 2 with AB-212, all with standard SSM
  16 Frigates: 6 with Otomat 2 SSM, 4 with Aspide SAM and 4 with Sea Sparrow SAM
  8 Corvettes
  7 Hydrofoils with Otomat 2
  2 Fleet auxiliary craft
  22 Minecraft and vessels.
  14 Destroyers/frigates/escorts
  2 LST and 19 LCM amphibious ships
  1 Marine infantry group with 30 VCC-1, 10 LTVP-7 APCs, 16 81 mm mortars, 8 106 mm RCL, and 6 Milan ATGM.
  2 Maritime patrol aircraft squadrons with Atlantic
  30 SH-3D Sea King, 53 AB-212

Peace-keeping:
  Lebanon (Unifil): 48
  Sinai MFO: 90: 3 Minesweepers

Probable maximum out-of-area contingency forces in Italy:
Land Forces
  2 independent mechanised brigades
  4 independent motorised brigades
  1 airborne brigade
  2 amphibious battalions
combat and service support forces
  1 wing of AB-204 and AB-205 helicopters (54 aircraft)
  1 CH-47 squadron
  1 light aviation force.

Air Forces
  1 Tornado and 2–3 G-91/AMX light attack squadrons
  1 F-104G recce squadron
  2 SAM groups with Spada
  1 C-130H and 2 G-222 transport squadrons

Source: Adapted from the IISS, *Military Balance, 1985–1986*, and John Chipman, *French Military Policy and African Security*, Adelphi Papers, 201, IISS (London, 1985), p. 20.

could often provide good support to an allied task force, and Italy's large number of mine vessels might be very useful in helping to clear Middle Eastern LOCs, but all would require external air cover and missile defences.

Italy also does not have 'blue water' capability outside the Mediterranean. Its ships and fleet are heavily optimised to operate from nearby land bases and facilities. Further, it lacks the kind of support ship strength and replenishment/resupply capability needed for extended out-of-area operations. It can support limited special purpose missions like mine clearing, but not task force missions or extended combat operations by more than a few of its larger vessels.

Finally, Italian amphibious lift is comparatively limited and better suited to moving forces to friendly shores than to forced entry. Like other NATO forces, Italy would require substantial air and naval gun-fire support to deal with the risk presented by the land-to-ship missiles, heavy anti-tank guided missiles, amd medium- and long-range artillery weapons now common in Middle East forces. Overall survivability would be very low in the face of any organised land forces or without clear regional air superiority. Even terrorist or limited land fire could produce significant casualties, particularly in low level operations where any casualties could produce significant political backlash.

Italy could theoretically deploy two to three motorised or mechanised infantry brigades and one to two wings of tactical aircraft without seriously weakening its contingency capabilities for NATO. It now, however, has no major regular combat units organised and equipped for power projection to the Middle East. It also lacks the lift assets and combat, service, and logistic support organisation for such missions.

There is sufficient standardisation and interoperability between the US and Italian forces to allow the US to provide such support and lift, but it is important to note that this would have to come at the expense of diverting assets from the support of US forces, and that it would require major reorganisation, re-equipment, and retraining of the selected Italian units to allow them to operate in a contingency where a Middle Eastern nation could use its heavy armour and modern tactical air power. Tunisia and Lebanon are virtually the only states in the Middle East which do not have major armoured and modern fighter forces.

Italy has some excellent units or special forces units and anti-terrorist forces. These include one airborne brigade, two amphibious battalions, and one marine infantry group. These forces are already flexible enough to provide considerable contingency capability and could be rapidly re-equipped with more anti-air and anti-tank weapons and LAVs and all terrain support vehicles suited for operations in North Africa. They would still, however, require the creation of new support forces of equivalent strength and cost before they could sustain extended low-level combat.

In a practical sense, therefore, Italy's contingency capabilities are, and will probably remain, best tailored to action in nearby states and to those peace-keeping or anti-terrorist/subversive operations which do not involve armoured or air threats. Italy can support collective NATO naval action in the Mediterranean but its naval forces are not suited to independent action or even a small carrier task-force sized operation. In spite of Italy's considerable ground and air potential, it is probably not capable of supporting a combat presence of more than one to two brigades and two to three squadrons.

Turkey
Turkey is already 'out-of-area' in the sense it has common borders with Iran, Iraq, Syria and the Southwestern USSR. In this sense, up to half of its armed forces could play an out-of-area role in defending eastern and southern Turkey. Turkey has 45 000 men in Eastern Turkey, and its Third Army has more than six bases around Erzerum, with six more strung out along the 160 mile highway towards Agri. It is conducting active operations against the Kurds in the area around Hakkair and Chirze. In the spring of 1985, it sent some 30 000 men to reinforce units on the Syrian and Iraqi borders, and it has steadily built up the capability of the Third Army over the last year.[8] Turkey is expanding its strategic road net near both the Syrian and Iraqi borders, and its steadily increasing its ties to the Northern Gulf states. It has developed stronger trade relations with the Middle East, and with Iraq and Iran in particular. It deployed forces equivalent to two divisions in Iraq in 1983, with Iraq's consent, in a military operation against the Kurds.

While Turkey would normally have to keep most of its forces deployed to meet the threat of Soviet or Greek action, Turkey could deploy at least six mechanised and/or armoured divisions in operations near its borders with Iraq and Iran or Syria (up to 500 tanks, 800 AFV/APCs and 400 artillery weapons). Turkey also has one command and one parachute brigade it could commit, and could deploy at least one mobile Gendarmerie Brigade with V-150 and UR-416 APCs suitable for light paramilitary action. The Turkish air force could deploy up to five fighter squadrons, one recce squadron, and two to four Rapier/Redeye units (twenty-four fire units), and is improving its C^{3}I net, military facilities and air bases in Eastern Turkey.[9]

It is important to note, however, that Turkey is severely short of mobile combat and service support assets. It has a very poor communications net, lacks the logistics and infrastructure for extended power projection much beyond its border areas, and badly needs modern anti-tank weapons, portable artillery and other combat gear for mountain and urban warfare. Turkey would experience severe operational problems the moment it shifted from border or territorial defence to operations beyond its border. Turkey has no real power projection capabilities and would require full-scale external support for any operation outside its border areas.[10]

Turkey has also carefully avoided taking any political or military action implying its forces could play any regional role other than self-defence. It still is deeply committed to Cyprus, and faces a massive Soviet and Bulgarian threat on its northern borders. It would probably avoid taking any action in a contingency that did not directly threaten Turkey, and would almost certainly avoid playing any role in an Arab-Israeli contingency even if it involved a substantial Soviet presence in Syria. Turkey's willingness to intervene in the event of the collapse of Iraq or a Soviet move into Iran is unclear. Turkey has publicly declared its facilities in Eastern Turkey are not US or NATO contingency facilities for action in the Gulf, although such declarations are deliberately ambiguous.

France

France and Britain still have major naval capabilities in the Mediter-ranean, and France normally deploys a two-carrier fleet in the Mediterranean and could mobilise a fairly substantial mix of land forces and naval transport and support ships for operations anywhere in North Africa and the Eastern Mediterranean.

Britain and France are also the only Western European nations that still deploy substantial out-of-area forces in the Middle East, Gulf, Red Sea, and/or Indian Ocean. It is important to note, however, that these British and French forces in the region are relatively small, and will normally play only limited roles in very low-level conflicts. They do not have the strength or sustaining power to engage in armoured, air, or naval combat in the Gulf, except against low-level threats like the Dhofar rebel units in the Peoples Democratic Republic of Yemen (PDRY) or as part of a regional or US led force. They have limited SAM, EW, and recce aircraft capabilities, but lack advanced sensor and intelligence systems other than maritime patrol aircraft, photo recce, and land/air/ship-borne ESSM.

Table 3.5   French contingency capabilities in the Middle East: 1985–95

Forces normally deployed in the area:
Mediterranean Fleet:
   2 SSNs
   9 submarines
   2 carriers
   14 Destroyers/frigates/escorts
   5 Mine countermeasure ships
   5 Amphibious ships

Peace-keeping
   Lebanon (UNIFIL): 1,380: 1 infantry and 1 logistic battalion
   Sinai MFO: 40: 2 Twin Otter and 1 C-160 aircraft

Djibouti
   Total manpower: 3,800 men
   Permanent and prepositioned forces:
      10th BCS (Command and Services Battalion)
      5th RIAOM (Overseas Regiment)
      13th DBLE (Demi-Brigade of the Foreign Legion)
         –ALAT (Army Light Aviation Unit) with 5 attack and 5 medium
            transport helicopters
         –CDMB (Engineering Company)
      1 motorised company
      Army equipment includes AMX 13 light tanks, AMX with SS-11 AFVs,
         105 mm battery, 1 AA arty battery
      1 Mirage IIIC squadron with 10 fighters, and air elements with 1
         C-160 transport, and 2 Allouette helicopters
      Naval elements with 1 Atlantic MPA
   Rotated Units (every four months): 1 motorised company.

ALINDIEN: Indian Ocean Inter-Service Overseas Command
   Total manpower: 1,400
   5 frigates, 3 minor combatants, 1 amphibious and 1 support ship

South Indian Ocean Joint Service Command: La Reunion and Mayotte
   Total manpower: 2,200 men
   Permanent and prepositioned forces
      53rd BCS
      2nd RPIMA (Marine Parachute Regiment)
   Rotated units: 1 parachute company

Probable maximum out-of-area contingency forces in France:
Rapid action force
   1 Parachute division (13,500)

    1 Air portable marine division (8,500)
    1 Light armoured division (7,400)
    1 Air mobile division (5,100)
    1 Signals regiment

Foreign Legion Force
    1 armoured, 1 parachute, 4 infantry, and 2 engineer regiments

Independent Army Elements
    1 support brigade and 2 mixed regiments

Naval Forces
    2 carriers with 20 Super Etendard, 4 Etendard IV or 7 F-8E
    5 ASW and 2 AA destroyers with Exocet, Crotale, and Malafon
    8 Frigates with Exocet
    2 Amphibious assault ships with 9 LCM or 2 LST
    2–5 Diesel or nuclear submarines
    11 Support ships
    5 Maritime patrol aircraft

Air Forces
    3 Mirage and 3 Jaguar squadrons
    1 Mirage III recce squadron
    6 Crotale batteries (8 fire/4 radar units)
    1 DC-8 and 2 C-160 transport squadrons
    60–80 armed Alouette II, Puma, and Gazelle army helicopters, some with
        HIT ATGM
    2–5 transport helicopter squadrons

Source: Adapted from the IISS, *Military Balance, 1985–1986*, and John Chipman, *French Military Policy and African Security*, Adelphi Paper 201, IISS (London, 1985), p. 20.

Current French capabilities and trends are summarised in Table 3.5. France's main contingency forces now in the region consist of its forces in Djibouti, its Indian Ocean Command (ALINDIEN), and its South Indian Ocean Command. France could also deploy substantial land and air forces, including elements of the FAR (*Force d'Action Rapide*), and up to a two-carrier task-force to the Gulf in an emergency. France has some particularly well-trained elite units for such operations, including the Foreign Legion.

France has shown on many occasions that it can project small forces effectively – although it generally needs US assistance in strategic lift for significant long-range troop movements. For example, the US provided a C-5A for the recent operations in Chad because French C-160 Transails cannot carry large weapons systems such as the Hawk missiles France used for air base protection.[11] It also

showed it could quietly provide significant internal security assistance
to Saudi Arabia when it had to suppress radicals who seized the
Grand Mosque in Mecca in 1982. France has, however, faced growing
political problems in sustaining out-of-area operations in cases like
Chad. It is increasingly doubtful that the French public would support
any intervention that produced significant casualties or required a
sustained military presence in the face of hostile forces.

Any notable out-of-area deployments would also mean cutting
France's capability to support the defence of the Central Region in
areas where the Supreme Allied Commander Europe (SACEUR)
and the Supreme Allied Commander Atlantic (SACLANT) have
declared NATO has major deficiencies in ship strength to meet
critical defence missions. The US would have to provide substantial
air-lift and resupply for combat operations, and would have to provide
intelligence support and air cover in the face of a Soviet or well-
equipped Third World air threat with long-range air or ship-to-ship
missiles.[12]

France spent some 2.5 billion French francs on out-of-area operations in 1985, of which 555 million francs was spent overseas. This
included costs for the French forces that were in Lebanon, the
protection of the Embassy in Beirut, the French presence in Chad,
French operations in New Caledonia and the creation of a new base
there. France, however, is experiencing steadily greater budget
problems in out-of-area operations. While France now seems likely
to remain in the Indian Ocean and Djibouti through 1995, it may
well have to phase out one of its three carriers and/or delay
construction and production of new carrier aircraft. Since the Super
Etendard, Etendard, and F8Es on French carriers, and much of the
C[3]I and air/missile defence gear on French ships, are already obsolete
or obsolescent, French carrier task force contingency capability is
likely to drop to a one carrier demonstrative deployment only
sometime between 1990 and 1995.[13]

France should, however, still be able to fund the deployment of
more advanced maritime patrol aircraft, modern fighter-recce aircraft,
and better ESSM systems. It plans to upgrade the surface-to-air
missile defences on many of its ships, to include better close in
protection. It will deploy improved SHORADs, but will have no
heavier land-based SAMs it might deploy to the Gulf. French carriers
are nuclear armed, and both French Mirage 2000s and Mirage IVs
could provide theatre nuclear support.

United Kingdom
British military intervention capability in the Middle East is more difficult to estimate. Britain can still deploy a large portion of its forces from the Atlantic to the Mediterranean. Although it officially is no longer 'East of Suez', it also provides a major advisory presence to many of its former Trucial states, and provides contract naval and air officers to Oman, as well as small SAS units.

British Conservative politicians have often suggested that Britain should strengthen its out-of-area role, and Britain has regularly deployed ships in cooperation with the US in the Gulf during the Iran–Iraq war. Britain also demonstrated excellent out-of-area contingency capabilities during the Falklands conflict. In practice, however, Britain has never provided the defence budgets necessary to maintain or expand its out-of-area contingency forces. Both its presence in the Gulf and total power projection capabilities have declined steadily since 1968, and are likely to continue to decline further.[14]

Table 3.6   British contingency capabilities in the Middle East: 1985–95

Forces normally deployed in the area:
Indian Ocean Squadron
  2 Destroyers/frigates
  1 Support ship

Oman
  SAS detachment
  RAF contract pilots
  RN seconded and contract officers

Diego Garcia
  1 Naval detachment
  1 Marine detachment

Cyprus
  UNFICYP: 750 men
  Army: (3,250)
  1 Infantry battalion less 2 companies
  1 Infantry battalion plus 2 companies
  2 Armoured recce squadrons
  2 Engineer and 1 logistic support squadrons
  1 Helicopter flight
  RAF (1,347)
  1 Helicopter squadron

Probable maximum out-of-area contingency forces in the UK:
Army

2 Armoured recce regiments
10 Infantry battalions
2 Paratroop battalions
1 SAS regiment
Scimitar, Ferret and Fox AFVs
FV-432, Saracen, MCV-80, Spartan APCs
2–4 Artillery regiments with 105 mm guns on AFVs or towed 155 mm
  howitzers
1 SAM regiment with Rapier
2 SAM batteries with Blowpipe and Rapier
30–40 Helicopters: Gazelle AH-1 and Lynx AH-1, some with TOW

Navy
  1 Commando brigade, 2 SBS assault squadrons with Blowpipe, 105 mm
    guns, Milan ATGMS
  2 Carriers with 10–15 Sea Harrier and Harriers, 9 Sea King
  5 Destroyers with Sea Slug, Sea Cat, and Sea Dart SAMs
  8–10 Frigates with Exocet, Sea Wolf, Sea Cat
  4–6 Nuclear and diesel submarines
  2 Assault ships with 4 LCM and 4 LCVP, and Seacat SAMs
  4 Landing ships
  15 Tankers, 6 store and 1 helicopter support ships.
  5 Nimrod maritime patrol aircraft; AEW-2 Sea Kings
  14 Commando and 20 ASW Sea King, 20 Lynx and Wasp helicopters

Air Forces
  2–5 Tornado, Jaguar, and Bucaneer squadrons
  1–2 Tornado and Jaguar recce squadrons
  1 Nimrod ECM aircraft
  1 VC-10 and 2–4 C-130 transport squadrons
  20–30 Wessex, Chinook, and Puma helicopters

Source: IISS, *Military Balance, 1985–1986*, pp. 41–43 and Peter Foot,
  Beyond The North Atlantic: The European Contribution, ASIDES,
  No. 21, Spring 1982, p. 28.

An estimate of British contingency capabilities is provided in Table
3.6. Both Britain's 5th Airborne Brigade (2nd and 3rd Battalions)
and the Royal Marines 3rd Commando Brigade (40, 42 and 45
battalions) are now specifically earmarked for out-of-area operations,
and the Parachute Regiment and a Gurkha battalion have out-of-
area experience. The 5th Brigade has been specially equipped for
such missions, and has been converted from an infantry to an airborne
unit during the last two years. It has a special landing battalion group
with artillery and combat engineer support designed for very rapid
long-distance deployment. Nevertheless, all such British forces have
been affected by Britain's budgetary problems and are short of the

air defence, armour, artillery and lift required for operations against armoured or mechanised Middle Eastern forces.[15]

Britain now has very limited carrier power, and would find it difficult to project more than one light carrier to the Gulf. Further, Britain would then be dependent on small numbers of comparatively short-legged Harrier and Sea Harrier aircraft. Even the coming refit of the *Invincible* will mean that Britain's largest 'carrier' can only deploy a total of eight Harrier VSTOL fighters and twelve Sea King AEW and ASW helicopters. The *Invincible* is being expanded to allow the storage of missiles for more extended operations and is being given a new 12 degree ski jump to extend Harrier range, a modern Type 996 three-dimensional radar, and three Goalkeeper 30 mm guns for terminal missile defence. Nevertheless, a British carrier task force would require US air/missile defence coverage against a Soviet or sophisticated Third World threat, although the Sea Harrier now has improved air defence avionics and air-to-air combat capability.

Britain probably would also require US logistic and fuel support for any extended naval operations outside the Mediterranean and probably emergency supply of munitions and critical contingency-specific parts and equipment. This US supply was vital to British operations in the Falklands, and Britain has not been able to fund most of the post-Falklands improvements it originally sought in its power projection capabilities.

British amphibious capability is especially tenuous. The *Atlantic Causeway*, the sister ship to the *Atlantic Conveyor* which was sunk in the Falklands, was converted to an amphibious helicopter ship capable of carrying several hundred Royal Marines and heavy lift helicopters. It now, however, is laid up along with *Hermes*, Britain's only dedicated commando carrier. It is doubtful that Britain will replace its aging amphibious assault ships, the *Fearless* and *Intrepid*, although both are already obsolete. Britain lacks modern amphibious dock ships (LPDs) and landings ships (LSLs). These create serious problems since Britain experienced major difficulties in trying to land in bad weather in the Falklands and could not conduct amphibious landings on the Danish coast in a 1984 Bold Gannet exercise because of bad weather.

Britain lacks the ability to deploy more than light armour in Gulf contingencies, and this situation is unlikely to change. Even a reinforced battalion-sized movement of mechanised British forces would now require either US air-lift or sea-lift. British land forces will, however, steadily improve their AFVs, holdings of Milan and improved TOW ATGMs, and modern SHORADS, like the improved Blowpipe and improved Rapier.

Table 3.7   Potential Soviet forces for the Middle East

Naval forces normally deployed:
Mediterranean squadron (SOVMEDRON)
   45 Ships on continuous deployment
   8–10 SSNG/SSN/SS
   8 Principal combatants
   2 Amphibious ships
   1 Mine counter-measures vessel
   17–25 Auxiliaries
   Regular exercise with Syrian and Libyan navies

Caspian Flotilla (HQ Baku)
   5 Corvettes
   30 Minor combatants
   7 Principal auxiliaries

Indian Ocean detachment of the Far Eastern Fleet (SOVINDRON)
   20–30 Ships on continuous deployment
   2–3 Regular and cruise missile submarines
   8 Principal combatants
   2 Amphibious ships
   12 Support ships

Land and air forces normally deployed:
Afghanistan
   115,000 men (10,000 MVD/KGB)
   1 Army HQ (Kabul)
   3 motorised rifle and 1 airborne division, 2 motorised rifle and 1 air assault
      brigade
   1 Air army HQ (Kabul Bagram) 257 aircraft and 245 helicopters:
   – 4 FGA regiments: 80 MiG-21, 40 MiG-23, 80 Su-17, 30 Su-25
   – 2 Recce battalions; 15 MiG-21R and 12 MiG-25R
   – 4 Helicopter regiments: 140 Mi-24; 105 Mi-28, 40 Mi-6, 40 Mi-2
   – An-22, VTA, and aeroflot aircraft in support

Algeria
   1,000 Advisers

Ethiopia
   1,500 men plus mine countermeasure vessels, 8,500 ton floating dry dock,
   helipads, IL-38 aircraft, and naval infantry detachment at Dahlak Island
   (guided missile cruiser and SSN port of call)

Iraq
   600 Advisers

Libya
   1,400 Advisers, including combat pilots
   IL-38 May MPA aircraft
   3 SA-5 Gammon units

Syria
  2,500–4,000 Advisers (1,100 ground, 800 air force, 100 navy plus 600 Men in air defence and 200–500 in 2 SA-5 Gammon units)
  IL-38 May at Tiyas
  Submarine tender, yard oiler and water tender at Tartus

North Yemen/YAR
  500 Advisers

South Yemen/PDRY
  1,000 Advisors
  IL-38 May at Al-Anad airfield
  Radio and ELINT facility at Bir Fuqum
  Berthing and anchoring space at Aden and Socottra

Regional mobilisation/front capabilities
*(Threat to Iran and Eastern Turkey and Pool for Power Projection)**
Land Forces
  2–3 Fronts with 9 all-arms armies, 5,500 main battle tanks, 6,300 artillery and MRL larger than 100 mm, 100 FROG/SS-21, 70 Scud, 1,600 SAMs
  2–3 airborne divisions
  1–2 Naval Infantry Regiments (Each with 3,000 men, 3 infantry, 1 tank and 1 artillery battalion, 31 tanks, 10 light tanks/MICVs, 30 122 mm SP howitzers, 6 MRLS, 6 MICVs with ATGM, 4 SP AA Guns, 4 SP SAMs
  3–4 Regular and 1 naval Spetsnatz Brigades

Tactical Aviation
  420 aircraft, 160 helicopters

Strategic Aviation
  60 Medium bombers
  30–40 SU-24 long range attack fighters

Naval Forces
  1–2 Light carrier task groups with one 65,000 ton carrier by 1988.
  – 7–10 combatants and 5–10 support ships each
  nuclear submarines
  1–2 Ivan Rogov, Alligator and Ropucha class amphibious ships
  60–100 Backfire B/Tu-22M, Badger C and Blinder bombers with AS4, AS-5, and AS-6 missiles

Cuban Forces
  Up to 45,000 men
  2–3 Mechanised or infantry divisions
  1 Naval infantry battalion
  100–150 combat aircraft, 25–50 helicopters

Notes: Author's estimate based upon IISS, *The Military Balance, 1985–1986*, and Department of Defense, *Soviet Military Power, 1985*.
*Does not include Bulgarian, Rumanian, and Soviet forces likely to be deployed primary against NATO's Southern Flank, including Turkey.

Soviet Problems and Capabilities

Like the US, there are many ways Soviet power projection capability in the Middle East can be calculated. Table 3.7, for example, lists the major Soviet forces now in the area including land, naval, and advisory forces. It also provides a rough indication of the total strength the USSR can deploy against various parts of the Middle East.

There is no question that the USSR has large additional forces it can redeploy from throughout the Soviet Union. This can lead to very high force counts, as an excerpt from Secretary Weinberger's FY 1987 posture statement indicates:[16] 'The primary Soviet threat to Southwest Asia during a global confrontation would be some 25 ground divisions and 900 tactical aircraft now based in the Turkestan and Caucasus Military Districts. Selected Soviet long range bomber and naval forces could also be deployed to disrupt our power projection assets.'

At the same time, Secretary Weinberger's posture statement goes on to note that,

While their proximity to the region provides an advantage in the balance, in any attempt to secure Southwest Asia's oil fields, the Soviets would still have to maintain lengthy lines of communication that would be subject to interdiction by our air and unconventional warfare forces. It is likely that a substantial portion of their ground forces would be needed for local security, and difficult terrain would limit their ability to bring additional forces to bear. Consequently, we believe that we could conduct a successful defence of Southwest Asia with substantially fewer ground forces than the Soviets, provided that our forces are heavily supported by tactical air.

In practical terms, the Soviet Union would also face major support and readiness problems. Most Soviet units near South-West Asia are Category III divisions with equipment numbers and types inferior to those in Soviet forces opposing NATO. The USSR would normally have to risk drawing down on its most combat capable units, and moving them to the area of combat. And it would still be base and facility limited, even in striking into adjacent areas such as Northern Iran.[17]

This is why even the more modest estimate of total Soviet

capabilities in a Gulf contingency shown in Table 3.8 probably exaggerates the size of the forces the USSR could deploy, even in a contingency where it could attack across its southern borders. In other contingencies, the USSR would be far more limited in terms of available forces tailored to the region and contingency, in both strategic air and sea-lift, and in the ability to protect that lift.

There is, however, no way to predict the time the USSR would have to build up its forces. The USSR could obviously take advantage of months or even years of presence in an area to create very large regional forces, or to create a mix of specially tailored high technology Soviet forces, local forces, and/or proxy forces. Similarly, there is no way to predict the pattern the USSR would follow in a given case.

Table 3.8   Soviet power projection forces for a Gulf contingency

Service and forces	Personnel and equipment
Army	
1 Tank division	11,000
21–22 Motorised rifle divisions	152,000
2 Airborne divisions	15,000–18,000
Naval Infantry	
2 Regiments	5,000
Frontal Aviation	
2 Tactical air armies	6 Fighter regiments
	6 Fighter-bomber regiments
34th TAA in transcaucasus MD	300 MiG-21, 23, 27; Su-24, 25, 27
6th TAA in Turkestan MD	175 MiG-21, 23, 21R, Mi-8
Naval Aviation	
Long-range bombers and anti-ship air-to-surface missile carriers	Over 100 on short notice
Navy	
1 Small ASW carrier task group	Would depend on contingency
Several guided missile task groups	
Nuclear and conventional submarines with long-range missiles	
Landing port dock (550 man lift) and maximum of 8 Alligator-class LSTs (325 men/26 tanks each)	

Source: Anthony H. Cordesman, *The Gulf and the Search for Strategic Stability*, Boulder: Westview, 1984, p. 818; and the IISS, *Military Balance, 1985–1986.*

The Regional Balance

These difficulties in assessing Soviet strengths and capabilities help explain why it is difficult to talk about the overall balance of Western and Soviet intervention capabilities without adding so many caveats that the discussion becomes almost meaningless. In broad terms, however, the military balance is fairly clear when it comes to contingencies involving high-level conflicts. These are generally less subject to the impact of regional forces, and more likely to be dominated by the forces the Eastern and Western blocs can deploy. The Mediterranean, for example, remains a 'NATO lake'. The USSR can threaten and can inflict damage, but it still lacks both a survivable naval presence and any major operating bases that can support major air operations or protect naval forces in port.

Similarly, the Soviet presence in the PDRY and Dahlak Islands off the coast of Ethiopia does not provide survivable bases capable of supporting major combat operations, and the Soviet Indian Ocean/Red Sea fleet cannot hope to survive an engagement with US naval forces even if it is fully reinforced by the USSR's new carrier and supporting forces. Accordingly, the main risks from high to moderate level Soviet intervention lie in those areas where either the USSR has a special geographic advantage or a combination of Soviet and indigenous forces present special threats. These contingencies include (1) a major crisis or war affecting Syria or Libya that led to demands for a major Soviet military presence, (2) an attack on Turkey, or (3) an attack on Iran.[18]

If the current political situation should change enough for Syria or Libya to seek Soviet military forces, the USSR could use excellent air bases in both Syria and Libya. It could make use of existing surplus land forces equipment capable of equipping one division in the case of Syria and two divisions in the case of Lybia. It could rapidly upgrade and man the extensive SAM and C^3I/BM net in each country, and use several major and well-sheltered air bases in each country. It is important to note, however, that it would take several months for the USSR to correct the severe technical and operational problems in the logistic, service and combat support systems in each country. Provided that combat occurred before this preparation was completed, the USSR would probably rapidly lose its air defence net and ability to operate air units if the US committed large-scale air and naval power.

The outcome of the land fighting would be more uncertain, but Israel and Egypt could almost certainly provide sufficient defensive land strength to deal with threats to these countries. The key vulnerabilities would lie in a joint Soviet-Syrian move on Jordan, increased pressure on the Gulf, and a Libyan-based attack on Tunisia or support of civil war in the Sudan and/or various revolutionary movements in sub-Saharan Africa.

A major Soviet attack on Turkey would be an attack on NATO, and any Soviet threat designed to occupy Turkey would be far more likely to come along the Black Sea coast than try to penetrate through the mountainous areas of Eastern Turkey. However, the main risk of Soviet military action against Turkey stems more from the escalation of fighting over Iran, leading to limited attacks on Turkey, than from a full-scale Soviet invasion, whatever its source and direction.

The critical vulnerability in such a contingency would be the fact there are only three to five main operating bases from which the US and Turkey could deploy air power efficiently in Eastern Turkey. At the same time, however, the USSR would also be base limited, with only seven to ten air bases, and the outcome of any such escalation would again depend heavily on each side's willingness to take risks rather than on military strength *per se*.

This raises the issue of a major US and Soviet land conflict in the Gulf. Such a conflict would almost certainly be fought over control of a northern Gulf state, and most probably over Iran. Such a conflict would allow the USSR to operate directly from its own territory, and take advantage of its land routes of communication and large amounts of theatre lift.

A rough estimate of the balance of US and Soviet forces that might be involved in such a war is shown in Table 3.9, which also helps illustrate part of the reason why the European contributions described earlier are not likely to be critical in shaping the outcome of a moderate to high level conflict in the region. A clash in Southwest Asia involving the superpowers could easily escalate to a major war engaging divisional and wing-sized units. The pace and technical level of such a war, and the fact that the US would be lift-limited, would give the US far more advantages from relying on its own forces than having to deal with the different level of technology in a relatively small allied contingent. This might not be true of British escorts – which could operate effectively with US carrier task-forces – or specialised forces like French mine warfare ships, which could perform

Table 3.9 Comparison of US and Soviet forces available for a Gulf contingency: 1986

US combat forces		Soviet combat forces	
Service and units	*Personnel*	*Service and units*	*Personnel*
Army		**Army**	
82nd airborne	16,200	1 Tank division	11,000
101st air assault	17,000	22 Motorised rifle divisions	
24th mechanised division	12,300		152,000
Ranger battalions (2)	1,200	1 Airborne divisions	9,000
Air cavalry brigade/		3 Artillery divisions	
special forces	2,500		15,000–18,000
Amphibious assault		Amphibious assault	
1 Marine amphibious force		2 Naval infantry regiments	5,000
(Division/air wing)	47,500		
Air Force		Air Force	
7 Wings plus 3 wings reserve		*Frontal aviation*	
including:		2 Tactical air armies	
F-15 (1 wing)	72	(6 Fighter & 6 fighter bomber	
F-111A (1 group)	144	regiments)	
F-4E (1 wing)	72	34th TAA (Transcaucasus MD)	
A-10 (1 wing)	85	with	
	373	MiG-21, 23, 27, Su-24, 25, 27	
			300
B-52H (2 squadrons)	35	6th TAA (Turkestan MD) with	
		Mig-21, 23, 21R, Mi-8	175
		Long-range aviation	
		Tu-95, Tu-16, Tu-22,	
		Tu-26 bombers	100+
		Naval aviation	
		Naval bombers	100+
Navy		Navy	
2–3 Carrier air task forces		1–2 ASW carrier task groups	
Combat aircraft	258	Combat aircraft	28 VSTOL
5 ASW aircraft squadrons		2–3 guided missile task groups	
Prepositioned ships	17–21	1 Naval infantry regiment	
1 MAB amphibious lift		Amphibious lift	
? Nuclear missile submarines		? Nuclear missile submarines	

Source: Adapted from Anthony H. Cordesman, *The Gulf and the Search for Strategic Stability* (Boulder, Colo.: Westview, 1984), p. 818, and the IISS, *The Military Balance, 1985–1986.*

missions where the US is poorly equipped. It will, however, be true of most combat operations.

These difficulties in estimating force strength are matched by the difficulties in estimating comparative build up, support, and re-supply capability. Table 3.10 illustrates one aspect of the latter capabilities: the balance of strategic lift. These capabilities could be critical in any major Middle East contingency, and would be crucial in a major Gulf conflict.

It is important to note that the US has an advantage in long-range lift capacity, but that this theoretical advantage is crucially dependent on the timing and details of a specific contingency. A lead by one side of several days could be critical in putting brigade-sized elements in place, deploying air defence systems, etc. Both sides can also massively re-supply a local force by air, move whole combat air units into regional bases in days, or provide critical additions of technicians and technical upgrades to improve local capabilities.

The outcome of any conflict involving Iran would probably be as dependent on lift and mobilisation capabilities as on the US-Soviet military balance *per se*. Even in the case of Iran, the USSR now lacks significant numbers of combat ready divisions, high quality tactical air assets, and major basing facilities along its border with Iran to support a major invasion without high risk or long preparation and warning. Similarly, the US would be heavily dependent on full access to bases and staging facilities in Oman, Turkey and Saudi Arabia, and to friendly ports and air bases in Southern Iran. Much would then depend on the reaction of Iran.

The key issue would be the problem of local attitudes and alliances mentioned earlier. It would be the attitudes of roughly 50 million Iranians, over three million of whom are now in active military service or play some form of paramilitary or security role. There is no question that the USSR could rapidly seize the Caspian coast of Iran, just as the US would have the edge in seizing Iran's Gulf coast. Both sides, however, would face the problem of penetrating and surviving in the mountain or desert areas and in the major population centres.

The Iranian population is ideologically alienated from both East and West. As the USSR has learned in Afghanistan, and the US in Lebanon, land wars do not involve passive populations and these can rapidly form major guerrilla forces. In this kind of contingency, the unpredictable currents of the Iranian revolution and the resulting 'taking sides' within Iran would be as important to the military

Table 3.10   US versus Soviet strategic life for a Gulf contingency in FY 1987

Type of Lift	US Forces		Soviet Forces	
	Number	Type	Number	Type
Military Airlift				
Strategic	319		335	
Tactical				
Active	216		320	
Reserve	323		88	
Total	539	a	408	a
Utility/Cargo				
Helicopters[b]				
Active	5,548		2,100	
Reserve	40			
Total	5,588		2,100	
Civil Fleets/Other[c]				
Cargo	67	Long Range	1,400	Medium and Long Range Transports
Passenger	227	International		
Total	294		1,400	
Tankers	185[d]		125	
Military Sealift				
Active/Reserve				
Cargo	21/97		158/—	
Tanker	21/73		71/—	
Prepositioning Ships (PREPO)[e]	8/—			
Maritime Prepositioning Ships (MPS)[e]	13/—			
NDRF	—/137			
Total	63/307		229/—	
Merchant Shipping[f]				
Misc.	—	—	1,900	
Dry Cargo	184	—	(17)	
Tanker	112	—		RO-RO
Total	296	—	1,900	
Amphibious Lift[h]				
Helicopter Carriers (LPH, LHA)	12		0	
Amphibious Command Ships	2		0	
Amphibious Cargo Ships	6		0	
Amphibious Transport (LPA/LPD)	11		2	
Landing Ship Dock (LSD)	11		0	
Landing Ship Tank (LST/LKA)	23		32	
Landing Ship Medium (LSM)	54		45	
Total	119		79	

Notes:
[a] Sources conflict on smaller aircraft.
[b] No accurate way exists to compare US and Soviet helicopter capabilities or readiness.
[c] The US Civil Reserve Air Fleet is roughly similar to Aeroflot, which is shown as the Soviet reserve force above. The Long Range Air Force (LRA) also, however, has major transport resources with 200 Cubs and Candids and about 1,000 medium and long-range passenger transports.
[d] Rough estimate. SAC has an additional 615 KC-135 A/Q and 24 KC-10 tankers.
[e] No clear statistical basis exists for comparing the impact of US and Soviet civil sea-lift.
[f] Soviet resources do not include 56 hovercraft and 56 LCUs. US resources do not include minor utility vessels.

Sources: *Soviet Military Power, 1984*, pp. 82–6; IISS *The Military Balance, 1984–1985*; *DoD Annual Report, FY 1986*, pp. 72–5, and *OJCS, Military Posture, FY 1986*, pp. 199–203.

balance as US and Soviet strength. The Vietnam and Afghan conflicts would be low-level struggles in comparison to the potential local threat from Iranian factions, and the risk both sides would run of repeating Xenophon's retreat would be very serious indeed.[19]

An Iranian contingency, however, is only the most dramatic illustration of the high probability that any prolonged intervention in a land conflict is likely to lead to a split within a given country, with some factions supporting the Western force involved and others opposing it. The issue is rarely likely to be the Western versus Soviet bloc military balance. It is much more likely to be the particular character of a given contingency, local attitudes and forces and a mix of Western and Soviet bloc/proxy military forces and advisory and military aid efforts. It is comparatively easy, for example, for the US to destroy the military facilities in the PDRY. It is much more difficult to create the effective political and military conditions needed to intervene in a full scale conflict between the PDRY and the YAR.

Further, the resulting 'taking sides' is likely to be extremely unstable and often to be driven by cultural and political pressures which even area experts might fail to predict before Western intervention. The Shah's fall is only the most recent example of a case where area experts completely failed to predict the true pattern of social change and revolution. The 'Xenophon Syndrome' has been operating in the region for well over 2000 years: today's friend can quickly be tomorrow's enemy. As the US learned in Lebanon, it is also far too easy to assume the West can impose its objectives on a local war or crisis. In practice, regional conflicts may well end in dragging Western military forces into local conflicts and impose their own political logic on the West. Escalation is easy; escalating in a manner that has strategic purpose and a reasonable probability of success is extremely difficult.

II USING AND SUPPORTING WESTERN POWER PROJECTION CAPABILITIES

Strategic Mobility Support

Table 3.11 illustrates both one of the most critical US problems in using force in the Middle East, and one of the most important roles European states could play in a moderate to high level conflict, particularly in a contingency involving the Gulf or emergency re-supply of Israel. As has already been explained, the main constraint shaping the US deployment of force in the Middle East is the size of US strategic lift. As table 3.11 shows, this lift is equally dependent on strategic bases and contingency facilities.

Table 3.11   US Military contingency facilities in the Near East

Base	Status
North Africa and staging points:	
Morocco	
Slimane	Former B-47 base now being modernised to support C-141 and C-5 operations
Navasseur	This base or Rabat may be given similar modernisation later
Liberia	
Monrovia	Contingency use of international airport for staging air operations. Expanded to allow use of C-5s, C-17s, and C-141s
Portugal	
Lajes	Negotiations were completed in 1983–4 to keep Lajes as a major air staging point for US air movements Fuel, runway and other facilities have been upgraded
Eastern Mediterranean and Red Sea area:	
Egypt	
Suez Canal	US granted tacit permission to move warships through Canal
Cairo West	US normally deploys about 100 men. Used for joint F-15 and E-3A AWACS operations
Djibouti	Access agreement and arrangements with French allow port calls and access to maritime patrol aircraft
Turkey	
Mus	Three Turkish air bases near the Soviet border, Iran, and
Batman	Iraq being expanded to allow deployment of US heavy lift
Erzurum	aircraft and fighters. No formal contingency arrangements exist
Gulf and Red Sea:	
Diego Garcia	Used through a long-term lease with the UK signed in the mid-1960s. The base provides 12,000 foot runways and facilities suitable for B-52 and heavy airlift facilities, and is where 7 US prepositioning ships in the Gulf are now deployed
Seychelles	Satellite tracking and communications base
Kenya	
Mombassa	Potential staging point, maintenance facilities, and port
Moi Airport	call. Facility expansion programme completed in 1983

Base	Status
Kenya Naval base	
Somalia	
Mogadishu Airport	Staging facilities for US air and sea movements. Limited repair capability. Expansion completed in 1983
Berbera	
Oman	
Al Khasab	Small air base in the Musanda, Peninsula near Goat Island and Strait of Hormuz. Limited contingency capability Largely suited for small maritime patrol aircraft
Masira Island	Airfield expanded to a major $170 million air and naval staging point. Limited deployment of prepositioning ships
Thumrait & Seeb bases	Major Omani air base facilities. Used by US maritime Airpatrol aircraft. Available for US use in a contingency
Saudi Arabia	No formal basing agreements, but the US has deployed F-15s, KC-10 and KC-135 tankers, and E-3A to Saudi air bases in emergencies, and operates E-3As from Riyadh. All Saudi major air bases have the sheltering and facilities to accept extensive US air reinforcements and/or support US deployment of heavy lift aircraft
Bahrain	US has a 65-man US support unit ashore. US Middle East Force deploys 'near' Bahrain although formal basing agreements have ended

Source: Adapted from material provided by USCENTCOM, and from Barry M. Blechman and Edward N. Luttwak, *International Security Yearbook, 1983/84* (New York: St Martin's Press, 1984), pp. 154–9.

NATO European nations can still play a critical role in determining the success or failure of US action. Further, this may involve far more than simply providing key staging points. US ability to rapidly redeploy forces and equipment from Italy, the FRG, and UK may be critical. So may the ability to temporarily draw down on the inventories of NATO countries with key items of supply or combat equipment needed by the US or friendly Middle Eastern states. For example, temporary US drawdowns of key parts in the FRG and UK was often necessary during the Vietnam conflict. Similarly, the US quietly supported its re-supply of Israel with drawdowns of equipment deployed in the FRG during the emergency re-supply effort to Israel in 1973.

The practical problem for NATO European states is that such arrangements are best handled quietly and on a bilateral basis. Few moderate to high level contingencies can be expected to induce a NATO-wide consensus, or even political consensus within a given state. Some may also present serious political problems in terms of European-Arab relations, and an increasing threat of the revitalisation of the 'oil weapon' by the early to mid-1990s.

It is important, however, that Europe realise that it cannot leave the US with responsibility for most uses of force in the Middle East and then second guess every action or hope to preserve a risk-free security while the US does the fighting. Force rarely is applied in neat packages with clear moral positions, easily predictable consequences, and the certainty of success without political backlash.

Burden Sharing

Like strategic mobility, burden sharing does not involve the active European use of force in the Middle East. As commonly defined by the US, it is also a military chimera. No NATO European state is really going to increase its defence expenditures and assume a larger role in the defence of Europe. Virtually all NATO European states are now committed to a budget trend which makes it difficult or impossible for them to preserve their current level of force numbers and technological sophistication, and all face Warsaw Pact threats that are growing faster than NATO capabilities.

At the same time, however, 'burden sharing' is vital to the extent it leads to a *de facto* European recognition that the US may have to draw down temporarily on forces in Europe or forces committed or earmarked to NATO in the US; Europe must face the fact that it cannot have it both ways. The US is also unable to increase its forces and to fund incremental power projection forces adequate to meet contingency threats in the Middle East without using any of its forces for NATO. Europe must accept the fact that it will at least indirectly share the cost and risk of any major US use of force in the Middle East, and that this is one 'out-of-area' contribution it must make.

Intelligence Sharing

The US, Britain and France already benefit a great deal from sharing 'out-of-area' intelligence on the Middle East. This sharing is limited, however, by differences over US support of Israel and a number of parochial issues, including arms sales and traditional, low-level rivalries in given Middle Eastern states. It is unclear that much can be done to further improve this situation, but it is clear that intelligence cooperation could be critical in many uses of force.

British and French area expertise and HUMINT could be critical to properly characterising local force capabilities, internal politics, and threats, particularly in nations where either has a major advisory or arms sales presence. The US can often provide high technology reconnaissance and intelligence collection assets that Britain and France do not possess. The carefully tailored fusion of intelligence can be a major 'force multiplier' once combat occurs, and critical to crisis prevention or management, when accurate assessments and warnings are essential to limiting or avoiding the use of force.

Intelligence sharing is not, however, an area suitable for broad collective efforts. To put it bluntly, the bulk of NATO has no need to know, and no member of the alliance with good regional collection capability is likely to take the risk of regular data sharing in a NATO forum. Intelligence designed for tactical support or crisis management should generally be confined to multilateral or bilateral groups with special elements tailored to the needs of a given contingency.

Arms Transfers and Advisers

While not usually considered as part of out-of-area operations, Western European provision of military advisers, arms transfers, and arms sales may provide Europe's important long-term 'out-of-area' contingency support in the Middle East. This kind of European support is also likely to be the most enduring. It is driven by the economic interests of key European states, it is not dependent on the circumstances surrounding a given contingency, and it is not as subject to the slow political attrition in current Allied ties to former colonial states that is inevitable.

Building up regional forces is also a sound alternative to both US and European out-of-area forces, and does not conflict with the defence of NATO. It places regional forces in the position of having to assume not only the military cost of their own defence, but the political risks and uncertainties. Further, it generally ensures the development of sufficient forces, infrastructure, basing and other support so that the US or Europe can deploy relatively limited numbers of high technology military forces in more serious contingencies rather than the full mix of forces required for full-scale land/air/naval operations.

The recent trends in world arms sales reinforce the potential benefits of Allied advisory and arms transfer efforts. The fighting in the Falklands, in the Iran–Iraq War, and in Lebanon have all raised out-of-area demand for Western technology. At the same time, there are many states which are reluctant to become dependent on the US because of their fear they will be seen as having taken sides in the conflict between the US and USSR, or because of their opposition to various US policies.

This is of special importance in the case of the Middle East. A number of states are reluctant to do anything that would further target them in terms of Soviet or radical pressure, and operate under political conditions which make it impossible or difficult for them to deal with the US, particularly given the reluctance of the Congress to authorise arms sales on a consistent and predictable basis.

These factors also help explain the trends shown in Table 3.12. The US is a relatively minor arms supplier to Africa. While its sales have increased over the last two years, it still sells less than one-tenth of the arms that the USSR sells to African states. The bulk of Soviet sales, however, go to two African states: Algeria and Libya. As Table 3.12 shows, Britain, France, West Germany and Italy are all significant suppliers to the Middle East and serve as an important counterbalance to the problems the US faces because of its close relations with Israel.

It is important to note that Egypt is now the only state in the Middle East that maintains 'correct' relations with Israel, and that no state in South-West Asia has friendly relations with Israel. The end result is a four-fold problem for the US. The US cannot sell arms to many Middle Eastern states without threatening Israel's security, US Congressional politics preclude any orderly US arms sales and advisory policy in dealing with those states which are actively hostile to Israel, many key oil suppliers and strategically important states cannot buy from the US or must diversify their purchase of arms and military advice, and most of the allies are reluctant to deal with the US in any contingency where support of Israel might threaten their trade or oil supplies.

Table 3.12 also reflects the importance of the military relations between individual European states and the individual nations of Southwest Asia and the Gulf. The European states sell roughly the same amount of arms to the region as does the United States. France, in particular, has become a major supplier to Iraq and the Southern Gulf states, and is now the principal arms supplier to all the smaller Gulf states except Oman. Saudi Arabia has chosen France as its

Table 3.12   Major country activity in arms sales and military advisory efforts: 1979–83

Country	Arms supplier									
	Total	Communist				Major NATO				Other
		USSR	Eastern Europe	PRC	US	France	UK	FRG	Italy	
Egypt	5,645	40	50	300	2,400	1,200	575	210	320	550
Israel	3,805	—	—	—	3,800	—	—	—	—	5
Jordan	3,430	230	—	10	975	1,000	1,100	5	—	110
Lebanon	395	—	5	—	250	90	10	—	10	30
Syria	10,530	9,200	520	90	—	200	180	40	—	300
Subtotal	23,805	9,470	4,375	400	3,625	2,490	1,865	255	330	995
Bahrain	120	—	—	—	10	40	—	40	10	20
Iran	5,365	975	45	2,600	1,200	20	140	5	150	2,600
Iraq	17,620	7,200	1,290	1,500	—	3,800	280	140	410	3,000
Kuwait	450	30	—	—	180	—	50	70	110	10
Oman	565	—	—	5	80	20	430	—	10	20
Qatar	765	—	—	—	10	440	310	—	—	5
Saudi Arabia	12,125	—	—	—	5,100	2,500	1,900	525	200	1,900
UAE	620	—	—	—	20	350	90	110	30	20
North Yemen	2,355	1,200	260	—	200	30	—	10	5	650
South Yemen	1,510	1,500	—	—	—	—	—	—	—	10
Subtotal	41,495	10,905	1,395	4,105	6,800	7,200	3,200	900	925	8,235
Algeria	3,660	3,200	—	—	—	30	50	300	—	80
Libya	12,095	5,800	1,115	310	—	850	40	380	700	2,900
Morocco	1,785	—	50	—	430	950	—	5	50	300
Tunisia	385	—	—	10	110	130	5	20	70	40
Subtotal	17,925	900	1,165	320	540	1,960	95	705	820	3,320
Total Near East	83,225	21,275	6,935	4,825	10,965	11,650	5,160	7,020	2,075	12,550
Afghanistan	1,830	1,800	20	—	—	—	—	—	—	10
Ethiopia	1,900	1,800	10	—	—	—	—	—	20	70
Somalia	580	—	10	50	30	5	5	—	410	70
Sudan	640	—	60	70	110	10	10	270	10	100
Turkey	1,865	—	—	—	750	10	5	850	150	10
Total Other	6,815	3,600	100	120	890	25	20	1,120	590	260

Note: Numbers are estimated based on ACDA, *World Military Expenditures and Arms Transfers, 1985*, and are shown in current US dollars.

second source of arms in addition to the US, and France has outstripped Britain since 1982 as the major European arms supplier to the region.

There is, therefore, a high priority to finding ways in which such European arms sales and advice can be coordinated with US efforts to build regional security, and to do so in ways which do not involve high demographic and economic costs to Third World states. While some competition between arms sellers will always be inevitable, it should still be possible to work together to develop local forces that cooperate on a regional basis.

The US needs to encourage European arms sales that involve some degree of standardisation or interoperability for over-the-horizon operations, and to consider whether they could back their arm sales with special reinforcements or high technology forces for contingency operations. Arms sales cooperation may be difficult in a West which is far more oriented towards sales than strategy, but it offers great long-term potential.

Demonstrative Uses of Force

Britain, France and Italy are all capable of supporting the US in demonstrative use of force, and can still act independently in those cases where a limited naval or air/ground presence will be an effective deterrent or demonstration of solidarity. Oman, Bahrain, the UAE, Djibouti and the Red Sea, and Tunisia seem to be good cases in point. A few ships, a battalion of paratroopers or a few squadrons of fighter-bombers might tip the balance between regional conflict and/or escalation and peace.

There are also many possible scenarios where it would be desirable to have a multilateral demonstration of Western solidarity – for example the British-US patrols through the Straits of Hormuz to deter Iranian action – or where it would be desirable to avoid US action because of the increased risk of triggering a Soviet response or because of regional sensitivities arising out of US ties to Israel. The key problem in such European uses of force will lie in the risk of escalation and the growing vulnerability of such forces.

Regardless of which Western nation is involved, it will be important to avoid political delays, divisions, or limitations on Western action. It seems very doubtful that the West would benefit from a NATO multilateral force or efforts to create too broad a multilateral support for a given form of Western action. The end result is likely to be too much delay, too much public hand wringing, too many limitations, and too many small military elements whose loss could trigger internal problems within NATO or a given European state that far outweigh their somewhat tenuous political and military benefit.

The US needs to learn this as well. As the US demonstrated in Vietnam and in the peace-keeping effort in Lebanon, it has an unfortunate tendency to seek allies first and then worry about the political consequences of seeking joint action or consensus later. The practical result is often to make the US seem ineffective or impotent, make the West seem divided rather than strong, and produce a new round of mutual recriminations.

In general, the West will be far better off if it limits any demonstrative use of force to those nations which have clear national interests in the use of force and which are capable of staying the course if anything goes wrong. Attractive as joint action and public consultation may seem in theory, they are likely to be counter-productive in practice.

Counter-Terrorism

Counter-terrorism is so scenario and case dependent that virtually any generalisation is likely to be wrong. There are, however, several factors which Western nations need to take into careful account in considering any military action or cooperation in this area.

The first such factor is that counter-terrorism is rarely a good area for overt cooperation beyond information sharing and police-level action. Terrorism is best dealt with by either treating the cause of terrorism or through the creation of an effective set of internal security and police systems that can hunt down terrorists before they act or contain the results of their action with minimal international publicity. The most useful role each Western nation can play in fighting terrorism is to look after its own territory while cooperating in intelligence operations with other states. Reducing vulnerability and limiting impact in the West is far more critical than out-of-area adventures.

Second, when terrorism must be dealt with in a given Middle Eastern state, it will generally best be dealt with through cooperation between a single Western state that preserves its freedom of action and a friendly regional state. 'International' or 'NATO' anti-terrorist forces belong to 'B' movies and comic books. One of the most important aspects of anti-terrorism is to deny the terrorist public impact and to act with success. This generally involves carefully chosen acts of violence executed by a single unified group, and – ideally – where no terrorists survive to stand trial and no one else is injured. A committee approach is almost guaranteed to end in delays, publicity for the terrorists, more innocents killed, and the kind of public trials that breed what they are intended to prevent.

Third, the West is inherently divided in its treatment of terrorism in the Middle East because of US ties to Israel. This division is compounded by the fact the US has no serious economic ties to radical nations like Libya, but is the natural target for any anti-Western action. In many cases, terrorism will be targeted against the US to the exclusion of most or all European nations.

The US will thus have to treat many movements as terrorist that European nations will not. The US will also often be a target when Europe is not. There is no purpose to be served in implying unity of purpose when it does not exist. Further, public efforts to create such unity may end in reducing intelligence and police cooperation that can go on at a low level as long as the issue does not become a political crisis.

Cooperation could be useful within NATO, where improved intelligence, special counter-terrorism equipment, and common training facilities may help individual nations solve their self-defence problem. There may also be considerable value in reaching a quiet multilateral agreement that France, Britain, Italy and Turkey should strengthen their ability to provide unilateral out-of-area support in the form of training of friendly counter-terrorist forces and the capability to take military action in selected states.

France and Britain have already done a great deal in this area, and have a number of special 'police' missions in key Middle Eastern states. The French Army, Foreign Legion and intelligence services can provide useful support to both the Francophone countries and key conservative Gulf states like Saudi Arabia. The British Parachute Regiment, Royal Marines Special Boat Squadron and Special Air Service all can play a useful role in many Middle Eastern countries, and elements of these forces and various British and French intelligence and police services have already played a useful role in Kuwait, Bahrain, the UAE, Qatar and the PDRY.

It is unclear whether further collective encouragement is required, but both Britain and France play a vital role in this area and one the US cannot – again because of its ties to Israel and status as a 'superpower'. Italy might also be encouraged to tailor part of its paramilitary security forces and elite forces like the San Marco Marines, paratroop units, or Alpine troops to play a similar role in quietly supporting a key state like Tunisia.

As for Turkey, it already is quietly playing a role half-way between anti-terrorism and internal security support for Iraq and should be encouraged to continue. The whole Kurdish issue is extremely dangerous in terms of its potential to undermine both Turkey and Iraq and serve as a lever for Soviet intervention in Iran. While every effort should be made to preserve Kurdish rights, the whole idea of an independent Kurdestan in any form threatens Western interests and offers the Kurds nothing other than the hope of a puppet state that will rapidly exchange one master for another.

Promoting Internal Security

Like anti-terrorism, support of Middle Eastern states in improving internal security and in dealing with coups and revolutions does not lend itself to collective Western action. Western consensus will always be far less important than political and military success. Cooperative efforts are again an almost certain recipe for delay, coordination problems and additional political constraints.

In most cases, the West will also have to act by pressing for key internal reforms, by providing intelligence support and warning to a friendly Middle Eastern state, and by providing advisory groups and arms tailored to deal with local threats and problems. Britain and France already do this with considerable success, and with an inherently lower profile than the US. Direct military action will generally only be possible when there is a clear outside sponsor or foreign-supported coup that occurs without broad local support, and where the West can intervene quickly and decisively before any such revolution, insurgent effort, or coup takes hold.

The West would also often benefit from providing mobility and other support to a local power like Jordan or Egypt, or by backing local military forces with airpower, advanced sensors, and other indirect forms of military action than by deploying its own forces. There will always be cases like Oman, where even limited SAS elements could still play a critical role in blocking PDRY-sponsored infiltration, but Western ground troops lack the political background, language skills and regional knowledge to be useful in true revolutionary conditions.

Above all, the West will need to remember the key lesson coming out of the fall of the Shah of Iran. The answer to the question of who should, and could, have saved the Shah is simple: it was the Shah. Nothing is more likely to end in failure than a Western military effort to prop up an unpopular leader after the political fact.

Protecting Naval Lines of Communication

Britain, France and Italy can all join the US in protecting lines of communication (LOCs) in the Mediterranean, and Britain and France can play such a role in the Gulf. Unlike direct task-force operations, LOC protection often involves specialised roles like mine detection and clearing. The US has a serious shortfall in mine warfare ships and equipment which are available in all three allied navies, and non-US forces would often be less provocative, or less likely to lead to escalation, than US forces.[20]

British, French and Italian naval forces could also be useful in providing pickets and performing various inshore patrol functions where there was only a limited air or anti-ship missile threat. Once again, all three fleets have more light patrol vessels than the US, and the deployment of non-US forces could again have the same general political benefits.

Depending on the scenario, allied forces could also help in securing lines of communication in contingencies involving the risk of Soviet initiation of submarine warfare where the primary threat is submarines and not aircraft. They would not, however, be suitable for independent out-of-area operations without direct US navy recce and intelligence support, and all three allied navies will slowly drop in capability during the late 1980s and early 1990s as the USSR acquires more sophisticated SSNs, submarine launched missiles, and satellite targeting systems. While individual European ships may have high capability, the Soviet submarine threat is advancing to the point where only the US can fully support fleet operations outside the Western Mediterranean and Atlantic.

Organising Joint Naval Task Forces

NATO is well organised to conduct joint naval operations in support of the defence of the Atlantic and the Mediterranean. The weaknesses in European naval and naval air forces are generally offset by US C^3I/BM capabilities and ability to provide a comprehensive ASW/air defence/missile defence screen. In practice, however, only the British,

French and Italian navies could provide ships that would be useful in a major out-of-area naval task force which faced a serious naval, air, or missile threat of the kind already common in the Eastern Mediterranean and Gulf, and which is likely to be characteristic of all major Middle Eastern states by the early 1990s.

The European role in such a task force would also generally be limited to providing the kind of specialised ships discussed earlier plus the most modern escorts with the most advanced mix of air and missile defences in a given European navy. Even then, these would often suffer from the inability to tie in to US navy sensors and defence systems.

The Falklands fighting, for example, exposed severe weaknesses in the fire control and sensor integration of the most modern British escorts, even within a ship, and these ships could not operate as a fully integrated air and missile defence force. Most French and Italian ships are even less sophisticated in this respect. It also showed that the US had to provide fuel, military satellite communication links to handle long-range communications, and a number of other services and special equipment that were not available in forces tailored for missions in the North Atlantic.

Most of these military limitations in European naval forces reflect a realistic set of trade-offs for forces which are not designed to support operations close to a hostile shore against a dense air threat capable of conducting simultaneous attacks, or within range of shore, small vessel based, or fighter launched air-to-ship missiles: their basic mission is ASW in waters where the primary air threat is Soviet naval bombers. These trade-offs do, however, impose severe limitations on out-of-area capabilities.[21] The West cannot ignore them in moderate to high intensity naval operations.

Conducting Limited Land/Air Operations

Britain, France, Italy, Turkey and the US could all conduct limited land/air operations in support of friendly states in the Middle East. The key issue will always be their relative ability to deploy and sustain operations in a given area and contingency. The broad limitations affecting each power have already been described, and it should be clear that no European state can now easily intervene unilaterally outside its own territory – if indeed the US can. The trend in the regional military balance will also move steadily against the West in the sense that local elements will continue to improve in force strength and in relative ability to use their military technology.

Launching Major Land/Air Operations

The broad problems in major multilateral Western military operations in the Middle East have already been discussed. There seems little reason why a NATO-wide or NATO-blessed operation would offer any advantages or have more than marginal military credibility. Britain, France, Italy and Turkey could all furnish useful force elements to a US dominated operation, but only Turkey could hope to conduct division sized or major air operations without extensive US support, and then only in the region near its borders.

The practical problem for both the European states involved in such operations and the United States would be the value of external political support versus the political and military problems of conducting joint operations with high risks and high potential casualties. In most cases, it seems likely that the US would not gain in force effectiveness unless the Allied forces involved were operating near or in territory and bases standardised around European equipment or – as in the cases of Oman and Djibouti – still capable of directly supporting British or French operations. In other cases, the US would have to divert lift, munitions and support resources to units which would generally be worse equipped than US forces; lacking standardisation in US munitions, spares, operations and maintenance, and tactics; and with different C^3I/BM systems. Further, the US is probably the only Western state which could absorb the political cost of a major defeat or reversal in such an operation. Any British, French, Italian or Turkish defeat would probably bring down the government supporting such a military operation and possibly undermine or sever ties to NATO.

III   REGIONAL SCENARIOS FOR THE USE OF FORCE

There is no question that the West faces the certain prospect of future conflict, violence, and terrorism in the Middle East. The US Department of Defense recently calculated that one out of four of all the world's nations are currently involved in at least low-level internal conflicts or episodic military engagements with other states.[22] At least one out of two Middle Eastern states are involved in such

Uses of Force in the Middle East

conflicts. As shown on Table 3.13, the use of force has become virtually a way of life in several Middle Eastern states, and the Iran–Iraq War and Afghan conflict have already lasted longer than the Second World War.

The discussion of Western power projection capabilities has already described many of the costs and benefits of using force in given types of contingencies. It has also illustrated some of the risks of trying to

Table 3.13   Current and probable levels of violence in the Middle East: 1985–95

Country	Current and probable levels of violence						
	Civil war	Terrorism Internal	Terrorism External	Low-level border conflicts	Major war with neighbours	Conflict involving NATO European states	Conflict involving super- powers
Mauritania	M	M	L	O	L	L	L
Morocco	M	H	O	O	M	L	L
Algeria	L	M	L	H	M	L	L
Tunisia	M	H	L	M	M	L	L
Libya	M	H	O	H	M	M	H
Egypt	L	O	O	H	M	L	L
Israel	L	O	O	O	H	L	L
Syria	M	O	O	O	H	L	M
Jordan	L	O	O	H	M	L	L
Lebanon	O	O	O	O	L	L	L
Iraq	M	O	O	—	O	O	M
Iran	O	O	O	O	O	M	H
Kuwait	L	O	O	O	M	L	L
Bahrain	H	O	O	O	M	L	H
Qatar	L	L	M	M	L	L	L
Saudi	L	L	H	H	M	M	M
UAE	M	H	H	H	M	M	M
Oman	L	H	H	H	M	M	M
PDRY	O	O	L	H	M	M	M
YAR	M	M	O	H	M	L	M
Ethiopia	O	O	O	O	M	L	M
Somalia	H	O	O	O	M	L	M
Sudan	O	O	O	O	M	L	M

Note: O = ongoing; H = high probability; M = moderate probability; L = low probability. Involvement with NATO Europe or superpowers involves conflict, joint military action, military intervention or support with combat forces, and excludes arms sales, provision of non-fighting advisors and demonstrative use of force.

prejudge the value of given uses of force by trying to predict the circumstances in which it must be used. It is all too easy to exaggerate either the advantages or disadvantages of using force by selecting a given scenario. It is exceedingly difficult, if not impossible, to predict the match between Western military forces and the needs of a given contingency. Yet, it is this 'force-contingency match' – not capability in some carefully chosen theoretical scenario – that will determine the real world value of force.

It is also extremely difficult to actually analyse a given scenario realistically without developing a full-scale contingency plan. The simple assertion that one outcome may occur rather than another is not a substitute for looking at the full range of alternatives that may occur and examining potential forces and military encounters in detail. Nevertheless, it is possible to make broad observations about key scenarios or contingencies that help illustrate the West's options.

Iranian Crisis Leading to Soviet Intervention

There are countless scenarios for a Soviet intervention in Iran. Some, such as the slow build-up of a major Soviet military presence at the invitation of a united Iranian government, simply cannot be countered by Western military action. Others, particularly civil war scenarios involving strong pro-Soviet factions in the North, probably involve too much risk. In any case, the US will have to bear the weight of virtually all Western military action, and the most it can hope for is limited Turkish, British and French support. In most cases, access to Turkish bases, to Diego Garcia, and to NATO staging points, will be far more critical than the forces European states can deploy. This is a case where broad Western solidarity might have a powerful impact in limiting Soviet action. As indicated earlier, however, the key determining factor will be the dynamics of the Iranian revolution and the attitude of the Iranian people and military forces. The US-Soviet military balance *per se* – like most of the balances in the region involving Western or Soviet bloc forces – will probably only be incidental to the outcome of any fighting or crisis unless the Iranian people are paralysed by their own divisions.

Israeli Defeat, Soviet Intervention and Superpower Confrontation in the Middle East

There is little reason for direct Western intervention in most Arab-

Israeli conflicts. Most of the probable outcomes of such conflicts are only of peripheral strategic interest to the West, and Western military involvement is usually likely to make the problem worse rather than better. The two exceptions are a catastrophic Israeli defeat or a major Soviet military move into the region.

In both cases, the US would almost certainly have to act unilaterally. Table 3.14 shows that the level of forces engaged in the region is rising steadily, and since their technology and weapons quality is already roughly equivalent to that of most Western forces, it is clear that most European task-forces would have little military value and would be then highly vulnerable to both hostile Arab troops and any Soviet units that moved into the region. The US could accomplish more to help Israel by using all its available land and air facilities and strategic lift to deploy its own forces than by diverting basing and lift capability to move less well-equipped European troops.

There is also a good military case for decoupling NATO and Western Europe as much as possible from any such action. The risk of a new oil crisis or embargo, and of identifying Europe with any such US military action, more than offsets the tenuous benefits of trying to develop European support for the US. Even a high profile attempt at obtaining such support might simply highlight the US need to draw down on forces and equipment in Europe, and to use European staging points. Further, it would discredit the option of Western Europe assuming a negotiating or peace-keeping role, and increase the risk of horizontal escalation which could involve NATO and the Warsaw Pact.

The US must keep its moral and political commitments to Israel. While an Israeli defeat and Soviet intervention now seem unlikely, another Israeli-Syrian war could lead to a Syrian defeat, to the kind of Lebanese crisis described by Cottam, or to a process of politico-military escalation that led to direct Soviet involvement in support of Syria or some other radical Arab state. Any such Soviet action would at least force a major US show of military force in support of Israel.

The US has, in fact, been forced to consider this kind of contingency as the military build-up on the Golan has escalated and the prospect of a new Syrian-Israeli conflict has become more likely. The essentially opportunistic character of Soviet policy might well exploit any conflict that gave the USSR the position of appearing to rescue an Arab state from a US backed Israel or even promised to provide major basing facilities in the Eastern Mediterranean. Nevertheless, the fact remains that the Levant is a strategic side show to the West, and Israel will remain a strategic liability to the West until it achieves a broader peace settlement with its Arab neighbours. Both the US and its European allies need to accept this reality.

Table 3.14   The force trends shaping a future Arab–Israeli war

Category	Israel 1982	Israel 1986	Syria 1982	Syria 1986	Jordan 1982	Jordan 1986	Egypt 1982	Egypt 1986
Total:								
Defence spending ($ billions)	6.1	3.6	2.4	3.3	0.4	0.5	2.1	4.1
Manpower (1,000s)								
Active	174.0	142.0	222.5	402.5	72.8	70.3	452.0	445.0
Conscript	120.3	—	120.0	—	—	—	255.0	250.0
Mobilisable	500.0	512.0	345.0	673.0	107.8	105.3	787.0	825.0
Army:								
Manpower (1,000s)								
Active	135.0	104.0	170.0	210.0	65.0	62.8	320.0	320.0
Conscript	110.0	88.0	120.0	135.0	—	—	180.0	180.0
Total mobilisable	450.0	400.0	270.0	55.0	—	—	620.0	643.0
Tanks	3,600	3,650	3,990	4,200	569	795	2,100	2,159
APCs	8,000	8,000	1,600	3,000	1,022	882	3,030	2,750
Artillery/MRLs	960	1,000	2,100	2,300	274	239	2,000	2,100
Air force and air defence forces:								
Manpower (1,000s)								
Active	30.0	28.0	50.0	130.0	7.5	7.2	113.0	105.0
Conscript	7.0	2.0	—	—	—	—	60.0	60.0
Total mobilisable	35.0	65.0	—	—	—	—	133.0	117.0
Total combat aircraft	634	684	450	583	94	121	429	427
Bombers	—	—	—	—	—	—	14	13
Attack interceptor	432	402	—	—	—	—	—	103
Attack	174	130	205	193	29	68	218	73
Interceptor	28	25	—	10	—	—	45	36
Recce/EW/AWACs	—	—	—	—	20	15	—	—
Other combat unit	42	90	16	100	—	8	24	48
Armed helicopter	42	90	16	100	—	8	24	48
Major SAM battalions Battery sites	15	15	75	126	5	5	151	100
Navy:								
Manpower (1,000s)								
Active	9.0	10.0	2.5	2.5	0.3	0.3	20.0	25.0
Conscripts	3.3	3.3	—	—	—	—	15.0	10.0
Total mobilisable	10.0	10.0	5.0	5.0	—	—	35.0	40.0
Submarines	3	3	—	—	—	—	12	14
Guided missile ships	27	24	18	22	—	—	19	30
Destroyer/escort/ frigate/corvette	2	6	2	2	—	—	8	10
Small combat ships	44	45	12	19	9	9	56	104
Amphibious	7	12	?	2	—	—	20	21

Source: Adapted from various editions of the IISS *Military Balance* and the JCCS *Middle East Military Balance*. Note that these figures do not show equipment in storage. They include estimates which often do not reflect actual readiness of manpower and equipment, and dated material. For example, the IISS data for Israel reflect virtually no updating between 1982 and 1986 and grossly exaggerate the size of Egypt's operational forces and equipment holdings in both 1982 and 1985. In fact, virtually no Soviet supplied equipment in Egyptian forces is combat operational and the true strength of Egyptian forces is less than one-third the totals shown. These figures are deliberately presented as a contrast to the trend curves shown earlier which reflect more substantial adjustments by the author.

Table 3.15   The trends in Iranian and Iraqi military forces: 1980–6

Force category	1980		1986	
	Iran	Iraq	Iran	Iraq
Total active military manpower suitable for combat:	240,000	242,250	750,000–930,000	520,000–755,000
Land forces:				
Regular army manpower				
Active	150,000	200,000	250,000–355,000	475,000
Reserve	400,000+	256,000	NA	230,000
Revolutionary Guards		200,000–300,000		
Basidji People's Army		70,000–100,000	404,800	
Hezbollahi (Home Guard)		2,500,000		
Arab volunteers			6,000?	
Division equivalents				
Armoured (divisions/brigades)	6 + 4	12 + 3	?	7
Mechanised	3	4	3–4?[a]	5
Infantry and mountain	—	4	9–12/1[a]	10 + 9[b]
Special forces/airborne	—	—	0/2	0/3
Pasadran/people's militia	—	—	9?/?	–/15
Major combat equipment				
Main battle tanks	1,740	2,750	900–1,250	3,750–4,220
Other armoured fighting vehicles	1,075	2,500	1,190–2,000	3,250–3,800
Major artillery	1,000+	1,040	1,000–1,360	2,500–3,500
Air forces				
Air force manpower	70,000	38,000	35,000	40,000
Combat aircraft	445	332	80–105[c]	520–580[d]
Combat helicopters	500	41	50?	144–171

Force category	1980		1986	
	Iran	Iraq	Iran	Iraq
Total helicopters	750	260	150–370	360–409
Surface to air missile batteries[e]	—	12	75	—
Naval forces:				
Navy manpower	26,000	4,250	20,000	5.000
Destroyers	3[f]	—	3[f]	—
Frigates	4[g]	1[h]	4[g]	1[h]
Corvettes	4	—	2–4	[i]
Missile patrol craft	9[j]	12[k]	3–7[j]	10[k]
Other patrol craft and gunboats	—	83	38	—
Mine warfare vessels	—	5	8	—
Hovercraft	14	—	10	—
Landingcraft and ships	—	17	2–3	—
Maritime patrol aircraft	6 P-3F	—	2 P-3F	—

Notes: [a] Estimates differ sharply. One detailed estimate shows 7 mechanised division with 3 brigades each and a total of 9 armoured and 18 mechanised battalions. Also 2 special forces divisions, 1 airborne brigade, and 8 division-sized revolutionary guard formations organised in battalions.

[b] Includes 5 infantry divisions and 4 mountain divisions. There are also 2 independent special forces divisions, 9 reserve brigades, and 15 People's Volunteer Infantry Brigades.

[c] Includes 35–50 F-4D/E, 17–50 F-5E/F, 10–14 F-14A, and 3 RF-4E. Large numbers of additional combat aircraft are in storage due to lack of parts. Some Argentine A-4s and PRC or North Korean F-6 and F-7 may be in delivery. The number of AH-1J attack helicopters still operational is unknown.

[d] Includes up to 7–12 Tu-22, 8–10 Tu-16; 4 FGA squadrons with 48–800 MiG-23BM/MiG-27, 6 with 75–95 Su-7 and 50–80 Su-17/20, and 1 with 12–15 Hunter FB-59/FR-10. 5 Super Etendard with Exocet have been replaced with 18 Mirage F-1 with refuelling probes and Exocet. There is 1 recce squadron with 5 MiG-25; and 5 interceptor squadrons with 25 MiG-25, 40 MiG-19, 150–200 MiG-21, and 45–55 Mirage F-1EQ, 5–15 extended range Mirage F-1 with Exocet, and 4–10 Mirage F-1BQ. Figures for Mirage strength vary sharply according to assumptions about delivery rates and combat attrition. Typical estimates of combat helicopters are 50 Mi-24, 70 SA-342 Gazelle, and 24 MBB BO-105.

[e] The number of operational SAM units on each side is unknown. Many of Iran's 12 Hawk batteries are not operational. Iraq has shown very limited ability to use its Soviet made SAMs and some sites do not seem to be fully operational. Counts of Iraq's missile strength are controversial but Iraq seems to have roughly 20 SA-2, 25 SA-3, and 25 SA-6 batteries.

^f 3 equipped with Standard Arm SSMs. One battle-class and two sumner-class in reserve.
^g Equipped with Sea Killer SSM.
^h 4 Lupo-class Italian made frigates on order.
ⁱ 6 Wadi-class Italian made 650-ton corvettes on order.
^j Equipped with Harpoon surface-to-surface missiles.
^k Equipped with Styx missiles.

Source: Adapted from various editions of the IISS *Military Balance*, Jaffe Center for Strategic Studies, *The Middle East Military Balance*, and work by Drew Middleton for the *New York Times*.

Iraqi Collapse

The West can do a great deal through arms transfers and economic policy to prevent an Iraqi collapse in the Iran–Iraq War, but very little in direct military terms. No Western state is willing to deploy major forces, and once a military or political collapse occurs the internal forces unleashed are likely to be nearly as decisive and massive in scale as those in the Iranian intervention scenario.

Table 3.15 illustrates this point. The military forces in Iraq and Iran are simply too large for Western intervention in a case involving civil conflict or a war between the two states. Once Iraq is in the actual process of military defeat, it will be too late for effective Western action. No new arms transfers by France or any group of Western nations will rescue Iraq. Iraq has demonstrated all too clearly that massive Western and Soviet arms transfers do not produce sudden shifts in Iraqi military capabilities. No demonstrative Western action will greatly inhibit Iran, and it is unlikely that the West will then be willing to even take the risk of alienating a victorious Iran. The US and France would probably support Turkey in any action it chose to take – possibly with British and German support – but it seems unlikely that Turkey will be particularly adventurous given the uncertainities and risks involved.

The Iran–Iraq war is a classic case of a vital Western strategic interest in which military action after the political and economic fact will be an extension of the failure of diplomacy by even worse means.

Attempt to Block Shipping in the Southern Gulf

An Iranian air/naval attack on the Southern Gulf states or attempt to block shipping is a good illustration of both the potential value of European forces in demonstrating solidarity with the US, and of their military limitations. Britain and France could both provide escorts, and might be able to take on the present Iranian air force and navy near the Straits of Hormuz, but neither could safely have acted independently at the start of the Iran–Iraq war or will be able to do so once Iran re-arms. Decisive Western action would also have to be US action, and would require full-carrier task-force sized units.

Protection of Kuwait

The West might well, however, be able to protect Kuwait against the consequences of an Iranian victory over Iraq or a shift in Iraq's attitudes. While Iraq and Iran have massive and combat trained military forces, neither state is experienced in projecting power and both now have considerable respect for what Western airpower can do to their ground forces. If the West could deploy several squadrons into Kuwait and operate larger air forces out of nearby Saudi bases, this might well be enough to halt any Iraqi or Iranian threat, provided that Western units were present in place before the invasion began. Weak as Kuwait's own military forces may be, it is far from clear that Iraq or Iran would take a military risk that brought it into direct confrontation with the West.

The practical problem will be Kuwait and Saudi Arabia's willingness to seek Western aid in time – particularly since the US would be the only Western power capable of deploying and supporting the forces required. US unwillingness to sell arms to Kuwait has led to considerable low-level hostility between Kuwait's ruling family and the US, and this may delay Kuwait's asking the US for help until it is too late. Unfortunately, this is also the case where Europe probably no longer can help. The days in which token British deployments would be sufficient are over, and France has no historical or advisory presence in Kuwait.

Internal Strife in Saudi Arabia

Saudi Arabia is lightly populated, its centres of power are far from its borders, and it is comparatively stable and unified. It is doubtful that any coup or other threat to internal security could take hold before the West could deploy major forces, particularly as long as the Saudi Air Force supports the regime and Western forces can move by air.

The level and type of Western military response required, however, will again be scenario dependent. In many cases, small French or British forces of squadron or battalion size might be enough to tip the balance – particularly with US logistic and lift support. In other cases, the conflict could be severe enough to require the support of US forces. Either a US airborne brigade with support from the USAF, or a Marine amphibious brigade with Marine and Navy airpower, would probably be sufficient to deal with any combination of hostile internal radicals and elements from nearby radical states.

In general, the key problem will be to foresee the threat in time to act before it grows or escalates, to ensure that any Western force works as closely with friendly Saudi military elements as possible, to keep the Western force as small as possible, and to leave as soon as possible. It is also important to point out that future success will depend on the Saudi regime retaining its current popularity and support within the military and internal security forces. As France has already quietly demonstrated, the West can help Saudi Arabia deal with an isolated coup attempt or a limited insurgency like the Eastern province riots or the effort to seize the Grand Mosque. It could certainly help deal with any infiltration from the PDRY or any other current regional threat. The West cannot, however, hope to save an unpopular Saudi regime from the Saudi people.

Other Internal Crises

The West's ability to act in other Middle Eastern internal security crises or coups will follow the patterns described earlier. The issue will always be the size and political position of the local military, popular opinion, access to ports and air facilities, attitudes towards the US and other Western states capable of military action and the probability of successful intervention versus the risks.

The main dangers in such interventions will be twofold. First, the risk of failure or of becoming the sponsor of an unpopular regime. Second, the illusion on the part of local rulers that Western military capability can save them from the processes of social and political change and the need for economic reform. This will present major, if not insuperable, problems if the internal divisions in states like Egypt, Morocoo, Tunisia and Bahrain should come to a crisis.

The West will almost certainly accomplish far more with economic and military aid before a crisis than it can accomplish with military forces once a popular revolution begins. Unfortunately, the West can only really hope to use military force successfully when a small elite attempts to seize power without major popular support – a contingency which is possible but less likely than a civil conflict growing out of the economic, political and religious problems affecting the moderate Arab states.

Peace-Keeping Operations

There are, however, some specific uses of military force that seem more likely than others. Some form of involvement in trying to keep peace between Israel and its Arab neighbours is a good case in point. The West has already been involved in several variations of Arab-Israeli peace-keeping options. British efforts failed from 1945–8, UN efforts failed in 1967, and US efforts failed in 1982–3. The West has been successful or partially successful in three cases: the original US intervention in Lebanon, the UN presence in Southern Lebanon, and the multilateral peace-keeping force in the Sinai.

All of these six cases illustrate the classic lessons regarding peace-keeping forces. The peace-keeping force could be successful when it did not have to take sides, when conflicting parties wanted an agreement or peace-keeping function to remain in force, and when the peace-keepers could avoid significant involvement in combat. They failed every time they did not meet all three of these conditions.

This pattern of past failure and success is likely to be equally valid in the future. A Western UN force can play a role in securing an Arab-Israeli peace settlement provided that that settlement is regarded as valid and desirable by both sides. It is almost certain to fail if it is not. The rules of the game in the Middle East have never protected peace-keeping forces which attempted to act as buffers between nations or movements which seriously want to fight, and such a peace-keeping force is almost certain to quickly be reduced to either impotence or taking sides.

A peace settlement on the West Bank or Golan would, however, present some problems for a Western peace-keeping force which are of special interest. A force identified closely with the US or NATO would be desirable to Israel, but probably be seen as pro-Israeli by at least Syria and the PLO, and possibly by Jordan. This could have advantages if Israel was willing to make major concessions on the West Bank or Golan, since a US peace-keeping presence in the area might act as both a credible substitute for Israeli forces and as a politically acceptable presence to the Arab states. It could also backfire if the settlement led to sustained guerrilla or low level operations by some element involved.

At the same time, no combination of European states could guarantee a peace settlement against an Arab or Israeli attack or crisis leading to war. It would take several armoured brigades and squadron equivalents to really deter military action. Further, it would take a major inspection force deployed throughout the confrontation states or a major arms control agreement to guarantee warning of a military build-up or deployment – barring US intelligence support using advanced technical means unavailable to most European states and too costly for France and Britain to deploy without major international funding. This means the US would probably have to participate at a C^3I/BM level, and act as the over-the-horizon guarantor of any agreement. Such a role, however, would require at least tacit Soviet backing to eliminate the risk of superpower confrontation and engagement.

These conditions seem likely to be typical of any Western peace-keeping role in the region involving states with major armoured and air forces, and this rapidly is coming to include virtually every country except Tunisia, Lebanon and the smaller Southern Gulf states. Accordingly, the litmus test will be whether a peace-keeping force can enforce an agreed peace or must try to create one. The West cannot afford the basic British out-of-area strategy of the nineteenth century: 'Blunder in, blunder on, but never blunder out!'

IV   LIBYA: A CASE STUDY OF COUNTER-TERRORIST OPERATIONS

Finally, the West still faces the very real threat of further escalation in the conflict between the US and Libya, or that the US will be faced with another hostage or terrorist crisis growing out of the rising Shi'ite and Palestinian extremism in Lebanon. This risk makes the lessons of the last US raid on Libya of particular interest.

The Impact of the Raid

The US raid on Libya involved less than twelve minutes of combat. It has, however, raised issues that the US and the West may spend years trying to come fully to grips with. The raid has also revealed a number of important lessons regarding both modern weapons and the fight against terrorism. While it is still premature to judge all of the lessons of the raid, several points have become clear.

The first is the problem of setting a clear military objective that has a credible chance of altering terrorist behaviour, as distinguished from simply enforcing punitive action. Many senior US military officers and defence officials privately felt that the raid on Libya lacked a definite objective, and that the US used military force without a clear purpose. Even Secretary Weinberger is felt to have been pushed into the raid by pressure from Secretary of State George Schulz and senior officials in the National Security Council.

The key uncertainty that surrounded US contingency planning before the raid, and which has re-emerged since, is whether it made sense to attack any targets other than Libya's oil export capability and Qaddafi, and whether the US could have accomplished more through covert action. The criticisms are twofold. First, many US experts and planners feel the raid was either much too large or much too small. On the one hand, it was not large enough to remove Qaddafi from power or to deter him from future 'adventures'. On the other hand, it was too large not to gain Qaddafi broader support in the Arab world and temporarily consolidate his people behind him. Many intelligence officials feel that a lower level effort to support his opposition would have been more successful – particularly since there had been several recent attempt to remove him from power.

Second, although few would say it publicly, many US intelligence officers and experts on the Middle East feel the raid was necessary because President Reagan and Secretary of State George Shultz had glorified Qaddafi by giving him so high a public profile, and by attacking him with broad unsubstantiated rhetoric that put leading officials on the same verbal plane as Qaddafi. These same experts feel that the US naval action in the Gulf of Siddra had the same effect. The US took on Qaddafi without damaging him, made him more of a hero with extremists in the Arab world, and encouraged him to launch the series of terrorist attacks culminating in the Berlin bombing. They feel that less publicity and more quiet support to Qaddafi's opposition could have brought him down long ago.

After all, there have been up to ten internal efforts to remove Qaddafi from power in recent years. Libya's current oil production is about half its 1978–80 level, the value of its exports has been cut in half, and its current account balance has gone from a $7.5 billion surplus to a deficit of over $1 billion. Qaddafi is nearly $9 billion behind in paying for foreign military and civil imports and services, foreign reserves have dropped from $14 billion to $2–3 billion, and the economy has contracted every year since 1980. Nearly a third of Libya's best educated managers and professionals have left the country, most industrial and consumer goods are in short supply, the political situation is so bad that even Libya's coffee houses have been closed to prevent public assemblies, and Libya is not meeting its payments even on its $4–5 billion arms debt to the USSR.

There are no easy answers to any of these uncertainties, which become much more pronounced when the same questions are raised about potential US or Western military action against terrorist activities that are sponsored by more powerful nations, like Syria. While the West can probably attack terrorist camps or facilities in areas like the Bekaa Valley with near impunity in terms of military reprisals, it is not clear whether such attacks will suppress terrorism and they may well lead to more terrorist volunteers and actions. Finding the proper level of military escalation to really deter future action will be difficult indeed – particularly if military action is not coupled with political action to remove either the causes of terrorism or the bulk of its popular support.

These uncertainties are reflected in the US reaction to the raid. Although Department of Defense officials publicly describe the raid as a success, most have pushed hard for shifting to covert action or for employing weapons systems like cruise missiles which might avoid US casualties. The end result is likely to be a continuing debate in which 'Hawkish' civilians in the State Department and NSC are often resisted by 'Dovish' officers and civilians in the Defense Department. Ironically, both are meeting some resistance in the CIA, where career intelligence officers are much more cautious about the ease and efficiency with which the US can use covert action than are officials outside the US intelligence community.

Lessons Regarding Consultation and Joint Action

One thing on which US officials do agree is that the US found both before and after the raid that it could not count on consultation with its friends and allies to yield more than token support. There is a great deal of high-level gratitude for the support of Prime Minister Thatcher, who one US Assistant Secretary of Defense described as 'the only real man in Europe' – a term he was conspicuously unwilling to apply to the leaders of the FRG and Italy. More broadly, many US officials now feel that consultation is at best suited for political and economic sanctions and is unlikely to produce meaningful political results when the use of force is contemplated.

Rather than deter US action, the political and public protests from Europe have tended to confirm the belief that neither the EEC or NATO will ever be meaningful forums for out-of-area action or anti-terrorism and that the US has been thrust into the position of having to act alone. The fact that the EEC imported some 10.5 billion ecus from Libya in 1985, and exported only 3.5, has not gone unnoticed in the United States. Neither has the lack of support the US received from France – which repeatedly has had to have US support and strategic lift for its own operations in Africa. Further, the highly negative public opinion polls in the FRG have tended to confirm the general US feeling that West Germany takes a firm attitude only in regard to its own defence.

This kind of thinking is scarcely likely to split the Alliance, but it also is unlikely to make the US take Europe seriously over any issue other than the defence of Europe. Regardless of the image building at the Tokyo Summit, the US increasingly feels that the steady roll-back in European out-of-area capabilities has thrust the US into responsibilities in the Middle East, Persian Gulf, South Atlantic and Pacific where all it can count on from its allies is criticism.

The Choice of Weapons

There is another kind of debate within the US, and this is a debate over what the raid says about the kind of forces and weapons that should be used for power projection and long-range strikes. Even some of the US defence officials who have fervently praised most the performance of US weapons during the raid privately acknowledge that it raised severe questions about the current US capability to carry out its 'quick strike' approach to low-level conflicts and terrorism and about the merits of trying to launch surgical strikes at long distances using existing types of US aircraft.

The US 'quick strike' concept essentially is the doctrine that the US cannot commit troops because of the political cost of involvement and casualties, or maintain a prolonged military presence to win minor gains. The lessons of Vietnam and Lebanon seem to be clear: the US public and Congress will not accept losses for confusing and uncertain political objectives. The US also cannot simply be reactive and let terrorists or minor Third World radicals choose their opportunities and targets. It must use all its intelligence resources to develop adequate warning and strike hard and decisively with advanced technology before its opponents act. It cannot take the time for consultation when this simply means leaking US intentions or arousing public criticism and it must keep US military and foreign civilian casualties to an absolute minimum.

The 'quick strike' concept itself is not at issue within the Reagan Administration – the majority of policy makers and military leaders support it. The question is choosing the right time and scenario for action and finding the right military means. Regardless of the political arguments surrounding the Libyan raid, a great many US experts are a bit stunned by the fact the raid required thirty-two bombers and nearly seventy support planes.

By the time all the forces are counted they include twenty-eight KC-10 and KC-135 strategic airlift tankers, twenty-four F-111E/F strike fighters, five EF-111 electronic warfare and jamming aircraft, several F-14A escort fighters, fourteen A-6E all-weather and night attack fighter bombers, five A-7E attack aircraft with HARM (High Speed Anti-Radiation Missiles) and Shrike shorter range anti-radiation missiles, six F-18A/Bs with Shrike, several EA-6B four seat electronic warfare and jamming aircraft, and four E-2C airborne control and warning and ESSM aircraft. The raid also required two-carrier task-forces, some seventeen ships carrying a total of 155 aircraft on their carriers, and total task-force manning of 14 700 men. What should have been a fairly simple operation ended up involving more aircraft and combat ships than Britain employed during its entire campaign in the Falklands!

Similarly, US experts are struck by the fact that so many carrier-based A-6s were not operationally available for use in the raid, and that the eighteen F-111s that were originally supposed to conduct strikes against Libya delivered only about half the planned tonnage. (One aircraft was lost over target, seven had to turn back, and two had avionics which did not function properly over target, and hence did not drop their bombs.) No one can deny that flying 2800 miles, carrying out four refuelings, spending six hours and twenty-four minutes on the way to target and then eight hours and ten minutes back to base imposes a near impossible burden. France's refusal to grant overflight rights forced the US to fly 1200 miles around Spain, and to use fighter-bombers to perform roles best suited for long-range interdiction bombers.

The broader point, however, is that the twenty-four-ton F-111 selected for the raid is not only the one US air force plane capable of both penetrating at 200–1000 feet and delivering its payload accurately at night, it is also the only high payload/long-range fighter-bomber in the US inventory. This inventory is not large for a global power – there are less than 300 F-111s in US tactical forces plus sixty-one in US strategic forces and thirty-six EF-111 electronic warfare aircraft. The F-111 is also a 1960s vintage aircraft optimised for nuclear strike missions, and which has never achieved great reliability in spite of constant upgrades and improvements. It is no longer in production and does not perform well enough to justify restarting production if the US takes heavy losses.

The US also cannot substitute bombers for long-range strike fighters. The B-52 is in its final years and no longer suitable for penetrating with conventional bombs against heavily defended targets, the B-1 is not optimised for conventional roles and will never be delivered in the numbers required, and the F-15E Strike Eagle simply does not have the range, payload, or night bombing capability for a wide range of interdiction missions.

The US is now discovering what one former commander of USCENTCOM long privately cautioned was a critical weakness in its force structure: the lack of a modern high-payload, long-range interdiction aircraft. Unfortunately, there have been many recent US air force advocates of advanced dogfighters, multi-role fighters and strategic bombers, but few advocates of long-range heavy strike aircraft. Now that the US needs one, it does not even have one on the drawing board! Europe faces quite similar problems. No European power now has a modern interdiction bomber, and only the Tornado has the range, payload, and low altitude penetration capability to rival the F-15E. European powers would generally have many more problems in refueling their aircraft, and would find long-range strikes even more difficult to support in the Middle East.

The US Navy encountered some disturbing problems of its own. Although Secretary of the Navy John Lehman has given several speeches claiming a flawless performance, the truth is that only the air defence and air defence suppression missions were really relatively trouble free. Two of the fourteen A-6s could not deliver payloads because they aborted as the result of mechanical problems. The entire A-6 force on the carriers *America* and *Coral Sea* had a relatively poor overall operational readiness for demanding attack missions. While many of the A-6 Intruders on the carriers are of relatively recent manufacture, the basic design is nearly fifteen years old, and the A-7Es and F-18A/Bs simply do not have the legs and avionics for long-range and highly demanding strike missions. These aircraft, however, out-perform the naval fighters and fighter bombers on any European carrier, and only France has any real remaining fixed-wing carrier strength.

Efforts to Limit Casualties

Some experts outside the Pentagon wonder, however, if many of the
problems the US encountered were not the result of overreaction to
the earlier US loss of two carrier-based fighters to SA-7s in daylight
missions over Lebanon. The US did, after all, have a very sophisticated range of other fighters, including the F-18A/B and A-7E. While
these are not suited to night attack missions, the carrier force might
well have been able to carry out a similarly effective strike in daylight
if it had used its entire mix of attack and air defence aircraft. The
US may have weaknesses in its power projection capabilities, but
there is no question that these capabilities are massive – particularly
against as poorly organised a defence as Libya possesses.

At least some observers feel that the only reason for not striking
during the day was the desire to avoid an all-out air suppression
battle, and particularly one that might have either led to US strikes
hitting large numbers of Soviet advisors or to revealing more electronic
warfare secrets in a comparatively low priority strike than the value
of the target justified. This, however, is a highly controversial area,
and many in the Pentagon would argue that the US simply used the
best available force mix. In any case, the issue is largely moot for a
European power. No European country has the mix of airpower and
electronic warfare capabilities to even attempt such a raid unless it
was willing to take very serious losses.

'Unmanaging' Escalation

One thing is clear. The combination of shortfalls in the aircraft that
were used in the Libyan raid meant both missed targets and a highly
unpredictable overall outcome to what was supposed to be a surgical
strike with carefully calculated effects. It raises serious questions
about how well the US can manage its 'escalation ladder' in tailoring
its use of force to a particular political objective. Even something
less than 50 per cent of the desired military effect may have been
better than the total failure of US battleships and carrier aircraft to
hit useful targets in Lebanon, but it is scarcely a desirable standard
of performance, and the US is almost certain to encounter other
overflight problems or needs for sophisticated attack profiles in the
future.

The issue of civilian deaths is also somewhat disturbing, although
more in terms of public and Congressional reactions than in terms of

unanticipated military effects. US planners had known from the start that some losses were likely, even under the most stringent engagement rules. Israel had already demonstrated in Lebanon in 1982 that a force trying its best to minimise civilian casualties will produce them in an environment where civilians, civilian technicians, terrorists without uniforms and military dependents move through the target area. While the US used its full range of technology to avoid such deaths, US policy makers had had prior warning that some civilian deaths are likely in virtually any military action against either terrorist units or their training camps and supporting infrastructure.

The problem in many ways is one of trying to fight with real weapons in the face of impossible political and moral demands. At least at the political level, the US experience reveals some very important lessons about escalation which affect any Western use of military force:

1. No technology can eliminate US military or foreign civilian losses.
2. No technology is good enough to produce surgical or fully predictable results.
3. No use of force can ever avoid at least some moral issues and contradictions.
4. Escalation is always difficult to control, produces unpredictable results and results in an uncertain mission.

This last problem is particularly important given the debate over whether the US did, or did not, try to kill Qaddafi or regarded him as a sort of 'bonus' target. Some area experts feel that the very ambiguity of the effect of US strikes may have had a damping effect on Qaddafi. Others feel that one of the key weaknesses of the raid is that no one now really understands what the US was trying to say or what would have happened if the US had hit all its targets.

Still other critics raise the issue whether the US simply ends in a kind of compromise position where it never acts decisively enough. They feel the US is so politically constrained that it tries to create finely calculated and fully coordinated patterns of escalation which simply lack coherence and purpose. There is also the feeling that an accountant's mentality has crept into US planning and that the US ends in overrefining its actions and in substituting bargaining theory for strategy.

This school generally supports the theory that the US should either have waited for still greater justification or simply gone for Qaddafi or for Libya's oil export capability. They argue that hitting Libyan and terrorist bases and camps is pointless, and at least some argue that much of the European and moderate Arab *angst* over the raid would have disappeared over night if Qaddafi had not survived or if there no longer was a mjaor Libyan oil export capability for Europe to worry about.

This US debate, however, reveals issues of equal importance for both European action and any efforts at collective action. The pressures on any single nation are the same, and they are likely to be compounded by efforts to organise cooperative endeavours or to obtain broad foreign support for specific courses of action.

In sum, the Libyan case study has broad implications for both the US and its allies. It is a very tangible illustration of the technical and military risks of projecting power into the Middle East, even to deal with relatively limited regional uses of force-like terrorism. It illustrates the difficulty of achieving a national, much less a collective, consensus over any course of action, and the difficulty of tailoring military action or escalation to produce predictable results.

V THE FORCES OF MILITARY CHANGE

These issues and problems will be reinforced by the steady growth of indigenous military forces and capabilities, in which the Middle East leads the Third World. Not only do all Middle Eastern states compete in some aspect of the regional arms race, that race is fuelled by the fact that arms sales to the region have become a significant item of trade for the US, Western Europe and the USSR, and a means of gaining political and military influence.

Arms and Technology

Table 3.16 shows the hard data on recent weapons transfers, which have enabled the creation of regional military forces with numbers of tanks and jet fighters approaching those of the larger NATO states. This table provides tangible evidence of why Western military forces lacking heavy armour and air support have lost much of their freedom of action. Furthermore, these arms transfers have increasingly given the Middle East near-parity with the first-line forces of NATO and the Warsaw Pact in many aspects of technology.

Table 5.10 Major weapons transfers to the Middle East by major supplier, 1979–85

Weapons type	Total	Supplier								
		USSR	Other Warsaw Pact	PRC	US	France	UK	Other NATO	Other Developed	Other Developing
Land weapons										
Tanks	7,708	3,330	1,400	405	1,333	70	260	20	890	—
APCs	11,472	4,440	155	145	5,352	595	125	270	390	—
Field artillery	11,319	1,530	470	715	1,959	195	90	4,365	1,995	—
AA artillery	11,472	4,440	155	145	5,352	595	125	270	390	—
Naval craft										
Major surface combatants	8	1	1	—	2	3	1	—	—	—
Other surface combatants	135	13	5	6	18	2	24	40	16	11
Submarines	4	—	—	2	—	—	—	—	2	—
Missile attack boats	32	14	—	—	3	6	9	—	—	—
Aircraft										
Supersonic combat	1,597	855	25	125	272	135	10	—	175	—
Subsonic combat	115	80	—	—	—	20	5	—	10	—
Other aircraft	302	60	90	—	22	15	5	15	5	90
Helicopters	634	445	5	—	4	80	10	80	10	—
Surface-to-air missiles	10,901	5,890	—	35	2,286	990	180	—	1,435	85

Source: Adapted by the author from data in ACDA, *World Military Expenditures and Arms Transfers, 1985,* and Richard F. Grimmit, 'Trends in Conventional Arms Transfers to the Third World, 1978–1985', CRS Report Number 86–99, 19 May 1986. The US data are for fiscal years and the other data for calendar years. Field artillery includes tubes, recoilless rifles, and MRLs over 100 mm. Air defence artillery includes weapons over 23 mm. Major surface combatants include aircraft carriers, cruisers, destroyers, destroyer escorts and frigates. Minor surface combatants include motor torpedo boats, subchasers, and minesweepers. Other aircraft include reconnaissance aircraft, trainers, transports, and utility aircraft.

While most Middle Eastern states cannot yet use the forces and technologies at their disposal with anything approaching the effectiveness of the best NATO and Warsaw Pact units, the recent fighting in the Falklands, the Iran–Iraq war, and the Lebanon conflict of 1982, show that Third World forces can use at least some of their modern weapons and technology effectively.

Moreover, the weapons systems being introduced into the area are highly advanced – in some instances more so than those available to Western forces, France, for example, has already offered to sell the Arab world more advanced tanks than it intends to procure for the French army. Italy is offering to sell ECM gear designed to defeat the Hawk missile. Britain is selling Saudi Arabia a somewhat gold-plated version of the Tornado with more avionics features than the standard aircraft sold to the RAF.

A similar upgrading of Soviet weapons systems can be anticipated; in fact, any forecast of the rate of technology transfer during the next decade is more likely to understate it than to exaggerate it. That transfer will be accompanied by a steadily greater regional capability to absorb and utilise such technology. Further, Middle Eastern states may often be in a position to combine Soviet-made weapons with the Western C^3I/BM, fire control systems, and other technology necessary to bring them close to par with the lead systems in NATO, or to buy a mix of the most advanced Warsaw Pact and NATO systems. Thus, the days of Western 'gunboating' – of successful unilateral Western intervention in the region – are over.

Cost and Resource Constraints

Both NATO and Middle Eastern forces will be resource constrained in the future. As has been mentioned previously, NATO now seems certain to fall far short of its goal of a 3 per cent annual rise in real defence expenditures, and of the investment levels necessary to maintain both its present mix of force numbers and level of technology. The Middle East faces grave uncertainties about oil economics, and is beginning to exhaust its credit and offset/barter options to buy more military goods.

Regardless of these trends, however, one thing is clear. Neither the West nor the USSR will lose its incentive to sell arms to the Middle East, and the competition involved is certain to ensure that Middle Eastern states increasingly can buy technology equal to that in first-line NATO and Warsaw Pact forces. The economics involved are illustrated all too clearly in Table 3.17. The Middle East is a far more important export market to both NATO and the Warsaw Pact nations than are the other states within the respective alliances, and the same resource pressures that drive NATO countries to reduce their out-of-area forces will drive them to increase arms sales to the Middle East.

In this connection, it should be noted that the USSR has, as indicated in Table 3.16, played a far more important role in actual weapons transfers than the dollar value of such transfers would indicate, and that Europe has transferred a relatively small number of major land weapons. This serves as a broad indication of the need for better Western efforts on force planning in improving the overall capabilities of friendly regional states. Far too many friendly forces are being supplied in a piecemeal fashion that deprives them of much of their effectiveness, while Soviet supplied forces tend to have a high degree of standardisation.

The Paradox of Force Ratios

In summary, the trends in the region seem likely to steadily increase the problems Western forces will face in operating in the Middle East over the next ten years, and the West's *de facto* reliance on the US for any use of military force in moderate to high level conflicts. These same trends will make any Western-Soviet bloc comparisons steadily less relevant. The issue will instead be the regional coalitions on each side, and the size of the combination of NATO and friendly regional forces versus the size of the combination of Soviet bloc and friendly regional forces.

The problem of force efficiency will also be important. The West is likely to retain a major edge in organisation and in the force-wide ability to use emerging technology and advanced C^3I/BM. By and large, however, only the US will be able to afford advanced power projection forces with tailored tactical technology. Western forces will also lose much of their advantage in C^3I/BM and manoeuvre capability if they suddenly have to assemble and fight multinational forces. While Britain and France will continue to have considerable capability in low-level conflicts, this is likely to slowly reduce their ability to operate effectively with the US in higher level operations.

The risks to the West will also increase in ways which make force ratios irrelevant. As more and more states acquire heavy anti-ship missiles, long-range attack fighters with advanced avionics, modern

Table 3.17 The Middle East's importance to the world arms market (market share of new arms export agreements to the Middle East in 1981–4 in $ billions)

Region	World total	Western							Communist		
		US	France	UK	FRG	Italy	Other NATO	Other non-communist	Soviet	NSWP	Other communist
Middle East	68.3	11.9	13.9	2.0	1.0	1.8	1.8	8.0	15.9	3.7	7.3
NATO Europe	20.1	15.3	1.1	0.5	1.7	0.3	0.5	0.6	0.0	0.1	0.0
Warsaw Pact	9.6	0	0	0	0	0	0	1.5	4.4	3.7	0.0
World total	175.3	53.0	21.4	5.0	7.3	4.2	4.0	18.2	41.6	10.7	9.9
Middle East as a % of world total	39	22	65	40	14	43	45	44	38	35	74

Note: Estimate by the author based on ACDA, World Military Expenditures and Arms Transfers, 1985, and working papers by Richard F. Grimmit of the Congressional Research Service.

third generation ATGMs and air-to-air missiles, and long-range artillery and multiple rocket launchers, they will be able to overcome more of the tactical and strategic barriers to striking at longer distances. They will also steadily increase the risk of 'wild card' damage to a Western carrier, or of significant land and/or air losses to a Western force.

This will further highlight the fact that force ratios are only meaningful to the extent they represent equal willingness to accept and sustain military losses. In practice, the national and political movements in the region seem likely to be willing to take far more initial and continued losses than the West. As the US experience in Lebanon in 1982 demonstrated, 'gun boating' depends on the virtual immunity of the gun boat and on the crew being able to inflict more damage than the forces on shore. Time seems decidedly to be on the side of the Middle Eastern forces on shore.

VI ISSUES BUT NO ANSWERS

The West's experience in Lebanon is a tangible warning of the fact that the trends within the Middle East and NATO do not favour alliance-wide attempts at the use of force, or efforts to expand the role of NATO to support 'out-of-area' operations. It is clear that there are powerful constraints on the value of multilateral operations in the Middle East. Military efficiency and freedom of action do not flow out of politically dominated efforts at any time, and this is particularly true when they require any kind of broad national consensus. Most NATO European forces are not really suited to operations in the Middle East, and most NATO European countries would be heavily dependent on US strategic air- and sea-lift, combat and service support and C³I/BM support.

The standardisation and interoperability problems of supporting Allied forces would often be more acute than the already serious problems in NATO, and many lack equipment and firepower equal to that of indigenous forces. The language and culture barrier problems would be sharply increased, and the already critical political problems in carrying out most low-level operations would be far more severe. Worse, even minor set-backs or defeats could have a serious political backlash that could threaten national support for the Alliance or create very serious problems for US relations with the nation involved.

Attractive as the idea of NATO action may seem to the advocates of closer cooperation within the Atlantic Alliance, the fact remains that most NATO states simply cannot play a role save that of peace-keeping and that only in those cases where the risk of escalation or even low-level military involvement is negligible. This is particularly the case when the politics of the situation divide the Alliance. This is likely to be true of all Middle East contingencies, but it is particularly true of scenarios involving the Arab-Israeli conflict and terrorism.

Efforts supporting collective military action in the West must also be balanced against the value of several alternatives that seem likely to produce more useful and tangible results:

1. Improved understanding by key Western nations of the US need for support in terms of strategic staging bases and strategic lift facilities.
2. A fuller European understanding of the fact that US use of US forces and equipment to support out-of-area contingencies upholds the Alliance as a whole and will be inevitable in the event of any major US action in the Middle East.
3. European acceptance of the fact that as Europe continues to shrink back to a purely regional defence role, the US must limit its consultation and search for consensus within NATO. Europe cannot fail to assume the military responsibility and assume that the US must act within a NATO political consensus.
4. US acceptance of the fact that no European state will increase its out-of-area forces during the next ten years or assume more of the burden in NATO by making real incremental increases in its forces or military expenditures.
5. A realistic focus on the role of the four key European states that can play an individual role in the Middle East, and on strengthening their individual capacities. In the case of Italy, this seems likely to mean peace-keeping and low-level intervention capabilities in North Africa and the Levant. In the case of Turkey this means strengthening Turkish forces in Eastern Turkey to provide *de facto* contingency capability in scenarios involving Iraq and Iran, and searching for arrangements that will allow the US to use Turkish facilities while minimising the risks to Turkey. It means supporting the continuation of the British and French out-of-area role as long as possible, and encouraging an expansion of their role in internal security and intelligence training in the GCC.

6. Efforts to provide better coordination in Western arms sales to key friendly and moderate states to ensure the success of technology transfer, interoperability and standardisation, and the creation of aids, such as advanced C^3I/BM systems, that will be helpful in any Western efforts at reinforcement from 'over the horizon'. This will become particularly important as the US loses its current market share in arms sales to the region, while still remaining the only state capable of serious military intervention.

These are not dramatic recommendations, but the time window for the Western use of force in the Middle East is closing. The practical reality is that the US is the only Western power capable of action in most scenarios which have real strategic importance, and its capabilities are limited. NATO is also already under severe resource pressure to deal with its own military problems, and must give these problems priority. Unfortunately, such pressures are almost certain to further reduce British and French power projection capabilities during the next decade.

These limitations on Western military power are matched by regional limitations on the West's ability to make the use of military power effective. In many contingencies, the endemic violence in the Middle East will not lend itself to useful Western military solutions. In most cases, Middle Eastern states will have to resolve the issues as well or as badly as they can. The fact that the West will experience strategic risks, that Western lives will be lost, and the West will suffer major economic costs, will simply be military facts of life that can only be resolved – if at all – by political and economic solutions to regional problems. Denying this reality will not make it go away or even succeed in hiding it.

The most desirable alternative for the West will be to deliberately strengthen friendly conservative and moderate states and to build up the regional power projection capabilities of states like Egypt and Jordan and collective forces like those of the Gulf Cooperation Council. In practice, however, the competition for arms sales is likely to paralyse both efforts at building up strong bilateral Western vendor–Middle East buyer relationships and any efforts at standardisation and interoperability with Western forces.

The key limiting factor on such efforts will be the Arab-Israeli conflict. Europe can largely ignore this conflict, but the US is the only Western nation with the military resources and reinforcement capabilities to build effective regional coalitions. Unfortunately, the US is also sharply limited in creating such regional coalitions or relationships by the politics of its relations with Israel. The US cannot even continue to sell major arms to friendly states like Jordan and Saudi Arabia. Barring an Arab-Israeli peace settlement, this means that Western capability to use or to support force in the Middle East is likely to steadily deteriorate throughout the next decade.

Notes

1. The detailed limitations in individual NATO ships can be found in *Jane's Fighting Ships, 1984–1985*. For a summary discussion of some of the issues involved see RUSI–Brassey's *International Weapons Developments* (London: Brasseys, 1980), pp. 62–92; and Doug Richardson, *Naval Armament* (London: Janes, 1981), especially pp. 16–58.
2. The US has made major strides in prepositioning and improving its air- and sea-lift. Nevertheless, it still will be very severely limited in this respect in any move of division or wing-sized USCENTCOM forces well into the mid-1990s. See Caspar W. Weinberger, *Annual Report to Congress, FY 1986* (Washington, DC; Department of Defense), February 1985 pp. 193–204; OJCS, *Military Posture, FY 1986* (Washington, DC; Department of Defense), 1985, pp. 49–50 and 69–76.
3. Estimate based on, *Military Balance, 1985–1986* (London: International Institute for Strategic Studies, 1986), and the data furnished by Department of Defence, Public Affairs, January 1986.
4. For an excellent recent treatment of US build-up capabilities in the region, see Thomas McNaugher, *Arms and Oil* (Washington, DC; Brookings Institute), 1985, pp. 53–89.
5. These comments and the following out of area force data are based on various editions of the International Institute for Strategic Studies: *The Military Balance*; Peter Foot, *Beyond The North Atlantic: The European Contribution*, ASIDES, Aberdeen, No. 21, Spring 1982; William T. Tow, 'NATO's Out of Region Challenges and Extended Containment', *Orbis*, Vol. 28, No. 4, Winter, 1985, pp. 829–56; Paul E. Gallis, *The NATO Allies, Japan, and the Persian Gulf*, Report No. 84–184F, Washington, Congressional Research Service, 8 November 1984; John Chipman, *French Military Policy and African Security*, Adelphi Paper 201 (London: International Institute for Strategic Studies, 1985); and Anthony H. Cordesman, *NATO Out of Area Contingency Options for the 1980s*, LASL (Los Alamos Scientific Laboratories) White Paper, 28 September 1984.
6. For a full description of the *Garibaldi* see Antony Preston and Antonio O. Ciampi, '*Garibaldi* – Pride of the Italian Fleet', *Jane's Defence Weekly*, 22 February 1986, pp. 318–19. Both British and French carrier groups have limited to moderate air and missile and AEW assets, but neither has sufficient assets to protect any significant number of allied vessels.

7. For a good discussion of the issues involved see Luigi Caligaris, 'Possible Scenarios for an Italian Rapid Deployment Force', *The International Spectator*, Vol. 20, Nos. 3/4, July–December 1985, pp. 64–87; and Maurizio Cremasco, 'An Italian Rapid Deployment Force: The Geopolitical Context', *The International Spectator*, Vol. 20, No. 2, April–June 1985, pp. 51–61.

8. Special Correspondent, 'Guarding Turkey's Eastern Flank', *The Middle East*, April 1986, pp. 9–10.

9. This estimate is based on working data from DMS, various editions of *Jane's Defence Weekly*, and the IISS, *Military Balance, 1985–1986*.

10. Andrew Borowiec, 'Turks Seek Aid to Upgrade Army', *Washington Times*, 16 May 1986, p. 7.

11. The Crotale is only effective to about 12 000 feet versus up to 52 000 feet for Hawk. As a result, the SAMs transportable on French lift aircraft cannot reach medium and heavy bombers. Although France deployed only 900 men, it also had to move its twenty-four armoured vehicles by land from the Cameroons since it lacked airlift for such vehicles (*Jane's Defence Weekly*, 15 March 1986, p. 454).

12. For a good recent description of the goals of the French Navy, see Pierre Lachamade, 'The French Navy in the Year 2000', *Jane's Naval Review* (London: Jane's, 1985), pp. 79–90. This precludes recent budget cuts but still indicates the probable future strengths and weaknesses of French naval out-of-area capabilities.

13. Jean de Galard, 'French Overseas Action: Supplementary Budget', *Jane's Defence Weekly*, 14 December 1985, p. 1281.

14. For illustrative British views see Lt. General Sir Geoffrey Howlett, 'NATO European Interests Worldwide – Britain's Military contribution, *RUSI Journal*, Vol. 130, No. 3, September, 1985, pp. 3–10; Simon O. Dwyer-Russel, 'Beyond the Falklands: The Role of Britain's Out of Area Joint Forces', *Jane's Defence Weekly*, 11 January 1986, pp. 26–7; 'Battle Continues to Preserve British Amphibious Warfare Capability', *Jane's Defence Weekly*, 8 February 1986, p. 185; 'UK's Amphibious Dilemma', *Jane's Defence Weekly*, 12 April 1986, pp. 661–2; Professor Neville Brown, 'An Out-of-Area Strategy?', *Navy International*, October 1982, pp. 1371–3; and Keith Hartley, 'Can Britain Afford a Rapid Deployment Force?', *RUSI Journal*, Vol. 127, No. 1, March 1982, pp. 18–22.

15. See Simon O. Dwyer-Russel, 'Marines Fear Loss of Capability', *Defence Attache*, No. 3, 1984, pp. 60–8; and 'Beyond the Falklands: The Role of Britain's Out-of-Area Joint Forces', *Jane's Defence Weekly*, 11 January 1986, pp. 26–7.

16. Department of Defense, *Annual Report, FY 1987*, Washington, 5 February 1986, p. 63–4.

17. See the author's *The Gulf and the Search for Strategic Stability* (Boulder, Colo: Westview, 1984), pp. 803–63 and Thomas L. McNaugher, *Arms and Oil* (Washington, DC: Brookings Institution, 1985), pp. 23–46.

18. For more detailed treatment of Soviet attitudes and methods of intervention see Stephen S. Kaplan, *Diplomacy of Power* (Washington, DC: Brookings Institution); Efraim Karsh, *The Cautious Bear*, Tel Aviv;

Jaffee Center, 1985, and Alex P. Schmid, *Soviet Military Interventions Since 1945* (Oxford: Transaction Books, 1985).

19. For more background see *The Gulf and Strategic Stability*, *op.cit.* (see Note 17), pp. 848–63, and McNaugher, *Arms and Oil*, *op.cit.* (see Note 4), pp. 23–87. Also see Robert P. Haffa, *The Half War: Planning US Rapid Deployment Forces to Meet a Limited Contingency, 1960–198.* (Boulder, Colo.: Westview, 1985), pp. 17–131.

20. For a good analysis of the role of Western forces during the mining o the Red Sea in July–September, 1984, see Captain John Moore, 'Red Sea Mines, A Mystery No Longer', *Jane's Naval Review* (New York Jane's, 1985), pp. 64–7, and Scott C. Truver, 'Mines of August: An International Whodunnit', *Naval Review*, May 1985, *Proceedings* Annapolis, pp. 95–117.

21. For a full discussion of the problems and issues involved see Bruce W Watson and Peter M. Dunn, *Military Lessons of the Falklands Island. War* (Boulder, Colo.: Westview, 1984), pp. 7–51, and 83–127, and Jeffrey Ethell and Alfred Price, *Air War South Atlantic* (London Sidgwick & Jackson, 1983), pp. 34–100 and 157–213.

22. Department of Defense News Release, No. 18–86, 14 January 1986, p. 1.

4 Do-it-Yourself: The National Approach to the Out-of-Area Question

Maurizio Cremasco

For historical reasons, and because of continuing political relations and economic ties, the European countries (France and Great Britain in particular) have a special interest in the geographical area stretching from the Persian Gulf and Red Sea regions to the Mediterranean Middle East and Maghreb regions. In fact, Algeria and Djibouti were French colonies, Libya and Somalia were Italian colonies, Syria and Lebanon were French mandates and Tunisia a French protectorate, while Jordan, Iraq and Palestine were British mandates. Finally, Egypt, Sudan and South Yemen, although technically not colonies, were part of the British domain.

The European countries have today, due to their growing integration within the EEC framework, larger common interests and are affected more than in the past by international crises, which have an impact on their foreign policy and their economic situation. Moreover, there is a growing awareness among the European states that the threats to their security stem less from the traditional scenario of a Soviet aggression and more from South–South or North–South crises in areas outside NATO's boundaries, leading to a Soviet-American, hence East–West, confrontation.

The European countries are also aware that situations of domestic instability in the 'grey areas' at the NATO borders could be exploited by the Soviet Union to expand its political and military influence. Furthermore, they recognise that oil from the Persian Gulf and other parts of the Middle East will continue to be of vital importance for their economic growth and that Soviet direct or indirect control of the 'oil faucet' in those regions will give Moscow an instrument of political pressure and jeopardise their independent industrial development. Finally, the nations of Europe know that the solution of Middle East political problems and the fight against the spectre of a spreading state sponsored international terrorism require a common effort and a closely coordinated policy.

Yet, nothing is more divisive in the Atlantic Alliance than out-of-area issues. Too often national – if not 'nationalistic' – approaches to these issues undermine a badly needed coherent 'European' attitude and put heavy strains on Euro-American relationships. Today, not only would it be impossible to expand NATO's area of responsibility[1] but also impossible to generate the political willingness to establish even the basic lines of a collective strategy to confront the most immediate and evident out-of-area challenges.

This chapter intends to describe the political framework for such a lack of foresight and political wisdom, and then to examine the specific positions of the European countries on the out-of-area question. The United States position is also analysed. In fact, the interests affected and undermined by out-of-area crises are collectively Western and not simply European, even though the European stakes might be higher. Furthermore, it would be very difficult to understand the complexity of Euro-American interface, interdependency and interactions without an explanation, though very schematic, of the United States' approach and attitude toward out-of-area issues. Finally, several case studies of real out-of-area crises are schematically outlined in search of a thread of common attitudes and responses, thus providing in the concluding section a tentative recipe for future use.

I   THE POLITICAL FRAMEWORK

The European countries recognised as early as the 1950s,[2] that their security could be deeply affected by developments in areas beyond the boundaries of the Atlantic Alliance as established in the 1949 Treaty. They indicated their concern for (and their interest) in the stability of those areas collectively in several key Alliance documents,[3] and in almost all final communiqués of the North Atlantic Council (NAC) meetings and individually, in a more concrete and direct way, through their foreign policies.

Historically, the focus of Alliance security concern has switched from area to area of the world in accordance with the changes in the international scene and the behaviour of the Soviet Union. In 1967 and 1973 the focus was on a Middle East in turmoil over the Arab-Israeli wars. At the end of the 1970s South-west Asia became the most important out-of-area issue due to a combination of events: the victory of the Islamic revolution in Iran; the Soviet invasion of Afghanistan, which brought the Soviet Army some 600 km from the Gulf, and thus within easy striking distance of the oil supply vital to Western industrialised countries; and the war between Iran and Iraq, which posed the threat of a closure of the Straits of Hormuz. In 1982, the Israeli military operations in Lebanon refocused European concern on the Middle East.

However, the European countries' openly expressed recognition of out-of-area challenges does not solve the problem of clearly defining what out-of-area really means in terms of collective or individual security interests, and what threats are such as to require an Alliance response. The need for wide-ranging consultation in case of a crisis is shared by all European states, as is the need to give priority to political and economic instruments over the employment of military power. But the problems of how to express political support for American policy and initiatives, of contingency planning for 'real case' scenarios – including the logistical and technical support of the American Rapid Deployment Force, and of 'division of labour' and burden sharing between the European countries and the United States are far from being solved.

There is an evident influence on European interests of the US global commitment and world competition *vis-à-vis* the Soviet Union. And there is also a clear influence on European interests of Moscow's foreign policy in areas where those interests are felt as vital. This has various implications. On the one hand the superpowers' confrontation in the Third World tends to turn any regional South–South crisis into an East–West conflict, a prospect which raises serious concern in Europe. On the other hand, the European countries seem to think that any threat to their particular interests in the out-of-area context can be better dealt with on a bilateral basis, unless there is an evident Soviet military intervention requiring a possibly collective Western response.

There is a general agreement between the United States and the European countries on the need to protect the West's vital interests in regions such as the Middle East and the Gulf. And there is a basic recognition that ensuring access to oil, maintaining Israeli security and setting limits to Soviet expansion are three elements essential to stability in the area. But there are also differences as to the best political and military means of achieving it. This does not mean that there exists a 'European' attitude towards out-of-area issues as opposed to an 'American' attitude, not only because complete agreement does not exist within the American Administration (the State Department's position does not entirely reflect the position of the Defense Department), but also because the opinions of the European countries differ, often considerably. (It could not be claimed that Margaret Thatcher's views resemble those of President Mitterand.) It can be said that whereas the United States tends to place priority on the 'Soviet threat', the European countries tend to be more concerned about the 'regional' elements, such as the factors causing internal instability, the persistence of the Arab-Israeli confrontation, the dangers of inter-Arab radicalisation, the effects of the failure to find a solution to the Palestinian problem, and so on. There is also a difference between the United States and its European allies (both politically and militarily) on how to define, evaluate and deal with the threat, which is not only and always Soviet. The threat of international terrorism is a good case in point.

This diversity in the lenses through which out-of-area challenges are seen is at the base of the very cautious wording of the official statements on the subject and the lack of real coordination within the Alliance.

The 'let us do the best we can' and 'if somebody wishes to do more let him' attitudes on out-of-area issues were already present in the 1967 Harmel report:

> Crises and conflicts arising outside the area may impair its [NATO] security either directly or by affecting the global balance. Allied countries contribute individually within the United Nations and other international organizations to the maintenance of international peace and security, and to the solution of important international problems. In accordance with established usage the allies, or such of them as wish to do so, will also continue to consult on such problems without commitment and as the case demands.[4]

They were even more evident in the final communiqué's of the North Atlantic Council meetings in the 1980s. Typical are the paragraphs on out-of-area threats from the final communiqué of the June 1983 North Atlantic Council (NAC) in Paris:

> The Allies recognize that events outside the Treaty Area may affect their common interests as members of the Alliance. If it is

established that their common interests are involved, they will engage in timely consultations. Sufficient military capabilities must be assured in the Treaty Area to maintain an adequate defense posture. Individual member governments who are in a position to do so will endeavor to support, at their request, sovereign nations whose security and independence are threatened. Those Allies in a position to facilitate the deployment of forces outside the Treaty Area may do so on the basis of national decisions.[5]

The only real agreement appears to be on the 'timely consultations' in case of crisis, even though it is not clear what 'consultations' are supposed to entail.

Out-of-area developments are normally discussed at ambassadorial level within the Atlantic Council framework. But these discussions are general in nature and amount to information gathering and perception exchanging sessions rather than to a real discussion of policy options. Furthermore, consultation, which is considered desirable, has often been carried out in a cosmetic way and very late with respect to the development of events.

The United States tendency has been more to inform its allies and seek their blessing than to consult, except in cases where it was felt that the issue had to be multilateralised in order to ensure military support and burden sharing. Even then, reliance has been placed on bilateral consultations with each European country, but with special treatment to 'special' allies, in terms of level of officials involved and amount of information provided. The US consultation process before the April 1986 air attack on Libya is a very good example of this.

Finally, the United States has, understandably, never been very willing, in the course of consultations, to provide details of the military operations being planned, or ready to be implemented. The risk of very damaging leakages is considered too high to be taken lightly, and information is passed on a selective basis, and only if and when necessary. Thus, again considering the April 1986 bombing of Libya, the information provided by the United States to the British Prime Minister, Margaret Thatcher, was more detailed than that given to French President Mitterand, which was, in turn, more ample than that submitted to the Italian Prime Minister, Bettino Craxi.

Furthermore, the statement of the 1983 NAC Final Communiqué on the need to maintain 'an adequate defense posture in the Treaty Area' implies a willingness on the part of the Europeans to fill the gap created by the possible redeployment of US forces and equipment from Europe, in case of an out-of-area contingency. This is far from being technically or politically feasible. The decision to facilitate the redeployment is recognised to be not an automatic response but a choice based on a case-by-case evaluation. This impairs its certainty and reduces its value.

But the significant words of the communiqué are 'if it is established that common interests are involved'. They are the key clue to the difficulties, a clear indication of the uncertainty of the European commitment, of the different national perceptions of out-of-area challenges, and of the blocks on the road to an effective and coordinated Allied response to crises outside the NATO-Warsaw Pact context. However, despite the cautious and ambiguous wording, the language on the out-of-area problem in the NATO communiqué has constituted the framework within which it was formally possible and politically feasible for the European countries to establish bilateral agreements with the United States on the utilisation of European facilities by the US Rapid Deployment Force (RDF) and on military compensation measures if US forces are taken out of Europe.

Paradoxically, the reasons at the base of the European concern for out-of-area crises are the same as those which limit the 'commonality' of the evaluation of the situation. First of all, each European country has specific political relations and particular economic ties with the countries of the Middle East and the Persian Gulf. Some are a heritage of the colonial past, or of the immediate post-war years. Some grow out of the economic and industrial development of the European countries and of their increased role as armament suppliers. These ties play a significant role in generating diverse European attitudes.

Second, European attitudes are influenced by energy dependence on Arab states. The situation today is admittedly different from that of the 1970s, marked by the two oil shocks of 1973 and 1979. The reduction of oil consumption, the establishment of strategic reserves, the present oil glut and the sharp dropping of its price have contributed to the lowering of oil vulnerability of European countries. However, continued oil flow from the Middle East-Gulf area will remain vital for the industrialised West. Any attempt by the Soviet Union to directly or indirectly control it, or any regional instability conducive to its interruption, would still be considered a very serious threat.

However, even this common perception, and the fact that it would be easy to draw detailed oil-related crisis scenarios, do not seem

ufficient to stimulate coordinated European contingency planning –
which, by the way, does not exist on anything else. Partly, this is
because the growth of strategic oil reserves has reduced the urgency
of taking action. The solution of any crisis involving the oil flow will
be viewed presently in a longer (from ninety to 180 days) and less
dramatic perspective than it would have been ten years ago, thus
further diluting the European willingness to consider the hypothesis
of a military intervention. Furthermore, this unwillingness is strengthened not only by a sense of the high political and military risks
involved but also by the lack of a 'real' military intervention capacity;
as Cordesman notes in Chapter 3, the forces suited to this purpose
are small indeed.

Finally, Europe's attitude is also conditioned by internal political
actors, particularly in those countries where foreign policy decisions
tend to have an abnormal effect on the domestic political situation,
countries in which, for example, the presence of strong Communist
parties means that such foreign policy choices can be utilised to create
extensive popular opposition. In any case, there is no doubt that
public opinion will have a significant impact on how the European
states react to out-of-area challenges. (It must be emphasised that
these domestic factors would have an effect even if the United States
and the European countries held identical views on how to deal with
out-of-area crises.)

A fairly clear example of the effects of these influences, and of the
difficulty of achieving a united Western position, was the abortive
attempt, at the time of the outbreak of the Iran–Iraq war, to set up
a multinational naval force for the purpose of keeping open the Strait
of Hormuz. The proposal put forward by the United States was
explicitly shunned by all the European Allies. The fact that two
European countries, France and Britain, did send warships into the
Arabian Sea and the Gulf (both in a strictly national capacity) does
not invalidate the argument. Rather, it serves to demonstrate the
differences of attitude and reaction between Europe and the United
States on out-of-area issues, and the foreign and domestic policy
restrictions which prevent European countries from associating themselves fully with US decisions and responding completely to US
requests for cooperation.

There are a number of elements which characterise the European
attitude towards the out-of-area question. No European nation, while
recognising the North–South and South–South dimension of its
security interests, and the possibility of a Soviet threat outside

NATO's area of responsibility, would agree to expand the presen Alliance boundaries. In fact, the Europeans seem to consider advan tageous the sharp delimitation of the NATO area, which permits ₐ more flexible approach to out-of-area crisis situations, an approach which can be portrayed as national and unilateral as opposed to ar Alliance approach which could be internationally interpreted as being the expression of United States policy. Even though the support of ₐ US military initiative could be better justified in the context of ar Allied response to a global security challenge, the European countrie prefer to maintain the freedom to play it in a unilateral or bilatera way. There is the evident concern that doing otherwise woulc entail the possibility of local crises escalating into an East–Wes confrontation.

For the European countries, the possibility of US unilatera initiatives in out-of-area crises undermining East–West relations anc increasing tension with the Soviet Union is of serious concern, anc tends to determine their supportive attitudes. This is particularly truc if there is disagreement on the evaluation of the Soviet role anc threat in the crisis. During the 1973 Arab-Israeli war the negativc attitudes of European states and their unfavourable responses to US requests for over-flight rights and other assistance were the resul both of preoccupations with the disruptive repercussions on thei relations with the Arab world and of a marked scepticism about the alleged Soviet threat.[6]

Moreover, the European countries do not wish to make commit ments in advance, particularly if these can be interpreted as full fledged support for US policy. They do not like to take public stand on out-of-area issues and prefer to act without too much externa and internal publicity.

No European country is willing to clearly define the criteria of out of-area security. Each country has its own perceptions and the genera feeling is that it will be a theoretical exercise anyway, due to the many different scenarios which could be drawn. The case-by-casc approach is the only one considered feasible and politically acceptable

However, each European power (with the exception of the Federa Republic of Germany) is preparing its armed forces to operate witl enhanced rapidity and increased flexibility far from their nationa borders. Since November 1983 the United Kingdom has developec a Rapid Deployment Force (RDF) of about 10 000 men. France i building up its own *Force d'Action Rapide* (FAR) 47 000 men strong Italy has constituted a *Forza di Intervento Rapido* (FIR) similar tₒ the English one. (For details, see Tables 3.4, 3.5, and 3.6, Chapter 3.)

The creation of these rapid employment forces has its rationale more in the need to adjust the military instrument to the changing threat environment, and on the need for a better defence of the national territory – even the French FAR can be seen in this light, considering that its priority employment is on the central front – than on the need to perform out-of-area missions. However, enhancing the mobility of some units, establishing a skeleton structure of C^3 for the force, and planning for integrated training exercises means creating the capability – and the mentality – to employ the military instrument rapidly, selectively, with specialised, mission-oriented forces. And these are the relevant features needed for many out-of-area military interventions in future contingencies.

To some extent the European RDFs are more shadow than substance, especially in terms of long-range air transport capability, logistic sustainability and specialised armament.[7] It would be naive to believe that they can effectively be employed in an out-of-area contingency different from simple peace-keeping operations, without being strengthened and supported by other national forces. However, the mere possession of a force which can be rapidly employed outside the national territory can have a deterrent effect, apart from any judgement of its true level of effectiveness and operational capability, which are always difficult to assess exactly.

It has been often suggested that over a long period the availability of rapid deployment forces, which due to their specialisation could be integrated in a single force, would facilitate the decision of the European countries to coordinate their military initiatives when confronted with out-of-area problems involving common interests. In fact, even though it is true that the integration of military units is easier when they have similar characteristics (in terms of organisation, equipment and training), the need to maintain tight political control, and the difficulty in finding a solution for the problem of military command in the field, will push toward the employment of the RDFs on a strict national basis. As the Lebanon MNF has demonstrated, even simple coordination among national forces is a difficult and politically biased task.

Finally, the European countries tend to prefer the United Nations as the organisational framework within which to act in case of out-of-area crises. The participation of European military contingents in multinational forces would be more likely if those forces were formed under UN auspices and if their task were clearly one of peacekeeping or peacebuilding. This is even more true today after the failure of the multinational force in Lebanon in the years 1982–3.

In summary, the European countries' reaction to an out-of-area challenge will be determined, influenced and limited by the following factors:

1. The type of threat involved and the importance of the out-of-area crisis in terms of international stability and of national interests.

2. The overall assessment of who is behind the crisis, or who is pushing for the intervention (for instance, is it advocated in the United States by the Israeli lobby?), who will eventually gain, and how the regional situation will be affected, will be strong determining factors.

3. The submission of a formal request to participate in the solution of the out-of-area problem either by the Third World country/ies directly involved, or by a Western nation (the United States or a European ally). In this context, a role will be played by former colonial-type relationships or by the existence of a 'special' relation with the United States within the transatlantic framework.

4. The threat of escalation, either due to the participation of other regional actors or due to the possibility of a direct or indirect involvement of the Soviet Union, conducive to an East–West confrontation.

5. The level, range and scope of the consultation process conducted by the United States with its European allies, prior to taking unilateral initiatives in an out-of-area contingency. The amount of flexibility available in responding to a US request for cooperation is an element which will have a direct bearing on the European attitude. Pre-commitments will not be accepted and the timing of the consultation will also be important. Late consultations will be interpreted as a formality and not as a true process aimed at searching for Euorpean advice and support.

6. The political acceptability and the military credibility of the rationale submitted to justify and sustain the need for an out-of-area intervention. In this context other elements will be important such as: the overall military capability needed; the size of the military operation, and then the size and type of armed forces to

be employed; the role these armed forces are supposed to perform; and the risks involved in terms of possible losses.

7. The domestic situation and the impact on the political system and on public opinion of the decision to participate in an out-of-area operation. This factor has a special significance in those European countries where strong opposition parties which are against out-of-area involvements – in particular the communist parties of the European Mediterranean countries – can rally vast popular support.

8. The eventual involvement of the United Nations, which offers the possibility of diluting the international and internal repercussions of an out-of-area intervention, and of presenting it as a supranational affair without any NATO or Western colouring.

9. The risk of retaliatory actions conducted by one or more countries involved in the out-of-area crisis or by international terrorism. This is a factor which will have a special meaning for the most vulnerable European Mediterranean countries such as Italy and Greece, whose long coastlines and many insular territories make them easy targets for hit-and-run terrorist attacks.

10. The consequences of not participating in the out-of-area intervention in terms of negative effects on the cohesion of the Western Alliance and on the relationship with the United States.

II NATIONAL POSITIONS ON THE OUT-OF-AREA QUESTION

France

France's policy towards Third World countries has shown a substantial continuity through the years. This policy was clearly outlined by President Mitterand in 1981 in a speech during his visit to Mexico. Its basic elements are: support for those populations struggling for freedom and social justice; reaffirmation of the concept that no international stability can be achieved without the contribution of developed Third World countries; refusal to accept the idea that conflicts arising in the South should inevitably and automatically have an effect on the East–West confrontation.

France is aware that it has limited means to fully implement this policy, particularly in terms of instruments to help the Third World countries free themselves from the tutelage of the superpowers. However, efforts have always been made to provide at least the intellectual and diplomatic framework within which solutions to regional crises could be sought.

In the Mediterranean area, which is considered vital to its own political and economic interests, France has been particularly active.

Since 1976 France has redeployed to Toulon in the Mediterranean Sea the bulk of its naval forces, including the two aircraft carriers *Foch* and *Clemenceau* and several ASW (anti-submarine warfare) and AD (air defence) warships such as the cruiser *Colbert* and the destroyers *Suffen* and *Duquesne*.

The links with NATO have been strengthened. The French STRIDA air defence system is tied in with the NADGE system. French liaison officers are assigned to the major NATO commands of the Southern Flank. French naval forces routinely participate in NATO naval exercises in the Mediterranean, while French maritime patrol (MP) aircraft cooperate with NATO MP aircraft under COMARAIRMED.

In 1980 France sent warships to the Gulf of Gabes following the attack on the Tunisian city of Gafsa by guerrilla forces reportedly supported by Libya. And it has supplied Tunisia with arms and military equipment.

Following Libya's incursion into Chad, France has reinforced its military presence in Central Africa. In 1983, it intervened in Chad with a 3000 man force, to stop the Libyan invasion (Operation 'Manta'). Presently, French military forces are deployed in the Central African Republic, in Gabon, in the Ivory Coast and in Senegal. Furthermore, France participated in the MFO in Sinai, in the MNF in Lebanon and in the mine-hunting operations in the Gulf of Suez, while its military contingent is still part of UNIFIL in Lebanon. Finally, France maintains a very important military presence in the Indian Ocean (five frigates, three minor combatants, one amphibious and three support ships), and in Djibouti (3800 men, whose main elements are two light tank regiments, one armoured squadron, one air squadron with ten Mirage-IIIC aircraft and thirteen helicopters). This is the only Western force stationed in the Horn of Africa.

Since the mid-1970s France has also directed its diplomatic and economic attention to the Persian Gulf region. Relations with Iraq have been strengthened, while economic and armaments supply agreements have been signed (1974, selling of helicopters and army guns; 1976, signing of the economic cooperation agreement; 1977, Iraqi order of thirty-six Mirage F-1 fighters; 1978, visit to Baghdad of French Defence Minister Yvon Bourges and new arms contracts; 1978, agreement for the delivery of a nuclear research reactor; 1980, Iraqi order of twenty-four additional Mirage F-1 aircraft, AMX tanks and Super-Frelon helicopters; 1982, visit to Baghdad of French Foreign Minister Claude Cheysson and Iraqi order of Roland and Exocet missiles; 1983, Iraqi order of Super-Etendard strike aircraft and Exocet missiles).

It is quite significant that France openly sided with Iraq after the outbreak of the Gulf war, while underlining the fact that it has friends but no enemies in the region. The delivery of very sophisticated weapons systems like the Super-Etendard aircraft and the Exocet missiles, giving Baghdad the capability to strike at the Iranian oil terminals on Kharg island, was a clear sign that France was ready and willing to support Iraq.

This French policy was based not only on economic interests – the oil factor was certainly pre-eminent when the French-Iraqi relations started to become tighter in the mid-1970s – but also on the political evaluation of the Gulf situation. An Iranian victory was seen as a dangerous and destabilising outcome. The unrestrained Iranian influence in the Gulf would have facilitated the spreading of Islamic revolutionary fundamentalism to the entire region and put an un-bearable pressure on the smaller Emirates and on Saudi Arabia. A possible formal alliance of Iran with Syria (and eventually with Libya and South Yemen) would have further complicated the situation radically, changing the strategic and political picture of the Middle East.

Iraq was not the only state to be the focus of French diplomacy in the Gulf. In the same period, Paris multiplied its relations with Qatar, the Arab Emirates and Saudi Arabia, particularly the latter.

In 1979 France quietly helped the Saudis during the attack on the Great Mosque in Mecca. In the same year Saudi Arabia ordered 200 AMX tanks and AS (air-to-surface) Exocet and SA (surface-to-air) Crotale missiles. In 1980, the French Minister of Defence Yvon Bourges visited Riyadh and a naval cooperation agreement was signed, including warship deliveries and training. Again in 1980 a bilateral agreement on internal security was concluded between the French and the Saudi Ministry of the Interior. In 1982 another accord was signed for the development of Saudi naval forces.

As has been said, even though the main stream of these increased relations with the Gulf countries was represented by the selling of French modern weapons systems (arms supplied to Iraq amounted to 40 per cent of the total French arms exports in the period 1980–2, reaching 40 billion francs), the political elements were clearly present. France is interested in the maintenance of its cultural, economic and military presence within its traditional sphere of influence (the Mediterranean Sea, with particular emphasis on the Maghreb and on Central Africa), and at the same time is interested in the stability of the Persian Gulf, a region economically very important both for oil imports (Iraqi oil amounts to 20 per cent of all French oil imports) and arms exports.

In summary, France is deeply involved in the Middle East-Gulf regions. It will very likely be directly concerned about any crisis involving the stability of the area or radically endangering the present strategic situation. Presumably it will be willing to take action, also of a military nature.

However, France has always stressed that an Alliance attempt to meet challenges or to control out-of-area instabilities would risk transforming them into East–West problems. France thinks that addressing out-of-area issues on a case-by-case basis, without any prior contingency planning, is the most effective way. Those European countries which have the interest and the capability of doing so should intervene, eventually by coordinating their political and military initiatives. However, intervention would be internationally plausible and domestically acceptable only if there were a request for help or support on the part of the country which is felt to be threatened. A bilateral framework is preferable, in particular if the country is a former colony and has maintained close post-colonial links.

Great Britain

England withdrew its forces from the East of Suez in 1971; however, not all the previous political and military ties have been completely cut. London maintains good relations with Egypt, Jordan, Saudi Arabia and the Gulf States, in particular Oman.

In the 1960s Britain helped Saudi Arabia to confront the incursions of South Yemeni Il-28 and MiG-17 aircraft (some reportedly piloted by Soviets) by supplying an air defence system. The delivery of radars, six Lightning interceptors, six Hunter fighter-bombers and a battery of surface-to-air Thunderbird missiles was organised and conducted under the code name of Magic Carpet by a purported civilian dealer. All weapons systems and equipment were taken from air force and army stocks, the personnel (pilots, crew chiefs, technicians and instructors to train the Saudi military) were former Royal Air Force and British Army officers and non-commissioned officers, and the agreement included a provision for British pilots to participate in operational missions.

As for Oman, Masqat's international relations were represented, when Sultan Said Taimur was in power, by his personal ties with Great Britain. These strong connections were also maintained when Sultan Qaboos Ibn Said deposed his father, breaking Oman's isolationist tendency. Britain helped Oman to fight and win the guerrilla warfare conducted by the PFLO (Popular Front for the Liberation of Oman) in the Dhofar, and the special link with London was maintained while Sultan Qaboos was strengthening his military-strategic relationship with Washington. The Omani army has been trained by the British, and the Baluchi regiments, the best in the army, are still commanded by British officers, while the air defence radar net is manned by British personnel.

In recent years, British military contingents participated in the MFO in Sinai, in the MNF in Beirut (a token force of 100 men) and in the mine-clearing operations in the Gulf of Suez. At the same time Britain has resumed its naval presence in the Mediterranean, though with deployments of short duration and limited to participation in NATO naval exercises. Furthermore, the strong military presence on Cyprus and the Sovereign Base Areas in the island play an important role in supporting British participation in peace-keeping operations in the Mediterranean region (UNICYP, UNIFIL and MFO), and any eventual military intervention requirements. On the whole, Britain considers that its overseas activities indirectly enhance stability and that its out-of-area military capabilities provide protection against challenges to the security interests of the Atlantic Alliance.[8] No doubt Britain shares with the United States a concern about out-of-area challenges and the need to strengthen the Western strategic posture in the Indian Ocean and the Gulf. The British-American agreement on the upgrading of Diego Garcia's facilities to better meet American RDF requirements should be seen in this context. But in line with the basic European attitude, the out-of-area threat is seen to stem more from regional instability provoked by domestic problems of the Middle East and Gulf countries than from a direct Soviet threat. (Obviously, the hypotheses of Soviet indirect interference or exploitation are not discounted.)

Britain feels that individual European countries should expand their security horizons and should take a more active part in responding to global security threats. However, the option of military intervention is considered viable only when vital national interests are at stake. (In this context, the Falklands campaign is a good case in point.) The possibility of an East–West confrontation is obviously seen as a concrete limiting factor. In any case, diplomatic, economic and military help in terms of arms deliveries is given priority over a direct military initiative.

According to former British Defence Minister Michael Heseltine, coordination among the European countries is deemed possible only in the long term. At present, no specific initiatives to improve coordination are seen as being feasible. However, it is important that the European countries understand that their interests extend outside the European continent.[9]

Michael Heseltine again stressed these points in the House of Commons in May 1985, in answering a question posed by the MP Bruce George on what discussions there were with the United States and the NATO allies in terms of operating outside the NATO area.

I think that it is quite wrong for major powers such as ourselves – not superpowers but major powers, for all that – to see no role for themselves on a world stage. That is not to say that you can have an orchestrated policy of working automatically with your allies. You cannot get this, it is not real. There is no way in which the Americans, or ourselves, or our European allies, are going to say in advance that they will cooperate in certain fields; they will not do it. However, there are countries of world significance, of a general good-neighbourly disposition, who will see if there is anything they can do to help, and try to work together.[10]

Furthermore, in another Commons debate, while disclosing that Britain was planning a big military exercise outside the NATO area, Heseltine declared: 'We must be prepared to bear our share of responsibility for protecting trade routes and for promoting peace and stability in those areas where local conflicts could spread and risk wider East–West confrontation.'[11] It is felt that this realistic assessment of the situation is still at the base of British out-of-area policy.

Italy

Since the end of the 1970s Italy has conducted a more active foreign policy in the Mediterranean area, with a higher profile and a more evident willingness to assume responsibilities and to make commitments.

In July 1979 an army helicopter unit (composed of forty-eight men and six AB-205 helicopters) was deployed to Nakoura as part of the United Nations Interim Force for Southern Lebanon (UNIFIL).

In September 1980, Italy signed with Malta a treaty for economic, technical and military assistance, assuming the commitment of safeguarding the neutrality of the island. The commitment has clear security implications, since it suggests that Italy is ready to confront any external threat to Malta's sovereignty. This is true even though the treaty does not provide for automatic military help in case of emergency, but does require prior bilateral consultations. As of May 1986, the arrangement was altered by former Premier Don Mintoff's decision to accept a Libyan offer for a parallel safeguard of Malta's neutrality, and by his request for more economic aid and his threat to break the Italo-Maltese agreement. The subsequent talks between the new Maltese Prime Minister Bonnici and the Italian Foreign Minister Andreotti redefined the terms of the agreement and a new treaty is pending ratification by the Italian Parliament. (A small group of Italian military advisors and instructors are still on the island, even though their support activity has been reportedly reduced.)

In March 1982, the Italian government agreed to participate in the multinational force designed to guarantee the full application of the peace treaty between Egypt and Israel resulting from the Camp

David agreement. The Italian contingent assigned to the MFO (multinational force and observers) was composed of three Larice class minesweepers and ninety-two men. The task of the naval group, which is today still conducting its daily patrolling mission, is to assure the freedom of navigation through the Tiran Straits and in the Aqaba Gulf.

In August and September 1982, an Italian military contingent participated in the two multinational forces which were deployed to Lebanon; first, to assure the safe withdrawal of the Palestinian fighters from Beirut and then, after the Sabra and Shatila massacre, to protect the Lebanese people and facilitate the regaining of authority by the legitimate Lebanese government. Finally, in August 1984, a naval force composed of three Castagno class mine-hunters, of the *Cavezzale* support ship and of 305 men was deployed in the Suez Gulf to search for the mines which had impaired navigation through that waterway.

Due to its geostrategic position, Italy is very concerned about the maintenance of stability in the Mediterranean region and does not underestimate the threat posed by crisis situations in the Gulf. It does, however, emphasise its position in the Mediterranean, an area where it has a comparative advantage for geographical and historical reasons with respect to other European countries, and where its military instrument can be most effective. But Italian officials, in particular Defence Minister Giovanni Spadolini, have stressed that Italy cannot play a realistic and effective stabilisation role unless there is an organic tie with Western strategy.

In general, there is a strong preference within Italian coalition governments (this has been a characteristic feature of all Italian governments) to participate in multinational peace-keeping or peace-building initiatives when these initiatives are conducted under United Nations auspices. In these cases, there will be a more pronounced willingness to send small military forces outside the Mediterranean. The Italian air operations in the Congo in the 1960–2 period is a good case in point.

On the other hand, bilateral US-Italian agreements have been reached on the eventual utilisation by US forces of Italian air facilities in case of an out-of-area crisis. But the right to use Italian airports as staging bases for the support of the RDF is not automatic and will be granted by the Italian government on a case-by-case basis.

Italy also considers that out-of-area challenges are most likely to stem from regional internal instability. However, the possibility of

Soviet supported or Soviet exploited domestic 'revolutions' is not excluded. Military intervention is considered the least likely option due to its multiple international political repercussions and escalatory risks.

Italy's willingness to participate in multinational actions aimed at defusing crisis situations in the Middle East and the Gulf is limited by several factors.

1. The endemic instability of the Italian political system; the overly large effects of foreign policy decisions on the coalition's cohesion and the tendency of all political parties to utilise foreign policy issues for their short-term domestic interests.
2. The tendency to devise Italian Middle East policy in the context of that of the EC.
3. The desire to avoid giving the appearance that Italian policy toward the Arab world is identified with US policy.
4. The negative effect of the failure of the MNF in Lebanon, which has cast serious doubts on the viability of multinational initiatives even when organised and conducted among allies.
5. The domestic political weight of the Communist Party, particularly its capacity to mobilise a large popular opposition to military 'adventures' within the Mediterranean (and even more so outside the area).
6. The still inadequate capabilities of the Italian armed forces in terms of long-range air transport, logistic sustainability and low percentage of volunteers. This element would pose a serious handicap every time the military force includes draftees (as it did in Lebanon), due to the inevitable public opposition to their employment for missions not directly connected with the defence of national territory.

The Federal Republic of Germany

The official position of the West German government can be summarised as follows:

1. Germany's position with respect to out-of-area challenges is very difficult both politically and psychologically.
2. France, Great Britain and the United States are permanent members of the UN Security Council, are maritime powers and possess a real capacity for force projection; thus, they can play a true political and military role.

3. The German Constitution forbids the deployment of German military forces outside the NATO area. There are legal experts who maintain that Article 87(a) does not necessarily preclude the employment of German units overseas where the missions are exclusively defensive. However, this school of thought has few followers and, as Rummel notes in Chapter 5, any attempt to employ German forces in any out-of-area context will face strong domestic opposition both within the political elites and from public opinion.

4. West Germany feels that having assumed the major burden for the defence of Europe it is paying a good share for overall Western security and it could not do more on the military plane, even without the binding Constitutional provisions.

5. The Federal Republic is more than willing to provide technical and economic aid to those countries which are seeking Western support.

In fact, West Germany has been (and still is) the European country which has provided the most extensive military aid to other countries in the Atlantic Alliance. Greece and Turkey have been receiving such help since 1964, and Portugal since 1978. Eighty per cent of this aid consists of the delivery of new military material, free of charge, and 20 per cent of the release of serviceable *Bundeswehr* surplus. The total value of German defence aid amounted to more than DM4 billion, as of December 1984. Turkey received deliveries for DM2920 million, Greece a total of DM802 million, and Portugal a total of DM292 million.[12]

Furthermore, West Germany has in recent years diluted the constraints formerly governing its arms exports. Contracts for the delivery of German weapons systems have been signed with several Arab and African countries: Tunisia, in 1980 (three Lurssen-57 fast attack craft); Saudi Arabia, in 1981 and in 1982 (seventy-two + 200 FH-70 155 mm howitzers); Cameroon, in 1981 (three Do-128 maritime patrol aircraft); Oman, in 1983 (two Do-228 transport aircraft); Nigeria, in 1985 (three Do-228 transport aircraft).[13]

Finally, the Federal Republic government feels that its contribution to out-of-area stability is also realised, aside from the measures of foreign economic and development policy, through military training aid. Thus, since 1981, about 1400 military personnel from fifty-three different countries of the Third World have received *Bundeswehr* training free of charge.[14]

In case of out-of-area crises, West Germany seems willing to participate in European supporting activities and initiatives, and to share part of the European burden if economic aid is to be an element of the European response. But it is very unlikely that the Federal government would agree on the participation of German military contingents in any multinational force destined to operate outside NATO's area of responsibility. This appears to be true even if the force is assembled under the UN auspices and is acting under a UN flag.

Turkey

Geostrategically, Turkey offers valuable advantages for out-of-area operations in the Middle East and the Gulf. Already in 1958, when instabilities in Lebanon and Jordan raised concern in the Eisenhower Administration about their eventual expansion to Saudi Arabia and Iraq, the Pentagon had outlined the need for prestocking equipment and war-consumable items in Turkish territory, and for staging rights at Adana airbase. The same requirements were expressed by the British military high command.

The strategic value of Turkish territory increased after the fall of the Shah of Iran and the Soviet invasion of Afghanistan, which has moved Soviet forces to within a short distance from the Persian Gulf. However, Turkey seems unwilling to be directly or indirectly involved in dealing with crises which are outside the traditional NATO-Warsaw Pact confrontation framework, as only these explicitly justify the commitment of Turkish armed forces.

Of course, Soviet military intervention capabilities and the general stability of the Middle East and the Persian Gulf are two elements which are necessarily a part of the Turkish security picture, especially if a crisis in those regions would be bound to lead to an East–West polarisation. If, however, the crisis did not stem from a direct Soviet military operation threatening vital Turkish interests, but from regional domestic instability, or from a South–South conflict, it is very unlikely that Ankara would consent to the use of its air facilities for the support of a US or Euro-American force. In these cases, consideration would be given to the presumed reactions of the Soviet Union and to its capacity to exert strong political and military pressure. The value and significance of Turkey's present political and economic ties with the Arab world would also be considered, with the aim of not undermining them.

These factors have seemingly influenced Turkish policies in the last two decades, as evidenced by:

1. The pro-Arab attitude assumed by Ankara during the 1967 and 1973 Arab-Israeli conflicts.
2. The diplomatic recognition of the PLO and the permission given to open an office of the organisation in the Turkish capital.
3. The economic and military cooperation agreement between Ankara and Tripoli signed in January 1979 during Premier Bulent Ecevit's visit to Libya. (After the increasing evidence of the role played by Libya in supporting international terrorism, this bilateral relationship has undergone a review and cooperation has been reduced.)
4. The extreme caution with which Turkey reacted to the Islamic revolution in Iran and to the Mujaheddins' raid on the United States embassy in Teheran, and the refusal to follow Washington in applying sanctions against Iran.
5. The Turkish condemnation of the Soviet invasion of Afghanistan, but the refusal to apply sanctions against Moscow.
6. Turkish neutrality in the Iran–Iraq conflict, and the increase in commercial and economic ties with both countries.

Furthermore, Turkey:

1. Was unwilling, during the 1973 Arab-Israeli war, to be directly involved in the US air bridge in support of Israel, while granting permission to over-fly Turkish territory to the Soviet transport planes directed to the Middle East.
2. Has required the Soviet Union's consent before complying with the United States' request, after the loss of US intelligence gathering stations in Iran, to let U-2 reconnaissance aircraft use Turkish airspace for the verification of Soviet compliance with SALT-II treaty provisions.
3. In the 1970 base rights agreement, has explicitly restricted utilisation of US military installations in its territory – reduced from twenty-six to twelve – to NATO military contingencies. (In June 1981, the Turkish Defence Minister Haluk Bayulken, referring to the possibility of making Turkish bases available to the US RDF, said explicitly that the bases on Turkish territory could be used by US forces only to defend vital NATO interests. The following year, reiterating the same concept, Turkish Premier Bulent Ulusu stated that Turkey could not associate

itself with actions that might jeopardise the security and interests of the Arab countries.)

It does not seem that this attitude has changed, so that Turkish participation and/or support for initiatives to meet out-of-area challenges should then be considered as a very dim prospect. However, if the out-of-area crisis were to touch vital Turkish interests, it is very likely that Ankara would review its attitude on the use of its bases and would react by utilising its military instrument in the mode and to the extent considered necessary. In this case, US military operations from Turkish territory, or Turkish-American military cooperation, could be possible.

The United States

In contrast to the European countries, the United States views its out-of-area interests in the context of its world-wide competition for influence and power with the Soviet Union. Thus, in the Middle East and the Gulf regions the United States tends to stress and give priority to the Soviet 'threat', while the European countries are more concerned about the regional sources of instability.

Furthermore, the United States' attitude and policy toward the Middle East and Gulf regions is based on several assumptions, some of which, as has been previously indicated, are not fully shared by its European allies.

1. The endemic instability of the Middle East-Gulf region will persist even after the solution of the Palestinian problem and the fading-out of the Arab–Israeli confrontation – two very difficult and long-term eventualities.
2. The Western nations can only hope to perform 'damage limitation' work in the region, not possessing the political and military instruments to truly influence the development of the events.
3. It is very unlikely that the Soviet Union will be willing to play a positive and stabilising role in the region, or that the Soviets will agree to a special 'code of conduct', involving, for example, the supply of arms.
4. Arms control negotiations will not solve the problems of the region and even proposals for an arms control regime in the Indian Ocean offer little prospect for enhancing Western security.
5. The pro-Western and friendly countries in the region will not

be able to confront their regional problems without external support. Thus, it is essential to demonstrate to the countries of the region that the United States is, and will continue to be, a reliable partner. The European allies should help the United States to perform this task. In this context, the special relationship with Israel should be closely safeguarded, since Israel is considered the only 'true' ally in the region.

6. The United States is expecting that in the event of a crisis the countries in the region with which it has signed agreements for the utilisation of air and naval facilities (Oman, Kenya and Somalia) will fully support US policy.

7. The United States will continue to build its force projection capability in order to be able to fight a limited war in the region. The European allies should be ready to cooperate with the United States, by providing direct operational support and staging facilities for the US RDF and by adopting measures for military compensation in Europe.

8. State sponsored international terrorism is to be confronted not only with diplomatic initiatives, but also with military actions. The states for which a supporting role has been unquestionably proven must bear the responsibility and pay a price for their actions.

There is no doubt that the United States intends to protect and defend its strategic interests in the region, utilising military force if and when necessary. The so-called Carter Doctrine has been explicitly restated and supported by the Reagan Administration. As recently as April 1986, US Vice-president George Bush reiterated, during a four-country tour of the Gulf, the US commitment to keeping open the Gulf shipping lanes, an endeavour in which it is currently engaged.[15] Furthermore, the Reagan Aministration has expanded the effort to build up a 'strategic consensus' in the region, by involving, besides Israel, Egypt, Tunisia and Morocco, where bilateral joint military commissions have been created. However, it should be underlined that the 'strategic consensus' policy and the stressing of the Soviet threat do not entirely reflect, and do not constitute the priority of, the more articulated US policy in the region.

Over the long run, the United States seeks, with the help of its allies, to create a more peaceful, stable and prosperous Middle East. Both as a means to this end, and because it is a long-term objective, the US wants the Allies to share the risks and the burdens of preventing further deterioration in the area: in this respect, its policy is aimed as much at Europeans as at the inhabitants of the Middle East.

For all the reasons given earlier, it is hard to develop a common Euro-American approach to the Middle East, especially with regard to the use of force. Moreover, the US propensity to employ force more readily than the Europeans, as in the attack on Libya in April 1986, has further undermined the possibility of harmonising policies and strategies in the area. Thus an obstacle to the implementation of US policy may be the inability to obtain European support in those few instances in which this may be crucial.

On the other hand, those factors which constrain European actions also affect US willingness to intervene in out-of-area crises. Apart from the possible lack of Congressional support for Administration policy, military interventions are limited by their eventual international repercussions and their economic and human costs. Thus, an air attack against Syria, if Syria were to be unquestionably identified as a state sponsoring international terrorism, would be something completely different from the case of Libya. In such an eventuality, however, European and US approaches might well converge, even though not in a fully coordinated way. And this means that the difference between the ways in which the United States and its European allies address the out-of-area question is not an organic feature of the question itself, but is wholly dependent on the type of crisis situation.

III WESTERN FORCES IN YESTERDAY'S CRISES

A Multinational Naval Force in the Indian Ocean

Speaking four days after the outbreak of the Iran–Iraq war on a TV channel in Wisconsin, President Carter declared that the United States would do everything necessary to keep open the Strait of Hormuz.[16]

Interviewed on 28 September 1980 on the CBS television news programme 'Face the Nation', Deputy Secretary of State Warren Christopher said:

> The Strait of Hormuz is an international waterway through which nations are entitled to send their ships. We intend to keep that

Strait open. We think that other nations have a very strong interest in doing so. Actually, the European countries have a stronger interest in that oil than the United States does, but working with our allies, we intend to see that what is necessary is done to keep the Strait open.[17]

On 3 October, a US State Department spokesman told reporters that the United States had talked with other nations about the possibility of joint naval action if there were a threat to shipping traffic through the Strait of Hormuz. However, he underlined that the talks were exploratory, 'simply one idea in a number of different ideas that have been discussed' and they should not imply that formation of a joint naval force was 'an imminent development'.[18]

In fact, the joint naval force was bound to be a non-development. The proposal put forward by US Secretary of Defense Harold Brown, which many within the Administration opposed, was put down by all the European Allies.

There were strong political reasons for the refusal. France, Great Britain and Italy felt that a formal Western military presence would have been a too evident sign of commitment, not welcomed by the regional states, and capable of polarising the Gulf crisis into an East–West confrontation by stimulating a stepped-up Soviet response. (In fact, Moscow had expressed its hostility to an integrated Western naval force in the Indian Ocean.) And, significantly, strong concern was expressed not only by the two belligerents in the Gulf, but also by the conservative, pro-West states of the region like Saudi Arabia and the Arab Emirates.

Additionally, a joint naval force in the Indian Ocean would have too much resembled NATO naval task forces such as STANAVFOR-LANT (Standing Naval Force Atlantic) or STANAVFORCHAN (Standing Naval Force Channel), giving the impression of a surreptitious expansion of NATO's area of responsibility.

Furthermore, the Allies were concerned with avoiding a too close identification with US policy. This was especially true of France, which was in favour of a demilitarisation process of the Indian Ocean that would exclude the presence of armed forces of the superpowers. In July 1980, after the visit to Paris of Secretary Brown, who met with the French President to brief him on the US plan to acquire base rights in Kenya, Oman and Somalia and on the creation of the RDF, an Elysee spokesman expressed the view that France could not consider the expansion of the US presence in the Indian Ocean a stabilising factor. Even though, due to the on-going Iran–Iraq war, the situation was now different, Paris was not willing to completely reverse its previous stand.

Great Britain was also very cautious about openly endorsing a proposal which provoked the opposition of the Labour Party and actually restricted the flexibility of British policy in the region. Italy reiterated that the Italian armed forces had solely a regional role and Minister of Defence Lelio Laporio went so far as to say that the Italian flag was in the Mediterranean and should remain there.

However, even though political agreement was not reached, events on a military level very quietly took a different course. Both Great Britain and France increased the level of their naval forces permanently stationed in the Indian Ocean and Gulf regions. Bilateral military consultations took place between French and British Defence Staffs and with the US Department of Defense, concerning naval movements and contingency plans for coordinated intervention.[19] A US–UK naval exercise was conducted in October 1980 in the central and north-west area of the Indian Ocean.[20] By the end of October 1980 there were about sixty Western warships and support vessels in the Indian Ocean and the Arabian Sea. French warships also cruised the Omani Sea, which was outside the traditional operational areas of the naval force based in Djibouti.

Thus, a Western force was present in the area and there is little doubt that the different national naval groups were closely in touch, exchanging intelligence information and data on reciprocal positions. The coordination not reached at the political level was thereby achieved at the operational level and the joint naval exercises conducted by British and US ships were a clear indication of that achievement.

This does not mean that, in case of an Iranian or Iraqi attempt to close the Strait of Hormuz, the European countries with a military presence in the area would have displayed the political will to take collective action. But at least, if the decisions were taken, the existing operational coordination would have facilitated military action. Moreover, even without operational coordination, the presence of sixty Western ships in the area was bound to have a military significance and a clear deterrent effect.

Even Italy, while refusing to send its naval forces outside the Mediterranean (the reasons were partly political and partly operational, due to the lack of staging bases in the Indian Ocean/Gulf area) was ready to indirectly support the United States' effort in line with the 'division of labour' formula. In fact, when the United States was forced to reduce from two to one the Sixth Fleet carrier battle groups in order to strengthen its naval presence in the Indian Ocean, the Italian Navy partially filled the gap by expanding its role in the Mediterranean.

The United States, France and Britain have maintained their military presence in the southern end of the Persian Gulf to prevent the Iranian Navy from challenging or intercepting their cargo ships passing through the Strait of Hormuz.[21] And in 1987–8 that presence was stepped up, ships sailing under Western flags (including Kuwait tankers transferred to US registry) were given naval escorts and the United States launched several retaliatory strikes against Iranian warships and offshore oil rigs in response to attacks on cargo vessels and to the laying of mines in the Gulf. Thus the pattern of independent but coordinated naval operations continued in the face of a new crisis.

The Multinational Force (MNF) in Lebanon (1982–3)

The MNF-2 was sent to Lebanon after the massacres of the Sabra and Shatila Palestinian refugee camps. The redeployment of the US, French and Italian military contingents was quite rapid – only six days after the complete picture of the events emerged between 18 and 19 September 1982.

The mandate was the same for all contingents: that of interposition in agreed areas to assist the Lebanese government and its armed forces in Beirut and the surrounding areas. This mission would facilitate the re-establishment of the Lebanese government's authority and sovereignty, thus assuring the safety of the population and the end of violence.

After the deployment, however, each country gradually began to develop a national interpretation of the mission, based on divergent perceptions of the policy necessary to solve not only the Lebanese but also the whole Middle East problem. Further complicating factors were the historically and politically different relationships that each country had with the participants in the Lebanese scene and the way they projected their short-term and long-term interests in the region

The United States saw the MNF as a way to further the Middle East peace process. The final aim was the withdrawal of both Israel and Syrian forces and a free, pro-Western Lebanon under the guidance of President Gemayel. This aim was evident in the explicit

US support given to Gemayel, in the effort undertaken to strengthen the Lebanese army by providing weapons and training, and in the willingness to openly confront the Syrian forces, in the later phases of the MNF stay.

France, a long-time friend of Lebanon and with a special relationship with Syria, strove to maintain an autonomous line of action, even though agreeing with the mandate for the MNF. It tried to emphasise its independent negotiating position, which included a PLO and Syrian role. Even when it used its military force in response to terrorist attacks, it conducted its retaliatory strikes in a fashion which tended to emphasise that they were somewhat different from the US ones.

Italy went into Lebanon with immediate expectations, convinced of the need to quickly re-establish peace and stability in the area. The emotional factor played a significant role in terms of political and public support for the deployment. The pre-eminence of the humanitarian role of the Italian contingent was reflected by its composition, which included a field hospital. However, like France, Italy felt that any long-term solution could be achieved only by taking into consideration the interests of the Palestinian people. Great Britain's military contingent, more a token presence than a real force due to its very limited size (100 men), was less the result of a specific commitment toward Lebanon than of the political need to be there. This was demonstrated by the limited support that the force was prepared to give to the Lebanese government. On the other hand, there were also the illusions and misperceptions of the Lebanese government about the role of the MNF, often considered as an instrument capable of serving the interests of Christian Maronite groups.

On the ground, not only political but also military coordination was substantially lacking. Each contingent, taking into consideration its own security requirements and defence needs, acted in a very independent way both in terms of relations with the population, with the different religious sects forming the complex Lebanese mosaic and eventually with Syria, and in terms of projection of their own image and military behaviour.

The deterioration of the local situation in Beirut and in the Shouf mountains, the increased threat to the MNF, the different way each participating country interpreted the mandate of the force, the further loss of authority of the Gemayel government, the ineffectiveness of the Lebanese Army, and the gradual withering away of the MNF's impartial status, were all elements bound to bring the MNF mission to an unsuccessful outcome.

The failure of the Euro-American attempt to act together in an out-of-area context to defuse a crisis situation underlines the political and military difficulties of a coordinated effort, in the face of differing perceptions and divergent foreign policy interests. Moreover, the Lebanese experience, apart from having a direct influence on the 1984 Western naval operations in the Suez Gulf, is bound to be recalled by the European states in any future out-of-area contingency in which they are asked to provide troops for a multinational operation.

The Mine Hunting Operation in the Red Sea (1984)

On 9 July 1984 an explosion damaged a Soviet container vessel navigating in the Gulf of Suez. More blasts – assumed to have been caused by mines – occurred in the same area towards the end of the month, followed by a series of similar explosions in early August, damaging seventeen merchant ships and oil tankers passing through the southern part of the Red Sea and the Suez Gulf.

From 28 July to 7 August Egyptian concern at the damage to merchant shipping and at the lack of success of its navy in ending the threat, led to a request to Western governments for help in clearing the vital waterways of mines. France and the United States were also asked by Saudi Arabia to help clear the sea approaches to Jidda and the oil port of Yanbu. Responding to the Egyptian request, the Western countries began to move.[22]

The United States was the first to be contacted and the first to react to the Egyptian request for help, sending a fifteen-member team of navy mine experts to Cairo (2 August), while preparing mine-sweeping helicopters to be deployed from Norfolk Naval Air Station to Egypt. The US force was eventually composed of eight RH-53D Sea Stallion helicopters, three support ships and over 1500 men. The United Kingdom moved to the Suez Canal the four mine counter-measures ships it had had in the Eastern Mediterranean since the height of the Lebanon crisis. A fifth was sent later. France deployed to the area four mine-hunters based at Brest, Toulon and Cherbourg; they were joined by a repair ship based at Djibouti. This force, in operation in the Red Sea and in the Suez Gulf by mid-August, was joined by the end of the month by three Italian mine-hunters and a support ship and, in early September, by two Dutch

minesweepers. Also three Soviet mine-hunters were reportedly operating in the Red Sea waters, searching in the Bab el Mandeb and
Aden areas.

The operation was far more difficult and complex than expected,
due to demanding weather conditions, to the partly rugged and partly
muddied characteristics of the sea bed, and to the great amount of
metal refuse. The search yielded poor results. Suspicious buried
contacts were blown up, producing bigger explosions than could have
been expected if they were just metal refuse but this did not constitute
hard evidence.

Only one mine was found: a recent Soviet-made mine retrieved by
a British ship. The condition of the mine substantiated the hypothesis
that it had been recently laid. But it could not be proved that the
explosions which had damaged shipping could be attributed to similar
devices. Moreover, it could not be proved that Libya was implicated
in the mining, even though some evidence was collected. By October
1984, the national naval forces were withdrawn. Again, it is not the
military aspects of the operation that are worth analysing, but instead
the political framework within which the operation was conducted
and the differing political approach of the Europeans in confronting
this new out-of-area crisis.

The recognition of the vital importance of the Red Sea and Suez
Gulf for Western commercial traffic and the need to intervene to
keep important sea lanes of communications free of any threat were
elements openly and commonly shared by all. An unrestrained flow
of oil traffic through the Suez Gulf was of paramount importance for
the Western nations, in particular after the entering into service of
the transarabic pipeline, with its Red Sea terminal, and the 'tanker
war' going on in the Strait of Hormuz. This was particularly true for
Italy, which in the 1980s imported about 30 per cent of the yearly 37
metric tons of oil passing through the Suez Canal.

However, while the United Kingdom was ready to participate with
the United States in the Egyptian Coordinating Committee (ECC)
established at Adabiyah, France and Italy refused to formally join
it, stressing the strictly bilateral framework of their participation in
the mine-searching operation. France coordinated directly with Egypt
and Saudi Arabia. Italy worked with Egypt only, sending a navy
team to Cairo to define the technical details of the operation (in
particular the search area to be assigned) prior to the agreement with
the Egyptian government. In any case, the Italian naval force joined
in the search only after the government decision was presented to,

and endorsed by, the Parliamentary Defence and Foreign Affairs Committees.

France's independent attitude was basically in line with its traditional foreign policy and thus did not specifically indicate a change in the French approach to attempts at coordinating Western operations in extra-European areas.

The Italian case was somewhat different. The caution expressed by the Italian government in dealing with the mine issue, after the apparent initial willingness to respond quickly to the Egyptian appeal was indicative of the impact of the Lebanon syndrome on the Italian political system. Apart from a repeated preference, and hope, for a United Nations role, Italy underlined not only the bilateral nature of the agreement with the Egyptian government, but also the 'technical' aspects of the mine-hunting operation in terms of support given to the Egyptian Navy, and the lack of any specific political significance thus suggesting that any eventual comparison with the Italian participation in the MNF in Lebanon was totally inappropriate. Likewise the time limit of the operation was emphasised, while no comments were made about the Egyptian allegations concerning the Libyan 'paternity' of the mines.

Even though the decision could have been regarded as falling within the perogatives of the Executive, the Italian government preferred to present the case to the House and Senate Defense and Foreign Affairs Committees. The attitudes of the political parties – not only the Communist Party's opposition but also the prudence of the Christian Democratic Party – were certainly influences on the difficult and slow decision-making process. This eventually brought – fifteen days after the other Western naval forces – the Italian minesweepers to the Suez Gulf.

As in the case of the MNF, the mine-searching operation provided some interesting hints of the politico-military pattern the European countries normally follow when confronted with out-of-area issues.

1. The Europeans responded only after the explicit Egyptian and Saudi request for help.
2. The 'national' character of the decision was strongly underlined even by Great Britain, the only European country to participate with the United States in the Egyptian Coordinating Committee
3. France, and Italy in particular, stressed that the operation was not to be seen as a repetition of the MNF and that the mine search was to be considered within the political framework of

technical support provided to Egypt, which did not possess a sophisticated mine-sweeping capacity.

4. There was the tendency, very evident on the part of Italy, to deny that the operation had any political implications, thus avoiding unwanted identifications with US Middle East policy.

5. The domestic political situation influenced, as was very evident, the role played in Italy.

Even the United States, for domestic reasons, downplayed its participation in the mine-hunting operation, which was basically justified in the context of a time-limited technical assistance given upon request by a friendly nation to keep an international waterway free. In this respect, the US attitude was quite similar to the European one.

Furthermore, some other general points are worth considering.

1. Egypt made an effort to treat the mine problem in a low-key fashion to avoid the impression that it was unable to cope with it and to reduce the negative impact on the level of shipping using the Canal.

2. The Western governments appeared more concerned with the alleged mines than the shipping companies, the insurance companies and official organisations such as the General Council of British Shipping.

3. In general, the negative effects of the explosions were less sharp than expected. By mid-August the traffic in the Suez Canal, which had had an evident drop in the early part of the month, was back to normal.[23] This could be partly explained by the Western countries' political need to show that they were ready and willing to confront any threat to international naval shipping, and partly by economic considerations based on oil dependency and the level of oil imports.

International perception of the motives for their intervention was of pre-eminent importance for all participating countries and determined their behaviour. Moreover, as on previous occasions, the image of an uncoordinated Western approach to an out-of-area issue did not completely overshadow the actual coordination reached at the operational level. As Scott Truver has noted: 'all the Western states worked within the framework established by the host government . . . Indeed, the objectives of the mine-hunting assistance never were debated or controversial.'[24]

The American Attack on Libya (1986)

On 5 April 1986 a bomb destroyed the 'La Belle' nightclub in West Berlin, frequented by US servicemen. The blast killed an American sergeant and a Turkish woman and wounded 230 others, among them some fifty US military personnel. The evidence that the terrorist bombing was planned and executed under the direct orders of the Libyan regime was defined by President Reagan as 'direct, precise and irrefutable'.[25] On the night of 14 April, US F-111 fighter-bombers based in England, and attack aircraft from the Sixth Fleet carriers operating in the Central Mediterranean just outside the Sidra Gulf conducted a series of air strikes against Libyan targets in the Tripoli and Benghazi areas.

The air raid was preceded by two events: the hastily summoned special meeting of the Foreign Ministers of the European Community held at The Hague on the morning of 14 April, and the European tour of the chief US delegate to the United Nations, General Vernon Walters, acting as President Reagan's special envoy. The aim of General Walters' visit to five European capitals in three days – Madrid, London, Bonn, Paris and Rome from Saturday 13 to Monday 15 April – was reportedly to present the Reagan Administration's position on Qaddafi's support for international terrorism and to press for stronger European sanctions against Libya.

The EC meeting, called by Italy and Spain following Libyan threats to attack NATO bases in the Mediterranean region, was to examine the issue of international terrorism and the mounting tension in the Mediterranean. The final communiqué of the EC meeting was again the result of a compromise among different views on how to deal with Libya, even though it was more explicit in linking Libya to international terrorism than the one produced in January, following the bloody terrorist attacks against the Rome and Vienna airports. This time Libya was mentioned and condemned for threats to the European Mediterranean countries, but no specific reference was made to its involvement in the most recent terrorist actions in Europe. The EC countries decided to take measures against Libya, such as restrictions on the freedom of movement of its diplomatic personnel, reduction of the staffs of diplomatic and consular missions in Europe, imposition of more stringent visa requirements and procedures, and a total ban on arms supplies. However, no agreement was reached on closing all Libyan embassies in the Community – as was proposed by the British Foreign Minister Sir Geoffrey Howe – or on imposing economic sanctions, a measure opposed by West Germany and Italy in particular.

While prudently condemning Libya, the European statement did not endorse or back a US military action. It underlined the need for restraint by all parties in order to achieve a political solution to the US-Libyan controversy and to avoid a military escalation of the tension in the Mediterranean.

Even though it is impossible to say whether stronger European actions would have stopped the US raid, certainly the EC decisions were perceived by the Reagan Administration as inadequate eleventh-hour initiatives, insufficient to forestall future Libyan-planned terrorist attacks.

As was easy to predict, national interests and national perceptions were at the base of the European collective response. The past impression of equidistance between the United States and 'state-sponsored' terrorism was partly dissipated, but the unwillingness to take stricter measures against Libya was a repetition of the show of caution and reluctance given by the European countries every time they are called upon to support United States policy in out-of-area crises.

The European reasons, however, were not at all negligible. France, which did not consider Libya to be the only supporter of international terrorism, was driven by its determination to preserve the independence of its policy and its links with the Arab world, by domestic constraints and by its preference for quiet diplomatic action. French reluctance to be directly involved in the US retaliation was probably due also to the need to protect the lives of the eight French hostages held in Lebanon. Thus France, while urging stronger anti-Libyan moves at the EC meeting, on Saturday 13 April rejected the US request to permit US fighter-bombers to cross its airspace.

The economic factor was very much present in the minds of the European ministers – in 1985 the EC had imported some 10.5 billion Ecus from Libya, while exporting only 3.5 billion[26] – together with the vulnerability factor and the commonly shared conviction that the military instrument was ill-suited to solve the problem of international terrorism. West Germany and Italy were particularly worried about their economic and commercial links with Libya, including an oil dependency which was particularly evident for Italy, about the fact that both countries had many of their citizens still working in Libya and in danger of becoming possible hostages and about their greater vulnerability to terrorist actions.

Only Margaret Thatcher's Great Britain was ready and willing to stand with the United States, not only advocating at the EC meeting a stronger Eueopean stance but also consenting to the use of British bases for the US air strike. This attitude was only partly the result of the role played by the 'special' relationship which has bound the United Kingdom and the United States since the Second World War. There was also full recognition of Libyan involvement in sponsoring terrorism in Europe, including support to the Irish Republican Army (IRA), and the awareness that it would be unfair to deny to a country such as the United States, so heavily involved in the defence of Europe, the help requested.

As far as the talks conducted by General Walters on the eve of the US attack are concerned, the impression is that they were not consultations *strictly sensu*, but just a way of telling the European allies about a decision already taken. In fact, by the time the Presidential envoy was in London and Paris the use of the British bases had been approved and the overflight of French airspace had been refused. And when he was in Rome on Monday evening, talking with the Italian Premier Bettino Craxi, the orders for the attack had been given and the operation was under way. As in the days and hours preceding the air raid, most of the European allies distanced themselves from the United States after the attack.

The French reaction was little more than a silence. In a twelve-line, 149-word statement released by the Foreign Ministry – but whose text was coordinated with Premier Jacques Chirac and President Mitterand – France admitted having been informed in advance about the US plan and said it had discouraged it. Furthermore, it deplored the fact that the escalation of terrorism had resulted in reprisal capable of setting into motion 'the spiral of violence'. Finally, it indicated that the European countries would be willing to take collectively appropriate responses in case of Libyan aggression against Italy or Spain.

It was a prudent way to express French 'dissociation' without explicitly approving or disapproving the US air strike, which was set in the generic framework of the action-reaction process stimulated by international terrorism. However, within the new majority there were also dissenting voices. Jean Lacaunet, President of the UDF, and Valery Giscard d'Estaing, former President of the French Republic, approved the US military action and regretted the government's decision to refuse the overflight of French territory to US aircraft on their way to Libya. Giscard d'Estaing went as far as to recall the United States support for the French military operations in Zaire in 1978 and to underline the need to show Western solidarity in the face of terrorism. There were also reports that France was unwilling to join the US initiative because the raid was considered too 'soft' to overthrow Qaddafi, and that had the United States decided to hit hard France would have been on the United States' side.[27]

The reaction of the government of the Federal Republic of Germany was characterised by a certain embarrassment. Even though he avoided explicitly criticising the raid, which was seen as a defensive action in the context of a struggle against a state continually preaching and practising violence, Chancellor Helmut Kohl stated that the Federal Republic was opposed to the use of force for the solution of international controversies. At the same time, he accused Qaddafi of being behind the West Berlin discothèque bombing, for which the German government had 'ample, independent evidence', and of having transformed his country into a nest of terrorists and a base for international destabilisation. The official West German attitude was thus one of 'understanding' but not of approving or backing the use of military force. On the other hand, the US air raid was condemned by the Liberal Party and by the SPD, which interpreted it as a new demonstration of how little the United States was listening to its allies.

Margaret Thatcher defended the US action as legal, and as justified on the basis of the inherent right of self-defence, recognised by Article 51 of the UN Charter, and on the basis of Libya being a proven sponsor of international terrorism. Apart from sharing the US attitude towards states supporting terrorism,[28] Thatcher defended her decision to allow the use of British airbases for several reasons. Over and above those already mentioned – solidarity for a country 'that has hundreds of thousands of forces in Europe to defend its liberty',[29] Libyan support for the IRA, recognition of the international legality of the US action, and the privileged link between the two countries – there was also the fact that the F-111 fighter-bombers were the only aircraft in the US inventory in Europe capable of carrying out such a difficult and demanding mission with good probability of keeping collateral damage to civilians at a low level. And there was the need to reciprocate in some way the support received from the United States for British actions in the South Atlantic during the Falklands war of 1982.

Disagreement was expressed not only by the Labour Party and the centre parties, but also by members of the Conservative Party. Attacks against Thatcher's policy grew following the killing of British hostages in Beirut, clearly showing the risks taken by Great Britain and the domestic repercussions of the issue of international terrorism.

However, the British cooperative attitude was not without 'qualifications'. On the one hand, the support was given on the ground that the military action would be directed against specific Libyan targets, demonstrably involved in the conduct and support of terrorist activities. In other words, it appears that the British government had a role in the selection of the Libyan targets. On the other hand, Thatcher was keen to indicate that the use of British bases could not be taken for granted, and that any future missions of the UK-based US aircraft would require another request and another specific authorisation.

The Italian negative reaction was the least nuanced among those of key European allies. On 15 April when talking in front of the Parliament, the Italian Premier Bettino Craxi said that 'notwithstanding the contrariety [*la contrarieta*] expressed by the Italian government and by all governments of the Atlantic Alliance and the European Community, the US government has maintained and realised its plan to attack Libya'.[30] Based on the common position taken by the EC and on views convergent with those of Madrid, Paris and Bonn, Craxi stated 'the disagreement of the Italian government with the American initiative' and outlined 'the responsibility assumed by the American government'.

Furthermore, Craxi said that the military actions, 'far from weakening international terrorism, run the risk of provoking a further explosion of fanaticism, extremism, criminal and suicidal actions'. Finally, he regretted that the position taken by the European governments was ignored by the United States, and that theirs was a 'decision which did not take into the right account the value of Euro-American partnership in front of important issues'.

The more evident Italian dismay and concern was related to several factors, similar to those of other European countries, such as wide economic and commercial relations and a large Italian working community in Libya. But it was also due to the peculiar geographical position of Italy, whose territory was very vulnerable to Libyan reprisals. In fact, only three hours and thirty minutes after Craxi's initial words, two Libyan missiles exploded close to the coast of Lampedusa island, where a LORAN station of the US Coast Guard, manned by US personnel, is located. The Libyan strike put Italy in the forefront of the US-Libyan 'war' and added the dimension of fear to the public perception of the Mediterranean situation, a dimension which the government and the political parties could not completely disregard.

In general, the attitudes of the European allies toward the US-Libyan crisis were determined by the usual mixture of heterogeneous elements: the economic interests to be safeguarded; the Alliance solidarity to be shown, but within the limits of a clear political unwillingness to adopt a truly coordinated policy; the perception of a US Administration not very often ready to listen to the advice of its allies, and very often ready to rely on its military instrument; the 'national' approach to out-of-area crises; and the concern about the deterioration in East–West relations resulting from a Soviet-US confrontation out-of-area. (The cancellation of the mid-May visit to Washington of the Soviet Foreign Minister Shevardnadze to arrange for the second Reagan–Gorbachev summit was seen in Europe as another negative repercussion of the raid.)

Other factors, however, influenced European attitudes, factors peculiar to international terrorism when considered as an out-of-area issue: the linkage of Arab terrorism with the political problems in the Middle East and the different US and European approaches to their solution; strong doubts about the utility and the applicability of the military instrument in confronting and curbing terrorism; the higher vulnerability of the Mediterranean European countries to terrorist actions and retaliations; the difficulty in finding unquestionable evidence of state-supported terrorism; the constraints imposed by the international situation when such clear evidence would eventually involve states more closely tied to the Soviet Union than Libya; and the concern about being directly called upon as NATO allies in case of an attack against US ships or aircraft in the Mediterranean, a case which would fall within Article 5 of the Treaty.

Notwithstanding European criticism of the attack, the United States preferred to downplay Alliance discord. It was a significant sign that Washington was aware of the peculiar position of Western Europe *vis-à-vis* the terrorist threat and was basically satisfied by the European willingness to expand the anti-Libyan measures and by the steps taken to fight international terrorism. However, it is felt that the European 'disagreement' will not be easily forgotten in the United States and that the issue of how to fight international terorism will be, in the future, another source of out-of-area differences between the two sides of the Atlantic and among European countries too.

IV   THE LIMITS TO WESTERN ACTION

The picture of Western attitudes and responses to out-of-area issues is one of complex and contrasting tones. The uncertain and cautious approach which has characterised the European politico-military reaction to out-of-area crises will form part of the picture in the future, as will the somewhat sharper approach of the United States.

Obviously, the European countries will evaluate their possible involvement in out-of-area contingencies first and foremost in terms of national interests, even though not narrowly defined. In fact, they will not only consider vital security and economic interests, but will also weigh the strength of the political and economic ties (former colonial or post-colonial) with the country or countries of the region where the crisis has erupted; the question of national prestige and the willingness to project an image of a power capable of intervening in the international arena; the relationship with the United States within and outside the Atlantic Alliance; and the assessment of how the eventual support of US initiatives in out-of-area regions would affect those national interests.

The political ties with the out-of-area country being threatened by domestic instability or by external pressures will undoubtedly influence the European response. We have seen this pattern in the past, both on the part of Britain toward Oman and Saudi Arabia and on the part of France toward Tunisia, Lebanon and the Central African States. On the other hand, economic ties could be an element of restraint in case of actions against an out-of-area country which is the alleged cause of regional instability; the lukewarm, if not implicitly negative, European reactions to the United States' policy against Libya, after the terrorist attacks at the Vienna and Rome international airports at the end of 1985 – and even more after the 15 April 1986 air raid – is a good case in point.

For the medium-sized European powers, the importance of regional ties will be enhanced by their willingness to continue to project themselves internationally as nations possessing the political and military capacity to be important elements in any out-of-area crisis. This sense of national prestige and the symbolic value of international commitments have been evident factors in French and British foreign policy, even in the post-colonial era. However, this should not be overestimated. Both France and Britain – and even more Italy and West Germany – understand quite well the limits on their foreign policy and the political and military cost of too explicit out-of-area commitments, in particular in a supporting role for the US global competition with the Soviet Union.

On the military plane constraints are also obvious. France and Britain – and Italy to a lesser degree – possess naval forces capable of fulfilling the roles and the missions typical of out-of-area operations requiring a maritime component. They have the proven logistical capacity to sustain limited naval forces at long-range, regardless of local resources. But, apart from Britain, France and Italy have inadequate long-leg air transport capacity, and airlift over long distances will either require the utilisation of staging facilities en route to the crisis area or the use of the US air transport assets. Furthermore, any out-of-area military commitment, particularly if it is of some size and of long duration, will have to be considered in the context of its possible detrimental effects on the Alliance's conventional capabilities in Europe.

Finally, the utilisation of naval forces as a foreign policy instrument to exert pressure or influence ashore, in other words their contribution to the solution of out-of-area contingencies, has been shown to be seldom effective and always very costly. On the other hand, air forces can be utilised effectively to transport troops and supplies but their employment in an attack role or in support of troops on the ground (as in Lebanon) has the dubious effect on the political environment typical of many out-of-area scenarios. And the employment of ground forces would be likely only in peace-keeping or peace-building type operations, unless vital national interests are evidently at stake.

Outside the recognised and accepted need to defend these interests, the weight of the opposition parties and of public opinion will be limiting factors in the European countries' attitudes towards out-of-area crises. As has been demonstrated in the course of the Lebanese crisis in 1983, both US and European public opinion played a manifest role in the decision to withdraw. People are less and less willing to agree that the integrity of Lebanon, or the maintenance in power of Arab kingdoms in the Gulf, or the future of Chad should be part of their country's military concern. They are less and less ready to accept the human and financial cost of operations which cannot be easily explained in terms of national security. This is even more evident if, as in the case of Italy, the military force that will be eventually employed is composed of draftees who do not take very lightly the fact of a compulsory military service which includes the possibility of being killed, not for the defence of the homeland but for the stability of a distant and unknown country.

In conclusion, the European countries' approach to out-of-area issues will be one of political caution and calculated military risks. The United States will be disappointed if it expects explicit Allied support in case of out-of-area crises. Past events have shown that Europeans are not willing to endorse and uphold US policy in the Middle East-Gulf regions, particularly if the possibility of an East–West confrontation is part of the crisis scenario.

This does not mean European inaction, even though the preference would be for a so-called 'division of labour', whereby the United States would take care of out-of-area problems, while the Allies strengthen their commitments in the European theatre. Another preferred policy seems to be that of helping pro-Western states in the region both economically and militarily, thus strengthening their ability to act as stabilising factors and to intervene in support of other friendly countries. The military support provided by Iran to Oman in 1975–6 and by Egypt to rebel forces in Chad in 1981 and to Sudan in 1983 are considered good examples of a policy which could be endorsed as an alternative to direct European intervention.

The Europeans will eventually do their part. In many cases their part will take the form of an autonomous initiative rather than a coordinated response and it will be more likely conducted on a bilateral than on a multilateral basis, unless the United Nations is able to intervene. In this respect, the insistence on a UN role is sometimes assumed by the Europeans as an alibi for not taking difficult initiatives. On the other hand, the UN umbrella helps domestically to justify more easily a policy of out-of-area intervention.

Even in those cases where direct participation with United States forces would not be politically feasible or militarily possible, the Europeans could choose the way of indirect support, using their diplomatic and economic instruments and/or permitting the utilisation of their facilities by the US RDF. This may not appear much of a policy and it is probably inadequate to confront the out-of-area challenges of the next decade. But asking for more will eventually mean introducing into the Euro-US relationship new elements of misunderstanding and friction.

How to Do It Together

This being the picture of the overall European attitude, is it possible to envisage different ways of dealing with the out-of-area question? The first important point is for the European countries to intensify their intelligence collection effort in out-of-area regions and then share the information with the most concerned and involved allies. This would be particularly useful for fighting international terrorism and for coping better with the local situation in cases of participation in multinational peace-keeping forces. Thorough intelligence in Lebanon in 1982–3 could have probably enabled a better defence against the bloody terrorist bombing attacks at the US Marine and French paratroop compounds. France has acquired with the Spot satellite a good capability for high-resolution photographic survey of areas of interest. European countries could jointly develop a more sophisticated military reconnaissance satellite capable of providing precious intelligence.

The second point is related to the necessity for European governments to show greater determination in addressing out-of-area crises. The sad picture of hesitation and ambiguity shown by the EC in the aftermath of the terrorist massacres at the Vienna and Rome airports in December 1985 should be avoided. European action in such cases is important as a political deterrent and as valuable, even though indirect, diplomatic support for the country that eventully will decide to act autonomously in an out-of-area contingency. In other words, it is not always necessary to have a common European response; sometimes, joint actions might have an adverse effect on the development of the crisis situation. But a coordinated attitude in terms of diplomatic support and collateral initiatives is bound to buttress the action taken by a single country.

The third point is related to the European rapid employment forces. It would be useful if these forces could train together in specifically devised exercises, in a way similar to the training conducted by NATO ACE Mobile Force (AMF). If the possession of a rapid employment force increases the capability to deter threats to Western interests by the ability to intervene if necessary in an out-of-area crisis – even within the operational and logistic limits previously outlined – common training will facilitate a coordinated military response if and when it becomes politically feasible. In the long term, the European rapid deployment forces could constitute the hard core of a truly 'European' military intervention capacity in out-of-area contingencies involving vital European interests.

The fourth point concerns intra-European political coordination during the development phases of an out-of-area crisis, even though it should be underlined that even timely and thorough coordination would not overcome the road-blocks represented by differences of priorities and objectives. In recent years, several European countries have created high-level crisis management centres. Their inter-connection and closer linkage with existing US centres by technologi-cally advanced communication means would be very important for the rapid transmission of information, for quick consultations and for real-time coordination of military initiatives. In the post-*Achille Lauro* affair, when US F-14 fighters forced the landing at the Sicilian airbase of Sigonella of the Egyptian aircraft with the four Arab terrorists on board, the communications between Washington and Rome were far from perfect, and the high-level exchanges reportedly were complicated by translation problems. The ability of the top decision-making bodies of the countries of the Atlantic Alliance to directly and fully communicate outside the NATO framework would enhance a badly needed timely consultation and coordination process, thus indirectly strengthening, at least at the 'technical' level, the Western response capacity to out-of-area crises.

The fifth point regards the possibility of coordinating European arms transfers to Middle East, Gulf and North African countries in such a way that these could be utilised to consolidate regional stability, to isolate trouble-making countries, and to support pro-Western nations threatened by neighbouring countries. Obviously, this can be realised only within the framework of a truly common Western policy towards those regions, an objective still very far from being realistically attainable. However, the European countries should try to impose on themselves at least a certain degree of unilateral restraint, especially in those cases – and toward those countries – where for political reasons other Western nations are imposing limits on their arms exports. In other words, the European countries should at least try to consider not only the economic, but also the political implications – and the effects in any future out-of-area crisis – of their arms transfer policy.

These few points might seem inadequate to change the Western approach to out-of-area question. In truth, the measures recommen-ded are basically technical in nature and do not and cannot solve the most important out-of-area problem, which is political and refers mainly to the lack of political will of European countries to develop and carry out a coordinated policy. No technical fix can replace the political will needed to effectively deal with out-of-area issues. In this respect, much needs to be done.

At present, however, the words of the 1967 Harmel report 'without commitment and as the case demands', referring to an eventual out-of-area involvement, appear to represent the basic policy of the European countries. The do-it-yourself syndrome is still to be overcome. But another dichotomy in the out-of-area response between the European countries and the United States may well definitively transform the US sense of isolation into isolationism with dramatic repercussions on the Atlantic Alliance. Thus much must be done, if the Alliance is to continue.

Notes

1. In this respect, it is worth remembering an historic precedent. After the accession of Greece and Turkey, Article 6 of the North Atlantic Treaty was modified to include their territories and the Mediterranean Sea. However, interestingly enough, as a symbol of then US sensitivity to out-of-area issues, the British bases in Cyprus, Wheelus air base in Libya and the French colonial bases in Algeria were not included in NATO's area of responsibility. See Major James H. Williams, 'NATO Out-of-Sector Interests in the Middle East', *The Military Review*, Vol. LXV No. 10 (Fort Leavenworth, Kansas: US Army Command and General Staff College), 25 October 1985, pp. 54–5.
2. Paragraph 5 of the NAC final communiqué of the meeting held in Paris in December 1956 reads: 'The Atlantic Alliance is primarily concerned with the threat to security of the NATO area. The Council discussed the threat which Soviet penetration of the Middle East would present for NATO. In view of the fact that the security, stability and well-being of this area are essential for the maintenance of world peace, the Council agreed to keep developments in this area under close and continuing observation.' See *NATO Final Communiqués, 1949–1974*, (Brussels, 1975), p. 101.
3. Reference to the out-of-area issue can be found in: the *Report of the Committee of the Three* (Gaetano Martino, Italy; Halvard Lange, Norway; and Lester Pearson, Canada) of 1956; the *Report of the Council on the Future Tasks of the Alliance*, also known as the Harmel Report, of 1967; the *Ottawa Declaration* of June 1974; and in the final communiqué of the Bonn summit in 1982.
4. Paragraph 15 of the Harmel Report, *NATO Facts and Figures* (Brussels 1971), p. 367.
5. *Notizie NATO (NATO News)*, October 1983, p. 35.
6. On the negative impact of the 1973 Arab-Israeli war on Euro-American relations see the vivid account of Raymond L. Garthoff in his *Detente and Confrontation. American-Soviet Relations from Nixon to Reagan* (Washington, DC; Brookings Institute), 1985, pp. 401–5.
7. However, it should be noted that Great Britain, in order to enhance rapid and long distance deployment, has purchased the Tristar aircraft as a tanker for in-flight refueling.
8. *Statement on the Defence Estimates 1986*, HMSO, Vol. 1, London, 1986, p. 21.

9. Michael Heseltine, interview, as reported in Maurizio Cremasco, 'La pace dal terrore al disarmo', *ADN Kronos*, Rome, 1983, p. 192.
10. *House of Commons Report*, 8 May 1985, p. 82.
11. John Carvel, 'British Army in Practice Run for Oil War', *The Guardian*, 13 June 1985.
12. The Federal Minister of Defense, White Paper 1985, *The Situation and Development of the Federal Armed Forces*, Bonn, 1985, p. 122.
13. Michael Feazel, 'New liberal arms export rules force review of German policy', *Aviation Week and Space Technology*, 2 December 1985, pp. 27–8.
14. *White Paper, 1985*, op. cit. (see note 12), p. 122.
15. 'U.S. to keep Gulf lanes open, Bush says,' *International Herald Tribune*, 9 April 1986.
16. *Le Monde*, September 28–29, 1980, p. 2.
17. United States Information Service, *Daily Wireless File (DWF)*, 30 September 1980, pp. 4–5.
18. *DWF*, 288, 6 October 1980, p. 21.
19. *Le Monde*, 22 October 1980.
20. *Middle East Economic Digest (MEED)*, 24 October 1980, p. 10.
21. On the near confrontation between Western and Iranian warships see Christopher Dickey, 'West sails close to confrontation with Iran in Gulf', *International Herald Tribune*, 20 November 1985.
22. For the best and most informed account of the mine-hunting operations, see Scott C. Truver, 'Mines of August: An International Whodunit', US Naval Institute, *Proceedings*, May 1985, pp. 95–117. See also John Moore, 'Red Sea mines a Mystery No Longer', *Proceedings*, May 1985, pp. 64–7.
23. Truver, 'Mines of August', p. 108.
24. Ibid., p. 108.
25. President Reagan's nationwide television statement in *DWF*, 70, 15 April 1986, p. 2.
26. Anthony H. Cordesman, 'After the Raid: The Emerging Lessons from the US Attack on Libya', unpublished paper, May 1986, p. 4.
27. William Safire, 'Tough talk by France: is it serious?', *International Herald Tribune*, 19–20 April 1986.
28. On 15 April, in front of the Parliament, Mrs Thatcher, referring to state-sponsored terrorism, said: 'If one always refuses to take risks because of the consequences, then the terrorist governments will win and one can only cringe before them', Harvey Morris, 'UK defends use of bases on its soil', *International Herald Tribune*, 16 April 1986, p. 1.
29. Ibid.
30. This and the subsequent quotations are translated from Mr Bettino Craxi's speech in front of the House of Representatives on 15 April 1986. *Parliamentary Records*, 471, 15 April 1986, pp. 31–3.

5 Political Perceptions and Military Responses to Out-of-Area Challenges
Reinhardt Rummel

This chapter looks at resources for defence – not military budgets, soldiers or weapons, but rather the resources of the confidence of the public in the wisdom of their governments' defence policy, and in the adequacy of the support this implies.

The early 1980s have seen large popular demonstrations against NATO policy (mainly because of opposition to the deployment of intermediate range nuclear forces) and marked divergencies of West European and US policies toward the Soviet Union and its satellites (concerning the gas pipeline and Poland). Both cleavages, government/public opinion and the transatlantic cleavage, undermined the cohesion of the Alliance and placed the West in a weaker and more vulnerable position *vis-à-vis* the Soviet bloc. From these experiences, the West has learned to pay more attention to the national security consensus and to invest more into ways and means of overcoming policy differences within NATO.

In the field of out-of-area threats, policy cohesion among allies should also be a key word, but has been long underestimated. Deterrence in Europe and in critical regions of the world will only work, and defence can only be successful, if one has the appropriate means of response as well as the political will to use them. Thus, public support for governmental action can be decisive and the cooperation among Western allies for the purpose of countering extra-NATO threats may well prove indispensable. Western responses to threats in the Middle East are good examples of these interactions and provide a test of Alliance solidarity in the matter of out-of-area challenges. They also demonstrate the differing ways of decision making and implementation in Western countries as well as the peculiarities and traditions of the use of military means. Given those structural divergences it does not come as a surprise that the common denominator for collective Western reaction to extra-NATO threats is rather small.

The out-of-area challenge has to be regarded from different angles of analysis to understand at least part of the complexity and, indeed, inconsistency of various viewpoints in NATO countries. The next sections will describe the factors influencing foreign policy and the use of force and give a picture of Western public perspectives:

1. on the scope and the nature of the threat arising from the Middle East;
2. on the political concepts to cope with these threats, especially on military responses as one of the major components of action;
3. on the procedural and organisational set-up to coordinate and implement Western responses.

I   FACTORS INFLUENCING POLICY ON THE USE OF FORCE

The use of military force in international relations is a question of efficiency as well as ethics.[1] Each country of the Western Alliance has developed a tradition of its own concerning the mix of these two demands. Moreover, support of or objection to the use of military force in the Middle East will depend on the particular circumstances of a given contingency, such as the scope of perceived threat, the intervention capabilities available and the experiences in the past. Public opinion and government action in the United States as well as in Western Europe tend to be based on all of these factors.

No doubt, the United States has the strongest intervention forces in the world and its government is tempted to use them for political purposes. In post-Second World War history, Washington has gone through some experiences of military intervention abroad. Today political elites and general public opinion in the US will mainly recall the Vietnam experience and will hence be very cautious in supporting military responses at a given moment or at a certain level of involvement, but this does not mean that the US government will eschew all military action, as Grenada in 1983 and Libya in 1986 have shown.

European nations have a different historical record. Except for relatively small international involvements of French and British forces, most European countries have eschewed military missions outside their territories. Security elites and the broader public opinion in these countries have ceased to contemplate far away military adventures. The case of West Germany is telling in this regard.[2] Rearmament after the Second World War was a difficult political problem for the Federal Republic. Legally the *Bundeswehr* is restricted to contingencies within the NATO framework and NATO's territorial limits. Sound military reasoning will argue against a deployment of West German troops away from the central front. But the problem goes deeper: precisely because the strictly limited employment area of West Germany's armed forces has become fully accepted by the German people, any attempt of a Bonn government to use its armed forces elsewhere would require a major change of public attitudes.[3]

Thus each individual NATO ally has its particular level of predisposition for and its particular scope of belief in military responses to regional threats. Erstwhile colonial powers may have kept a certain degree of preparedness for intervention by force in order to protect their former colonies while the United States feels both close emotional ties to Israel and a mission to help those countries in the Middle East that are victims of aggression.[4] Other NATO members do not stand idle in these cases but they will hardly include military means in their consideration of actions to be taken. This assumed pattern of behaviour in the North–South context is certainly influenced by the traditional East–West perspective, where 37 per cent of Germans hold the view that military force should never be used, while in the US, in Great Britain, in France and in the Netherlands the figure is between 4 and 9 per cent.[5] The justification of the use of military force in these four countries certainly differs, but they seem to be more prepared than others to defend their vital interests with weapons.

Differences in political culture among Western countries come into play when analysing military responses to out-of-area contingencies. In the United States foreign policy decisions tend to be based on pragmatism rather than on programme and concepts.[6] It is the reverse in most of the European countries' decision-making processes. Translated into Middle East policy this means a rather frequent shift of Washington's focus: Iran, Afghanistan and the Soviet Union in 1979/80; internal regional changes in Lebanon and the Gulf from 1982–4, terrorism and Qaddafi in 1985/6. European governments tend to be less issue-oriented and seem to prefer continuity and to take a broader perspective. By the same token, US administrations are more under public pressure to produce quick results than are Europeans – and a military reaction to a particular external challenge often offers some good chances for a short-term solution to a security problem.

It is probably safe to assume that a majority of the public opinion in all NATO countries tends to rally around the government, if in a question of really vital security interests a limited military operation seems unavoidable, as was the case in the Falklands campaign, the Grenada operation and the raid on Libya. It is true that not all the people in countries of the Western Alliance felt equally involved emotionally in what the British did over the Falklands and the Americans did over Grenada and Libya. Geographic or emotional closeness remain decisive factors in the instinctive reaction of public opinion, and they cannot be spread evenly over sixteen nations of the Western Alliance. However, public confidence seems to be the most reliable in the country directly involved in a conflict. Moreover, each of the cases mentioned was limited in scope and successful in the short run.

Can public confidence in Western societies be maintained if things go badly, given the pressure of the free press, the ubiquity of the electronic media, and particularly the general aversion to war in all Western countries? The cases of Lebanon and, on a much larger scale, Vietnam come into mind. There is a widespread belief that the US is no longer capable of waging a protracted war, particularly one that is complex and difficult to understand. The media has a major role in deciding this question: if there had been no critical reporting, no pictures about the misery of war, so the argument goes, Vietnam might not have been abandoned to the Communists and, in turn, the public uneasiness in the United States about the protracted presence of the Marines in Lebanon would have been felt less acutely.[7]

As a consequence of Vietnam, the US President's freedom of military action abroad has been narrowed legally, politically and psychologically. Congress has acquired a bigger share in the decision-making process, based among other things on its huge build-up of sources of information. The Reagan Administration has tried to redress the power balance between President and Congress but the decisions on how to cope with Nicaragua are still taken under the nightmare of the Vietnam experience. Those European publics who had joined US opposition towards military involvement in Indochina, today again side with those in the US who want to exclude all military engagement in Nicaragua, or elsewhere in Central America, for that matter. People remember the painful process of sliding into a morass once the threshold of military involvement had been passed.[8]

The last case in which European governments had to take the United States' criticism of military action into account dates back to Suez in 1956.[9] Since then, West European governments are primarily constrained by their internal public opposition – if they are constrained at all, because foreign policy decisions are not as much a public affair in Western Europe as they are in the United States. The European media are less aggressive and there is relatively little debate among extra-governmental experts. While these factors seem to give European political decision makers a relatively free hand, other elements of their political culture will bring limitations, as do coalition governments, the parliamentary system and the general reluctance to use military power. In 1983, when France had to intervene in Chad against a Libyan supported insurrection, Mitterrand preferred to follow cautious domestic considerations and traditional French concepts of how to deal with Colonel Qaddafi than to take Washington's advice and act quickly and massively in order to punish the Libyan leader.[10]

In turn, Washington does not seem to follow European advice either, when the decision for military intervention in a region outside the NATO borders is taken. In cases like Grenada, Nicaragua and Libya the US President has acted against the expressed views of a majority of the Europeans. He even used the fact of a reluctant European audience as an argument for US intervention policy, claiming that the United States had to balance the unwillingness and complaisance of the Europeans. Recent experiences confirm that many other factors in the US decision-making process rank before the opinion of the Europeans: Congress, the military, US public opinion, the Jewish and the Arab lobbies, the reaction of the Soviets and of key Middle Eastern countries, etc. Moreover, this particular US administration, and especially its President, have a well-known political goal, to redress US power in the world, and Ronald Reagan does not exclude the use of force as a means of achieving this goal.

As we have witnessed, the personality of the President may be decisive in critical foreign policy situations. His ability to counter massive domestic and international lobbies, to manipulate influential groups and to appeal to the public is always an important factor. (This remark, of course, also tells something about the stability of public attitudes and the reliability of opinion polls.)

The use of military force is not an everyday decision. For reasons of efficiency such a decision has to be taken clandestinely but once it has been implemented its implications quickly affect the emotions of people. Shifts of attitudes may occur abruptly. It is therefore necessary to be careful in generalising about views on the behaviour of decision makers and of the public in NATO countries and to be even more careful in extrapolating from these views to judgements concerning attitudes and responses in particular cases.

II   ASSESSMENT OF THE NATURE AND SCOPE OF THE THREAT

One factor affecting both attitudes and responses is views about threats to national interests. How do Western allies view the nature and the scope of today's and tomorrow's threat in the Middle East? Is the threat increasing or decreasing? In what ways and on what levels does the threat occur? Is there a congruency among the Allies on the types of threat, if not on the amount of danger? Does the United States feel a more immediate threat than neighbouring countries like Turkey or other Mediterranean NATO partners like Italy? Do we find the usual fact that the public opinion lingers behind the relatively high degree of governmental threat awareness? These are only a few of the questions that must be answered in investigating Western opinion on the character of the threat from the Middle East.

The out-of-area question first surfaced during Atlantic Charter discussions in the late 1940s. At issue was the protection of the colonial empires of Britain, France, the Netherlands and Belgium. The question was largely abstract and the US Senate was not in favour of extending collective defence to areas beyond the North Atlantic Ocean and the Mediterranean Sea.[11] The Korean, the Indochinese and the Suez crises served as the first test cases for more realistic Allied reflections on the type of threat to vital interests for which the West had to prepare. Opinion on both sides of the Atlantic began to change in a reverse direction. The US Senate came out in favour of collective operations beyond the NATO treaty boundaries fixed in Article 6, while some of the European Allies viewed US involvement in North-east and South-east Asia with concern.

Since these embryonic reflexes, the definition of regional threats to Western security has become ever more sophisticated. Today, all member states of NATO share the view that events in the Middle

East may affect Western interests in many ways and at various levels. Public perceptions, however, are not unanimous on the nature and the scope of regional threat. In this regard official NATO communiqués on the subject may not represent the whole range of varying assessments which exists in Allied countries.[12]

Threats within an East–West Context

The period of *détente* in the 1970s was not strong enough to avoid souring of East–West relations in the 1980s. This includes also the question of regional stability. Today, the situation is characterised by the assumption that an eventual military conflict between the two antagonistic blocs would more likely start from a crisis situation in the Third World than from an aggressive Soviet move on the Central Front.[13] Most of the Western public perceives the Middle East as the critical region where such a war might start. The combination of local war, permanent conflict and numerous reasons for instability in the Middle East has contributed to fostering the image of a powder-keg. There seems to exist no reliable means to control situations that may grow out of hand.[14]

The foremost threat to Western interests in the Middle East seems to be the tilt of the world-wide power balance in favour of the Soviet Union. The regional display of Soviet power puts stress on the limited Western defensive capabilities. Since the fall of the Shah and the Soviet intervention in Afghanistan a majority of the public in the United States is convinced that Moscow will further profit from instabilities in the Gulf to move southward. Military cooperation agreements with fairly important strategic countries of the region (Syria, North and South Yemen, Ethiopia) and newly acquired maritime mobility in the Indian Ocean give the Soviet Union power projection capabilities which are perceived as a major strategic threat to US influence in the region and on the global level.[15]

The European public has not overlooked the signs of Soviet power projection in South-west Asia (and the Mediterranean for that matter) but has tended to point to the risks and constraints which the Soviet Union has to include in the power equation.[16] Europeans stress the historical fact of low Soviet risk-taking as well as the limits to Soviet intervention capabilities and the lack of reliable local support.[17] Moreover, European minds are less oriented toward an interregional challenge than are US minds, which are affected by a constant media and policy coverage of the world's most dangerous 'choke points'.[18]

Another security concern stems from Soviet behaviour *vis-à-vis* countries in the Third World and local actors. In the Middle East the danger is less the Soviet support of revolutionary Communist regimes and the corresponding ideological change of socieites but rather Soviet support of leaders and groups inclined to be critical of Western countries and their policy in the region. Moscow and other members of the Warsaw Pact have tried to stimulate anti-Western coalitions and to profit from regional polarisation to enhance Soviet influence. NATO members are unanimous on this particular kind of threat, although more voices in Europe than in the United States hint at the relatively poor results of Soviet coalition building and subversive activities. Indeed, some sections of Europe's policy elites are inclined to assume that Moscow interprets the seizure of Kabul as a mistake and will henceforth act even more cautiously, a view seemingly borne out by the next Soviet agreement to withdraw its troops from Afghanistan.[19]

Along with the lack of constructive involvement of the Soviet Union in the Middle East and increasing Soviet intervention capabilities the vulnerability of vital Western lifelines is a threat, which people know well from their experience with the oil crisis. All OECD countries depend to a certain degree on the Middle Eastern markets, with crude oil being the major strategic good. It is not economic competition which frightens Western industrial nations but the nuisance instruments which the Soviet Union holds in its hands and may abuse in order to undermine the continuous flow of trade between the Middle East and the West. The present oil glut and the structural change on the petro-market have deemphasised the particular threat of an interruption of the oil flow but they have not ended it. The European public felt more threatened by the insecurity of oil supply in the 1970s than the US people; consequently Europeans have reacted with rather successful adjustment and diversification strategies to lower their dependency on Middle Eastern oil.[20]

Given the political and military presence of the Soviet Union in the Middle East and the vital Western connections with the Arabian-Persian Gulf, the region has been regarded as one wherein the USSR could exert political-military pressure against the West. Thus the Gulf has assumed a function which West Berlin used to have in the 1950s and 1960s: that of a lever which the Soviet Union could pull at will. This assessment, which was given occasionally in the US public, was never shared in Europe. The European 'softness' on Afghanistan stemmed mainly from a rather sober calculation: the Soviet move into Afghanistan seemed to further undermine the achievements of *détente* in Europe. These achievements were regarded as an integral part of the overall security balance sheet. While the European public continues to be more eager to decouple East–West relations from Soviet behaviour in critical regions outside Europe, the United States audience tends to relate the two and to support a threat assessment which is based on a linkage perspective.[21]

Threats within the West–South Context

In contrast with the East–West context, the relations of Western countries with the Middle East itself are neither characterised by antagonism between military-political blocs nor distorted by the existence of an ideologically aggressive superpower which demands military and political parity with the United States. In this analytical perspective, the Soviet Union stays rather in the background, supports regional actors, or uses windows of opportunity. Western relations with regional powers are characterised by the military and technological superiority of the West, by unilateral post-colonial dependencies and by economic interdependencies. Asymmetries in these relations are the roots of major tensions between some members of the Atlantic Alliance and some Middle Eastern states.

A major security factor in this regard emanates from local conflicts which theaten to spill over the Europe and the Atlantic community. In recent years, crises like the Israeli-Arab-Palestinian conflict, the overthrow of the Shah, the Soviet occupation of non-aligned Afghanistan, the war between Iraq and Iran, the ethnic-religious group fighting in Lebanon, the political and social instability of a number of key countries like Saudi Arabia and Egypt, and the subversive role of Qaddafi have all demonstrated a potential for uncontrolled escalation. Neither the superpowers nor regional or global organisations have been successful in dampening those conflicts nor has the West succeeded in hedging against their potential consequences.

Southern European countries are highly sensitive to a geographical widening of local Middle East conflicts. Turkey is, of course, the most exposed to this type of infection. But as critical periods during the October War, the Iranian revolution and the Gulf war have shown, many other NATO nations may be affected and fear being dragged into an unwanted war. Once the superpowers are involved in active regional fighting, the European and North Atlantic theatres cannot be isolated from events in the Middle East. Public opinion in Europe is particularly impressed and even shocked in this respect by

US contemplation of 'horizontal escalation' as a reasonable concept for coping with regional aggression.[22]

A particular threat which follows from local conflict is the loss of an important partner or stronghold in the Middle East. Those members of the Atlantic Alliance such as France, Great Britain and the United States, which have close military ties with Middle East countries and governments, cannot afford to sit idle while adverse forces turn these Western oriented partners into hostile actors. However, the public moods within these three NATO members vary over time. The British people did not show much regret when Aden established contractual relations with Moscow after London had given up this stronghold but twenty years later London would welcome a more influential role in the Middle East.[23] The French have regarded unrest in Africa (Chad, Djibouti, Ethiopia) as a threat to the francophone realm. The United States has developed a widely supported, close relationship with Israel ('strategic cooperation'), and some close links with Arab countries such as Saudi Arabia and Egypt. The development of such relationships was not deterred by the loss of Iran, the former cornerstone for the United States' security setting in South-west Asia.

While some of the NATO member states are anxious to safeguard their special military-political relationships with some of the Middle Eastern countries, other members of the Alliance tend to be ambivalent about the value of these connections. They regard them as a political source of threat. They feel that these connections might drag others into military conflict or divert forces from the defence in Europe. This concern is particularly strong in West German public opinion.

A deep feeling of vulnerability is responsible for a widespread threat perception which may arise in the West European public because of disturbances of economic-political West–South relations. The Iran–Iraq war is a good example of such a danger. One can easily calculate the damage which the seven-year-old war could have brought to the world oil market and to the world economy if the war had started a few years earlier. The type of contractual commitment which some West European states (especially France) were ready to accept in the 1970s in order to try to guarantee the oil supply has to be regarded as a measure of the perceived threat. At that time, public opinion in France was almost unanimous in its support of this approach, rather than supporting the counter-cartel International Energy Agency (IEA).[24]

In the last few years political terrorism has become a major threat element. It occurs in the region itself as well as outside and often in the hearts of Western countries. Terrorist threats have a special twist because people feel directly and personally endangered and Middle Eastern terrorism is connected with organised crime and indigenous terrorist activity within NATO countries. West European countries have been hit by the bulk of these terrorist aggressions and public opinion ranks these threats relatively high.[25] Americans seem to suffer particularly from anti-Israel and Libyan supported terrorism. However, they and the Europeans have also been victims of Shia inspired terrorism in Lebanon and other places, supported by Syria and Iran. France has especially to cope with Armenian terrorism. All Western nations are affected in one way or another.

Threats in the West–West Context

'Threat' in this context is perceived as a striking lack of cohesion, a disruptive divergence of view and policies within the Alliance. Both indigenous events in the Middle East and Soviet regional behaviour have the potential to undermine NATO's cohesion and to drive wedges among the Allies. This threat seems to be a particular concern of the US public and political elites, given the fact that NATO's leader quite naturally asks for support of its positions and demands solidarity from its allies.[26] Most Europeans, however, seem to be more concerned with their emancipation from Washington in an area which is not a NATO responsibility *per se*.

Major divergences can be found in the transatlantic assessment of the threat in the Middle East. A majority of Americans will stress the Soviets as a prime factor among the multiple sources of threat in the region. Moscow is regarded as a fundamentally aggressive military power, which uses every opportunity to expand its empire and to profit from Western vulnerabilities. Most conservatives and parts of the liberal spectrum in the US hold this view. The assessment by European publics underlines the fact that most conflicts in the Middle East stem from indigenous factors. The Soviet Union appears in most analyses as a hegemonial power in decline, lacking ideological and economic attraction but managing rather successfully to drag the United States into a military power game. Some portion of US liberals share with the European public this dominant view. It does not come as a surprise that policies which are based on such diverging

threat assessments turn out to go in different directions and to cause
controversy and mistrust among NATO allies.

Differences in the political culture of Americans and Europeans
tend to enhance these cleavages. Europeans will assert that they
know the Middle East better than the United States does, given
the 'neighbourhood backyard' situation and historical interactions.
Obviously, some of the Europeans (colonial powers like Italy, France,
Great Britain) are more familiar with the region than others. A
country like West Germany will rather side with the United States
on this point, having gained its Middle Eastern insights mainly from
business contacts and a special relationship with Israel and Turkey.

Another dividing factor is the continuous quarrel over the purpose
of NATO with respect to out-of-area questions in general and the
Middle East in particular. While the US government (supported by
most political commentators in the United States) usually perceives
NATO as the central organisation to coordinate Western responses
to regional threats in the Middle East, most Europeans (governments
and publics alike) do not believe in the usefulness of NATO for most
of the realistic contingencies which may come about in the Middle
East. The function of NATO after the establishment of the US
Central Command (CENTCOM) remains a matter of Alliance
controversy. In a realistic view, the Alliance has never enjoyed a
golden age, but there is danger that criticism and disaffection become
constant and growing attendants of NATO. The Soviet Union is not
unwilling to exploit this.

III PUBLIC OPINION AND THE USE OF FORCE IN THE MIDDLE EAST

Is the West determined to counter the various Middle East threats
discussed in the previous section? Can Allied governments count on
broad public support for military as well as non-military actions?
How does the predisposition among some security elites to respond
by force work? In recent years some of the NATO member countries
have been involved in the Middle East militarily: do public attitudes
in these countries vary from those of Allies who did not deploy forces
outside the NATO territory? What kind of action is regarded to be
'military': outright intervention, over the horizon presence, military
cooperation with local actors, dispatch of peace-keeping forces,
weapons transfer or the denial thereof?

Answers to threats in the Middle East follow largely the pattern of threat perception by Allied countries. The United States displays a tendency to aim its policy predominantly at the Soviet Union almost irrespective of the kind and the origin of the threat. Washington has to show that it can successfully compete with the other superpower everywhere and on each level in the world and the US public is in favour of keeping the image of a strong United States in world affairs. Thus, most Americans support a strategy of keeping the Soviets away from the Middle East and of neutralising Moscow's influence. President Carter's attempt (early in his term) to cooperate with the Soviet Union on the Palestinian issue and on the concept of the Indian Ocean as a 'zone of peace' seems to be the exception rather than the rule in US Middle East policy.[27] President Reagan not only endorsed and broadened the Carter Doctrine on the right of passage through the Arabian-Persian Gulf he also managed to interpret Soviet behaviour (notably the invasion of Afghanistan) in a way which prepared the ground for beefing up defence budgets in general, establishing CENTCOM, and strengthening strategic relationships with friends in the Middle East.

The 'European approach' (as represented by the multilateral foreign policy cooperation of the Twelve) is less guided by a fixation on the Soviet Union. Europeans are in favour of a balanced and comprehensive Middle East policy. 'Balanced', stands for cooperating on equal terms with all countries in the region, friend or foe. 'Comprehensive', means including any relevant actor in the search for peaceful conflict resolution (including the USSR and the PLO). *Vis-à-vis* the Soviet Union, the Europeans favour a kind of Harmel concept for the Middle East which combines defensive measures with a permanent proposal of cooperation. They detest US 'overreaction' and would like to see Washington concentrate on the 'real' threat, which is the myriad of indigenous conflicts. Yet, there are limits to cooperative minded governments in Europe. The French security elite as well as a majority of the general public opinion did not support President Giscard d'Estaing on his meeting with Brezhnev in Warsaw shortly after the Soviet invasion of Afghanistan. Likewise, President Mitterrand's meeting with Colonel Qaddafi in Crete during the Libyan aggression in Chad in 1983 was not applauded by his fellow citizens.[28]

Two recent events may have, however, shifted US policy slightly toward the European concept. In the course of the Iran–Iraq war, the US noticed that both superpowers have no real influence on the development of the conflict. Lebanon's civil war told Washington that there are situations where even an offer of the best services can be harshly rejected. Today, more American voices than before seem to support a policy which recognises that the Middle East itself is a mess, independently of Soviet behaviour. At the same time the evidence has grown that this mess is not only a problem for the United States but for the Soviet Union, too.

These experiences have prompted US diplomacy to try to establish some constructive contacts with the proponents of steadfastness over Palestine and confrontation with Israel (mainly Syria and Iran). Parallel to this evolution, however, Washington and the whole American nation continued to condemn the involvement of Syria, Iran and Libya in political terrorism; thus the new approach is a mixed one.

IV   MILITARY FORCES AS A REGIONAL DETERRENT FACTOR

Contingency planning for the Middle East has been a prominent as well as controversial subject in US and European debates of the early 1980s. The discussion circled around three different strategies.[29] One approach aimed at having Western forces stationed permanently in the Arabian-Persian Gulf (in contrast to over the horizon). The implementation of such a strategy demanded an infrastructure which would far exceed the existing access to facilities in Egypt, Oman, Somalia, and Kenya; therefore additional partners such as Saudi Arabia, Bahrain and Turkey (expansion of NATO facilities in Eastern Anatolia) had to be considered. US critics of this concept argued that a massive military Western presence would help to counter a certain level of aggression but by the same token would create a new series of instabilities in host countries. In Western Europe this critical view was widely shared. People also did not believe that a large European participation in such US plans would render a Western military presence more acceptable and digestible to receiver countries.[30]

A second strategy intended to avoid the problem of acceptance by turning over the main task of securing Western interests in the Arabian-Persian Gulf to the US Marine Corps. This model was built primarily on a deployment and support of ground troops from the sea and would rely to a large extent on rapid deployment forces built around maritime capabilities. This concept was rejected on the ground that it would not deter the Soviets from marching to the 'warm waters' if they really wanted to.

A third strategy was more directly tailored to deter the Soviet Union. Proponents of this approach pleaded for a small, efficient intervention force, able to seize the oil fields in a crisis situation and thus to demonstrate the vital interests of the West. If this 'trip wire' failed, the United States would answer with an expansion of the conflict: i.e. horizontal and/or vertical escalation. As stated above, the Europeans were not very fond of this version of deterrent strategy against a potential aggressor in the Middle East. Moreover, many US commentators doubted that the United States was realistic about its capability to follow up horizontal escalation and whether vertical escalation was an altogether wise move in this context.

In France the establishment of the *Force d'Action Rapide* (FAR) did not cause the same amount of controversial discussion because of the different military-political set-up of the country and the dual purpose of these forces, for use in the European theatre as well as abroad. The French public will support the FAR as a deterrent to local indigenous aggression but probably only for francophone countries and with some differentiation with respect to the kind of regime and the type of leader who would profit from such deterrence capabilities.[31]

The mood of the British government and public on deterrent forces outside NATO has undergone considerable changes. While London had practically left 'East of Suez' in the 1960s and had started to reduce also its naval forces during the 1970s, the 1980s – boosted by the Falklands surprise – have seen a selective come-back of British interest in regional conflict management by force. Italy, too, in the 1980s has tended to become more active militarily, mainly in the Mediterranean neighbourhood. Public opinion in these countries has examined these changes with a critical eye but has endorsed the underlying trend.

In Germany, no change has taken place; the government, pushed by an anxious people, will voice some understanding of the creation of CENTCOM to contain the Soviets but will make clear to Washington that local instability cannot be controlled by military deterrence. Turkey, which is supposed to play a major additional role within a regional deterrence strategy, holds basically the same view. Both countries will reject participation in a multilateral deterrence policy unless a common NATO strategy for the Middle East were to be hammered out – an approach which, in turn, they do not promote.

Forces as a Means of Intervention

Intervention outside NATO is the business of only a few member states, acting individually. Except for the Libya raid in April 1986 the United States has not undertaken an outright intervention in the Middle East, but has used US forces in various ways. President Carter was basically supported by most of the American people when he launched a desperate rescue operation to free US hostages in Teheran. The US invasion of Grenada, in October 1983, a more clear-cut intervention case, occurred right after the Beirut disaster and seemed to be an appropriate opportunity to redress the United States' image of a credible watch-dog of Western interests. But when Ronald Reagan subsequently tested the waters in El Salvador and Nicaragua he appeared to be operating from a position that is too far right for the US public, even though that public has itself been moving to the right in recent years.

While in the case of Central America we may find a relatively broad Euro-US coalition of public opinion opposing intervention, the Middle East is a different story, especially when it comes to fighting terrorism. On the one hand, European governments were supported by their publics when they used military or para-military means to defend their own interests in the Middle East. Some of these countries (particularly France) even counted on US help to their actions. On the other hand, the Europeans, governments and publics alike, displayed opposition to Washington's use of military power.

The French population by and large has supported its President, liberal or socialist, in cases of intervention in Africa. Operations in Zaire, Tunisia and Chad have enjoyed broad political consensus in France, the only exception being the Communist Party. Thus, Paris can keep up its intervention forces in several corners of Northern Africa. Moreover, the assignment of French police to advise and aid Saudi forces that stormed the Great Mosque in Mecca did not stir up public opinion very much, while the Greenpeace affair revealed an even further understanding of the French public when it comes to defending national interests by forceful means.

Great Britain, too, has helped to settle minor incidents in the Gulf and would certainly do more if necessary. The Falklands case shows not a unanimous but a substantial public support for using force in the event of international aggression. Italy may be more difficult to categorise. One cannot easily see where Rome would intervene (despite the scope of the guarantee of protection to Malta) and how the Italian public and political elites would react, but there are indications that the Italian people would follow if the government were to save Italian citizens or to protect vital territorial interests via military force. Even West Germany mobilised its para-military task force 'GSG 9' to stop aircraft hijackers at Mogadisco back in 1977. This response, however, stemmed from a direct and immediate threat to German nationals (if not to broad German interests) and is not, as shown below, typical of responses when the threat is less salient.

V   PUBLIC OPINION IN PREVIOUS CASES OF THE USE OF FORCE

The Multinational Naval Force

When the US Secretary of Defense Harold Brown, after the outbreak of the Iran–Iraq war, launched the idea of a multinational naval force in the Indian Ocean the test case for a collective Western response to a potential Middle East threat, the closure of the Strait of Hormuz, was presented. While France, Great Britain and Italy found a way of rejecting the concept but cooperating congenially with US naval forces in the area,[32] the German government and public reacted nervously. The Federal Republic felt pressure from its allies to take part of the burden and to send warships to the Persian-Arabian Gulf to defend access to oil sources. Chancellor Helmut Schmidt expressed a willingness to provide West German forces to fill gaps in European defences that could be created by the presence of Allied units in the Indian Ocean but he ruled out for legal reasons the use of West German armed forces outside the geographical area of the Atlantic Alliance.[33]

   A series of newspaper commentaries began to challenge the notion that the German Constitution actually bans such an involvement. It was argued, for instance, that nothing in the Constitution specifically states that West Germany may not operate outside the NATO area. The *Frankfurter Allgemeine Zeitung* wrote that if the Government was willing to send warships into the North Atlantic and the Norwegian Sea, which are far from the West German coast, then 'there can be no constitutional reservation about deployment in other oceans'.[34] Some Christian Democrats were reported to have said privately that they thought a symbolic West German naval presence in the Gulf would be a valuable gesture of solidarity towards the United States and NATO. But they have been reluctant to take such a position in public, apparently because they judged it as potentially unpopular.

The whole debate had started already in February 1980, when plans for sending the two cruisers *Luetzen* and *Bayern* to the Indian Ocean had become public. The Soviet press had criticised these plans as German 'participation in dangerous preparations of war outside the NATO area'. German media, too, had questioned whether the sending of ships to a crisis area was a legal and altogether opportune move. But the German Defence Minister Hans Apel, made clear that year after year ships of the *Bundesmarine* were undertaking journeys to faraway countries and continents. He saw no reason to stop this kind of regular friendship visit, despite the current problems in the Gulf region. However, Apel and other members of the Social Democrats attacked the Bavarian Christians Socialist Union CSU, when it included a passage in its July 1980 security programme calling for an end to geographical boundaries and political constraints on the employment of the *Bundeswehr*.[35]

Anti-terrorist Operations

Middle East-based political terrorism has become a growing problem for Western countries.[36] The *Achille Lauro* event, the Rome and Vienna airport bombs and the Berlin discothèque explosion were attributed to terrorists from the Middle East. The US was particularly furious about the Libyan Colonel, who was accused of having supported these acts of terorism and was denounced for 'criminal outrages by an outlaw regime' (Reagan). The President was largely backed (if not pushed) by the US public to impose a total economic boycott against Libya and to take further steps if these measures did not end Qaddafi's terrorism. When US planes bombed airfields, government command posts and suspected terrorist training camps in Libya to 'pre-empt and discourage' terrorism, Reagan was applauded by the majority of his fellow countrymen.[37]

By contrast, the European allies all along declined to join the US appeal for a boycott and eventually stronger action against Libya. Every European country seemed to have an approach of its own.

For Germany past experience had shown that sanctions had never had the desired result and had often produced the opposite effect. Italy had the same kind of doubts about economic sanctions but undertook some minor measures to let the United States not be alone this time. Spain and Portugal disassociated themselves from the idea of economic sanctions for political reasons. Greece appeared more concerned about a possible US military strike against Libya than about Qaddafi's alleged harbouring of terrorists. Britain, which broke off diplomatic relations with Libya after a London policewoman was slain by a gunman hiding in the Libyan embassy in 1984, also was unenthusiastic. Turkey, together with the Islamic Conference, declared its solidarity with Libya in case of a US intervention.

In short, none of the European NATO allies was ready to boycott Libya economically or even think in terms of military retaliation. The European Political Cooperation (EPC), which argued for 'quiet diplomacy' instead and for initiatives to settle the core conflicts in the Middle East in order to deprive terrorism of its political motivation, expressed the general mood of the European public.

When the US raid on Libya occurred, almost all Europeans united in an outcry of disapproval and a reference to the United States' 'Rambo' instinct. Margaret Thatcher, who had allowed the US air force to conduct part of the raid from British airfields, was under heavy attack in the Commons, mainly from the opposition parties, but there were pertinent questions from the Conservatives, too.[38] According to the Harris Institute not even one-third of the British population regarded the US bombing as justified, and seven out of ten UK citizens condemned Margaret Thatcher's support of Washington.[39] While she managed to counter part of the criticism by referring to US solidarity and help during the Falklands conflict, she and her foreign secretary were blamed for breaking the rules of European foreign policy cooperation.

Opinion in France was split over the US attack on Libya, but a significant majority of Frenchmen approved of the Government's decision not to allow US bombers to use French airspace. A poll of the political weekly *Le Point* indicated that 40 per cent of Frenchmen disapproved of the US raid, compared with 39 per cent who approved. Fifty-five per cent of those polled (a representative national sample of 800 people) supported the Government's refusal to allow French airspace to be used, compared with 26 per cent who took the opposite view. These findings appear to be contradicted by another poll published in *Newsweek*, which suggested that as many as 66 per cent of the French people approved of the US action, compared with only 32 per cent who opposed it.[40]

While it is difficult to judge which of the two polls provides the more accurate picture of French public opinion concerning the raid on Libya, it is significant that there have been no big anti-Reagan demonstrations in Paris, unlike the situation in most of the other European capitals. But then France has always been the 'odd man out' in Europe when it comes to 'peace' marches. In Italy, where the government took a critical stand on the US military move, the parties of the left not only supported Bettino Craxi but organised demonstrations all over the country. In these demonstrations it was Reagan rather than Qaddafi who figured as the rascal.

In the European Parliament (EP) the Socialist Group heavily disapproved of Washington's military action against Libya. The Socialists regarded the US reaction as unlikely to reduce terrorism and as a totally inappropriate punishment of its initiators. The EP Christian Democrats, on the contrary, avoided mentioning the United States and showed understanding for those fighting the new type of state terrorism. The Liberals in the EP felt that one cannot blame a power if it reacts strongly when threatened by terrorism. All groups of the EP deplored the repeated unilateral actions of the United States and the disregard of European views – the Europeans had hoped until the last minute to keep Washington from going military by adopting sanctions against Libya.

Peace-Keeping and Mine Sweeping

NATO countries have had a mixed experience with peace-keeping forces in the Middle East. While the Sinai Multilateral Force and Observers (MFO) was a success, the Beirut Multinational Force (MNF) was a failure. The MFO was an integral part of the Camp David process, which public opinion in the West broadly supported.[41] People, especially in the United States, were keen to bring peace to the Middle East, even if they, like most of the Europeans, preferred a more comprehensive peace process. The European debate on how to contribute to the MFO without giving up the fundamentals of the Venice Declaration mainly took place among diplomats and foreign policy elites and hardly touched the wider public.[42] Europeans mainly felt that they should support Sadat's bold policy of reconciliation.

Initiation of and participation in the MNF was more controversial. It also shows changes of political attitudes over time. Initially the

MNF – composed of US, French and Italian troops and later joined by a small British detachment – was set up to guarantee the evacuation of the PLO from Beirut and protection of Palestinian civilians in Beirut once the armed PLO forces had left the city. In both Europe and the United States the public supported a joint peace-keeping mission aimed at avoiding further armed conflict in Lebanon.[43] Once the PLO completed its withdrawal, however, the United States decided to pull its marine contingent from the Multinational Force ahead of time, prompting Italy and France to follow suit and causing some public questioning in Europe of Washington's real goals and commitments in this matter.

Shortly after the MNF had withdrawn from Lebanon, newly-elected President Bashir Gemayel was assassinated, and the Israeli Army, then surrounding Moslem West Beirut, invaded the city. In the wake of this event, in September 1982, Christian Lebanese militiamen entered the Palestinian refugee camps of Sabra and Chatila. That operation ended in the death of several hundred Palestinian civilians, prompting the return of the MNF. While nobody in the West was complaining of the humanitarian role which brought the MNF back to Beirut, a debate started over the political ends of this new mission. A change of US policy seemed to put the MNF directly in support of President Amin Gemayel's minority Christian government. This turned the peace-keeping force into a target for the Moslem majority that had originally welcomed it to the country.

It did not take long until the Western public sensed that the atmosphere in Lebanon had changed and that the mission of the MNF was increasingly blurred. The first protests emerged in the United States. When the US troops were put into a situation where they were seen as siding with one party to the conflict, with the danger of being dragged into a quagmire, Congress and the American people supported the withdrawal of the marines and the President followed suit, especially after the car bomb explosion which killed some 240 Americans.

France was eager to be present in the Middle East on another peace-keeping mission after its enduring participation in UNIFIL since 1978. While the MFO was successful and was elegantly used by the new Socialist government to change France's Middle East policy toward the US approach, Beirut became a failure for Paris, as well.[44] The extent, however, to which the French public supported its government on this matter is reflected in the fact that right after the attack on the US and the French headquarters in Beirut a public opinion poll in France showed a 51 per cent majority for staying on the peace mission.[45] Criticism came from the Communist Party (at that time still part of the coalition government) asking for the immediate withdrawal of the French contingent and arguing that France had intervened in inner-Lebanese affairs, especially since it had allowed its troops to launch retaliatory blows. The Gaullist RPR, in turn, renewed its demand for a more clear-cut definition of France's role in a militarily confused situation and asked that attacks against the MNF be answered appropriately. Yet Mitterrand knew that this mission was doomed to fail. For face-saving reasons he kept his troops in Lebanon till the end of March 1984, hoping to repair the French image among the Arabs by trying to launch a UN-monitored peace concept for Lebanon.

The government in Rome, too, but to a lesser degree than in the case of France, was supported by the Italian public in its intention to take over more responsibility in Mediterranean security and to participate in both the MFO and the MNF peace-keeping missions.[46] In Western Europe, except for Germany, peace-keeping seems to be a rather acceptable if not attractive way of using armed forces in the context of Middle East conflict control – even among Northern European governments and their people. Given the low level of their involvement, these countries do not seem to be constrained by domestic and international suspicion of escalating their engagement: the European public displays more confidence in European peace-keeping forces than in American ones.[47]

This judgement is somewhat confirmed by the handling of the mobilisation of a multinational mine-sweeping operation in August and September 1984 to try to make the approaches to the Suez Canal and the waters of the Red Sea safe for shipping after incidents of ship damage in the areas. As indicated by Cremasco in Chapter 4, Italy and France were willing to answer calls for help from the Saudi and the Egyptian governments but strongly emphasised the bilateral character of their mission. Still holding a bad memory of what had happened in the multinational force in Lebanon, Rome and Paris did not want 'to appear to be associated in any American crusade in the Red Sea'.[48] They felt that neither public opinion in their countries nor that in Arab countries would appreciate the re-establishment of the MNF in a new fashion. The crucial point to them was not whether or not to send mine-sweepers but how to discontinue any collective Western approach. In consequence, only Great Britain collaborated with the United States in this operation.

VI ORGANISING THE WESTERN RESPONSE

How useful is NATO in organising out-of-area responses? If we find no consensus among the Allies for an expansion of NATO's territory as well as duty, do the Allies agree on a specialised out-of-area organisation instead? Is the multinational approach altogether useful? Are military reactions more acceptable in a collective approach than in an individual policy? Is it of relevance that the use of force in the out-of-area question means more than just assuring deterrence? Are NATO allies happy with the new structure: US CENTCOM – compensation within NATO? Will the European public endorse support of CENTCOM in a hot crisis?

NATO's Role in Out-of-Area Activities

NATO is by function and character a defence organisation oriented toward the Soviet Union. The Alliance is not equipped to contain Moscow in the Middle East, let alone to cope with the complexity of regional conflicts. The structural problem of NATO (to be confined to the Treaty area) does not in principle impinge on the West's ability to act collectively, if a situation in the Middle East demands such action but so far, the framework and the procedures for military protection of Western interests in the Middle East are in flux. The consultative infrastructure is impressive, but the outcome is poor.[49] There are a number of bilateral settings and multilateral arrangements on the operational level but no joint management based on a common political denominator. Not even the Mediterranean rim countries have developed a concerted approach, much less joined together with the United States, which has both interests and forces in the area.[50]

Today, neither Allied governments nor the public in Alliance countries seem to support the geographical and functional expansion of NATO to include out-of-area defence tasks. No prominent representative of a member country has recently proposed a transatlantic defence community for regional security nor has there been a public debate on that sort of suggestion. Discussion has concentrated, instead, on assigning to NATO some complementary functions in dealing with out-of-area questions: consultation, regional deterrence, compensation.[51]

Public opinion in the United States as well as in Europe has never objected to the consultative function of NATO.[52] Criticism has referred to the sometimes erratic and incomplete method of consultation rather than to consultation as such. When it comes time to act militarily, experience shows that each member country will guard its freedom of manoeuvre anyway.

To the extent that NATO is regarded as deterring Soviet actions against the Southern Flank, its member countries seem to have gradually changed their view. While NATO policy and strategy remain oriented to the Central Front, the flanks have received more attention in recent years. People seem to accept, at least theoretically, that the defence of Western interests has to widen once the Soviet threat widens geographically. However, countries like Greece and Turkey, which for obvious reasons should play a key role in this regard, have been reluctant to take a much bigger share of the military and political burden that the strategic overlap of the Southern Flank and the Middle East region implies.

Between 1980 and 1985 NATO has been the framework in which the sharing of the out-of-area burden among its members was discussed. They agreed to compensate for gaps opened up by the establishment of CENTCOM and the possible redeployment of US troops to the Middle East in time of crisis.[53]

For those allies who have no intervention forces of their own, or do not want to send them to the Middle East, the concept of compensation within NATO might be an elegant way to gain Alliance solidarity without straining their national security consensus. Yet, some of the major problems of this 'solution' may still lay in front of us: to what extent will the US be distracted from the defence of Europe? Do we witness the slow but steady decoupling of the United States from the European theatre? Will efforts for a further conventionalisation of Europe's defence be undermined? Is the US using CENTCOM unilaterally while implying the multilateral support of its allies via compensation? Given the many transatlantic divergences on the Middle East threat perception and policy, each of these questions may raise some doubts as to the solidity of the out-of-area defence structure.

The United States and Europe: Cooperation or Competition?

The history of joint European-United States intervention is a mixed success story. Suez, the October War and the MNF are highlights of conflictual as well as cooperative activity in the Middle East. The United States, as well as the European countries, know that they have to find a *modus operandi* in response to Middle East challenges. Do they need a setting which enables collective action beyond NATO limitations?

Washington has been inconsistent in wanting the Europeans as a partner. European countries have been hesitant in tying their regional policy to a superpower which is regarded as being oriented toward quick military fixes. The United States – for good reasons – has often gone it alone; Europeans would also desire this ability but lack the means and the will.

Most European countries dream of more self-reliance, some in terms of Europe as a civil power, others in terms of a European rapid deployment force. Most have managed so far to find a common line for political-economic approaches to Middle East contingencies. but there is no unanimity in the circles of the Twelve on intervention or weapons transfer policy, let alone on acting in a concerted manner. Cooperation among the Europeans seems to be limited to non-military instruments and policies. The European Parliament (EP) is one of the few actors in Europe who have devoted time and energy to thinking about collective defence capabilities for regional threats. Traditionally, members of the European assembly have favoured (under various conditions) European security arrangements – rather for the sake of constructing the 'United States of Europe' than in order to cope with a particular military problem.[54] After the Soviet move into Afghanistan and the outbreak of the Iran–Iraq war a minority of the European Parliament proposed forming an operational military structure to protect the supply lines from the Gulf. Given the relatively low influence of the EP in such matters the proposal did not get very far in practical terms.[55]

Even within the smaller group of states belonging to the West European Union (WEU), regional security cooperation has not gone beyond paper work. Theoretically the WEU could provide the framework for the coordination of the use of armed forces because it does not have territorial restrictions, but when the subject came up during the recent revitalisation period of the WEU it was marginalised and eventually turned down.[56] The Assembly of the WEU has, in fact, discussed all security related events in the Middle East and has produced thorough reports on subjects like 'European Security and the Mediterranean', 'European Security and the South Atlantic', 'Situation in the Middle East' and 'European – United States Cooperation for International Peace and Joint Security', but as its impact on the European public is even smaller than that of the

EP, a more widely supported debate never took off.[57]

As Edwards points out in Chapter 6, European agencies are based on complicated decision-making procedures and are rather compartmentalised (EC, EPC, WEU, EUROGROUP); hence, one cannot see how an efficient European-United States cooperation in the field of regional security could materialise even if public opinion on both sides would favour it. More problems would be raised than solved by squeezing the two sides into a tight multilateral partnership. Models like the 'principal nations group' or a 'NATO consultative group on out-of-area challenges' therefore have remained wishful thinking.

Experience points to a less multilateral direction.[58] Joint *ad hoc* operations on the practical level seem to be by far more acceptable than pre-planned procedures for collective action. A good number of contingencies in the Middle East, especially those not directly related to the Soviet Union, simply do not lend themselves to multilateral approaches. A cost benefit analysis will probably not encourage investment in Western cohesion and in the establishment of common public support for such cases. For the sake of efficiency, the West will have to live with cross-cutting public attitudes in these cases.

VII THE LIMITS TO CONSENSUS

Since the beginning of this decade, NATO and its members have been confronted with a new wave of out-of-area questions related to the Middle East. To the extent that military answers were given or contemplated, a wider public debate has been initiated on the appropriateness of the use of force in a regional security context. This discussion was parallel to and intertwined with the problem of reassuring a Western security consensus at large and of managing the future of the Atlantic Alliance.[59]

In the United States, where this debate was relatively rich, a majority among conservatives pleaded that more attention be given to the instruments of military power, while many of the liberals cautioned the US government not to believe in military solutions to regional problems. In Europe, so far, opposite attitudes have existed between nations rather than between like-minded political groups. Certainly, one can mention the general opposition of West European left-wing parties (some socialists but especially communists) to the use of force in international relations, but the main cleavage is between a country like France, whose government can count on a broad public support during French interventions in Africa, and a country like West Germany, where the use of military power – except for deterrence purposes – is almost taboo. In both countries, a shift of the political majority from left to right has not substantially altered the country's attitude on out-of-area actions. Other European countries have to be ranked in between these two extreme positions. The picture of the public treatment of the out-of-area question among the Allies is, therefore, everything else but unamimous.

Nevertheless, events in the Middle East have raised the degree of Allied preoccupation with out-of-area questions and have led to a more sophisticated perception of threat among the informed Western public. The salience of regional threats, and the scope of public and elite debate on this topic in Italy, certainly contributed to Rome's taking a higher level of responsibility in the field of Mediterranean and Middle Eastern security. This is not the case for Greece and Turkey, where public opinion continues to be captured by the Greco-Turk dispute, which does not seem to permit a glimpse beyond the national horizon. The American people, to the contrary, have reminded foreign policy analysts of the unpredictability of a nation's threat perception: though located on a distant continent and equipped with an enormous military force, the people of the United States felt strongly threatened by such unequal events as the Soviet strategic gains in South-west Asia and the terrorist attacks on US citizens abroad.

Concerning public attitudes and the employment of military means, the experience of the 1980s demands a differentiation between deterrence purposes, intervention goals and peace-keeping missions. While all Alliance members accept the build-up of military forces as a deterrent to the Warsaw Pact in Europe, only some NATO countries seem to support the adaptation of deterrence capabilities for an out-of-area region, such as the Middle East. And even there, one finds more support among the Western public for those regional deterrent strategies which are oriented toward the Soviet Union than for a strategy which includes the deterrence of local indigenous aggression. In other words in both the United States and Western Europe a majority goes along with the US CENTCOM's function as a clear signal to the Soviets but is reluctant to have it displayed as a means of restraining indigenous conflict or major internal changes, including that of a friendly regime or government.

Ad hoc military intervention in the Middle East and North Africa has been largely accepted by former colonial powers and by the public in the United States. Other NATO allies showed criticism and aversion. They would not allow their governments to facilitate or support those interventions. The attitude of publics; can however, change – see the hijacking of the German Landshut airplane in 1977 – when fellow countrymen are directly endangered. If not, even 'interventionist-minded' publics may oppose a military move in the Middle East of an Allied country, a specific case being France's refusal to support the US during its raid on Libya.

Low-key interventions have not encountered much opposition among Western publics; sometimes they are even met with some sympathy (see the French Mecca action or the US capture of the *Achille Lauro* hijackers). The scope of the US attack on Libya (like the Grenada mission) seems to be a tolerable measure of intervention. In this case, President Reagan did not need European support of his decision because he had the articulate mandate of the US public. (The reason for including Great Britain in the move is open to political explanation beyond the military-technical needs.) Larger style US interventions will probably meet more substantial opposition in both Western Europe and the United States, if one can trust the debate over the establishment of and the missions for the US Rapid Deployment Force. In this case, European attitudes are likely to be shaped by the view that there are no major contingencies in the Middle East without repercussions on the central front, while the US public will recall Vietnam as a constraint. (Moreover, the political availability of facilities in host countries has been a critical point of uncertainty for Washington's decision makers and publics.) In this regard, public opinion may grant France, which is not officially integrated into the military command structure of NATO, more freedom of manoeuvre for large-scale interventions than the United States.

Peace-keeping missions of European countries are regarded as positive and morally acceptable as such. They enjoy the support even of Europeans on the far left, of the Scandinavian countries and of smaller European countries like the Netherlands and Greece. Even West Germany has – so far with no result – debated participating in peace-keeping missions, provided they are under UN auspices. On the contrary, US peace-keeping activities encounter a more mixed reception among the public in the United States, as well as in Europe. People seem to hold the suspicion that Washington has an inclination to go beyond the purposes of a peace-keeping intervention.

While the present US President has a surprisingly high potential to manipulate the US public, he also has to consider massive public, and especially Congressional, opposition to US military involvement in critical regions, the Beirut operation being a case in point. In France, the other Western power with a high propensity to undertake military missions abroad, more or less the same pattern applies. The French President can claim the overall national interest for interventions outside France but cannot altogether ignore emotions in the public, as the recent taking of French hostages by Shi'ite groups in Lebanon or the withholding of Madame Claustre in Chad back in the 1970s have proven.

The experiences of the 1980s do not allow us to conclude that a collective Western approach to the inclusion of military means in Middle East policy, as compared to individual actions, would render the use of force more acceptable to the Western public. The maximum of collectivity tolerable seems to be a common Soviet related threat assessment in NATO as well as an understanding among the Allies that the Southern flank should be strong and that Moscow should not be allowed to become a hegemonial power in the Middle East. The practical consequences of these imperatives – consultation, facilitation, compensation – touch on national sensitivities which imply uncertainties for a wider Western consensus. This is even more so if institutional arrangements for jointly dealing with out-of-area questions are considered – France being the leading opponent in this regard.[60] The smoothest and most efficient handling of military actions in the Middle East seems to be the unilateral approach, concerted on the operational level, if need be, with other partners. It is therefore doubtful whether it is worthwhile to invest in the development of a wider Western security consensus as far as out-of-area questions are concerned.

On the other hand, out-of-area contingencies obviously are not the subject for 'making the Alliance work';[61] they have rather the effect of disturbing or even destroying the 'internal fabric of Western security', especially if regarded as test cases for the security consensus in NATO proper.[62] It seems that the out-of-area question is more controversial a topic and Allies are more extensive adversaries in this field than in the traditional East–West political-military antagonism.[63] Western Europe, itself a many-coloured collection of nation states, cannot be much more than a 'partial partner' to Washington,[64] while the United States will not persuade European minds of the appropriateness of military responses to regional Third World threats.

Notes

1. Stanley Hoffman, *Duties Beyond Borders* (Syracuse: Syracuse University Press, 1981).
2. Peter Schmidt, 'Public Opinion and Security Policy in the Federal Republic of Germany', *Orbis*, Vol. 28, No. 4, Winter 1985, pp. 717–42.
3. Gebhard Schweigler, *West German Foreign Policy. The Domestic Setting* (Washington, DC: Praeger, 1984).
4. 'Ultimately, two factors will bring Europe and the United States into conflict in the Middle East. One is the contrast between their vulnerability and their capability, the most vulnerable actor being the least powerful. The other stems from a different emotional relation to Israel.' Dominique Moisi, 'Europe, the United States and the Middle East Conundrum', *Atlantic Quarterly*, Vol. 2, No. 2, Summer 1984, pp. 161–82.
5. Heinrich Siegmann, *The Science Center Berlin Mail Survey of Security Policy Elites in Five Nations: Codebook and Marginals of Responses* (Berlin: Publication Series of the International Institute for Comparative Social Research, 1983), p. 22.
6. Gebhard Schweigler, 'Pragmatik statt Programme', *Die neue Ordnung*, Vol. 37, No. 3, June 1986, pp. 209–20.
7. Christoph Bertram, 'Public Confidence and Western Defense in the 1980s', *Atlantic Quarterly*, Vol. 2, No. 2, Summer 1984, pp. 133–43.
8. Leslie H. Gelb, *The Irony of Vietnam: The System Worked* (Washington, DC: Brookings Institute, 1979).
9. Richard E. Neustadt, *Alliance Politics* (New York: Columbia University Press, 1970).
10. John Chipman, *French Military Policy and African Security*, Adelphi Paper No. 201 (London: International Institute for Strategic Studies, 1985).
11. Theodore Achilles, 'US Role in Negotiations That Led to Atlantic Alliance', *NATO Review*, 1979, No. 5, pp. 1–5.
12. An analysis of communiqués from NATO bodies since 1949 shows a gradual development of a common threat assessment among member-states' representatives in the North Atlantic Council and the Defence Planning Committee concerning events outside the Treaty area. The official recognition that those events may affect their common interests as members of the Alliance is one reality, the other consists of public opinion and political groupings within NATO countries whose positions are likely to be less unanimous. See NATO Information Service, *Texts of Final Communiqués*, Brussels, Vol. I (1949–74) 1975, Vol. II (1975–80) 1981. For more recent communiqués see *Atlantic News*, Brussels, various numbers.
13. Even in a geostrategically exposed country like West Germany more than 60 per cent of the national elites in 1980/81 believed that a major war could start from an oil supply disruption or a regional war of superpower proxies while only 20 per cent of the same group saw a

conventional Soviet breakthrough or a strategic nuclear strike as a cause for a possible third world war. See Dietmar Schoessler, Matthias Jung, SIPLA-Umfrage 1980/81 (Tabellenband), University of Mannheim 1982, pp. 164–17.

14. Miroslav Nincic, *How War Might Spread to Europe* (London and Philadelphia: Taylor and Francis, 1985).

15. Fred Halliday, *Soviet Policy in the Arc of Crisis*, (Washington, DC: Institute for Policy Studies, 1981).

16. Certainly part of the US public and some of the experts have held a similarly cautious position. See Joshua M. Epstein, 'Soviet Vulnerabilities in Iran and the RDF Deterrent', *International Security*, Vol. 6, No. 2, Fall 1981, pp. 126–58.

17. Hannes Adomeit, *Soviet Risk-Taking and Crisis Behaviour – A Theoretical and Empirical Analysis* (London: Allen & Unwin, 1982).

18. To mention just one current example: 'Reagan's Choke Points. Passages Cited by Reagan Hold Key to Defense Operations Around World', *International Herald Tribune*, February 15–16, 1986, p. 3.

19. Edward Pearce, 'The British Labour Party and Defence', *Atlantic Quarterly*, Vol. 2, No. 2, Summer 1984, pp. 143–52. Heinrich Winkler, 'The German Social Democratic Party and Defence', *Atlantic Quarterly*, Vol. 2, No. 2, Summer 1984, pp. 153–60.

20. The US, too, worked to lower the dependence on Middle Eastern crude, especially since it became obvious that the United States' economy would suffer from price related effects of a disruption in the same approximate range as would the European allies. Stanley R. Sloan, *Western Vulnerability to a Disruption of Persian Gulf Oil Supplies: US Interests and Options*, Congressional Research Service, Report 83-24F, Washington, 1983.

21. 'Linkage' was a widely shared concept among Americans during both the Carter and the Reagan Administrations. Zbigniew Brzezinski, 'Crises regionales: Gerer l'imprevisible', *Politique Internationale*, Vol. 6, No. 30, Winter 1985/86, pp. 189–200. See also Foreign Secretary George Shultz's speech at the RAND/UCLA Conference in Los Angeles on 19 October 1984.

22. Washington's reaction to the Soviet intervention in Afghanistan and the war mongering rhetoric of the early Reagan Administration certainly contributed to an unprecedented peak of 32 per cent of the European Community population in 1981/82 who regarded a new world war in the next ten years as likely. See Peter Schmidt, *Public Opinion and Security Policy in the Federal Republic of Germany: Elite and Mass Opinion in a Comparative Perspective*, RAND Paper P-7016, Santa Monica, 1984.

23. The unequivocal response of Britain to the Argentine invasion of the Falklands shows that a majority in the United Kingdom is again aware of regional threats to vital Western interests.

24. France's entanglement in the Gulf war via arms trade has its roots in economic and political considerations during the 1973–74 oil crisis. This subject is treated from a French point of view in Basma Kodmani, *Quelle sécurité pour le Golfe?* (Paris: Editions Economica, 1984).

25. According to the Center of Strategic Studies of the University of Tel Aviv the following percentages of all terrorist attacks in 1984 were given:

40.5 in Western Europe, 20.6 in the Middle East, 16.5 in Africa, 13.6 in South America, 2.9 in Central America, 1.5 in North America, 0.2 in Eastern Europe. See Gerd Langguth, 'Origins and Goals of Terrorism in Europe', *Aussenpolitik*, Vol. 37, No. 2, 1986, pp. 162–74.

26. The US concern over transatlantic cleavages in both East–West relations and out-of-area questions is expressed paradigmatically in hearings and reports of the United States Congress. Two examples: United States Senate, Committee on Foreign Relations, *NATO Today: The Alliance in Evolution* (Washington, DC: US Government Printing Office, 1982). United States Senate, Committee on Foreign Relations, *Crisis in the Atlantic Alliance: Origins and Implications* (Washington, DC: US Government Printing Office, 1982).

27. Seth P. Tillman, *The United States in the Middle East* (Bloomington: Indiana University Press, 1982).

28. David Yost, 'French Policy in Chad and the Libyan Challenge', *Orbis*, Vol. 21, No. 4, Winter 1983, pp. 967–97.

29. Gene I. Rochlin, *US Military Forces and the Persian Gulf*, (Berkeley: University of California, 1982).

30. Alvin J. Cotrell, Michael L. Moodie, *The United States and the Persian Gulf. Past Mistakes, Present Needs* (New Brunswick and London: National Strategy Information Center, Transaction Books, 1984).

31. David S. Yost, *France and Conventional Defense in Central Europe*, EAI Papers No. 7, Spring 1984.

32. See Chapter 4.

33. Chancellor Schmidt was not alone in this position. Defenders of his line argued against the use of a West German force outside what they consider to be the NATO geographical area with a reference to Article 87 A of the Constitution. This says that 'Apart from defense, the armed forces may only be used to the extent explicitly permitted by the Basic Law'. Such possible additional employment of the armed forces is taken to mean service in natural catastrophes or domestic disturbances. They argued further for a close interpretation of Article 115 A of the Constitution, which links 'the determination of a state of defense' to an attack on West German territory or the imminence of such an attack. Opposite positions, instead, stressed that Article 24 of the Constitution, which permits the country's membership in a military pact, also allows it to 'consent to such limitations of sovereignty as will bring about and secure a peaceful and lasting order in Europe and among the nations of the world'. This reading even sees a mission for the Federal Republic to become militarily active and take responsibility in certain cases, though not on a unilateral basis.

34. Guenther Gillessen, 'Das Grundesetz sagt nichts ueber den Indischen Ozean', *Frankfurter Allgemeine Zeitung*, 3 October, 1980, p. 3.

35. A key argument in this context was that all German troops are assigned to NATO and can only be deployed in accordance with collective Allied decisions.

36. Assembly of the West European Union, *Security and Terrorism*, Report of the Commission of General Affairs, Paris, 29 April 1986.

37. According to a *Newsweek* poll, 71 per cent in the United States approved

of the raid; other surveys showed up to 83 per cent approval. See *Newsweek*, Vol. 57, No. 17, 28 April 1986, pp. 10–14.

38. 'Howe Urging Further Moves', *The Times*, 24 April 1986, p. 4.
39. 'Rambos Tochter und die blumigen Grusse aus Washington', *Frankfurter Rundschau*, 18 April 1986, p. 3.
40. 'France the odd man out in bombing protests', *The Times*, 21 April 1984, p. 1.
41. The Multinational Force and Observers (MFO) was to guarantee the centre-piece of the bilateral Egyptian-Israeli peace treaty, the total withdrawal of Israel from the Sinai.
42. Alfred Pijpers, 'Die europaische Beteiligung an der Sinai-Friedenstruppe (MFO)', *Europa Archiv*, Vol. 38, No. 21, 1983, pp. 675–84.
43. The Multinational Force (MNF) was formed in August 1982 after the US government mediated a cease-fire between Israel, which invaded Lebanon in June of that year, and the PLO, whose leaders and guerrillas were cornered in Beirut as a result of the invasion.
44. Helmut Hubel, *Frankreichs Rolle im Nahen Osten* (Bonn: Europa Union Verlag, 1986).
45. *Quotidien de Paris*, 26 October 1983, p. 1.
46. For more details on the Italian position during the two MNF missions see Chapter 4.
47. David Allen and Alfred Pijpers (eds), *European Foreign Policy-Making and the Arab-Israeli Conflict* (The Hague/Boston/Lancaster: Martinus Nijhoff Publishers, 1984).
48. Loren Jenkins, 'Allies Shun Concept of Multinational Force', *The Washington Post*, 29 August 1984, p. 1.
49. Thomas J. Kennedy, Jr., *NATO Politico-Military Consultation: Shaping Alliance Decisions* (Washington: National Defense University Press, 1984).
50. See Chapter 6.
51. Charles A. Kupchan, 'Regional Security and the Out-of-Area Problem', in Stephen J. Flanagan, Fen Osler Hampson (eds), *Securing Europe's Future* (London/Sidney: Croom Helm, 1986), pp. 280–301.
52. Fredo Dannenbring, 'Consultations: The Political Lifeblood of the Alliance', *NATO Review*, No. 6, 1986, pp. 1–7.
53. Until 1982 the US administration favoured a direct support of US Rapid Deployment Forces in the Middle East. The extremely small echo of this appeal heard in Europe – among other reasons – prompted Washington to switch to a more acceptable solution: the compensation approach.
54. Carsten Lehmann Sorensen, 'A European Security Policy? The Attitudes of Candidates for the European Parliament', *Scandinavian Political Studies*, Vol. 3, No. 4, 1980, pp. 347–71.
55. Henri Labrousse, 'Contribution de l'Europe a la sécurité dans le Golfe', in B. Kodmani (ed.), *Quelle sécurité pour le Golfe?* (Paris: Editions Economica, 1984), pp. 177–92.
56. Two main reasons were mentioned in this context: (1) the WEU has transferred all its military forces and commands to NATO; (2) the WEU treaty refers to 'defence' as the main purpose of the Union which – in a

narrow interpretation – would exclude the projection of military power.
57. Western European Union, *Index of Presidents, Chairmen and Reports of the Assembly of Western European Union*, Paris, 1983.
58. Karl Kaiser, Winston Lord, Thierry de Montbrial and David Watt, *Western Security* (New York: Council on Foreign Relations, 1981). Phil Williams, 'Revitalising the Western Alliance: Proposals for Change', *Atlantic Quarterly*, Vol. 2, No. 2, Summer 1984, pp. 119–32.
59. Christopher Coker, *The Future of the Atlantic Alliance* (London: Macmillan Press, 1984). Lawrence Freedman (ed.), *The Troubled Alliance* (Guildford: St Martin's Press 1983); Baard Bredrup Knudsen, *Europe versus America: Foreign Policy in the 1980s* (Totowa, NJ: Rowman and Allanheld, 1983).
60. Dominique Moisi, 'Superpower Stakes in the Middle East: A French Point of View', *AEI Foreign Policy and Defense Review*, Vol. 6, No. 1, 1986, pp. 43–9.
61. Gregory G. Treverton, *Making the Alliance Work: The United States and Western Europe* (Ithaca, NY: Cornell University Press, 1985).
62. Gregory Flynn, *The Internal Fabric of Western Security* (London: Croom Helm, 1981).
63. Simon Serfaty, *The United States, Western Europe, and the Third World: Allies and Adversaries*, The Center for Strategic and International Studies, Significant Issues Series, Vol. II, No. 4, Washington, DC, 1980.
64. Edward A. Kolodziej, *European Perspectives on Europe's Roles in the World: The Partial Partner*, The Wilson Center, Working Paper No. 17, Washington, DC, 1981.

6 Multilateral Coordination of Out-of-Area Activities
Geoffrey Edwards

Ringing declarations and exhortations to consult closely and to develop more harmonious if not harmonised positions have regularly emerged from the multilateral fora of Western Europe and the Atlantic. In 1951, for example, it was declared that:

> There is a continuing need . . . for effective consultation at an early stage on current problems, in order that national policies may be developed and action taken on the basis of a full awareness of the activities and interests of all the members of NATO. While all members of NATO have a responsibility to consult with their partners on appropriate matters, a large share of responsibility for such consultation rests on the more powerful members of the community.[1]

Much the same could be, and is being, said today both on matters coming within the NATO area and especially on matters that fall outside it. And yet the channels of multilateral consultation have grown considerably, not only between those countries that make up the European Community but also between Western Europe and the United States. Such multilateral channels are, of course, in addition to those bilateral links that the countries of Western Europe have maintained with the United States. The existence of such a multitude of channels raises expectations that consultation will take place. Disappointment and some resentment is often the result when it does not. Equally, perhaps, when consultations do take place, they raise expectations that the views of those being discussed will be taken into account. Again, resentment is caused when they are not.[2]

The fact that multilateral channels are not always used to the full, particularly, but not exclusively, on out-of-area activities, suggests that NATO allies (and EC partners come to that) frequently prefer to rely upon their own initiatives and their own resources, consulting others and calling for their support only when it is necessary. The latter may more often be a matter of necessity for Europeans (French policy in Chad notwithstanding) but even for the United States, unilateral action in the Middle East and North Africa has rarely achieved the results expected or even hoped for. The United States may be indispensable to the peace process in the Middle East and to the maintenance of security but even its powers are circumscribed. At the same time, of course, the countries of Western Europe have both significant interests in the Middle East, not least oil, and have shown a determination to protect them, by one means or another – precisely which means, of course, being a frequent source of conflict in Euro-US relations.

This chapter examines the ways in which the United States and the countries of Western Europe seek to inform, consult and, if necessary, act together in the light of events which directly or indirectly threaten their interests in the Middle East. It focuses therefore on both intra-European cooperation and Euro-US co-operation, the means available to them and the use made of those means. Inevitably, different procedures will be used depending on the nature of the threat, its immediate seriousness and its possible ramifications. Problems in the Union of Arab Emirates (UAE) in 1978, for example, or in Mecca in 1979 led to the brief involvement of the UK and France respectively. The Camp David Accords led both to the Venice Declaration of the ten members of the European Community in 1980 and to the establishment of the Multilateral Force and Observers (MFO) in 1981. The Soviet invasion of Afghanistan led, after a considerable delay, to the introduction of sanctions against the Soviet Union of varying degrees of insignificance; the Iran–Iraq war has led to anxious inaction (except in terms of arms deals). All but the first two cases were discussed at length in the Community and in European Political Cooperation (EPC: the foreign policy coordination process of the members of the European Community as distinct from EEC procedures) and in NATO. It would appear, at least from the UAE case, that relatively minor post-imperial matters tend to be left to the discretion of the former colonial power to deal with unilaterally, unless it raises the issue with others. Other matters are frequently subject to close scrutiny, debate and negotiation among partners or allies or, of course, both. The question then arises of which forum is the most appropriate for which issue. Is there, for example, a rule of thumb which suggests that a crisis in the Middle East which has a strong East–West element to it should be discussed immediately in the NATO framework (although not necessarily exclusively: the Twelve may wish to raise it first or at the same time in EPC), while other issues may more suitably be discussed in another forum, perhaps a purely European one? Or should less critical issues be dealt with bilaterally, with any other European country, or the United States, or more widely, in association with other countries at, for example, the United Nations?

The answer does not, of course, depend only on the seriousness of the threat or its implications for East–West relations; important too will be the type of reaction required. A diplomatic *démarche* may be the most appropriate response, in which case action by the Presidency of EPC might be considered – with or without any supplementary unilateral action by one or more of the Twelve. If any economic instruments of policy are envisaged, such as the withholding of aid or the postponement of trade agreements, then obviously the European Community is involved – with or without any supporting action in terms of declarations by EPC. If any form of military response is envisaged beyond, that is, an interruption in military assistance or the sales of arms, then the Alliance is involved, at least if significant numbers of troops are to be withdrawn from the NATO command for any length of time – with or without any action being taken elsewhere. However, such neatness of course belies reality; a general untidiness in policy formulation predominates, both in Europe and in the United States.

I BILATERAL AND MULTILATERAL APPROACHES TO COORDINATION

The capacity or incapacity to react to a threat to its interests will naturally influence each individual West European state in its attitude toward the various consultation procedures. The military capacities of NATO members are discussed elsewhere in this study; what is significant in the context of multilateral coordination is the willingness and/or ability of each member to use its resources. West Germany, for example, has the military capacity to contribute some forces to out-of-area activities. It is, however, constrained by a much debated constitutional limitation that its forces can only be used on NATO business. Much discussion has therefore taken place over Germany's role within the Alliance in possibly compensating for the temporary withdrawal of other countries' troops, and on the ways in which Germany could use its economic strength. British, French and Italian forces are not subject to any similar constitutional restrictions, and Britain and France have been called upon to fulfil some post-imperial responsibilities, even if they have eschewed, albeit sometimes with reluctance, the role of general international policemen. Both, moreover, have displayed a willingness to use what means have been at their disposal, including military forces if necessary, 'without complexes' as one official put it. Successive Italian governments have gone still further, seeking to heighten their profile in the Middle East, on the ground that the Mediterranean has become a part of the central front of the Alliance with the southern flank now stretching from the Horn of Africa to the Gulf.

The Bilateral Dimension

While such differences of view inevitably make themselves felt in the various international fora, they are also, of course, continuously being questioned, reviewed, refined and perhaps even modified in discussions with other governments on a bilateral basis. Although this chapter will concentrate on multilateral fora, the importance of bilateral relationships in underpinning the multilateral process cannot be under-estimated. A realisation that the bilateral dimension has too often been overlooked in discussions on European integration has led to increased (academic) attention in recent years, reinforced, no doubt, by the growing number of bilateral summits introduced over the last decade.[3] The Franco-German relationship for example has always been seen as of profound importance to the evolution of a more united Europe.[4]

While the UK sought to establish close relations with Germany and often worked in close harmony within NATO and the Western European Union, bilateral ties at the highest level were not established until 1975. Britain's refusal to join, and then its exclusion from, the European Community contributed to the delay. Britain's preoccupation with domestic and budgetary issues then prevented the 1975 agreement from fulfilling many peoples' hopes. Qualitatively, relations between Britain and West Germany, and France and West Germany have been very different, with one West German official quoted as saying that the relationship with the UK was a business partnership and that with France, a marriage.[5] Annual meetings between French and English leaders were established in 1976. Significantly, it was another five years before summit meetings were arranged individually by the UK, France and Germany with Italy.

By that time, the UK, France and Germany were also meeting on a trilateral basis with increasing frequency – and indeed, sometimes with the United States – on issues including Berlin but also stretching very much wider. Italy's exclusion was perhaps most clearly brought home after a series of secret meetings among the Three during 1980 had led to Lord Carrington's visit to Moscow in pursuit of peace in Afghanistan. Italian outrage required that the British Foreign Secretary return via Rome so that the Italian Prime Minister could be fully briefed. Not only, therefore, have bilateral relations to be taken into account, the evolution of a directory of the bigger European states has also had important ramifications, a point taken up in the concluding section of this chapter.

Europe and the United States

European attitudes towards the use of force and, indeed towards coordination with the United States have to be set against both the state of particular bilateral relations between the countries of Western Europe and the United States and the general condition of Euro-US relations. It has become increasingly clear over the last decade that there are differences of interpretation over the nature of the threat to Western interests as well as the best means of protecting them. As Sir Geoffrey Howe gently reminded readers of *Foreign Affairs*: 'The world threat posed by the Soviet Union, its allies and its clients has been clearer than ever. So has the complexity of the sources of instability; the variety of local factors involved and the difficulties of calculating the best Western response in each instance.'[6] Such differences flow perhaps ineluctably from the fact that Europe and the United States have different interests. The Middle East is very much more important to Europe in terms of oil and markets than it is to the United States. The Middle East is also more important to some Europeans than it is to others, which has also caused problems. Each is in competition with the other and subject to various domestic pressures which emphasise national interests above all else. This is common everywhere, although it is a frequent complaint (made not solely by Europeans) that the US is particularly susceptible to domestic lobbies, whether in its treatment of Israel or its approach to, for example, Libya. But the point at issue here is that different perceptions of the threat have caused problems for coordination, especially between Europe and the United States.

There is of course considerable common ground: regional stability,

the maintenance of oil supplies and markets, the denial of the area
to further Soviet influence and the need to combat terrorism could
be and, indeed, have been, agreed as common aims. However, there
have been differences over priorities which inevitably spill over into
policy divergences. The need to try to maintain or re-establish the
territorial integrity of Lebanon in 1982 led as we have seen to the
Multinational Force (MNF). The initial purpose of the MNF may
have been relatively clear, even if the motives which led France and
Italy to participate alongside US troops may not have been identical.
There was very much less identity of purpose to complicate the
position of MNF-II. The rapidity with which the MNFs were
assembled may explain some of the divergences, but at a more
general level, there appears to be little argument on the extent, and
even the desirability, of contingency planning for the use of Western
forces. Among some European governments especially there has
been a belief that too obvious an indulgence in contingency plannings
for the use of force could be counter-productive. Treverton has put
it succinctly:

> Western military force was at best tangential to the real problems
> of stability in the region. Worse, there was the possibility that the
> effort to build that force would become a factor for instability, not
> stability, by identifying friendly Arab states too closely with the
> West in general and the US in particular, thus providing targets
> for internal dissidents.[7]

Thus while there could be general agreement on the three-pronged
approach adopted by the United States, of support for pro-Western
regional powers, direct military sales and assistance, and a commitment to employ force if necessary and at the request of the local
government, the European emphasis has been consistently placed
(British and French actions in Chad or the Falklands notwithstanding)
on preventing the need for force. Given local sensitivities, the stress
on the military options contained in Secretary of State Haig's 'strategic
consensus' was regarded as wholly inappropriate for the Middle East.
The rather more relaxed approach of Shultz eased West–West tension
somewhat after a particularly difficult period. Discussions on an
acceptable division of labour in the Middle East which included a
strong element of burden-sharing among the Allies were none the
less protracted. Moreover, much of the work on facilitation carried
out in NATO, which allowed for overflights and access, appeared to
be of questionable value given the reaction of most European

countries to United States action in Libya in April 1986.

In these as in other negotiations, the countries of Western Europe have, with varying degrees of consistency and intensity, maintained their bilateral links with Washington. They have also, of course, sought to coordinate their views, whether first or at the same time, in a European Community and an EPC context. They have used the NATO forum, and the opportunities provided by the meetings of the Western Economic Summits. Other possibilities have also been suggested, at least for European coordination, such as the use of a revived Western European Union. Such a myriad of opportunities can cause confusion, perhaps even immobility, as discussion in one forum inhibits discussion in another, or disagreement in one spills over into another. Profusion can also encourage bargaining, etc. over a wide variety of issues, with the Americans as well as the Europeans talking sometimes together, sometimes to only one or two others and so on.[8] To discern clear patterns in such circumstances is difficult; pragmatism and '*ad hocery*' appear to be the norm.

II THE EUROPEAN COMMUNITY[9]

Given Europe's emphasis on 'preventive' measures, that is to say, measures designed to encourage and maintain stability in the Middle East, its efforts to coordinate trade and aid policies are of primary importance. The European Community has a wide range of cooperation agreements with the countries of the Maghreb and the Mashreq (Libya being the exception). It is also negotiating an agreement with the Gulf Cooperation Council, a joint ministerial meeting in October 1985 concluding that a comprehensive agreement between the two somewhat disparate bodies was possible and desirable.[10] The Community's Cooperation agreements with the countries of the Mediterranean typically allow for industrial free trade, some, usually limited, agricultural concessions and the provision of aid or access to credit. They also provide for Cooperation Councils as well as, for example, working and export groups.

The Mediterranean Cooperation agreements provide the commercial and aid policy instruments at the disposal of the EC, or, in other words, the armoury of Europe as a 'civilian power'. The concept of a civilian power was suggested in the early 1970s and still has its supporters.[11] But it was also increasingly deprecated and ridiculed as the 1970s wore on.[12] Modest though such instruments obviously are, they have not lain wholly idle. On Israel's invasion of Lebanon, for example, the Community postponed the scheduled meeting of the EC-Israel Cooperation Council and, somewhat more significantly perhaps, delayed signature of a new Financial Protocol. At the same time, the Community and the Ten condemned the invasion, called on Israel to withdraw and offered Lebanon humanitarian aid. That this had little if any effect on Israel's action is incontestable – although no-one else was either able or prepared to exercise enough influence to halt the Israeli invasion.

The Community's efforts have not always been restricted to the postponement of meetings. A very clear example of the Community's use of trade as an instrument of foreign policy (albeit outside the framework of a Cooperation Agreement) was during the Falkland Islands conflict in 1982. Sanctions against Argentinian exports were introduced by the Community under Article 113 of the Treaty of Rome. They were supported by coordinated action on the part of the Ten at the United Nations and, eventually, backed up by the use of force by the UK at which point the consensus began to evaporate.[13] One might conclude that, temporary though such unity of purpose may have been, it is suggestive of what is possible. On the other hand, it could equally well be argued that the Falklands' case was peculiar since it involved aggression against a territorial possession of a Community member state. In other instances of the Community imposing sanctions, against, for example, the Soviet Union over Afghanistan and Poland or against Iran, agreement was achieved only with considerable reluctance and imposed only half-heartedly – and usually at the behest of the United States.[14]

In these latter cases, a number of issues were at stake beyond the value of the trade involved or the possible effects of its embargo on member state economies. Most importantly, they revealed a fundamental difference between the United States and most Europeans over the principle of sanctions and their efficacy as a foreign policy instrument. Few Europeans believe that sanctions have the desired impact on the recalcitrant state and most hold that the greater effect is likely to be felt by the country imposing the embargo. Sanctions have greater value as a symbol of involvement and commitment. Such an argument was regarded as particularly applicable in the case of sanctions against the Soviet Union. It has been less convincing, especially in US eyes, in the case of Libya. The inability of the Community to agree on economic sanctions as part of a package of measures to bring about the end of Libya's role in international terrorism was seen in the United States as a sign of major weakness and raised once again deep disquiet over the Euro-US relationship and the future of the Atlantic Alliance.

At a more mundane procedural level, the growing number of occasions on which sanctions have been discussed in the Community indicated most clearly the impossibility of divorcing external economic relations from foreign policy. While highlighted in emergencies, the intimate linkage of the two has been increasingly recognised and accepted by the member states.[15] The use of aid and trade policies to supplement and extend diplomatic or other moves has been marked at all levels. Since 1974, for example, the Community has been involved in the so-called Euro-Arab Dialogue, which was set up in the aftermath of the Arab oil embargo, within the framework of European Political Cooperation. The dialogue had a useful role from the point of view of the Nine, in maintaining high-level links with the Arab League, while concentrating as far as possible on economic and technical issues, of industrial development and energy supplies and on cultural relations. For the Arabs, while such cooperation was seen as useful, it was none the less secondary to the political thrust of the dialogue, the reason why it was coordinated within the EPC rather than the EC framework. Progress has been limited even at the technical and cultural levels. The Ministerial meeting agreed to in principle for 1980 fell victim to the disarray within the Arab League after the Camp David Agreement and the expulsion of Egypt from the Arab League.

In the Mediterranean context, too, the usefulness of the Community's cooperation agreements have been reinforced by the growing habit of adding a 'political' dimension to meetings of Cooperation Councils. In May 1982, for example, the Belgian President of the Council of Ministers used the meeting of the EC–Egypt Cooperation Council to hold a discussion with the Egyptians on the situation after the death of President Sadat. Similarly, when France held the Presidency, Cheysson (then French Foreign Minister) invited his colleagues to discuss Middle East issues with the Israeli Foreign Minister after the formal sessions of the EC–Israel Cooperation Council. This general trend towards the closer integration of the economic and political dimensions of external relations was formalised in the EPC's London Report of 1981.

While Community policy is formally determined by the Council of Ministers on the basis of proposals put forward by the European Commission, a distinction has always been made between external economic relations, a Community responsibility, and foreign policy, a perogative of the member states. The latter have, of course, been attempting to coordinate their foreign policies (see part III of this chapter) but the Commission, initially at least, was largely excluded from the procedures of EPC. The greater recognition of the interrelationship between EC and EPC business allowed for the fuller involvement of the Commission in the workings of EPC, an involvement specifically referred to in the 1981 London Report and in the 1986 Single European Act. One consequence of this has been that the Commission's views, determined not only by its particular area of competence but based also on its own sources of information, have been brought to bear in both Community and EPC contexts. The Commission's sources of information are extensive: there are now Commission delegates in most of the countries of the Middle East and there is also an Information Office in Washington, a most useful addition given the diverse sources of intelligence on US policy. Conversely, most Middle East countries have some form of representation to the Community in Brussels, as does the United States. The Commission's increased involvement in EPC has added an extra dimension, in that an official in the US Mission to the Communities now has specific responsibility for EPC affairs.

At another level, the artificial distinctions between EC and EPC matters which plagued the Nine during the 1970s and which may have confused and bemused those with whom Europe negotiated, rarely inhibited the European Parliament from discussing both. The European Parliament (or at least a majority of its members) has also been to the fore in calling for a greater European security and defence identity, particularly by using its right of 'own initiative' to institute debates and reports.[16] In this way the Parliament has sought to involve itself as fully as possible in policy debates and in setting at least the wider framework within which policy is actually decided, thereby enhancing its own position. This is not the place to discuss the development of the European Parliament or to exaggerate its present role, although it is probably held to have greater influence on policy by those outside Europe. Nevertheless, the Parliament has been extremely active. Its reports, and the resolutions that have accompanied them, have not only been in response to specific events in the Middle East such as the invasion of Afghanistan, the Iran–Iraq war and the situation in the Lebanon; they have also sought to encourage the member states of the Community to play a full part in forwarding the peace process (as in, for example, the Pender's Report of 1982),[17] to coordinate their policies in protecting the sea lanes (as in the Diligent Report of 1981),[18] and to coordinate national policies on arms sales, this as part of a wider development in both the industrial and the security fields (as in the Ferguson Report of 1982).[19]

The European Parliament has sought to play a wider international role by means other than reports and resolutions. It has, for example, attracted widespread attention by offering itself as a public platform. A number of heads of state and government have been invited to address it, among them President Sadat in 1981 and President Reagan. The impact of these speeches may have been limited, although that of President Sadat created additional complications for the Euro-Arab dialogue. In addition, the Parliament has maintained close links with other parliaments. Meetings of delegates from the European Parliament and from Congress, the latter often including Committee chairmen, take place twice a year and a report of their work is published as an official document of Congress. The meetings have generally provided a useful forum for wide-ranging and informal discussions.

III THE EUROPEAN POLITICAL COOPERATION[20]

The Middle East has played a highly significant role in the development of EPC even if the efforts made by the member states to coordinate their views and positions have not always been successful.[21] The EPC process itself is usually characterised as one of gradualism and incrementalism; since it is based on consensus, it necessarily moves at the pace of the slowest. Several member states were initially reluctant to forgo orthodox Community decision making, although for the most part the critics were reconciled by the end of the 1970s, in part because of EPC's seeming success (relative at least to the Community) and also because of the gradual breakdown of the barriers between EPC and Community decision making referred to above. For Italy, as well as some of the smaller member states, EPC became a particularly valuable part of their foreign policy. This was clearly revealed on the part of the smaller countries by their willingness to indulge in what has been described as 'political tourism', frequent fact-finding missions in the Middle East.[22] For West Germany, EPC has had additional value in providing a vital Western framework to its policy to complement its *Ostpolitik*. For the British and French, the situation has been slightly different; while both have developed what might be described as an EPC reflex, EPC has been regarded essentially as an additional means of preserving their international status.[23] Lord Carrington's Presidency of the Council of Ministers in 1981 provides a good illustration of the British case; he unsuccessfully sought a particularly active role over Afghanistan and, equally unsuccessfully, in the Middle East peace process.

Events in the Middle East have all too often revealed the vulnerability and the impotence of the European member states, and this has inevitably been reflected in EPC. The Middle East has, perforce, been on EPC's agenda since the beginning, with all levels, from working group to the European Council, involved. Much has been written in the context of EPC on the value of exchanging information, the primary task of the many working groups of EPC. It is, clearly, extremely useful both for smaller states whose own resources may be limited and for the larger, in providing a broad picture of mutual concerns and priorities. However, the transparent inability of the Ten to react with any promptness or coherence to the Soviet invasion of Afghanistan showed only too clearly the limitations of the process when governments are caught off guard and unprepared. There is no effective forward planning within the EPC structure; even the meetings of national planning staffs appear limited in their results, in part because they do not all have the same planning focus nor do they all carry the same weight. Little provision (particularly in terms of time) is made for the correspondents, the political directors, or Foreign Ministers to look far ahead, except perhaps at the latters' more informal 'Gymnich-type' weekend meetings.[24]

Afghanistan, however, did achieve one breakthrough; it led to agreement on measures to be taken in times of crisis. While discussions on crisis management had been held intermittently since 1974, the London Report of 1981 outlined certain procedural measures to be adopted: a meeting of political directors and/or Foreign Ministers had to take place within three days if so requested by three member states. Although perhaps not formally used in 1982 over the Israeli invasion of Lebanon as Foreign Ministers were already together to discuss other matters,[25] the procedure was used twice in 1986, first to deal with the question of sanctions against Libya, and then with the aftermath of US action. In each case (and in that of the Falklands which also involved emergency procedures) the role of the Presidency was highly significant in responding to the request for a meeting and preparing for it.

EPC–US Coordination

While the inevitable conclusion must be that procedures are no substitute for policy, they can, in some cases help to facilitate agreement or, in others, help to contain disagreement. A myriad of procedural channels and devices exists by which the Europeans within EPC and the United States can inform or consult each other on issues of mutual interest and importance. The Middle East in fact played an important part in setting up the most important, the so-called 'Gymnich formula' agreed in 1974, i.e. in the aftermath of the disastrous results of the Year of Europe that had been launched by Henry Kissinger in 1973.[26] Under the Gymnich formula, the Presidency of the Council or its designated representative meets US officials to discuss the agenda for the forthcoming meeting of the Political Committee. The Presidency then relays US views to the Committee and, finally, reports back on the meeting to the US.

The formula was deliberately designed as a flexible response to US concern over the evolution of EPC. Once it was accepted, and once, it has been suggested, the US realised how limited agreement was in EPC, US attitudes became more relaxed. In addition, there are frequent contacts between US embassies and the government holding the Presidency and between the embassy of the Presidency and the US State Department, particularly at the beginning of each six-month term of office. There are also the meetings in New York between the caucus of EPC member states and the US Mission at the United Nations, usually held in September. Significantly, perhaps, it was only in 1982 that more institutionalised meetings at Political Director level became established, although they are still not formalised in any declaration or agreement. Luncheon meetings and many other more informal discussions are also held. This growing frequency of meetings and increased familiarity with procedural devices have overcome some of the irritation and bewilderment – though perhaps not all – aroused when interlocutors change twice a year and sometimes appear in formations of three under the so-called troika system.[27]

In the EPC process, therefore, the Presidency is central. Its role goes beyond that of being an interlocutor; it is both manager and administrator in addition, tasks which have sometimes fallen particularly heavily upon the smaller member states.[28] During any Presidency, much depends on the policies of each member government, the commitment of the Foreign Minister, and the

organisational support provided. Continuity cannot therefore be
assured, although the introduction of a small Political Secretariat
now that the Single European Act formalising the political role of
the European Community is ratified may well make a contribution.
As yet, since the Presidency is held only for six months and is far
from being the sole interlocutor between Europe and the US, a weak
or inactive Presidency need not have any great impact. (This is
especially true since the introduction of the troika principle of the
immediately past and immediately succeeding Presidencies assisting
the incumbent.)

IV   THE WESTERN EUROPEAN UNION[29]

With the agreement on the London Report in 1981, EPC appeared
to have reached a certain plateau. The need for the closer integration
of EPC and EC procedures had been recognised – even if every
effort was made to continue their separation in Atlantic relations.
What was lacking was agreement on how to develop EPC further.
Many governments sought to bring about a closer identity on defence
and security policies within the EPC framework. The Genscher–
Colombo initiative of 1981 gave expression to this but it resulted only
in the Solemn Declaration of 1983 which went little further than the
London Report.[30] The need for unanimity prevented anything more
being agreed. Given the seeming impasse in EPC, an existing if
somewhat neglected organisation with a specific mandate to discuss
security issues suddenly appeared more attractive and ripe for revival:
Western European Union (WEU).

   While WEU needs to be considered because of its Treaty responsibilities in the defence field, it remains of potential value only despite
its already long history. Moreover, there are a number of limitations
on even a potential role, the most important of which is that under
its Treaty, its defence functions were largely transferred to NATO
in order to avoid duplication. Furthermore, the first task given to the
institution after its revival in 1984 was that of bringing about a
coordinated response to the Strategic Defense Initiative of President
Reagan. It was one almost guaranteed to deflate those optimistic
about a new role; it was clear at the outset that agreement was
impossible.

   If, therefore, against current odds, the revival of WEU proceeds, there will be certain problems, not least of coordination *vis-à-vis* EPC and NATO. If successful, WEU will, of course, attract greater attention from non-members, especially but not exclusively those who are also members of EPC and NATO. Portugal has already submitted an application to join; others may follow. Some, for example, Turkey, may regard it as a half-way house between NATO and EPC, much as it was regarded for a short while in 1968 by the British and Germans before the French defeated the idea. But while the enlargement of WEU might be its undoing, the rationale for WEU's revival – that the Seven are 'like-minded' and therefore will be able to act in unison more often – might also be questioned. Under Article 5 of the WEU Treaty, of course, the guarantee of aid and assistance is more automatic than in NATO. But this is confined to attacks in Europe. The question of any threat to the member states' interests outside Europe therefore remains open. Moreoever, while six of the seven members might provide forces on an individual basis in pursuit of a policy discussed within the WEU Council (although it is difficult to imagine the WEU being used either primarily or exclusively as a forum for discussion or vehicle for any action) there remains the constitutional limitation on West German forces being deployed outside Europe.

In some respects therefore the WEU might already be too large. The spectre, if not the existence, of a smaller directory of three or four states is no new phenomenon. Italy and the Benelux countries have been irritated in the past by the actions or concerted positions of the other three. WEU, as yet at least, does not provide an institutional framework sufficiently compelling to counter-balance the forces making for a directory.

The prospect of WEU's revival none the less re-aroused a concern in the United States that a more formalised caucus was to be established with a built-in anti-American bias. This was in part because of the timing of the initiative and in part, too, because the initiative appeared to be a French one; a profound suspicion of France appears to permeate the US policy-making machinery. It is perhaps ironic that one of the motives for reviving WEU – cited by Mitterand as well as others – was to demonstrate to US opinion, particularly in Congress, that Europe was taking defence matters seriously.

As yet, WEU remains marginal. By 1986, despite the considerable energy of its Secretary General, Cahen, the revival seemed to have fulfilled its gesticulatory purpose. And yet its potential remains. If demands for a closer defence identity revive, it exists; it does not have to be re-invented.

V THE ATLANTIC ALLIANCE[31]

This chapter began with a quotation from a NATO report prepared in 1951, then repeated in 1956 by the Three Wise Men in their report on non-military cooperation. The latter came after one of the worst examples of division among the Allies, and one caused by a crisis in the Middle East, Suez. The Three Wise Men went on to recommend that: 'a member government should not, without adequate advance consultation, adopt firm policies or make major political pronouncements on matters which significantly affect the Alliance or any of its members unless circumstances make such prior consultation obviously and demonstrably impossible.'[32] There is no need here to go into the history of the Alliance and the reasons why it was restricted to the North Atlantic areas and stretched only to the northern littoral of the Mediterranean. There are now many – not all concentrated in the Pentagon – who perhaps rue the logic of the United States' earlier anti-colonialism. But it was not only a question of avoiding any entanglement in Europe's colonial problems. The initial proliferation of commands in the Mediterranean region reflected 'less the primacy of their roles than the conflict over their missions';[33] they were very much the product of Anglo-French and US rivalries. But although other areas were clearly regarded as peripheral to the European front, it was acknowledged almost from the beginning that events 'out-of-area', particularly in the Middle East, could intrude onto the NATO agenda. In many ways, Suez, by far the most difficult out-of-area issue for the Allies to resolve, symbolised the eclipse of the traditional great powers of the region. In replacing them, the superpowers created a new strategic balance that inevitably affected Europe. However, while most of the NATO allies recognised the growing significance of the possible threats to their security in the Middle East, there was, and as we have seen, there remains, little agreement on what should be done about them – beyond, that is, to inform and consult each other 'in accordance with established usage' as the Report of 1967 put it.[34] NATO, in other words, provides a forum for discussion; it does not provide a basis for action.

The Consultative Framework

An elaborate system for discussion and consultation has gradually been built up over the decades of NATO's existence. At Ministerial level, for example, there are the twice-yearly meetings of Foreign Ministers in the Atlantic Council and of Defence Ministers in the Defence Planning Committee. The meetings of Foreign Ministers have also been supplemented since 1982 by more informal gatherings similar in a sense to the Gymnich meetings of EPC Ministers, which were introduced because, as one Canadian commentator put it, 'Consultations in Brussels have grown too stately'.[35] There are then the Permanent Representatives and their deputies who meet weekly and regional expert groups that meet half-yearly. In addition, there is the Atlantic Policy Advisers Group (APAG) made up of representatives from national planning staffs. While this is subject to some of the limitations of the group of planners within EEC, it has been described by one enthusiastic participant as 'unique', in that its meetings: 'provide the only opportunity where national views on important trends and developments can be discussed in their long-term perspectives within the framework of the Alliance'.[36] Unfortunately, APAG meets only annually.

Within the Alliance-wide system, the European Allies have also evolved their own consular procedures, especially among Defence Ministers, notably the Eurogroup and the Independent European Programme Group (IEPG). While both, particularly the IEPG, were designed to improve and encourage closer collaboration in relation to armaments, the Eurogroup has retained much of its original informal character (it was established in 1968 at the dinner table of the then British Permanent Representative to NATO, Sir Bernard Burrows) and its discussions have therefore ranged somewhat wider. However, Eurogroup itself has certain limitations to its effectiveness. Most importantly, France rejected membership of the Eurogroup from the outset; it was, after all, established only two years after the French had withdrawn from the integrated military structure of NATO. And although France became a member of the IEPG (on the condition that it was entitled the 'Independent' European Programme Group), it has continued to stand aloof from the Euro-Group. France's absence has inevitably blunted the political impact it could make. In addition, while the Eurogroup provides a valuable informal forum for the exchange of views among Defence Ministers other than the French, there has been a reluctance to move too far –

at least publicly – into more 'foreign policy' fields. Nevertheless, the Eurogroup has been in a useful position to discuss such issues as facilitation and compensation and to put its views forward to the Americans. The latter has been regarded as a particularly important part of its functions. Michael Heseltine, for example, wrote an appreciative piece on the Eurogroup in 1984 when he was British Defence Minister, pointing out that: 'One of the principal concerns of the Eurogroup has been to ensure not only that the Europeans play a full part in the strengthening of the Alliance's military capabilities, but that that contribution is fully recognised and understood in North America.'[37]

The Alliance and Its Divisions

In picking out the need to explain Europe's role in the defence system, Heseltine reflected a growing concern over the divisions within the Alliance. Although the various groups, committees and the Council have provided the opportunities for discussion, there remains a problem of understanding and/or of acceptance of the differing perceptions of the Soviet threat both in Europe and more globally. While the Soviet invasion of Afghanistan diverted attention towards out-of-area activities, the longer-term reactions of the Allies need to be set alongside other causes of disquiet within the Alliance. A number of issues had arisen that gave concern, particularly the dual-track decision on INF modernisation and the situation in Poland. The INF modernisation, however much a European initiative, was increasingly surrounded by political difficulties – with a breakdown of the 'defence consensus' and the emergence of the peace movements. In addition, there was a growing tension in and about Poland and the role and continued survival of Solidarity. The imposition of martial law in December 1981 caught the West largely off-guard once again and *inter alia* led to the interruption of the Madrid follow-up meeting of the Conference on Security and Cooperation in Europe, with West–West differences being aired almost as loudly as East–West differences. These 'European' problems were important in creating an atmosphere that was far from conducive to an enthusiastic acceptance of US leadership outside Europe. There was, in a sense, a belief that NATO in Europe had enough problems to face without being asked to tackle others.

But the Soviet invasion of Afghanistan could hardly be ignored. The problem was, as usual, what to do about it. On the one hand, the Allies' lack of preparedness and consequent disunity created a widespread recognition that a somewhat greater commitment to, at the very least, full and timely consultations was required. The British White Paper of 1980 summed up the attitude of most of the Allies when it declared:

> changes in many areas of the world, together with growing military readiness to exploit it directly or indirectly, make it increasingly necessary for NATO members to look to Western security concerns over a wider field than before, and not assume that these concerns can be limited by the boundaries of the Treaty area.[38]

On the other hand, it remained a question of 'looking to' out-of-area security concerns rather than a commitment to any significant action. Then, and again in 1986 over the US strike against Libya, Administrations on both sides of the Atlantic must suffer a strong sense of *deja vu*. When, for example, only Portugal of the European Allies had allowed the United States to use refuelling and other facilities during the Yom Kippur War of 1973, intense irritation had been caused and charges of cravenness levied, but the consequence then, as later, was a call for further consultation. Under the Ottawa Declaration of 1974, the Allies had agreed:

> to keep each other fully informed and to strengthen the practice of frank and timely consultations by all means which may be appropriate on matters relating to their common interests as members of the Alliance, bearing in mind that these interests can be affected by events in other areas of the world.[39]

In general, it might be said, protestations on the need to consult increase as European and US attitudes diverge. The efforts made in the aftermath of the Soviet invasion of Afghanistan to bring about closer cooperation within EPC were not matched at the NATO level. Nearly all the members of the Alliance (the Greeks being somewhat out on a limb) agreed that after the invasion it could not be a case of 'business as usual' with the Soviet Union. However, few other than the United States were convinced of the appropriateness and efficacy of sanctions against the Soviet Union. It was the same in the aftermath of the imposition of martial law in Poland, when the situation among the Allies was made even worse by the Administration's efforts to extend US jurisdiction over European corporations. As the *Report on the Allied Contribution to the Common Defense* put it in 1982:

United States and European views on how best to counter the Soviet threat remain divergent, in spite of major United States efforts over the past year to portray the threat graphically to European elites and publics . . . Europeans believe Soviet policy can be moderated through traditional forms of social, economic and political contact. They are less enthusiastic than the United States about the build up of military force as a counter to the Soviet challenge.[40]

For Europeans, such a military emphasis gave rise to considerable concern. This was especially the case when, in addition, the US appeared insistent that *détente* was indivisible – the logic of that meant re-importing tension into Europe. The prospect was profoundly unwelcome not least because of the widespread belief that *détente* had brought very real (and not only tangible) benefits to Europe. Yet as one German commentator suggested, the reverse of the US argument that *détente* was indivisible was that tension, too, should be indivisible.[41] Nor was there any question for the Europeans of extending the NATO area to encompass the Middle East. European and US interests appeared too divergent, as were perceptions of the threat to them. European governments have tended to take a very much more pragmatic view of the factors creating instability. And, at the Bonn NATO Summit of 1982, their views appeared to predominate since – at least in terms of the official communiqué – greater prominence was given to the Allies' purpose of working 'to remove the causes of instability such as underdevelopment or tensions which can encourage outside interference . . .' rather than to military measures.[42]

Such attitudes reinforced the concern of many in the US already perturbed by Europe's defence posture. For some Americans, the European argument that *détente* could be 'divisible' had profoundly adverse consequences on opinion in the US, consequences according to one commentator that 'have undermined the shared sense of danger that was the alliance's original *raison d'être*'.[43] It was no longer a question of Congress looking askance at Europe's contribution to its own defence, it was now resentful that Europe was seemingly unprepared to protect its interests elsewhere. The position was put most succinctly by Irving Kristol who declared: 'If American force intervenes somewhere and our European Allies simply stay aloof, there will be overwhelming support in Congress and public opinion for the removal of American troops from Western Europe.'[44]

The proposal put forward by Senator Nunn for a conditional troop withdrawal from Europe reflected such a mood – although equally importantly, it also sought to stave off pressures for withdrawals and even more fundamental changes in NATO that were not contingent on Europes' increasing its defence expenditure.[45]

The Nunn Amendment gave rise to considerable resentment in Europe as well as concern. While Europeans had frequently complained that their position was misunderstood, the Nunn Amendment appeared to mark a significantly deeper lack of understanding. Efforts were made, therefore, especially by Europeans, both to damp down thoughts of a crisis in the Alliance and to explain Europe's position more clearly (by means of articles in US journals, etc.).[46] The revival of WEU was also, in part, a response.

However, it was also clear that more had to be seen to be done by the Europeans. In the immediate aftermath of the invasion, President Carter had made clear that he would expect a great deal from the European Allies if there was a direct threat to Gulf oil supplies. Some measures were indeed undertaken by Europe. According to Caspar Weinberger, in his 1983 *Report on the Allied Contribution*, a number of measures had been taken since Afghanistan such as: the deployment of forces in the Middle East by France, Italy and the UK; closer security arrangements in the region had been undertaken by Britain in Oman and France in Djibouti; UK support in the use of Diego Garcia; and over-flight rights, shipping supplementation, etc. had been discussed.[47] The list was neither particularly long nor perhaps particularly impressive and did little to silence the critics.

NATO and the South-west Asia Impact Study

Other steps were also taken. After Afghanistan, Robert Komer, then US Under-Secretary of Defense, had told his NATO colleagues that he would expect them 'to take up the slack' in Europe if US forces were required elsewhere.[48] And as Weinberger was reported as saying in 1982:

> I have said many times that I think NATO should begin to plan for this possibility in the Middle East . . . because access to the oil fields is vital . . . I think just ordinary contingency advance planning would dictate that NATO give some consideration to the possibility that some of its forces may be needed there.[49]

The result eventually was the South-west Asia Impact Study. It is, so far, the only example of contingency planning for out-of-area activities.[50] The study is also based on a worst-case scenario that war is being fought in Europe as well as in the Middle East, so that forces would not be withdrawn from Europe but reinforcements from the United States might be sent to the Middle East, in which case Europe would have to compensate for them.

The study outlines the measures that could and/or should be taken, including logistic as well as combatant support. Given the supposition that those with forces capable of being deployed elsewhere might have to deploy them, many of the compensatory measures fall particularly to West Germany to implement. In addition to outlining the measures that might need to be taken, the study also deals with the mechanics of bringing them about, including, of course, the issue of communications and consultation. Since the study deals with decisions on out-of-area activities, consultation is to be on a bilateral basis rather than an Alliance-wide one. As the communiqué issued after the Lisbon Atlantic Council Meeting in June 1985 put it, the Allies:

> will engage in timely consultations on such events if it is established that their common interests are involved. Sufficient military capabilities must be assured in the Treaty area to maintain an adequate defense posture. Allies who are in a position to do so will endeavor to support those sovereign nations who request assistance in countering threats to their security and independence. Those Allies in a position to facilitate the deployment of forces outside the Treaty area may do so, on the basis of national decision.[51]

Useful though the South-west Asia Impact Study may have been, both in terms of breaking new ground and in concentrating the Allied mind, the approach remains a pragmatic one. Moreoover, the study is based on a worst-case scenario; questions, perhaps doubts, remain about Allied reactions over the whole gamut of cases up to the worst, including those suggested elsewhere in these papers. All that has been agreed, as one British defence official put it:

> is for the Allied members of the Alliance acting as Allied members but not the Alliance (and that is the distinction that is drawn) and obviously [sic] one cannot apply therefore the same processes of planning and operational exercises, training and so forth in that regard as one could to the normal NATO force requirements.[52]

Force requirements resulting from the study have indeed been 'folded into' requirements, yet the Allies on both sides of the Atlantic have very carefully eschewed committing themselves in advance to precise actions. While there remains such differences in approach to Middle East issues, such a reluctance is inevitable.

The extent of such differences was clearly shown in the reactions to the Libyan strike. It was none the less, surprising, and to United States opinion shocking, that despite the work done on out-of-area activities and the intense exchanges of information and views, the Alliance should have fallen apart quite so spectacularly. There had, of course, been differences in the past over US policies towards Libya. But it had been felt in the US that there had also been increasing common ground with Europe on the need to counter terrorism, and to use the NATO forum as part of the effort – particularly after NATO itself bacame the target of terrorist activity. And yet it was clear that intergovernmental cooperation was being discussed and introduced only hesitantly. This was in part because of national sensitivities about their own security forces but it was also because a number of governments were not convinced that NATO was the most appropriate forum, even for discussion.[53]

Should NATO be Reformed?

It is interesting to note in such circumstances that the Rapporteur of the North Atlantic Assembly's committee which looked into out-of-area activities, Herrero Rodriquez de Minon, found little dissatis-faction with existing consultation procedures.[54] Others have been somewhat less sanguine, regarding them as far from adequate even as a basis for full discussion, let alone for action. Still others have been even more critical, suggesting a need for a profound reorganisation of the Alliance. According to Sir C. Rose, a former British Permanent Representative to NATO, the Alliance has 'failed to work out an accepted basis for genuine consultation' about how to deal with out-of-area issues.[55] He has therefore made a number of suggestions such as the establishment of a link between EPC and NATO, regular summits and the greater use of *ad hoc* groupings (discussed below).

But there are a number of problems which make for discord and suspicion that are not easily resolved. One such problem, to which, among others, General Farrar-Hockley has drawn attention, is the position of SACEUR. SACEUR, who is also Commander-in-Chief of US Forces in Europe, might:

be required to take overall command of contingency forces sent to, for example, the Near East because his national fief is more extensive than his Allied one. This arrangement not only gives hostages to the opponents of NATO but intermittently an uneasy feeling also to those wholly committed to it. The fact that the incumbents, past and present, of the dual appointments have never compromised the integrity of either makes no difference. The arrangement occasions friction. It inhibits the evolution of planning for out-of-area activities.[56]

General Rogers was, of course, in command of US forces during the strike against Libya. It was significant that because of the known hostility of the European Allies to military action, he did not as a matter of policy inform Lord Carrington, the Secretary-General, in order not to compromise him. One proposal to overcome the problem was that put forward by Henry Kissinger in a *Time* article in March 1984 that there should be a European SACEUR and a US Secretary-General.[57] The proposal, designed to show more clearly Europe's commitment to its own defence, was not considered particularly helpful at the time. It remains unattractive, especially to those concerned about the pressures for US 'de-coupling'.

However, Kissinger's articles and speeches retain a certain authority and need therefore to be considered. In drawing a distinction between the blow dealt to Europe by the United States in 1956 at Suez, and Europe's blow to the United States in 1986, he wrote:

> When the United States thwarted Europe a generation ago, it was accelerating an inevitable process of decolonization. When Europe disassociates itself from the United States today, it challenges a concept of global defense and therefore, indirectly, the psychological basis for American commitments even to the defense of Europe.[58]

Such statements – and Kissinger's formulation is by no means an extreme one – raise once again the issue that it is not simply a question of events outside the NATO area affecting the security of NATO members by interrupting oil supplies or whatever; it is also a question of those same events affecting the continuation of NATO in its present form. Another of Kissinger's proposals was to set up a high level group of the European participants of the Western economic summits together with the US (Canada appears to have been consigned to limbo) under Lord Carrington's chairmanship to examine Euro-US differences on out-of-area issues. Whether or not the work of such a group would be helpful, Western economic summits themselves have begun to tackle some of the issues raised, including terrorism.

VI THE WESTERN ECONOMIC SUMMITS

Western economic summits need to be included in a discussion of Euro-US processes and procedures because of their growing political significance. Early summit meetings were fairly strictly confined to economic issues, important and relevant though these might be from the point of view of this study (*viz*, consideration of energy issues at both the Bonn and Tokyo summits). More 'political' discussions were limited to bilateral meetings among Heads of Government or very much to the margins of the meeting. This pattern began to change after 1979, in part because the Heads of Government not invited by France to the meeting in Guadeloupe in that year were determined to prevent an inner political directory being established from among their number. The Soviet invasion of Afghanistan also played a part. None the less, discussion of political issues remained limited, largely because of the attitude of successive French Presidents.

The French position appears somewhat paradoxical. On the one hand, there is the French propensity to seek to settle the 'big' issues at the highest political level. In order that this should be possible, heads of government need the maximum freedom of manoeuvre; they should not, that is, be subject to limitations imposed by over-detailed preparatory work of the kind that was demanded by, for example, President Carter. On the other hand, the French have been suspicious that the United States might attempt to 'bounce' an issue through a meeting if preparations have not been thorough enough.

Others of the seven industrialised countries of the West have been very much more favourably disposed to political discussions. At the London Summit of 1984, for example, largely at the insistence of Margaret Thatcher and despite French reluctance, international terrorism was discussed. The result on that occasion was a somewhat patchy document that reflected a lack of consensus although it listed a number of general areas which 'found support'.[59]

Terrorism featured even more prominently at the summit of 1986 in Tokyo. Again, at least according to the English press, Thatcher was particularly active in pursuing agreement.[60] Certainly, in the aftermath of the US action against Libya and the acrimonious exchanges it had given rise to, most participants were resolved to give at least the impression of unity restored. Most were also keen to declare their determination to step up the fight against terrorism, the Japanese having perhaps most doubts about the statement that was issued. That they eventually agreed on a joint statement – that included naming Libya as a sponsor and supporter of terrorism – endorsed a general conclusion on the usefulness of the summits: that they tie the Japanese into the political as well as the economic debate. The French, who could have been expected to register at least disquiet, appeared somewhat muted. Led by Mitterand, with Chirac also present, they appeared constrained by the pressures of the 'co-habitation' of a Socialist President and a right-wing Prime Minister. Both, moreover, favoured rebuilding bridges with the United States after their refusal to allow US planes to fly over France during the strike against Libya. As Mitterand was reported to say: 'France, while ever vigilant of its sovereignty, did not want a crisis in relations with the United States.'[61]

The statement on terrorism, while obviously a compromise document, was one much tougher than many had expected (including, it appears, the so-called 'sherpas', the officials who were responsible for drawing up initial drafts of communiqués, etc.). It did not, as perhaps the United States had still hoped, include support for economic sanctions. None the less it was welcomed by the United States as endorsing its policy towards Libya. The statement itself included the pledge 'to take maximum efforts' to fight terrorism; to collaborate with others in relevant international organisations; increase the exchange of information; deny opportunities and means to terrorists; refuse to export arms to states sponsoring or supporting terrorists; place strict limits on the size of diplomatic and other missions; and to deny entry to those expelled for terrorist activities by another state. It ended with a plea for the closest possible bilateral and multilateral cooperation.

Although increasingly familiar in the international network, Western economic summits, because they are only annual events and involve heads of government, continue to arouse certain expectations that agreements will emerge. The wish to meet such popular or media demands has variable strengths but few heads of government are totally immune from it. At the same time, of course, summits provide the opportunity not only for heads of government to meet but also Finance Ministers and Foreign Ministers as well as many top officials from national capitals and the European Community. Preparations at all levels have become generally extensive. Such institutionalisation may undermine the original purpose of a frank exchange of views among leaders of the Western World. On the other hand, the summits continue to demand time and effort and therefore attention. They continue, as one official has suggested:

> to serve as a regular reminder of common interests in trans-Atlantic relations which transcend specific differences; they offer a channel at the highest level between the European Community and the United States; and they help to guard against a return to the mistrust and the frustration which marked Dr. Kissinger's abortive 'Year of Europe'.[62]

VII MULTINATIONAL COORDINATION IN PAST CRISES

The Multinational Forces and Observers

It was only with considerable difficulty, and after some highly charged exchanges between Carrington and Haig, that the Reagan Administration achieved its objective of European participation in the MFO. Lord Carrington, via the Presidency, had attempted to distance both the UK and the Ten from the Camp David process, to the extent that the United States had to exercise no little pressure on the Israelis to accept European contingents. US pressure on Europe was equally clear, although a number of other factors were also involved. The French, for example, agreed largely because a more sympathetic attitude had been adopted towards Camp David – as part of a wider peace settlement – by the newly-elected French President, Francois Mitterand. It was a view that the President and several of his leading ministers sought to explain very carefully to Arab leaders, including Mubarak. The Italian position, under the generally pro-US government of Spadolini (he was to show his Atlanticism even more strongly over the *Achille Lauro* affair when his temporary resignation threatened to bring down the government of Craxi), was favourable to participation although certain conditions were mooted, including endorsement by the Ten. The Dutch position was partly determined by memories of the oil embargo of 1973/74. It was also complicated by difficulties with the US over cruise and

Pershing missiles which suggested that it would be politic to receive
the US request for Dutch participation sympathetically. In addition,
the Dutch agreed to take part in order to forestall what appeared to
be the emergence of a directory of the larger member states. To this
end, the Dutch also insisted that participation had to be endorsed by
all the member states of the Community.[63]

. An endorsement by the Ten was complicated by a number of
factors but most notably by the positions taken by Greece and
Ireland. The newly-elected Greek Government of Papandreou was
generally pro-Arab, and was determined to remain in the vanguard,
as it were, on the question of Palestine. The Irish Government had a
very different problem which stemmed from its dislike of any peace-
keeping activities outside the strict framework provided by the
United Nations. A consensus was finally achieved under the British
Presidency in November 1981, largely on the ground that for the
Europeans to be unable to reply to the invitation to participate would
undermine any credibility that the Venice Declaration had won in
the Middle East. Thus, in addition to the individual statements of
the four participating states, the Ten, somewhat weakly and with
obvious reluctance, gave their endorsement.[64] The actual basis on
which the peace-keeping forces were provided remained an individual
one, with each of the four member states negotiating directly with
the US on the units to be contributed.

The Multinational Force in Lebanon

The way in which MNF was formed bore only slight similarity to that
establishing the MFO, which suggests that the impact of the latter
experience had been limited. The parts to be played by national
contingents were worked out bilaterally with the United States and,
of course, with the Lebanese Government. But whereas nearly all
European governments had been reluctant to participate in the MFO,
both France and Italy were favourable to the US initiative to establish
the MNF, as were the British, although they contributed no forces
to the first MNF because of their commitments elsewhere (particularly
the Falklands). The role of EPC was also limited. According to one
observer: the positive responses to proposals for a multinational force
in Lebanon came as quickly as they did in part because of the
prior vetting of the question in political cooperation.[65] Certainly, the
MNF fitted into the parameters set by EPC declarations, whether
those of Foreign Ministers or of heads of government – with the

French especially to the fore in pressing for agreement on the conditions for the withdrawal of Israeli and Palestinian forces. However, there was no statement that gave formal endorsement to the MNF. Even after the Sabra and Chatila massacres which led to the return of the MNF contingents – together with a small British unit – the Foreign Ministers expressed only their readiness to support additional steps, including the strengthening of UN observers and the possible employment of UN or multinational forces.[66]

The member states attempted to keep the situation in Lebanon under constant review within EPC but it was a far from easy task. As confusion in Lebanon increased, the problems besetting the MNF increased. The aims and objectives of the MNF, particularly of MNF-II, were vague, which exacerbated the problems of liaison and coordination among the participating governments, as Cremasco has indicated above.[67] In Beirut itself there were two coordinating groups, one of the military commanders, the other of ambassadors. There was also a more loosely structured group in Washington which was primarily concerned with trying to find out what was going on. There was no consensus on a more formal grouping, the French especially being adamantly opposed. Each contingent pursued its own role, attempting to implement the priorities determined for the most part by its own individual government. As the situation in Beirut became more complex, so priorities diverged further, with the French in particular determined to avoid too close an identification with US policy. The attacks on both US and French personnel appeared to negate French policy even while they encouraged further efforts at differentiation. Caligaris has been particularly critical of the member states for failing to reassess their operations and their basic political and military aims after the Israeli partial withdrawal.[68] But it was not, of course, merely the French who failed adequately to liaise with the other participants. Few if any participating governments, for example, gave more than a mininal indication that they were about to withdraw their troops, including the British.

Mine-Sweeping in the Red Sea

The absence of any formal liaison among the participating states also characterised the mine-hunting operation of the summer of 1984. Each government responded separately to the Egyptian call for assistance, with, as Cremasco has pointed out, only the UK and the US participating in the 'Egyptian Coordinating Committee'.[69]

Reference to EPC was scant and without significant impact. Information was, of course, exchanged among governments but usually on an informal bilateral basis.

The Fight Against Terrorism

The MFO and the MNF were examples of largely US initiatives to which European governments responded with varying degrees of reluctance or willingness. Acceptance – even if minimal or tacit – was achieved in part because both operations were peace-keeping efforts, albeit outside the United Nations framework, and, more cynically, because costs were limited or minimal. US initiatives to combat international terrorism have been regarded in a wholly different light. A considerable degree of common ground has emerged from the various discussions held at all levels – among the Twelve, the Twelve and the United States, the Sixteen of the Alliance and the Seven of the Western economic summits. Yet profound differences remain, not least over the root cause of much of international terrorist activity, and therefore over the means to counter it.

Terrorism has been on the Twelve's agenda for many years. In 1976 the so-called 'Trevi Group' was established, largely in response to the growing international links between the various terrorist groups of Germany, Italy, France and Northern Ireland and the rising threat of airline hijacking. Much of the Group's discussions were limited to more technical aspects of counter-terrorism. As international terrorist activity connected with the Arab-Israeli conflict grew, so wider political aspects were inevitably introduced into the discussions. This trend was reinforced by the growing concern of the United States over the absence of any strong, political, counter-measures against states sponsoring or supporting international terrorism, most notably Libya. However, the Ten and later the Twelve stuck largely to procedural and diplomatic issues, agreeing in September 1984, for example, to take common action if one member state suffered serious attack involving an abuse of diplomatic immunity.[70] Economic sanctions were ruled out as inappropriate – they were also unobtainable on a common basis among the Twelve. The only sanctions agreed to entailed a ban on arms sales to countries supporting terrorism. These were agreed at the emergency meeting of Foreign Ministers in January 1986, but, as usual in the case of arms sales, the ban was left to the member states to introduce on an individual basis. At the same time, however, efforts were made to expedite agreement on a wider and more politically significant package of measures with the establishment of a new EPC working group to supplement the work of the Trevi Group.

The protracted nature of European discussions caused growing frustration within the US Administration, faced as it was with the increased brazenness of Qaddafi. US pressure, including the despatch of emissaries to at least some of the Allies to explain the US position and to urge stronger joint action, was not successful. On the one hand, there was a growing sympathy with the US against Libyan claims and actions and a need to agree on some joint measures was recognised. On the other hand, many Europeans remained critical of US policy; after all, the issue of Qaddafi's support for terrorism was hardly new. In 1982, for example, John Campbell had written: 'What European opinion questioned was the timing, the methods, the overblown publicity and the engagement of the President of the United States in a shouting match with such as Muammet Qaddafi.'[71]

Cremasco has pointed to some of the factors which influenced individual responses in 1986, including those which led Margaret Thatcher to allow British bases to be used in the US strike.[72] In general, Europe was concerned that the United States was placing itself in a position which, ineluctably, escalated the conflict with Libya. As a result, many in Europe saw a need to maintain a distance from US policy, especially when that policy appeared to ignore possible repercussions in the rest of the Arab world. These were views with which it was believed the British concurred; hence, the acrimonious reaction to the Thatcher decision. Most European governments tended to rationalise their position (their inaction and weakness in US eyes) by emphasising the need to tackle the basic issue of the Arab-Israeli dispute at the same time as attempting to deal with the terrorist activity it has inspired; to treat the cause, that is, as well as the symptoms. It was a view that had been expressed by the Ten (with Spain and Portugal) in December 1985 immediately after the terrorist attacks on Rome and Vienna and adhered to with some consistency during subsequent events, a factor which intensified the regret of several leaders that the United States should have so clearly ignored it. Transatlantic disagreement was fundamental and remained so despite the use of all the procedures and devices designed for consultation and cooperation.

Thus, the existence of such an array of procedures has not meant that misunderstandings are always avoided, even when the procedures are fully utilised. The internal workings of both EPC and the member

states on the one hand and the US administration on the other
are such that some misunderstanding is inevitable even when not
contrived. As suggested earlier, Europe's differing perceptions and
assessment of the elements that make up the Middle East conundrum
lead to divergent policy reactions that allow EPC–US links to play
only a limited role. Official reaction in the US has ranged from relief
to anger to derision depending on how united the Twelve have or
have not been and on whether the policy agreed on coincides with
that of the US.[73]

Implications for the Future

If one looks at the contingencies of internal strife in Saudi Arabia,
the possible collapse of Iraq or growing superpower confrontation
elaborated elsewhere, it is probable – and a legal requirement under
the Single European Act of 1986 – that the twelve EPC states would
attempt to coordinate their position. The emergency procedure for
calling a meeting of the Political Committee might be invoked, led
by France, for example, if the Iraqi collapse was precipitous, but
individual members would doubtless have been in less formal contact
by telex and telephone. In such preliminary discussions, most member
states would also have been in touch with the United States, whether
via the State Department or other channels – in the third contingency
of superpower confrontation, perhaps directly with the President.
These various contacts would then be placed on a multilateral basis,
bringing into effect the Gymnich formula and so on once discussions
began within EPC.

The intensity of subsequent transatlantic contacts would inevitably
depend on whether common action was being sought or undertaken,
or, of course, if Europe or the US were seeking to prevent or limit
unilateral action by the other. But at no time is it likely that relations
would be restricted simply to formal links. As one (US) official put
it:

> We might be concerned if EPC were to become monolithic and
> monopolistic, the only channel for United States contact with the
> European Community in political foreign policy questions, just as
> the Community would surely have cause to worry if its sole
> contact with the United States Government were through the State
> Department.[74]

Such conditions are not likely in the foreseeable future; nearly all the member states have their own contacts and channels of communication with the US Administration, which they jealously guard. It is none the less legitimate to ask of both the United States and Europe whether procedural arrangements might be improved so that they provide an incentive for governments to use them and not ignore them at the crucial moment.

VIII TOWARDS MORE EFFECTIVE COOPERATION

It has been the theme throughout this paper that there are plenty of fora in existence in which Europe and the United States can consult and coordinate their actions. The issue is whether the fora are used effectively. The factors that influence the Europeans, whether individually or collectively, or the Americans to use the various procedures are inevitably numerous. They might include the seriousness of the threat – whether it involves a single friendly state or dynasty, the stability of the region, or the East–West strategic balance; the type of reaction required and the resources available. Given the number of crises that have arisen in the Middle East, there is now a considerable body of experience, if not expertise, among the Atlantic Allies. There is, too, the constant interchange of information whether on a bilateral or multilateral basis. And yet, each new crisis reveals differences, both among the Europeans and especially between Europe and the United States. The conclusion seems inescapable, that existing channels of communication are not being particularly well used in 'normal' times and therefore cannot cope in times of crisis because governments do not wish to so use them.

To suggest that interests and policies are more important than procedures is hardly earth-shattering. Nor should one over-estimate the importance of multilateral procedures and processes as against bilateral relationships. It is possible to envisage tinkering, even extensively, with existing mechanisms to good effect, but unless one begins to think in terms of radical changes in the way Europe and the US formulate and execute their policies, that effect is still likely to be marginal.

However, there are a number of shortcomings and gaps that could be put right and so improve relations by creating at least a confident expectation that when used in an emergency, they will not break down. At that level it is, for example, worth noting that measures such as the introduction of the 'bi-cephelous' Presidency, the arrangement whereby the Community is represented by both the President of the Commission and the President-in-Office of the Council of Ministers, and the troika principle of representation have been useful in improving continuity and consistency. The establishment of a small EPC Secretariat may be of further help, in terms both of continuity and of providing an additional point of contact for non-EPC members. Again within EPC, the introduction of a 'reinforced' Middle East working group which periodically looked towards the future, at trends, interests, options, etc. could be useful. Given the almost Byzantine nature of US decision-making, a common processing of intelligence might be attempted to some value by means, say, of a working group designed for the purpose.

A very much more difficult issue is that of a greater European defence or security identity, whether within the framework of WEU or EPC. The limits in formal terms at least appear to have been reached, although the increased number of references to such issues in the work of EPC gradually widens the space in which to manoeuvre. Much, then depends on the Twelve's interpretation of 'the political and economic aspects of security', as the London Report puts it.[75]

The issue can, naturally, be approached at many different levels and not simply from that of a fully-fledged European Defence Community (a possibility that if realised would probably alarm many of the present critics of the European contribution to the Alliance). Sir C. Rose, for example, has suggested that a link could be established between EPC and NATO.[76] To the extent that issues discussed in EPC may afterwards be put forward at Atlantic Councils by the country that happens to hold the Presidency of EPC suggests the existence of some sort of link already – even if it breaks down every five or six years when the Irish hold the chair. A link at any other level might be more problematic, although it is likely that member states of both EPC and NATO will continue to put forward views on particular issues that have been coordinated in EPC (and may even retire temporarily from the Council to determine those views).

The Alliance itself could make greater use of its broad remit by discussing with greater frequency the interrelated issues of economic, political and military policies towards third countries. Such round tables, with the European Commission present, are not unknown and might prove educational for all. In addition the more frequent meeting of Heads of Government might also be worthwhile. Such meetings, at the beginning of a new US Presidency and perhaps three-quarters of the way through his term of office, could be in addition to those of the Western summits. The latter have become accepted as not only economic in character (although the extent to which they need to retain a strong economic thrust needs to be faced). They also have the great advantage of including the Japanese.

It used to be a concern frequently expressed by several members of the European Community that the Western summits included only the four larger European countries. That to a considerable extent was overcome by the involvement – albeit after considerable delay and some reluctance – of the President of the Commission and, if that office was not held by one of the Big Four, by the President of the Council. It gives a rather heavy bias to European views. None the less, the initial concern was symbolic of the perennial suspicion that the Big Three or Four, or even Five, of Western Europe were coordinating their views secretly or quietly together, with the others deliberately excluded. Certainly, the pressures on those who have or may have the ability and inclination to influence events to get together has not always been resisted. Coordination among the Big Three with the United States over Berlin, for example, or in the South-west Africa Contact Group, are but two examples that could be cited. It has indeed been suggested that this 'principal nation' approach is usually the most effective. In the report of the Four Institutes, for example, in 1981, it was concluded that:

> NATO and the Seven Nation Summits . . . are insufficient forums for consultation on political/security issues outside the Central Front. The primary mechanisms should be a group of the small number of *principal nations* which are concerned and prepared to take a direct role in dealing with a particular problem. The organizing principle would be to include only those countries which are able and willing to accept concrete obligations within the troubled area. Participation would be linked to the capacity and responsibility for action.[77]

While the success of the approach cannot of course be guaranteed (as we have seen in the case of the MNF), the pressures to adopt it and, for some, the attractiveness of it remains considerable. There are, however, problems involved for those who are not principals (on whatever flexible interpretation of the word) but who might yet have an interest in the outcome. Inevitably, there are occasions when some Community member states, for example, are not directly involved and are content with the policy being pursued, which presupposes perhaps relatively full information on the ends and means of the policy. It is when information is less full, when consultation has been limited and where there are differences of interests and so on that problems begin. It is then that questions tend to arise over the quality and efficiency of procedures.

Within the Atlantic relationship, two points stand out: Europe believes its interests in the Middle East are not always the same as those of the United States and agreement on policy cannot always therefore be expected and the United States, while preferring to involve its Allies, is willing to act unilaterally. Both sides are committed to consultations, but there are limits; as General Walters said over Libya: 'It's very difficult to allow someone else to have a veto over American foreign policy'. Over the Arab/Israeli conflict, while the Europeans have evolved common elements of a policy, it remains fairly limited and sufficient neither to influence the Arabs nor the Israelis, nor even the United States, who might then exercise leverage with the Israelis. Finally, over the security of the region in general, and the assessment of the political and military threats to it, differences remain profound; there may be an agreement (albeit reluctant) to discuss some elements of planning, and even to join in defensive measures on a cooperative basis, ahead of time about the circumstances which might require military action. The Europeans especially have insisted that in any threatening situation, time has to be allowed for the exhaustion of all diplomatic options. In such a situation, procedural improvements and a commitment to contingency planning in its broadest sense offer little to help alleviate some of the criticisms of European and US actions. Yet, inevitably perhaps, the final approach will remain a pragmatic one.

Notes

1. Text of the *Report of the Committee of Three on Non-Military Cooperation in NATO*, 1956.
2. As *The Financial Times* put it in its leader of 14 April 1986: 'If Washington had gone ahead with a unilateral military strike against Libyan targets just as soon as it was logically in a position to do so, Europe would not have had time to organize its disapproval . . . Yet the consultation process which has been set in train risks heightening the political disagreement between Europe and the US: for if the Americans do consult their Allies, the Europeans have a right to expect that their views will carry weight.'

3. See for example, W. Wallace, *Britain's Bilateral Links with Rivals in Western Europe: Britain, France and Germany* (Gower: London: 1986).

4. See H. Simonian, *The Privileged Partnership: Franco-German Relations in the European Community, 1969–1984* (Oxford: Clarendon Press, 1985).

5. Cited in W. Wallace, op. cit., (see note 3) p. 29.

6. Sir G. Howe, 'The European Pillar', *Foreign Affairs*, Vol. 63, No. 2, Winter 1984/85, p. 235.

7. Gregory Treverton, 'Defence Beyond Europe', *Survival*, Vol. XXIII, No. 5, September/October 1985, p. 219.

8. See D. Allen and M. Smith, 'Europe, the United States and the Middle East', *Journal of Common Market Studies*, Vol. XXIII, No. 2, December 1983.

9. The European Community was established under the Treaties of Paris, 1952 (which set up the European Coal and Steel Community) and Rome, 1957 (which set up the European Economic Community and the European Atomic Energy Commission). A customs union was created together with a common commercial policy. The formal decision-making procedure is that the European commission (made up of seventeen individual Commissioners and a supporting bureaucracy) proposes policy and the Council of Ministers (representing the twelve member states) makes the decision. For an introduction to the community, its institutions and its policies see H. Arbuthnott and G. Edwards, *A Common Man's Guide to the Common Market*, 2nd edn, 1989.

10. European Community, *The Nineteenth General Report of Activities of the European Community* (Brussels: 1985) p. 305.

11. In support of the concept see, for example, the *Report on European Political Cooperation and European Security* (Brussels: European Community, 1985) drawn up by the Political Affairs Committee of the European Parliament. The Rapporteur, the Danish MEP, Niels Haagerup, suggested (p. 44): 'It is fair to say that although the European Community always, and its member states usually, abstain from direct military intervention in Third World Affairs, the Community has considerable leverage by virtue of its economic powers to influence developments in various parts of the world.'

12. Against the concept see, for example, Hedley Bull, 'Civilian Power in Europe: A Contradiction in Terms', in L. Tsoukalis (ed.), *The European Community: Past, Present and Future* (Oxford: Basil Blackwell, 1983). Bull wrote (p. 151): 'Possession of scarce resources was a source of power to militarily weak states only so long as militarily strong states chose not to use their force. More generally, the power or influence exerted by the European Community and other such civilian actors was conditional upon a strategic environment provided by the military power of states which they do not control.'

13. For a discussion of the EC and the Falklands dispute see G. Edwards, 'Europe and the Falklands Crisis 1982', *Journal of Common Market Studies*, Vol. 22, No. 4, June 1984.

14. For a discussion of such divisions see C. Hill and J. Mayall, *The Sanctions*

Problem: International and European Perspectives, EUI Working Paper No. 59, 1983.

15. See, for example, S. Nuttall's chapters on 'European Political Cooperation' in successive volumes of F. Jacobs (ed.), *The Yearbook of European Law* (Oxford: Clarendon Press, 1981, ff.).

16. A number of reports on different aspects of security preceded that of Niels Haagerup (see note 11) including those by Lord Gladwyn and E. Blumenfeld in 1975, and E. Klepsch and T. Normanton in 1978. The latter was published in *Two Way Street: USA/Europe Arms Procurement* (London and New York: Brasseys/Crane Russak, 1979).

17. *Report on the Situation in the Near East* by J. Plenders, Rapporteur, 1982.

18. *Report on the Surveillance and Protection of Maritime Lines of Communication*, Rapporteur, A. Diligent, 1981.

19. *Report on Arms Procurement Within a Common Industrial Policy and Arms Sales*, Rapporteur, A. Fergusson, 1983.

20. European Political Cooperation was established on a modest scale by the then six members of the European Community in 1970 with the purpose of coordinating their foreign policies. It remained based on intergovernmental agreement outside the Community Treaty framework until the Single European Act of 1986. While the member states have gradually deepened their cooperation – as reflected in a number of reports such as the Copenhagen Report of 1973 and the London Report of 1981 and the Solemn Declaration on European Union of 1983, the procedure has remained based on unanimity. For a general introduction to EPC see D. Allen, R. Rummel and W. Wessels (eds), *European Political Cooperation* (Guildford: Butterworth Scientific, 1982).

21. See D. Allen and A. Pijpers, *European Foreign Policy Making and the Arab–Israeli Conflict* (The Hague: Martinus Nijhoff, 1984).

22. A phrase used by R. Rummel and R. Bourgignon in a paper 'The Role of the Ten in International Affairs: "Speaking with One Voice" and Beyond?' presented to the Trans-European Policy Studies Conference, organised by the Institut für Europäische Politik, Bonn, December 1985.

23. See Francoise de la Serre, 'The Scope of National Adaption to EPC,' in A. Pijpers, *et al*, *European Political Cooperation in the 1980s* (The Hague: Martinus Nijhoff, 1988).

24. 'Gymnich-type' weekends should not be confused with Gymnich formulas. The former merely denote the informal weekend meetings of Foreign Ministers named after the first such meeting at Schloss Gymnich in 1974. It was in fact at that meeting that the Gymnich formula for improving relations with the US was agreed upon.

25. S. Nuttall, op. cit. (see note 15), Vol. 2, 1982.

26. See M. Smith, 'From the "Year of Europe" to a Year of Carter', *Journal of Common Market Studies*, Vol. 17, No. 1, 1978.

27. E. Regalsberger, 'EPC: Contacts with Third Countries, Past and Present', in E. Regelsberger, P. de Schoutheete, S. Nuttall and G. Edwards (eds), *The External Relations of European Political Cooperation and the Future of EPC*, EUI Working Paper No. 172, 1985.

28. On the role of the Presidency and national approaches to it, see C. O'Naullain (ed.), *The Presidency of the European Council of Ministers* (London: Croom Helm, 1984).

29. The Western European Union was established in 1954 by a Protocol to the Brussels Treaty of 1948 extending membership from the original five countries of Belgium, France, Luxembourg, the Netherlands and the UK to include West Germany and Italy. It grew out of the failure of the proposed European Defence Community which had envisaged a European Army including West German forces and which had been rejected by the French National Assembly. WEU's major purpose was to allow for the rearmament of West Germany and its entry into the Alliance. It set up a Council and an Assembly – somewhat oddly composed of the same national representatives who attend the Council of Europe – and a small secretariat (located in London) together with an Arms Control Agency and a Standing Armaments Committee (located in Paris).

30. For a discussion of EPC and the Solemn Declaration see Nuttall, op. cit. (see note 15), Vol. 3, 1983.

31. The North Atlantic Treaty was signed in April 1949 with initially twelve members. Greece and Turkey joined in 1952, West Germany in 1955 and Spain in 1982. The Treaty established the North Atlantic Council composed of Foreign Ministers and the Council then set up the Defence Committee of Ministers of Defence. A Parliamentary body was established only in 1955 and meets annually. The literature produced on both sides of the Atlantic on the Alliance, its purposes and its problems, is now so vast that any suggestion for an introductory text would be wholly arbitrary. The organisation in fact produces its own very useful handbook: *The North Atlantic Treaty Organization: Facts and Figures.*

32. See note 1.

33. L. S. Kaplan, R. W. Clawson and R. Luraghi (eds), *NATO and the Mediterranean* (Wilmington, Del.: Scholarly Resources, 1985), p. 7.

34. NATO, *Harmel Report* (Brussels: NATO Information Service, 1967).

35. J. W. Holmes, 'The Dumbbell Won't Do', *Foreign Policy*, No. 50, Spring 1983, p. 19. The idea that informed exchanges necessarily lead to a constructive consensus was somewhat confounded at the June 1986 weekend meeting when according to *The Financial Times* the 'free for all' only hardened opposing positions (over the decision to breach SALT II).

36. F. Dannenbring, 'Consultation: The Political Lifeblood of the Alliance', *NATO Review*, No. 6, 1986, p. 5.

37. M. Heseltine, 'Strengthening Europe's Contribution to the Common Defence', *NATO Review*, No. 6, 1984, p. 18.

38. Defence White Paper, 1981 quoted in J. Baylis, *Anglo-American Defence Relations 1939–1984: The Special Relationship*, 2nd edn (New York: St Martin's Press, 1984).

39. Declaration on Atlantic Relations in *The North Atlantic Treaty Organization: Facts and Figures*, p. 293.

40. *Report on the Allied Contribution to the Common Defence 1982*, quoted

in *Assembly of WEU Report to the Committee on Defence Questions and Armaments*, Rapporteur, P. Wilkinson, Document 947, 18 May 1983, p. 18.

41. See, for example, Theo Sommer, 'Europe and the American Connection', *Foreign Affairs*, Vol. 58, No. 3, 1980.
42. *NATO Facts and Figures*, 1982, p. 299.
43. K. Holmes, 'Europeanizing NATO', *The Washington Quarterly*, Vol. 9, No. 2, Spring 1986, p. 61.
44. I. Kristol, 'Saving the Atlantic Alliance', *Current*, No. 248, December, 1983.
45. See P. Williams, 'The Nunn Amendment, Burden-sharing and US troops in Europe', *Survival*, Vol. XXVII, No. 1, January/February 1985, p. 5.
46. See, for example, Sir G. Howe's article in *Foreign Affairs*, op. cit. (see note 6).
47. Department of Defense, *Report on the Allied Contribution to the Common Defense, 1983*, p. 61.
48. *The Times*, 15 April 1980.
49. *The Times*, 9 September 1982.
50. Herrero de Minon, the Rapporteur, Sub-Committee in Out-of-Area Security Challenges to the Atlantic Alliance, *Charter Final Report*, May 1986.
51. Ibid.
52. *Third Report of the Defence Committee of the House of Commons on Defence Commitments and Resources and the Defence Estimates 1985/6*, HMSO, p. 57.
53. *The Times*, 29 May 1986.
54. De Minon, op. cit. (see note 50).
55. Sir C. Rose in *NATO Review*, No. 1, 1983, p. 5.
56. General Sir A. Farrar-Hockley, 'Problems of Over-extension: Reconciling NATO Defence and Out-of-Area Contingencies; Part I', in *Power and Policy: Doctrine, the Alliance and Arms Control*, Adelphi Paper 207, International Institute of Strategic Studies, Spring, 1986, p. 58.
57. H. Kissinger, 'A Plan to Reshape NATO', *Time*, 5 March 1984.
58. *Observer*, 11 May 1986.
59. See P. Wilkinson, 'State-Sponsored Terrorism: the Problem of Responses', *The World Today*, Vol. 40, No. 7, July, 1984, p. 297.
60. The English press was full of reports such as that headed 'Thatcher's Tough Image Kept Alive', *Financial Times*, 6 May 1986. Schulz was quoted as describing her as 'a terrific leader' and *The New York Times* reportedly quoted a US official as saying 'Margaret really wrestled old Francois to the mat' (both *Observer*, 11 May 1986).
61. English press reports of 29 April 1986 of the interview given by M. Mitterand to *Yomiuri Shimbun*.
62. N. Bayne, 'Western Economic Summits: Can They Do Better?', *The World Today*, Vol. 40, No. 1, January 1984, p. 11.
63. For an excellent survey of European positions on the MFO see Alfred Pijpers, 'European participation in the Sinai peace-keeping force (MFO)' in Allen and Pijpers, op. cit. (see note 21).
64. The Ten declared that the decision of the four member states to

participate 'meets the wish frequently expressed by the Members of the Community to facilitate any progress in the direction of a comprehensive peace settlement in the Middle East'.

65. An American Embassy official to a conference organised by the European University Institute, and the Institut fur Europaische Politik, Bonn held in Florence in 1984.

66. The communiqué of the European Foreign Ministers on 20 September spoke of their support for additional steps including the strengthening of UN observers in Beirut and the possible deployment of UN or multinational forces. *Agence Europe*, 21 September 1982.

67. See Cremasco, Chapter 4, pp. 174–5. Also R. W. Nelson, 'Multinational Peacekeeping in the Middle East and the United Nations Model', *International Affairs*, Vol. 61, No. 1, Winter 1984/85.

68. L. Caligaris, 'Western Peacekeeping in the Lebanon: Lessons of the MNF', *Survival*, Vol. 26, No. 6, November/December 1984, p. 265.

69. Cremasco, Chapter 4, p. 177.

70. S. Nuttall, op. cit. (see note 15) Vol. 4, 1984, p. 339. After outlining the main points agreed by the Ten, he goes on to write: 'this is among the first decisions taken within Political Cooperation which regulate relations among the Ten rather than the position of the Ten with regard to third countries or specific problems of international relations.'

71. J. Campbell, 'The Middle East: A House of Containment Built on Shifting Sands in America and the World 1981', *Foreign Affairs*, Vol. 60, No. 3, 1982, p. 623.

72. Cremasco, Chapter 4, pp. 181–4.

73. This is the conclusion of, for example, S. Hoffman, 'Western Europe: Wait and Worry', in 'America and the World 1984', *Foreign Affairs*, Vol. 63, No. 3, 1985, p. 648.

74. See note 38.

75. The 'London Report' appears as 'The Report on European Political Cooperation issued by the Foreign Ministers of the Ten on 13 October 1981,' *European Political Cooperation (EPC)*, 4th edition (Bonn: Press and Information Office of the Federal Government, Federal Republic of Germany, 1982, pp. 271–8).

76. Sir C. Rose, op. cit. (see note 55).

77. Karl Kaiser, Winston Lord, Thierry de Montbrial and David Watt, *Western Security: What Has Changed, What Should Be Done* (London: Royal Institute of International Affairs, 1981) p. 45.

7 Conclusions and Recommendations
Joseph I. Coffey

Although the Middle East does not fall within the area covered by the North Atlantic Treaty, it is of great importance to the members of the Atlantic Alliance. Its geostrategic position, at the juncture of Europe, Asia and Africa, is still significant, even in an age of intercontinental missiles. Through the Middle East run the sea lines of communication between Europe and East Africa, Europe and the Far East and even, around the Cape of Good Hope, Europe and the South Atlantic and over it pass the aerial routes linking these regions with each other and with the Middle East itself. Its proximity to NATO, whose zone of responsibility it borders both on land and on sea, means that events in the area can impact on the Alliance, directly or indirectly. And it is the location of the bulk of the world's proven reserves of oil and the source of some 60 per cent of the oil imported by the Western European members of the Alliance.

It goes, therefore, almost without saying that the West has vital interests in the Middle East, that these interests will be affected by developments in the area and that in some instances members of the Alliance may have to act, individually or collectively, to safeguard those interests. It also goes almost without saying that the preferred actions will be diplomatic or economic rather than military, that they will be aimed at heading off crises as well as at ameliorating them and that they will therefore be continuous, rather than intermittent; in fact, the real challenge facing the West is to devise, coordinate and implement a policy which will so engage the interests of the principal powers in the area that together they can bring a measure of peace and stability to that troubled area. But even if this formidable task is successfully carried through it will not put an end to crises and conflicts nor will it automatically insure that Western interests are secure against the vicissitudes of politics, against the effects of economic changes or against the shocks from social upheavals. There may, therefore, be occasions in the future, as there have been in the past, when one or more of the Western powers deems it necessary to employ force in defence of its interests or those of the broader community of which it is a member.

In previous chapters of this study we have attempted to define those interests, to indicate some of the threats that may arise, with particular reference to those likely to cause consideration of a military response, to outline the most important military and political factors that will influence responses – including those deriving from domestic political attitudes and political processes – and to describe the institutional structures, relationships and procedures which will also affect decisions on the use of force. Here we will summarise our earlier findings, as a prelude to the task of assessing the implications of selected uses of force both for the maintenance of Western interests and for the security and cohesion of the Alliance. And finally, we will suggest to the members of the Atlantic Alliance some factors they might consider if, as and when they contemplate employing the military instrument in the Middle East.

I WESTERN INTERESTS IN THE MIDDLE EAST

To speak of 'Western interests' is at one and the same time both correct and misleading. It is correct because the various members of the Alliance are in almost perfect agreement about their major objectives: insuring access to Middle East oil, safeguarding the security of Israel, preventing Soviet expansion in the area, and fostering stability[1] – which in broad sense requires also promoting peace, helping in economic development and supporting measures to enhance the well-being of those living in the area. It is misleading because the United States may differ from its European allies (as these do to some extent among themselves) about the priority to be accorded these objectives; for example, US leaders certainly attach more importance to (their version of) Israeli security than do West European authorities in general and those heading the Greek, Italian and Spanish governments in particular. Moreover, even when nations agree on the priority to be accorded a given objective (such as insuring the flow of oil) they may disagree as to the best means of attaining it – as was certainly true at the time of the Arab embargo in 1973–4. More importantly (at least for this study) is the pronounced preference of the European members of the Alliance for persuasion over coercion and their great reluctance to endorse the use of force, other than for internationally sanctioned peace-keeping operations. And though there is nothing intrinsically wrong with such predilections, they frequently result in divisions between Europe and the United States over how best to cope with threats to Western interests, a matter which will be taken up again after discussing the nature of these threats.

II THREATS TO WESTERN INTERESTS

Western interests are jeopardised in part because these interests conflict with those of other actors, who employ their power and influence to thwart Western policies or programmes. Partly, however, this jeopardy arises from the fact that these other actors, in pursuing their own interests, create situations which have an adverse impact on the West: thus attacks on shipping in the Persian-Arabian Gulf are not so much directed against the West as they are a by-product of the Iran–Iraq war. Moreover, as noted in Chapter 2, the forces of change in the Middle East operate at least quasi-independently of national actors – and perhaps even of sub-national ones. In earlier parts of this book we have discussed all of these factors; here we would like to single out the most significant, i.e. those most likely to lead to intrastate or inter-state conflict, on the not unreasonable ground that violence in the Middle East is most likely to generate a violent response by outside actors – which is the subject of our concern.

As Cottom points out, the Middle East is undergoing rapid change at an accelerating tempo, change which challenges social norms as well as authority structures and which generates both instability and uncertainty.[2] This is significant not just because turbulence is undesirable but because the process could lead to a change of regime in a 'moderate' country such as Egypt, Jordan or Saudi Arabia and consequent shifts not only in regional alliances but in the balance of influence between the West and the Soviet Union. Conceivably, the outcome could be not only a period of confusion and uncertainty but fresh inter-state conflicts, as national actors attempted to exploit new possibilities or to re-establish a stable situation in the area.

Moreover, most of the countries of the Middle East are engaged in a perpetual struggle for power and influence, marked by changing policies, shifting alliances and abrupt reversals of their affiliations with external actors, of which Sadat's switch from the Soviet Union to the United States circa 1974–5 is the most memorable but by no means the only one. Inasmuch as such swings are induced by political rivalries among national and sub-national leaders, as well as by regime changes, we cannot rule out further shifts of this kind. Barring, however, changes of alignment on the part of key actors such as Egypt or Syria, such shifts are likely to have less impact on peace and stability in the Middle East (and on Western interests in the area) than the regime changes noted previously.[3]

More far-reaching consequences have in the past resulted from armed conflicts in the region, such as the six Arab-Israeli wars, the perennial Lebanese civil war, with intermittent external involvement, and the Iran–Iraq war. This is true not only because such conflicts could lead to the defeat of one or another of the 'pro-Western' states (as was true of Jordan in the Six Day War) or to attempts to bring in the Soviet Union to redress the consequences of failure, as Syria did following the Yom Kippur of War 1973, but because they involve the West, in ways ranging from supplying weapons to providing peace-keeping forces to facing down the Soviet Union, as the United States did in October 1973. Indeed, *all* the allies are desirous of precluding or damping conflicts in the area which, by and large, can only be disadvantageous to, or even dangerous to, the West.

These threats to Western interests in the area are exacerbated by the fact that some of the local actors may receive diplomatic, economic and even military support from the Soviet Union. This makes harder the maintenance of a political and military balance in the Middle East and forces the United States (and sometimes other Allies) to make a larger investment of resources and a greater commitment of support to Israel or to 'moderate' Arab regimes than would otherwise be necessary. It also raises the possibility that the Allies – or at least the United States – may in time of crisis back such a regime against one supported by the USSR and hence find themselves in a local confrontation with the Soviet Union, which could conceivably evolve into a clash of arms, as it threatened to do in 1973. Confrontation or conflict might lead to 'horizontal escalation' elsewhere, with either the United States (as some Americans have suggested) or the Soviet Union (as Europeans fear) applying pressures in Europe to achieve the desired outcome in the Middle East. And finally, it is always possible that the Soviet Union might directly intervene in the region in defence of its own interests, because it sees an unique opportunity or, as some would have it, in furtherance of a 'Grand Design' – a concern that was most salient in Western minds immediately after the intervention in Afghanistan in 1979.

III   THE USES OF FORCE: AN OVERVIEW

The first thing to note is that the Middle East is one of the most heavily-armed regions in the world; the countries of the Gulf alone possess almost as many main battle tanks as do all the Allied units on the Central Front.[4] Although their operational readiness, sustainability and command, control and communications are not up to Western standards, the armed forces of the area are acquiring and absorbing modern weapons and equipment and increasing their ability to employ them. In Cordesman's words, 'the trends in the region seem likely to steadily increase the problems Western forces will find in operating in the Middle East over the next ten years'.[5]

The second thing to note is that the forces available to the West for operations in the Middle East are, on the contrary, shrinking. Although Britain, France, and Italy all possess 'Rapid Deployment Forces', and Turkey has units that could be employed in this role, these are relatively small in size and sometimes unsuited for operations in the Middle East. As Cordesman points out,

> Most NATO squadrons cannot move most of their service C^3I/BM assets. Most NATO ships lack adequate naval replenishment and repair facilities to provide even limited endurance in the Middle East without access to local ports and key docks. Most NATO ground forces lack training in low level war, support capability for desert, mountain or other special regional conditions, suitable long range air or sea lift, mobile stocks, and specialized armaments.[6]

Furthermore, even where trained and equipped units exist, as they do within the Central Command, a shortage of air- and sea-lift means that the United States cannot speedily redeploy division or wing-size units to the Middle East and sustain them in combat for any period of time.

A third point is that these shortfalls increase the need for local bases and facilities (which are not always easy to come by) and require the West to place greater reliance upon indigenous forces, which may be even less easily obtainable. This is due in part to the difficulties that countries like Egypt, Jordan and Saudi Arabia would find in openly committing their armed forces to Western-directed military operations, in part to the fact that most elements of these forces are even more closely tied to their own territories than are those of the European allies, and in part to the fact that their operational units are neither balanced nor sustainable.

A fourth point is that all this augurs ill for multinational operations, either among the Western powers or by a Western power and those countries in the Middle East likely to be on its side. The well-known problems of interoperability and intercommunicability among the members of NATO would be compounded by attempts to operate in an unfamiliar environment, which would impose special requirements on both troops and equipment. As for operations involving indigenous forces, only the happiest of accidents would make it possible for Frenchmen to talk over the radio to Egyptians or for Americans to refuel and rearm Saudi tanks. Militarily, this suggests parallel or cooperative operations rather than combined ones. It also suggests that those Allies not now possessing forces capable of operating in the Middle East would find it extraordinarily difficult to create them, other than as a token of their support. And both support for out-of-area operations and the forms that it should take are still subject of dispute within the Alliance.

IV RECONCILING NATIONAL APPROACHES

As indicated at the beginning of the chapter, all members of the Alliance desire a peaceful, secure, progressive Middle East, which would be not only a market for exports but a partner in development. By and large, they even agree on subsidiary objectives whose attainment would facilitate these larger aims: ensuring Western (and Japanese) access to oil, preventing Soviet expansion in the area, promoting stability and safeguarding the security of Israel. The problem in developing and reconciling approaches to securing these objectives is that some (like the prevention of Soviet expansion) are made more difficult by the pursuit of others (such as maintaining the inependence and integrity of Israel) and that the Allies differ not only over the priority to be given potentially conflicting objectives but over the ways of achieving them – and both of these will affect their willingness to sanction and/or to support the use of force.

Broadly speaking, the US sees the Middle East in the framework of the global competition with the Soviet Union, which means that gains in power and influence by that state or its clients are, as in a zero-sum game, losses for United States. Moreover, changes are viewed in terms of how they show up on the 'global scoreboard', where they take their place along with Angola and Ethiopia, Nicaragua and Grenada, and in terms of how they affect the over-all image of the United States. Sometimes this leads the US to attach to developments in the Middle East an importance disproportionate to their implications in the area (and for the Western Alliance) and to respond in ways which almost inevitably put in a confrontational posture *vis-à-vis* the actors in the region, as did the Carter Doctrine of 1980 (which stated that 'an attempt by any outside force to gain control of the Persian Gulf region will be regarded as an assault on the vital interests of the United States of America and such an assault will be repelled by any means necessary, including military force') and the Reagan corollary of 1981, which expanded this to cover threats to the Saudi regime from any source whatsoever.

Both this view of the situation and domestic political factors have led the United States to emphasise the military instrument, which is deemed both the most important and the most effective. Much attention has been paid by the Reagan Administration (as by its predecessors) to helping selected allies such as Egypt and Israel to bolster their military capabilities, to arranging arms sales to 'moderate states' such as Saudi Arabia and Jordan, to obtaining bases in Egypt, Djibouti, Turkey, Somalia and Oman, to prepositioning stocks of equipment for utilisation in an emergency, as at Diego Garcia and at Masira Island in Oman, to exercising US (and Allied) forces, as in Egypt, etc.; in fact, the only new Unified Command created by the United States since 1950 is the Central Command, whose primary concern is that of preparing for operations in the Middle East.

This does not mean that the United States has eschewed the use of diplomatic, economic and other instruments but rather that these too are employed largely to maintain the political balance in the area rather than to deal with regional problems. There is no 'Grand Design' such as from time to time has marked US policy toward Latin America, no significant attempt to work with the Arab League as the United States has done with an (admittedly more acceptant) ASEAN. The major diplomatic activities, aside from those aimed at securing the release of hostages, have been those intended to bring about a settlement of the Arab-Israeli dispute. However, partly as a result of domestic political influences, partly as consequence of prior efforts to include the Israelis to engage in bargaining, the US has given the latter a virtual veto not only over the outcome of any negotiations but over the conditions for their initiation. And while this approach may reflect reality, that reality is a stark one.

The Europeans may be equally pessimistic about the prospects for achieving common objectives in the area but this is in part because they consider the US approach to be sometimes counter-productive. As Rummel phrases it,

> The 'European approach' (as represented by the multilateral foreign policy cooperation of the Twelve) is less guided by a fixation on the Soviet Union. Europeans are in favor of a balanced and comprehensive Middle East policy. 'Balanced', stands for cooperating on equal terms with all countries in the region, friend or foe. 'Comprehensive', means including any relevant actor in the search for peaceful conflict resolution (Soviet Union and PLO). *Vis-à-vis* the Soviet Union the Europeans favor a kind of Harmel-concept for the Middle East which combines defensive measures with a permanent proposal of cooperation. They detest American 'overreaction' and would like to see Washington concentrate on the 'real' threat which is the myriad of indigenous conflicts.[7]

Particular differences exist with regard to the Palestinian question. Many deem the virtual 'blank cheque' which the United States has given Israel as enabling that country not only to avoid meaningful negotiations and to perpetuate its control over territory and peoples not properly part of its domain but also to utilise force freely against its neighbours, as in the bombing of the Iraqi reactor at Baghdad and the 1982 incursion into Lebanon. The principal countries of Europe are on record as believing that the Palestinians are entitled to a homeland and that that homeland should encompass (some portion of) the West Bank and the Gaza Strip. Moreover, most governments recognise the PLO as the legitimate representative of the Palestinians, not because they love Yasir Arafat but because they see no other figure accepted by the majority of the Palestinians. These approaches lead not only to an exacerbation of US-European relations (such as followed the Venice Declaration of 1980) but also to significant differences with respect to the conditions and circumstances under which the Allies will endorse military actions aimed at helping Israel – a view which has not changed significantly since 1973, when several countries denied over-flight rights and the use of air bases by US planes flying weapons to the Israeli army and air force. (Even more recently, the Turks have indicated that bases on their territory could be used only to defend vital NATO interests and that Turkey could not 'associate itself with actions that might jeopardise the security and interests of the Arab countries'.[8])

More significantly, the West Europeans view force as an inappropriate and largely ineffective instrument of policy and deem the allocation of resources to the build-up of military establishments in the region as a diversion of monies badly needed for other purposes. This view reflects both their predilections for economic (and political) measures and their judgement that many problems arise out of the low level of economic and social development in the Middle East: only with progress will the prospects for peace and stability improve. When to this is coupled the greater European dependence on imported oil, the close relations that some countries maintain with the states of the region (as France does with Iraq and Britain with Oman) and the fact that West Germany has *no* 'power projection capacity', those of Britain and Turkey are limited and those of France and Italy are confined largely to the Mediterranean littoral, it is understandable that the Europeans may not share the US opinion concerning the utility of force in the Middle East.

Furthermore, there is a belief in some quarters in Europe that the United States is too bellicose, too 'quick on the trigger', too much given to acting in ways which could not only sacrifice *détente* but actually jeopardise security, all in furtherance of its competition with the Soviet Union. These views are held even more strongly by publics and by non-governmental elites than by those holding positions of authority; as Rummel points out, 'European minds are less oriented toward an inter-regional challenge than are American minds'.[9] By and large, West Europeans tend to see the Soviet influence as less pervasive than do US publics and to view the Soviets as more cautious than do many of their US counterparts; moreover, Europeans, and particularly West Germans, are 'more eager to decouple East–West relations from Soviet behaviour in critical regions outside Europe'[10]; i.e. to practice selective *détente*. On other threats (and responses) European opinion tends to divide somewhat along national lines; thus, the French public tended to support both uses of force by their government in Djibouti and in Saudi Arabia and the refusal of that government to join in other proposed uses, such as counter-terrorist operations, while the British government was much more concerned over the Argentinian take-over of the Falkland Islands than over the Communist take-over of Aden. As for the West Germans, Rummel concludes that 'any attempt of a Bonn government to use its armed forces elsewhere [than in Europe] would ask a major change of public attitues'.[11]

Were this all that could be said, the chapter could end here – and so could any possibility of inter-Allied agreement on out-of-area operations. There are, however, other factors which favour if not total agreement at least some degree of support for some uses of force in the Middle East.

One such factor is that, by and large, all the Allies recognise that threats to their interests have in the past arisen in the Middle East and that they can do so again. One such threat is the tilt of the world-wide power balance in favour of the Soviet Union, marked by and accompanied by its acquisition of 'power projection capabilities', by agreements for military cooperation with strategic countries of the region, such as Syria and South Yemen, by Soviet efforts to stimulate anti-Western coalitions and to enhance Soviet influence and by the potential ability of the Soviet Union to choke off the flow of trade between the Middle East and the West.[12] Furthermore, crises like the Israeli-Arab-Palestinian conflict, the overthrow of the Shah, the war between Iraq and Iran and the ethnic-religious group fighting in Lebanon all suggest that conflict may be endemic and that continuing conflict may not only spill over into Europe but may, in and of itself, jeopardise Western interests – as would the loss to hostile internal elements of an important partner or stronghold in the Middle East.[13]

Another factor is a gradual coalescence of views among those in power with respect to responses to threats. This is particularly notable with regard to terrorism where, despite criticism of the US bombing of Libya, the governments of Britain, France, Italy and West Germany, to name just the most prominent, have imposed new constraints on Libyan officials and businessmen on their soil, have intensified police operations against suspected or potential terrorists and have adopted a harder line toward states or organisations associated with the practice of terrorism. Similarly, there is seeming agreement among the principal powers that the collapse of Iraq would be detrimental, if not disastrous, to the West and that measures both to stave off such a happening and to guard against the consequences should it occur are desirable. Moreover, the West Europeans have always been inclined to view seriously overt Soviet military activities in the Third World, such as the invasion of Afghanistan, and hence are closer to seeing eye-to-eye with the United States on the need to deter Soviet aggression than on other measures to counter the spread of Soviet influence in the Middle East.

A third factor favouring agreement on a decision to use force is that the several states, recognising these potential dangers, have tried to devise an approach which would enable members of the Alliance to cope with them. This approach is embodied in the Final Communiqué of the June 1983 meeting of the North Atlantic Council,[14] which provides that individual members in a position to do so 'will endeavor to support, at their request, sovereign nations whose security and independence are threatened' and that those Allies in a position to facilitate the deployment of forces outside the area may do so if they choose. Although this communiqué (which is essentially a paraphrase of the 1967 Harmel Report) is permissive rather than consensual, it does give concerned countries a mandate to bring up problems for discussion, either in NATO councils or in other fora, allows them to negotiate in advance for overflight rights and the use of bases (so that the debacle of October 1973 will not be repeated) and encourages them to seek from other members commitments to offset transfers of armed forces from Europe to the Middle East, as one means of assuring 'sufficient military capability in the Treaty Area to maintain an adequate defense posture'. Whether this represents more than a papering over of differences remains to be seen but at least the Allies have agreed in principle that occasions could arise in which force might have to be used in defence of Western interests.

V AGREEING ON RESPONSES

Agreeing in principle that force could be employed if necessary may, however, be easy compared to agreeing on who should do what – and on what conditions. Here, moreover, a host of other factors enter in, ranging from the availability of troops to equity in sharing costs and running risks. As was noted earlier in this chapter, the numbers of men and weapons in the armed forces of the Allies mean very little when it comes to combat outside Europe. Most members of NATO lack the ability to intervene effectively in the Middle East: their units are neither trained nor equipped for operations there, they are tied down to commitments in Europe, they are handicapped by a lack of air- and sea-lift and they lack the capacity for sustained operations. Of the five countries that could contribute forces, the US has far and away the largest contingent, earmarked for service in the Central Command, though even its ability to deploy and sustain more than one division, with supporting air and naval forces, is doubtful. Next in line are France and Italy (though their capabilities are largely limited to the Mediterranean littoral), Turkey, whose ability to project power diminishes rapidly with the distance from its borders and the United Kingdom, whose navy is aging and whose interventionary unit, the Fifth Infantry Brigade, is part of the BAOR (British Army of the Rhine). Even if constitutional restrictions precluding the dispatch of troops outside the Treaty area could be lifted or circumvented, the Federal Republic has virtually no forces available and the contributions of other countries would probably be limited to tokens, as with the two Dutch mine sweepers sent to help clear the Red Sea in 1984. Of necessity, then, the United States must provide any force above roughly brigade level, or which has to operate against sophisticated air and air defence systems. And it must, moreover, transport, help supply and partially equip any Allied unit sent to the Gulf area.

This is a responsibility which the United States has assumed, though not cheerfully. For one thing, defence planners are concerned about the difficulty of preparing for sizeable operations in the Middle East while still maintaining divisions and air wings in, and/or earmarked for, operations in Europe; indeed, if any intervention in the Middle East involved more than two or three divisions, it would begin to cut significantly into the reinforcements earmarked for Europe and would, long before that, divert munitions, spare parts, transport aircraft and other logistic support likewise intended for Europe. For another, US defence (and budget) planners are concerned about the cost of maintaining the Central Command, especially when Western Europe is not only contributing little or nothing toward meeting threats to the Middle East but is not even meeting its force goals in Europe. For a third, the US does not, for political reasons, wish to be the sole 'guarantor of peace' in the Middle East and would prefer not to be the first; it sees no reason why the French could not again act in support of the Saudi regime, whose security forces they are training and advising, or the British, in the event of need, return to Oman two or three of the battalions employed there during the war in Dhofar Province. Finally, should there ever be a 'show down' with Soviet forces in Syria or elsewhere in the Middle East the United States would much prefer that the West provide a truly Allied contingent, indicative of NATO solidarity.

For their part, the countries of Western Europe that have developed interventionary forces have done so because of perceived need but this does not mean that they would interpret 'need' in the same way as would the Americans (or each other) or that they would reach the same decision as to the response to be made. Even if they did, they might not be able to act on it, either for political reasons or for military and technical ones; as Cremasco points out, the Italian government would have to consider whether to arouse political opposition by engaging draftees on missions not directly related to the defense of national territory or whether to accept the loss of military effectiveness resulting if these draftees were removed and replaced with volunteers from other units.[15] And while any forces dispatched might be willing to cooperate with a US (or other Allied) commander they are unlikely to subordinate themselves to one. Thus, entirely aside from the political decision to intervene, a military decision on how to carry out that intervention successfully might pose even greater problems.

This is particularly true since burdens and responsibilities fall unequally upon members of the Alliance. For example, though a small European power such as Belgium might benefit from actions designed to assure continued access to oil, it could make no force contribution and hence would incur no costs – since the maintenance of armed forces is a national responsibility. The absence of a voice in the conduct of operations might seem a small price to pay, especially since Belgium would retain entry to political decision making through NATO – or at least to 'timely consultation'. Only in the event that the Atlantic Alliance itself became committed – a possibility so remote as to be safely disregarded – or Belgium became involved in helping to 'maintain an adequate defense posture' would the direct financial burden fall on that country. This is precisely the aim of some planners, who would want the Belgians to replace the British Fifth Infantry Brigade should that unit be redeployed to the Middle East or the Federal Republic to mobilise two or three territorial brigades to make up for comparable units withdrawn from, say, the US Vth Corps and would ask both countries to activate additional units should the Warsaw Pact begin to make threatening gestures against any part of the NATO Treaty Area.

Even this, however, would not suffice to equalise the burden. In the past, most operations, such as those of the French and Americans in Vietnam, or the British in the South Atlantic, were clearly undertaken for national aims; hence the direct costs of those operations were expected to be borne by the countries engaged. Theoretically, however, some national operations in the Middle East would be carried out on behalf of NATO, a premise strengthened by the Paris Communiqué and by the many discussions within the North Atlantic Council about contingencies requiring the use of force. Thus at some stage, especially if operations are protracted and costly, the question of burden sharing is bound to arise in even a more exaggerated form than it does today. And, given the failure to resolve that problem when the threat is both obvious and proximate, and NATO is directly seized with the problem, one may imagine the difficulty of arranging for subventions to forces engaged in the Middle East – or even for 'offsetting contributions' which are regarded as equitable by all concerned.

What all this says is that marked differences in military capabilities, as well as in international responsibilities, are going to affect what each country will provide in the event of necessity. Moreover, these differences raise serious questions about the probable effectivenss of any force, especially as it gets much beyond the size of a division, about its military direction and control (especially if it is composed of contingents from more than one nation) and about the costs incurred – and the risks borne – by contributors to this force. All these issues may be impossible to resolve but this is a matter better known in advance than after the decision to employ force has been taken – an outcome to which this book will hopefully contribute.

VII ORGANISING FOR DECISION MAKING

The diversity of interests, perspectives and policies among the members of the Alliance in itself would make it hard to arrive at an agreed decision on how to employ force in the Middle East and how to equalise the resultant costs and risks. The problem of achieving and operationalising consensus is, however, made more difficult by the fact that there is no single forum wherein the issue can be discussed and a plethora of organisations wherein it is discussed – to say nothing of bilateral and *ad hoc* multilateral exchanges. As Edwards notes, much will depend on the type of reaction required.

> A diplomatic démarché may be the most appropriate response, in which case action by the Presidency of EPC might be considered – with or without supplemental unilateral action by one or more of the Twelve. If any economic instruments of policy are envisaged, such as the withholding of aid or the postponement of trade

agreements, then obviously the European Community is involved – with or without any supporting action in terms of declarations by EPC. If any form of military response is envisaged beyond, that is, an interruption in military assistance or the sale of arms, then the Alliance is involved . . . with or without any action being taken elsewhere.[16]

Given the concern shown by members of the Atlantic Alliance about threats to their interests in the Middle East, the potential implications for NATO of both threats and responses and the fact that it is the only umbrella group (other than the United Nations) covering all sixteen present members, NATO would seem a logical locus for decisions on the use of force in the Middle East. This is, indeed, the US position as reflected officially in Secretary of Defense Weinberger's call for contingency planning in September 1982[17] and more emotionally in press commentary to the effect that if the Alliance will not support the United States in coping with Soviet challenges outside Europe then it may not be worth having anyway. To the contrary, European members are by and large resistant to any extension of the Treaty area, some of the smaller powers because they are unwilling to be involved in out-of-area activities and some of the larger ones, like France, because they prefer to maintain their freedom of action.

The best the Alliance has been able to do is to come up with the formula expressed in the Paris Communiqué (and a half-a-dozen earlier ones) on the need for consultation and on the desirability of cooperation – but on a national basis and in support of national initiatives. This does not mean that the situation in the Middle East has been ignored; it has been discussed frequently in NATO fora, at both the Ministerial and Ambassadorial levels. It does not mean that NATO has not assessed threats and studied responses but rather that its attention has been focused primarily on the resultant impact on defensive capabilities if troops should be withdrawn from Europe and on the 'compensation' other member nations should and could provide in this event. As one British defence official put it, the matter is one for 'Allied members of the Alliance acting as Allied members but not the Alliance (and that is the distinction that is drawn)'.[18]

Nor is this necessarily bad: to add disagreements over the Middle East to those now extant over relations with the Soviet Union and the countries of Eastern Europe, over measures to bolster the conventional deterrent and over involvement in SDI might be the last straw for even that sturdy camel, the Atlantic Alliance. Moreover, to link NATO formally with out-of-area activities might be to increase the likelihood that any conflict there would escalate to an East–West confrontation, a possibility all would like to avoid. The issue is not really whether NATO can be extended to cover the Middle East or be saddled with the problems of the area, but what the member states can and will do to cope with these problems; if they are truly determined to cope with them, other means of reaching decisions can be found.

One other organisation that could be used for this purpose is the Western European Union (WEU), which is not only concerned with security but has the added advantage of not being restricted geographically to the NATO Treaty area. However, the first major task of a revitalised WEU – a task which may be a 'hardy perennial' – was that of developing a coordinated position on SDI, not that of assessing threats to security arising in the Middle East. Moreover, neither the United States nor some European countries of great importance, notably Turkey and Spain, are members of WEU; hence its competency to deal with such questions is limited. Finally, it must compete for position not only with NATO (of which it is, by incorporation, a constituent element) but also with the European Community, which includes not only all members of the WEU but most other states of Western Europe.

The European Community has utilised interactions with the Arab states on matters of trade, development, energy supplies, and so on to begin, as far back as 1974, an Euro-Arab dialogue, subsequently followed by less formal ones with individual Arab states and with Israel. But even though the European Community has a role to play in coping with threats to security in the Middle East, both by development and technical assistance programme and, in the event of crisis, by its ability to invoke sanctions (as it did at the time of the clash over the Falklands) its responsibilities are economic. True, the twelve member states have, by the Single European Act of 1986, 'legitimised' European Political Cooperation, which had formerly been an intergovernmental grouping of Ministers and officials, and have established a small secretariat to reinforce and support the Presidency of the Council (a rotating office) in its interactions with the Foreign Ministries of the several states (see Chapter 6, pp. 259–60). However, even though the EPC has devised important procedural improvements, all decisions must be made by consensus, a process which is difficult enough in economic matters but virtually impossible in political ones; the Irish, for example, are determinedly uninvolved in peace-keeping operations other than those sponsored by the UN and the Greeks are pro-Arab. Moreover, while the members of the European Community have grudgingly accepted its extension into the field of international politics, they have not approved its entry into the field of international security; hence it would have great difficulty in dealing with anything smacking of military affairs – a field in which, indeed, neither the staff of the European Community nor that of European Political Cooperation has any competence. And finally, the EPC would have to coordinate its policies and its operations with those of the United States and of other interested non-members such as Turkey.

All this has meant that while various organisations, with different memberships, functions and responsibilities, are seized of parts of the problem no one institution is seized of the whole. In consequence, the bulk of the efforts to cope with (or to prepare to cope with) the out-of-area question are conducted on a bilateral or a multilateral basis – to such a degree that the Directors of four eminent institutes for the study of foreign policy proposed in 1981 that a 'principal nation' take primary responsibility for a particular issue.[19] It has also led to 'shopping around' to find that forum in which a proposal is most likely to receive a favourable hearing, frustration at the division of functions and responsibilities among major organisations, of which we have discussed only a few, and a frequent inability to ascertain what is going on, in as much as the system of exchanges suffers from 'information overload'. That, however, may be both universal and endemic.

VIII CONTROLLING MILITARY OPERATIONS

So far we have dealt mainly with political decision making and not with the command and control of military operations; yet this issue could be crucial. (Whether it is in fact solvable is perhaps another question.) We should begin by noting that the much vaunted principle of 'unity of command' does not hold at the higher levels of the armed forces, as evidenced by the 'Chiefs of Staff' system established, in one form or another, by virtually every member of the Alliance.[20] Nor does it hold in operations marked by great political sensitivity, as would be the case with any intervention in the Middle East. The reasons for this are manifold and overriding:

1. There is no inter-Allied defence organisation with jurisdiction over the area, so that one cannot, as in NATO, establish a command structure in advance.

2. The threats are so varied, and so vague, that it is impossible to agree, as NATO has more or less done, as to military measures which the Allies must take in order to deter, or if necessary to counter, overt aggression; moreover, many of these threats are internal to the states of the area and hence even more difficult to define.

3. The Allies differ, as noted earlier, not only over the courses of action to be taken but over the roles their forces should play and the responsibilities they should assume.

4. Each of the Allies wants to preserve its own freedom of action both with respect to policy and with respect to the use of force in support of that policy; in fact, France is adamant on this point.

5. In any major military operation, the United States will necessarily contribute the bulk of the forces and hence might be reluctant to yield overall command to a national of another country – even though there is a precedent for this, as when a Brazilian general was placed in charge of the OAS 'peace-keeping' exercise in Santo Domingo in 1965.

In the past, therefore, military operations in the Middle East have been conducted as they have been arranged: by cooperative endeavours. For most purposes this would suffice in the future: one scarcely requires a SACGIOA (Supreme Allied Commander, Gulf and Indian Ocean Areas) to schedule the convoying of tankers through the Straits of Hormuz. One may, however, require someone on the spot with the authority to prescribe the conditions under which naval escorts may (or may not) fire on attacking aircraft and patrol boats, to authorise exceptions and to deal with the consequences. And with larger and more complex operations the need for a military command (if not a single commander) may well grow.

By and large, all this means that it is easier for the Allies to agree on small measures than on large, on actions largely risk-free as against those that could develop into a confrontation with the Soviet Union, on operations which have some degree of international sanction as compared to those that do not and on measures which follow a 'clear and present danger' rather than those that attempt to head off threats before they are full blown – findings which should come as no surprise to anyone. Even within this context, however, the degree of consensus will depend on whether the members of the Alliance are asked to participate in a multinational effort which has NATO blessing, to support and facilitate operations by one or more 'principal nations', to acquiesce in such operations without helping the participants or simply to comment on what is being, or what should be, done. As applied to actual situations, these can have very different connotations; thus it may be useful to look both at prior operations and at hypothetical future ones, in order to see how principles apply in practice.

IX LESSONS FROM THE PAST

Protection of Access to Oil

Access to Middle East oil, which is carried not only in Western vessels but in those flying the flags of every maritime country in the world, depends critically on the ability to load that oil without interference and to transport it safely through the Suez Canal or through the Straits of Hormuz. That access can be denied – or at least hampered – in a variety of ways and though local countries can, and should, deal with some of these threats to the transportation of oil, others may be beyond them; in fact on two occasions the Western powers have been forced to intervene, as they may again be.[21]

The first of these occurred after the outbreak of the Iran–Iraq war in 1980 when the United States expressed a fear, presciently as it turned out, that the forces of the two hostile powers might attack each other's oil refineries, terminals and loading facilities and the ships attempting to use the latter. Accordingly, the US government not only pledged that it would do everything necessary to keep open the Straits of Hormuz but called upon its Allies to participate in creating a joint naval task-force whose function that would be.

As Cremasco notes, this 'project was bound to be a non-development':[22] Moscow expressed its opposition to the idea, as did both radical and conservative states of the region; Britain and Italy felt that a formal Western military presence could turn the Gulf crisis into an East–West confrontation, France had already gone on record as favouring demilitarisation of the Indian Ocean area and other members of the Alliance expressed concern lest formation of a Middle East equivalent of the Standing Naval Force Atlantic might give the impression of a surreptitious extension of NATO's area of responsibility. But although they did not formally 'come aboard', both Britain and France dispatched additional warships and support vessels to the Persian-Arabian Gulf and the Indian Ocean to join the augmented US naval forces there, bilateral consultation between the defence staffs of the three countries took place and Italy, though not sending ships outside the Mediterranean, took over some of the responsibilities of the US Sixth Fleet when the latter sent one of its two carrier task-forces to the Indian Ocean. By the end of October 1980 there were present, in or near the Gulf, some sixty US, British and French naval vessels, whose commanders were undoubtedly closely in touch with one another, and even, on the part of Americans and British, held joint exercises.

The second operation, in August–September 1984, involved mine-sweeping in the Gulf of Suez and the Red Sea, where some seventeen merchant ships and oil tankers had been damaged by explosions, suspected to have been caused by mines. In response to a request by the Egyptian government, (and a separate one by Saudi Arabia for help in cleaning the approaches to Jidda and the oil port of Yanbu) mine-sweepers from five Allied countries, plus a separate contingent from the USSR, carried out operations during August–September, destroying a number of suspicious objects, and actually retrieving one recently laid mine.

The operation, though effective militarily, was less successful politically. First of all, the Europeans joined in only after the Egyptians and the Saudis had requested help. Secondly, only the British joined the Americans in forming an Egyptian Coordinating Committee, the French worked separately with Egypt and Saudi Arabia and the Italians with Egypt alone. Third, all of the Western powers (and particularly the Italians) emphasised the technical, non-political nature of the 'support' given to the Government of Egypt, which took the same approach. Thus, the consultations at the decision-making level did not result in a common approach, much less the establishment of anything like a coordinating committee, and the efficacy of the naval operations depended more on informal arrangements among the senior naval officers in the area than on guidance and direction from a single source.

The Multinational Force in Lebanon

Another experience in out-of-area operations from which lessons can be learned is that of the Multinational Force (MNF) in Lebanon, in 1982–3. US, French, Italian and later (a token contingent of) British troops were introduced into Lebanon following the Israeli invasion, withdrawn and then re-introduced after the massacre of Palestinian refugees in the Sabra and Shatila camps. Their mission, worked out in bilateral negotiations but falling within the general parameters earlier set by declarations of the EPC, was that of interposition between feuding factions, hopefully allowing the Lebanese government to re-establish its authority and, with the assistance of the Allies, to re-build its armed forces.[23]

But it quickly became apparent that the facade of agreement covered widely differing national aims. Those of France and Italy were to facilitate negotiations among all interested parties, including the Palestinians and the Syrians, whereas that of the United States was to bring about the withdrawal of Syrian and Israeli forces and to establish a pro-Western Lebanon under the guidance of President Gemayel – to which end it openly favoured and supported the Christian factions. Since the latter were trying to utilise the MNF for their own ends, the almost inevitable result was to antagonise various Moslem elements, who initiated attacks on the MNF, culminating in the car bombings of US and French military billets. The reprisals by elements of these forces achieved nothing save greater hostility; US public opinion (though not French) turned against the operation and the US withdrawal of the Marines was followed shortly by that of the other Allied units.

The difficulties deriving from very different rationales for participating in the MNF (with the British, for example, simply fulfilling a political obligation to demonstrate Allied solidarity) were compounded by a lack of unified direction, political or military. Partly because the French were 'adamantly opposed' to any formal arrangement, coordination of policy was left to a 'loosely structured group' in Washington and to the Ambassadors in Beirut of the four Allied powers. Similarly, coordination of military actions was left to the four senior officers present, which in effect meant that there was none: US shelling of 'rebel' positions in the mountains was initiated independently, as were French aerial attacks on 'terrorists' while the final withdrawal of troops took place with minimal notice – and no cooperation. The result was a débâcle which reflected little credit on any of those involved and which served to erode the public support for peace-keeping operations in Lebanon that had facilitated the initial decision to form the MNF.

The Bombing of Libya

On 14 April 1986 some thirty US fighter-bombers and attack aircraft, supported by some seventy other aircraft and a task-force of seventeen ships and almost 15 000 sailors and airmen, struck at five target areas in Tripoli and Bengazi, damaging Qaddafi's residence, military barracks, communications facilities and, regrettably, some civilian areas.[24] To many Americans these attacks were a logical and necessary response to terrorism, without which such terrorism might have further accelerated and without which US willingness to act in the event of threats might have been further discredited; to many Europeans, it was an unnecessary, ineffective and dangerous action, which could only accelerate 'the spiral of violence'.[25]

There are, as Cordesman indicates, some important military lessons to be learned from the Libyan operation.[26] One is the need to 'set a clear military objective that has a credible chance of altering terrorist behavior'. A second is picking the right level of operations to deter future actions, since too small an attack may be ineffective in convincing those conducting or supporting terrorist activities that they must change their behaviour and too large an operation may create sympathy for the 'victim' and perhaps inspire others to join the ranks of the extremists. A third is the difficulty of conducting 'surgical strikes' against terrorist bases in populated areas. And a fourth is that even a limited strike requires significant forces; in fact, the Libyan operation 'involved more aircraft and combat ships than Britain employed during its entire campaign in the Falklands'. It is, therefore, obvious that such an operation will not be lightly undertaken nor quickly executed once decided upon.

More significant, however, is what was learned about the limits of European support for counter-terrorist operations. Almost without exception, West European governments and peoples deplored the use of force, which was viewed both as an overreaction to terrorism (which had plagued Europeans for years) as unlikely to achieve the desired result of overthrowing or discrediting Qaddafi, and, as Prime Minister Bettino Craxi of Italy phrased it, as running the risk of 'provoking a further explosion of fanaticism, extremism [and] criminal and suicidal actions'.[27] Some officials deplored the lack of consultation by the United States (with General Walters' briefing of Craxi beginning after US planes were already in the air) and the fact that the decision taken by Reagan ran counter to the long-standing views of the leaders of Western Europe on the use of force; only Thatcher justified the legality of the US action, on the ground of the inherent right of self-defence. And though the Foreign Ministers of the European Community, meeting on 15 April under the aegis of the EPC, placed some restrictions on Libyan activities, these extended neither to the closing of all embassies nor to the imposition of economic sanctions.

The Europeans had many reasons for their behaviour: economic interests, the desire to maintain some independence of US policy, distaste for the use of force and concern about its consequences, a belief that the problem of terrorism could be solved only if one dealt with more fundamental issues such as the Palestinian question, and so on. In US eyes, however, these all added up to a rationale for inaction, leading to the conclusion that neither multilateral nor bilateral consultations were (or were likely to be) productive and that the United States would have to 'go it alone'. And given that the successful use of any other instrument of policy depended on cooperation, this almost compelled a resort to the use of force.

Interpretations

Although 'three swallows do not a summer make', these experiences bear out our earlier generalisations that the European members of the Alliance were more inclined than the United States to uphold the rights and the positions of the Palestinians and to attribute terrorist attacks to failure to resolve the Arab-Israeli dispute as much as to anti-Western attitudes *per se*. They were also more involved in, and dependent on, economic interactions with the countries of the Middle East (and North Africa) and hence more reluctant to impose sanctions or to endorse other measures that could jeopardise trade. For a variety of reasons, they were dubious about the effectiveness of the military instrument and more inclined than the United States to stress its adverse implications for relations with the Arab World, its impact on *détente* and the possibility that its utilisation could lead to a confrontation with the USSR. And they were very concerned lest they be too closely associated with US policies, even in those instances when they approved of them, lest this both damage their relations with the Arab world and antagonise elements of their own people.

Even though there were nuances in these positions, the overall differences between Americans and Europeans (and, to a lesser extent, among Europeans) meant that organisations such as the

European Community, the Western European Union and even NATO could not be utilised to formulate and coordinate policy; at best, issues were threshed out in *ad hoc* groups, and more usually in a series of bilateral meetings, whose participants attempted to formulate a common policy. Even in those cases where they succeeded in doing this, the Allies refused to set up any 'unified commands' in the Middle East, partly because of the difficulty of working out the arrangements and partly because each nation wished to maintain its freedom of action; in consequence, military operations were not always well coordinated. Fortunately, the forces involved were small and their employment limited so that this was not disabling, as it could have been under different circumstances.

On the positive side, it should be noted that European members of the Alliance did respond to some US initiatives, including three of the four we have examined which called for the use of force in the Middle East, and a fifth which occurred subsequently: the protection of shipping in the Gulf. Moreover, though most of the Allies disassociated themselves from the unilateral US action against Libya, some of them termed it a justifiable response to state-sponsored terrorism, and almost all joined in reducing the number of Libyan diplomats and officials on their territories, in imposing restrictions on travel and in taking other measures designed to inhibit terrorist activities. Thus in some ways and to some extent Americans and Europeans do agree on 'out-of-area' operations.

X APPLICATIONS TO THE FUTURE

How far this agreement will extend is, of course, conjectural; neverthless it seemed useful to us to examine several future 'contingencies' that could lead to the use of force by one or more of the Western powers, contingencies such as an internal upheaval in Saudi Arabia, an undesirable outcome to the Iran–Iraq war and an Israeli–Syrian clash leading to a superpower confrontation. As may be seen immediately, these contingencies have been selected as prototypical; they have also been chosen on the basis of likelihood and of potential consequences – with likelihood, though admittedly subjective, a determining factor.[28] In each case, we have attempted to define a threat that could adversely affect Western interests and to outline the kinds of military rejoinders that might be considered and the factors influencing a decision to utilise force. Our aim is not to predict outcomes, which would require a prescience we do not command, but to help policy makers understand the nature of the problems with which they may some day be confronted.

Coups and Counter Coups: The Case of Saudi Arabia

As noted in the previous section, the process of change has affected the stability of all the Arab regimes in the Middle East, traditional or national, and will undoubtedly continue to do so. Responses (barring the unlikely one of turning over power to radical religious elements, which is analogous to committing suicide in order to avoid being murdered) are also likely to follow prior patterns: building a network of family, tribal, ethnic and political loyalties; creating a competent technocratic elite; improving – and diversifying – internal security forces and domestic intelligence nets; attempting to create national loyalties that can override local ones and endeavouring to provide better material benefits to the people. In addition, some regimes, with President Saddam Hossein's unwise incursion into Iran in mind, will also pursue prudent foreign policies, seek to maintain good relations with such of their neighbouring states as they can and perhaps keep a foot in the camps of both East and West. Nevertheless, even the most stable and skillful of regimes can be vulnerable to the assassination of a leader on whom national unity depends, to a coup by ambitious elements of the armed services and/or to pressures by nationalist or religious groups.

Although both threat and response are generalised, these patterns apply specifically to Saudi Arabia. Furthermore, as Cottam has noted,[29] within Saudi Arabia there is both a strong receptivity to revolutionary leadership and a powerful individual, Prince Abdullah, who might be able to play that role. A coup led by him, or by any other change-oriented individual, could, if successful, result in a marked alteration in Saudi foreign policy, a shift in regional alliances and power balances and a significant erosion of US prestige and influence in the region; indeed, a successful coup, following on the heels of the earlier overthrow of the Shah, would deal a hammer blow to the United States. And a coup which only partially succeeded could lead both to calls for assistance from 'loyal' elements and to a very critical decision for the United States and its allies: whether – and if so how – to respond to such calls.

As Cordesman points out,[30] a military response by battalion-size British and French forces or, if necessary, by a US airborne brigade or Marine Amphibious Brigade would certainly be feasible and probably all that would be necessary – *if* the 'legitimate' regime retained some degree of popular support and the allegiance of key elements of the military and internal security forces, notably the Royal Saudi Air Force. If not, or if Western intervention should polarise publics, elites and members of the armed services, the consequence could be Western involvement in a civil war, with the 'rebels' obtaining help not only from radical regimes near by but conceivably from the Soviet Union. And though the United States could, within six weeks, bring to bear two or three heavily armed divisions, not even a force of this size could, as Cordesman comments, 'save an unpopular Saudi regime from the Saudi people'.[31]

Given that it has the ability, *will* the United States respond to a call for help from a strife-torn Saudi Arabia? In favour of 'doing something', even if that involved the dispatch of Marines to bolster the 'loyal' forces, are the ties between the two countries, the extent to which the US relies on 'moderate' Arab states in pursuing its Middle East policy, the untoward consequences of 'losing' Saudi Arabia, and the 'Reagan Corollary' to the Carter doctrine, which pledged that the United States would help mainain the Saudi regime. Against it would be uncertainty as to the outcome, the probability of intense reactions from other states of the region, ranging from a new oil embargo through intensified terrorist attacks to thinly disguised assistance, perhaps with covert Soviet support.

Against it also would be opposition of the European members of the Alliance to any sizeable Western intervention; as Rummel points out, European governments are more likely to underwrite paramilitary operations (such as the help France gave in recapturing the Great Mosque in Mecca in 1979) than military ones and European publics are more likely to acquiesce in them,[32] perhaps because of their small-scale and clandestine nature. Whatever importance the European allies attach to trade with Saudi Arabia, to the preservation of their influence there or to stability in the Gulf they also have other interests, such as avoiding any backlash from the Arab world, and other concerns, such as the feasibility of sweeping back a revolutionary sea with a military broom.

On balance, then, the decision is not likely to hinge on the availability of forces (which are at least potentially adequate to carry out the assigned tasks) but on the willingness of the West to run the risks and pay the costs of employing those forces. On this there will be differences within, as well as among, governments, with the ultimate determinant probably being the base of support of the 'revolutionary' elements. If these are made up largely of aggrieved ministers or dissatisfied officers, intervention is more likely to meet Rummel's criteria that it be 'short, selective and successful', and hence to be approved, but if the opposition is widespread, and includes religious elements such as the Shia in the Eastern Provinces, enthusiasm is likely to be lacking. Under these circumstances, it might well be counter-productive to raise the issue of intervention in multinational fora, though obviously intensive bilateral exchanges should precede any decision and continue throughout the operation. And probably the best the United States could hope for, should it decide to intervene, would be authority to use air bases and staging facilities in Europe (though perhaps not those on the territories of Greece, Spain and Turkey) and a degree of informal cooperation from the French mission engaged in training the Saudi Armoured Force – if indeed the latter had not already joined the rebels.

Local Conflicts: The Iran–Iraq War

Although the Middle East has witnessed a number of threats and demonstrations, such as those by Syria against Jordan during the 'Black September' of 1970, and some interventions in internal struggles, such as those by Egypt and Saudi Arabia in Yemen in the 1960s, there have been relatively few overt conflicts not connected with the Arab-Israeli war. Of these, the most serious is the war between Iran and Iraq, now in its seventh year. It is serious in part because of its magnitude (for which see Table 3.15, Chapter 3), its duration and its cost – in part because neither Arab efforts to bring it to an end nor those of other states have been effective, and in part because in some sense it is a struggle between 'radical Islam' (admittedly with strong overtones of Iranian nationalism) and the 'new nationalism' of Iraq. It is this latter aspect which makes the prospect of an Iranian victory so dangerous to Western interests: not only would this open many new options to the Iranian leadership but it would, as Cottam phrases it, encourage the internal forces of resurgent Islam in every Arab state.[33]

The danger is not that Iran will win a clear-cut victory but rather that continuing pressures and intermittent successes could lead to the collapse of the Iraqi Army, many of whose soldiers come from a Shia community basically sympathetic with the Islamic fundamentalists in power in Iran. So far, the Iraqi regime has been sustained by infusions of resources from oil-producing Arab states, which have enabled it not only to finance the war but to met the material needs of its own populace, by an effective system of internal control which ruthlessly employs terror when necessary and by the fear among secular elements of the consequences of change. These latter two supports are, however, weak reeds on which to lean, even in a country which makes its boats from reeds.

If an Iraqi collapse occurs, there would be relatively little the United States or others among the Western powers could do about it, other than to provide fresh assurances (and perhaps tangible evidences of support) to states like Kuwait, which could be faced with new dangers from a militant Iraqi government backed by an even more militant Iranian one. The question is what the Allies could – and would – do prior to such a collapse if the latter seemed a 'clear and imminent danger'.

One option would, of course, be to employ Western military forces (which in practice would mean those of the United States) to bolster Iraq, either directly (as by the dispatch of an airborne brigade to a threatened point) or indirectly, as by bombing Iranian troop concentrations, supply points and lines of communication. Entirely aside from the political consequences of such actions (which would undoubtedly be dire) they would be extremely difficult and perhaps ineffective militarily. For one thing, bombing attacks would require either that the US carrier task-force in the Indian Ocean expose itself to possible counter strikes by the (admittedly weak) Iranian air force or that land-based aircraft operate from Egyptian, Saudi or Turkish air fields, which might or might not be available. For another, given the size of the forces engaged on both sides, it is unlikely that 5–6000 lightly-armed men would make a significant difference to Iraqi capabilities – if, indeed, the appearance of Western forces did not lead to a change of heart (and allegiance) on the part of many Iraqi soldiers. For a third, the maintenance of US and/or Allied forces would necessitate not only relatively safe passage for transport aircraft but, if heavy equipment were required or substantial augmentation were needed, the use of sea lines of communication, either through the theoretically internationalised Suez Canal and across Jordan or through the Persian-Arabian Gulf, in the teeth of Iranian interdiction.

At the other end of the spectrum the West (especially France, which is a major supplier of Iraq) could certainly step up the flow of arms; delivery, however, is a slow process and effective absorption an even slower one. Moreover, as Cordesman points out, 'massive

Western and Soviet arms transfers do not produce sudden shifts in Iraqi military capabilities'.[34] Thus, exercising this option only when collapse seems imminent may be too late as well as too little.

This still leaves open the possibility of arranging for support by indigenous forces; in fact, a Jordanian brigade has been engaged on the side of Iraq and some elements of the Saudi army have at least been present in that country. However, the Saudi armed forces are too small, too poorly trained and too closely tied to their own territory to provide meaningful support. The Jordanian Army is larger, better equipped and more effective but it is questionable whether King Hossein could, or would, supply more than one division, especially since US efforts to arm and equip a Jordanian 'strike force' foundered on the rocks of Congressional opposition. As for Egyptian forces, they too are unlikely to be available in quantity and are even more remote from the battle area than those of Jordan and Saudi Arabia. While a force of two or three divisions from sympathetic Arab states might bolster Iraqi morale, and conceivably could contain any local Iranian attacks, it is questionable whether it would suffice to turn the tide of war; moreover, these Arab states would encounter political difficulties in organising what would in effect be a Western backed interventionary force.

There certainly are other possibilities, ranging from the stimulation and support of Turkish intervention to the establishment of a blockade of Iran but all present significant military difficulties, to say nothing of political and legal ones. Hence, even if one considers only the military factor, one inescapably concludes that whatever is done to safeguard Iraq from collapse should be done *before* that collapse is near – and by means which, though they may employ the military instrument, do not directly involve Western military forces in combat operations.

The reception accorded any measure to support Iraq will vary according to its type and scale of the intervention. Accelerated or expanded shipments of arms to the Iraqis, Jordanians and, should they need them, Kuwaitis, would undoubtedly be regarded by most members of the Alliance as a hedge against undesirable outcomes; in fact one could expect the French, and perhaps the British and the West Germans, to take part in such arms transfers. Actually equipping and maintaing a Jordanian 'strike force' or its Egyptian counterpart to fight alongside Iraqi soldiers is a very different matter; it is not only more likely to stir up Syrian opposition and widespread protests in the Arab world but would constitute an implicit commitment not only to Iraq but to those countries that provided the forces. If these should succeed in stemming the tide, well and good, but if they were caught up in a flood of onrushing Iranian revolutionaries, or if Iran exploited any success by undertaking or stimulating an assault on Jordan, the Western Allies would have no choice save to intervene militarily in defence of their surrogates, a prospect which might cause them to reject in advance any course of action likely to lead to such an outcome.

Similarly, the dispatch of, say, a UK infantry brigade to patrol Kuwaiti borders or a wing of US fighter planes to buttress Saudi Arabian air defences could also be viewed in the West (and perhaps in some areas of the Middle East) as a prudent safeguard. Actually deploying troops to Iraq, much less initiating air attacks on Iranian troops and bases, would be regarded much less favourably. To much of the Arab world this would smack all too loudly of 'great power imperialism' and their views would influence the judgements of some countries in Western Europe. More largely, the risk that any such action could precipitate indiscriminate terrorist operations against Westerners and perhaps even countervailing military measures (such as Syrian mobilisation on its frontier with Iraq) could induce a majority of members of the Alliance to oppose these measures. Furthermore, these also could fail, with even more dire consequences than the support of Jordanian and/or Egyptian troops.

If the latter two courses of action were contemplated, consultation would be unlikely to lead to consensus; whether an attempt is made to introduce the matter in NATO or in the European Political Cooperation depends on whether one wishes to cool down feverish impulses, as in Benjamin Franklin's analogy of pouring tea from cup to saucer and back again. Since, moreover, no country save the United States could undertake a 'rescue operation' of the type and scale indicated, the question of command and control becomes moot: if General Crist of the Central Command is not in charge it will only be because another American general or admiral is.

Obviously, the costs and the potential consequences of military intervention aimed at bolstering a tottering Iraq suggest that one employ measures other than the use of force and do so now, rather than when Iraq is on the verge of collapse. To some extent, the Allies have done this, with France, the Federal Republic and Spain all selling to Iraq substantial quantities of arms[35] and the United States providing intelligence useful in organising Iraqi bombing of Iranian oil terminals, refineries and other industrial facilities.[36] However, both the desire to see the war end in a negotiated peace, rather than a victory for either party, and the pursuit of other interests (such as the freeing of hostages) have induced some of the Allies to cultivate Iranian friendship; indeed, there is more than a suspicion that not only Western powers but 'moderate' Arab states such as Saudi Arabia and Kuwait have sought to 'hedge their bets' by cutting deals with Iran rather than by supporting only Iraq. Thus, one possible result of continued Iranian success in its war with Iraq might be an attempt at accommodation with the 'victor' rather than strenuous efforts to preclude that victory – a result which would militate against the kinds of military responses described earlier.

An Israeli–Syrian Clash and Superpower Confrontation

By common agreement, the greatest danger to Western interests would arise from a superpower confrontation in the Middle East. Such a confrontation would not only jeopardise peace and stability in that region but would have an impact on the cohesion and security of the Atlantic Alliance. While the US would obviously have to provide the prerequisite military force, actual or latent, Canada and the European allies would be immediately confronted with decisions on whether to support US actions and on the extent to which they should share the resultant burden, either by making available military forces or by taking offsetting measures (such as those envisaged in the US–West German Host Nation Support Agreement), the means that should be employed to maintain the deterrent in Europe, especially if the United States withdrew from there any combat or combat support units, and so on. Failure to render tangible, if limited, assistance could exacerbate US–West European relations but moves to do so would not only cause fissures within the Alliance (with Spain and Greece, for example, likely to oppose them) but could undermine *détente*, to the continuation of which the Federal Republic of Germany, at least, attaches great importance. More importantly, they could perhaps expose Western Europe to Soviet counter-pressures, including the threat of force, if not its use.

Obviously such consequences are so dire that everyone hopes a confrontation will never eventuate. There has, however, been at least one such confrontation in the past, at the time of the Yom Kippur War in 1973, and there could have been another in 1982 had the Soviet Union moved to support Syrian and PLO units under attack by the Israelis. A question for the future is whether the USSR would again be so forebearing if Israel attacked air bases deep within Syria (some of which are defended by Soviet-manned surface-to-air missiles), again tried to destroy that part of the Syrian Army based in Lebanon, as seemed possible for a few days in 1982, or attempted to 'cut the Syrian knot' by initiating a thrust at Damascus, which lies only some thirty miles from the Golan Heights. Though there is no indication that Israel is seriously contemplating such moves, miscalculations and misunderstandings, such as seemed possible in early 1986, could again lead Israel or Syria to attack the other. In such a case, as Cottam indicates,[37] the Soviets would almost have to give Syria the support needed to stave off another catastrophic defeat while the United States could neither accept an Israeli defeat nor stand idly by while Soviet tanks duelled with Israeli armour on the plains of Syria.

If any Soviet-American confrontation followed the pattern of 1973, when the Soviet Union communicated intent by internal troop movements and the United States showed determination by placing its strategic nuclear forces on first-stage alert, the implications would be serious but not demanding militarily. If, however, the United States had to dispatch troops to bolster Israeli units engaged with Soviet mechanised forces in Syria, or to check the pursuit of a defeated Israeli army, the matter would be entirely different: this would require sizeable ground, air and naval air forces. The latter would be available from the Sixth Fleet if the navy were prepared to risk it in the Eastern Mediterranean but the former would require redeployments from Western Europe, the United States or both. And though the Central Command is, as shown on Table 3.3 of Chapter 3, composed primarily of combat and combat support elements based in the United States, this is not true of logistic support, much of which would have to be provided by the Seventh Army in Europe. Moreover, most of the army and air force units assigned to Central Command are earmarked for redeployment to Europe in the event of war, so that employing them in the Middle East would diminish the ability to carry out the (already overly ambitious) build-up of US forces scheduled to take place in the first ten days of mobilisation. Thus, a confrontation would pose military, as well as political, problems for all the Allies.

Both for this reason and because the West Europeans are not as committed as the United States to the support of Israel, one could expect major opposition to US involvement: in NATO, in the EPC and nationally, at government levels and by publics. Only if the

Soviets themselves followed a defeated Israeli Army across the frontier, or precipitated combat with US units in the area, would such a feeling be likely to change and even then the Allies are more likely to provide offsets in Europe and/or to make available transfer facilities than to engage, say, the Italian navy alongside the US Sixth Fleet. In sum, this is both the most serious incident of those described and the one which could place the United States at greatest odds with its Allies, even with such a customarily staunch supporter as Great Britain.

Implications for the Future

Not entirely by chance, the three 'contingencies' analysed are more demanding than the four types of out-of-area operations examined earlier. This is not due primarily to the anticipated force requirements; even in the event of a superpower confrontation in the Levant, the Soviet forces now deployed or readily introduced into Syria could be matched by US troops available – to say nothing of the contingents at the disposal of Allies such as France, Italy and Turkey. (Moreover, in this as in other instances the existence of the strategic deterrent is likely to weigh more heavily in political calculations than are marginal military advantages on the ground.) Militarily, problems are more likely to derive from the nature of the mission (such as involvement in civil war or interposition between hostile armies) and from the associated needs for rapid deployment and sustained support than from the relative size of friendly and hostile forces or the comparative states of readiness of US and Soviet reserve divisions.

Even if this were not the case, the military issues pale before the political ones, which include reconciling interests that are not always congruent, overcoming differences with respect to the efficacy (and the risks) of force and altering both European beliefs that Americans are likely to act too rashly and US judgements that Europeans will not act at all. Obviously, success in achieving this (or even in avoiding obvious failure) will require extensive consultation, before as well as during any 'contingency'. It will also require the choice of fora which do not, by their very nature, 'load the dice' against one particular member of the Alliance, as could insistence on utilising the European Political Cooperation or the North Atlantic Council.

Above all, it will require action now: the Allies cannot pursue independent (and sometimes irreconcilable) policies in time of peace and expect to mesh these in time of crisis. Nor can they assume that the military alone can carry the burden of upholding western interests in the Middle East: avoiding a superpower confrontation may depend more on the restraint the US and the USSR exercise over their respective allies than on the balance of US and Soviet forces in the area or the volume of arms transfers to client states. And while no diplomat relishes upsetting current relations for the sake of avoiding a future unpleasantness which may never occur, it is not too early to start the difficult task of persuading one's counterparts in other countries (and one's superiors) that adjustments in policy may be a necessary means to this end.

XI 'TO DO OR NOT TO DO . . .'

In some sense the Atlantic Alliance is in a 'Catch 22' situation. On the one hand, undeniable threats to its interests can arise 'out-of-area' and especially in the Middle East, threats which, if not blunted, could jeopardise the economic well-being of its members, their political influence and conceivably their strategic position in an important area of the world. On the other hand, responses to those threats carry with them their own costs and risks which, to some members, under some circumstances, may outweigh the dangers arising from developments in the Middle East. The problem, as in most human affairs, is where to strike the balance between threat and response, a task which is most difficult when, as former Secretary of State Dean Rusk once said about problems reaching his desk, that balance is usually 51–49. The best we can do here is to cast some of the weights to be utilised in that balance.

One such weight is the reactions of actors in the Middle East, national and non-national. If the judgement is that some states may welcome uses of force – and even request them – or will silently approve even where they have not, this will be a positive factor. If, on the contrary, Western intervention is likely to arouse near-universal opposition, or to stimulate intensified terrorist operations and other forms of resistance on the part of particular countries, many in Western Europe will deem the political game not worth the military candle. And many, in the United States as well as in Western Europe, will ask what the intervenors propose to do politically and economically to capitalise on the use of force, which might on occasion be necessary but will almost never be sufficient.

A second influence will be the reactions of the Soviet Union, both in the area and out of it. If these are deemed likely to take the traditional – and prudent – form of transferring arms, dispatching military advisors and training teams, etc. then concern may be mitigated. If, however, the action proposed could involve one of the Allies in a major clash with Soviet forces in the region, or could trigger a Soviet counter-action, such as an incursion into Iran, then fears – and hesitancy – would increase. And if the judgement were that the Soviet Union might exert counterpressures against vulnerable points in Europe, then hesitancy could well become opposition.

It is for this reason that many in the Alliance place so much stress on maintaining its capabilities in Europe. Admittedly, most uses of force in the Middle East would have such a small impact on overall force postures that they could pass virtually unnoticed. Even the deployment from the United States of a fighter-bomber wing, a Marine Amphibious Brigade or the 82nd Airborne Division would not significantly affect the forces available for European missions, though the latter might delay further the time when the United States would have ten divisions on the central front. If, however, interventionary forces grow beyond that level and/or engage in sustained combat that consumes reserves of ammunition, spare parts and weapons then West Europeans will worry both about the implications for the military balance and about the requirement to 'compensate' for such withdrawals.

A final concern, with psychological as well as political implications, is the effect on the cohesion of the Alliance, Both Americans and West Europeans believe that the others are unappreciative of their contributions to the common defence and their sacrifices in support of the Alliance. Both Americans and Europeans see their Allies as economic competitors, if not granters of hidden subsidies and dumpers of underpriced goods in international markets. Some Americans see the Atlantic Alliance as irrelevant to (if not detrimental to) coping with the global problems that have assumed such great importance and some Europeans see the United States as determined to use the Alliance as a source of support for policies on which they do not agree, as in Central America. Whether these differences affect the cohesion of the Alliance depends largely on whether the member nations allow them to do so, with restraint and deference to the opinion of others as two means to that desired end.

XII WHAT TO DO?

Making suggestions is even more difficult than carrying out analyses, in part because their utility is dependent not only upon the accuracy of the assessment and the validity of judgements but because they imply that one can estimate correctly the future behaviours of a multiplicity of actors pursuing policies upon which they not yet decided in an unknown – and changing – environment. Obviously this is not possible, which is why the authors are so cautious in putting forward policy suggestions. Since, however, that is part of the desired outcome, here they are.

The first suggestion is that analysts, planners and policy makers take a longer-term perspective concerning instability in the Middle East. With the possible exception of a few decades under the Caliphate, turmoil has continued for centuries; even as the Turkish Sultan Soloman the Magnificent was readying an expedition to seize Cyprus from the Knights of Jerusalem he had to cope with a revolt in the Hejaz that jeopardised both the trade and the revenues of the Ottoman Empire. In more modern times we have witnessed the overthrow of Nuri Said in Baghdad, which undermined the Western position in the area, and the shift of Egypt from the Soviet to the American camp, which dealt the USSR a hard blow. While it is possible to conceive of events which could irretrievably damage Western interests in the Middle East, as could the coming to power throughout the area of radical Islam, many happenings are neither so dire nor so (temporarily) irreversible, as a look at Table 3.13, Chapter 3 will show. Furthermore, overestimating the significance of happenings causes over-reaction, such as rushing 300 million dollars worth of US weapons to North Yemen after the assassination of its premier some years ago.

A second suggestion is that the same categories of people look harder at both the requirements for forces in the Middle East and their availability. Although there are certainly some developments, several of which we have discussed, that could require expeditions of division size or larger, the bulk of the potential requirements would fall at or below brigade level. (To paraphrase an old German saying, 'The demanding is not likely and the likely is not demanding.') More importantly, any Western military responses would *have* to be limited to roughly division level; as Cordesman points out, even the United States would find it difficult to go above this range and still more difficult to do so quickly.[38] And though additional units are, or can be made, available, transport will remain a bottleneck for the foreseeable future.

The third suggestion is that one apply to the provision of forces for out-of-area operations the Marxist doctrine of 'From each according to his ability. . .' At the moment, the bulk of the capabilities for intervention are those which the United States has slowly and painfully built up under the aegis of the Central Command; none of the other major powers could make available more than a brigade or two and the Federal Republic of Germany has no rapid deployment force at all. While the build-up of larger and more quickly deployable forces of intervention is certainly possible this would be both costly, and in some cases, such as that of West Germany, politically difficult. Furthermore, there is a real question whether such a build-up might not divert resources from the primary mission of defending Europe. There are other ways in which those not possessing forces of their own can contribute, as by developing units to replace any transferred from Europe in time of crisis, by allocating additional monies to the NATO Infra-structure Program or even by increasing, to agreed levels and for defined purposes, arms transfers and/or economic and technical assistance to countries of the Middle East. (If participation by others in out-of-area operations is necessary, either to share the risk or to show solidarity, one can always revert to Marshall Joffre's suggestion in 1914 that he be given one British soldier, to be killed in the afternoon of the first day of battle!)

The fourth suggestion is to give up any idea of finding or creating a multinational decision-making organisation with responsibility for out-of-area matters; as Edwards has made painfully clear, neither one of these seems feasible. Instead, it is proposed that the Allies accept the 'principal nation' concept, under which countries with real interests and valid concerns assumed responsibility for employing force. This does not mean that they need do so on their own, as both the Paris Communiqué and the prior suggestion argues for their receiving 'compensation'. Nor does it mean that they should initiate actions without consulting with, and considering the inputs from, other states; as Cardinal Mazarin, Prime Minister of France at the time of Louis XIV, said on a somewhat different occasion, 'Above all, not too much zeal'. In this context there are three fairly simple procedural steps which might be taken:

1. One would be to hold regular (as well as emergency) meetings of the self-designated 'principal nations', whose number and

composition would vary with circumstances. At these meetings, emerging problems and new opportunities could be identified and possible responses discussed, without commitment to their acceptance but with some effort to reach agreement on the measures to be taken.

2. Another would be to apply universally within the Alliance, and not just within the European Political Cooperation, something like the Gymnich formula, whereby officials of other countries are informed in advance of these and other meetings, given an opportunity to make known their views and briefed on the results of the deliberation.

3. Given that military operations out-of-area may well create crises where none existed before, a third would be to consider seriously how to link together the national crisis centres now extant – beginning with the three in the United States!

Another suggestion is that we recognise the limits to improvisation in the planning and conduct of military operations and consider how these might be improved, without either prejudging the decisions to be taken or impinging on the freedom of action of any member of the Alliance. Means to this end might include:

1. Setting up, on a voluntary basis, an international group for contingency planning, perhaps drawn from the staffs of the national Rapid Deployment Forces and perhaps based in one of the several Defense Colleges, national or international.

2. Organising, on occasion, low-level combined exercises in the Middle East, perhaps with participation by units normally assigned to, or just rotated from, NATO elements such as the Allied Command Europe or the Standing Naval force, Atlantic.

3. Reporting to the 'principal nations' the results of these exercises and any contingency plans developed, and sharing these findings with corresponding elements in NATO.

A final suggestion is that the Allies recognise that force is not in all instances the best instrument of policy; security may be more readily enhanced by political and economic measures, carried out over time, than by the intermittent application of military power, or even its continuing presence in the region. Granted, diplomatic initiatives may not resolve disputes and programmes for economic development may not alleviate unrest, but neither may force. Granted, taking such initatives or formulating such programmes may be difficult but so will be reaching agreement on the application of the military instrument. Our purpose here is to call attention to the need to ready this instrument, not to argue that force alone is sufficient to achieve the goals of the Atlantic Alliance in the Middle East. If we have succeeded in the former task, perhaps others can take up the more difficult one of devising the non-military measures that are essential to this larger end.

Notes

1. Maurizio Cremasco, 'Do-It-Yourself: National Positions on the Out-of-Area Question', Chapter 4, p. 149.
2. Richard W. Cottam, 'Levels of Conflict in the Middle East', Chapter 2, pp. 17–18.
3. Ibid., pp. 27–8.
4. Anthony H. Cordesman, *The Gulf and the Search for Strategic Stability* (Boulder, Colo: Westview Press 1984), tables 13, 17, p. 529; *The Military Balance, 1985–1986* (London: The International Institute for Strategic Studies, 1985), p. 186.
5. Anthony H. Cordesman, 'The Uses of Force in the Middle East', Chapter 3, p. 139.
6. Ibid., p. 77.
7. Reinhardt Rummel, Chapter 5, p. 205.
8. Cremasco, Chapter 4, pp. 168–9.
9. Rummel, Chapter 5, p. 199.
10. Ibid., p. 201.
11. Ibid., p. 193.
12. Ibid., pp. 200–1.
13. Ibid., p. 202. See also Cremasco, Chapter 4, pp. 148–9.
14. Ibid., pp. 148–9. See also Geoffrey Edwards, 'Multilateral Coordination of Out-of-Area Activities', Chapter 6, pp. 248–9 and 252.
15. Cremasco, Chapter 4, pp. 163–5.
16. Edwards, Chapter 6, p. 229.
17. *The Times* (London), 9 September 1982, quoted in ibid., p. 247.
18. Quoted in ibid., p. 248.
19. Karl Kaiser, Winston Lord, Thierry de Montbrial and David Watt, *Western Security: What Has Changed, What Should Be Done?* (London: Royal Institute of International Affairs, 1981).
20. In the Second World War for example, the United States divided the Pacific Ocean basin into two theatres, one controlled by Admiral Nimitz, operating out of Hawaii, and the other by General MacArthur, operating out of Brisbane, Australia. Moreover, the latter theatre was further subdivided so that Admiral Halsey's fleet, and consequently operations on Guadalcanal, did not initially fall under MacArthur's command. Only after the army had taken over from the marines, and Halsey's ships had

moved away, did the South-west Pacific Theatre of Operations assume responsibility for the Solomon Islands.

21. Since this was written, there has been another instance of intervention, with Britain, France and the United States all escorting ships of their own flags – including, in the case of the United States, a number transferred from Kuwait – through the Persian-Arabian Gulf and sweeping mines both from entrances to ports and from ship channels.
22. Cremasco, Chapter 4, p. 172.
23. Ibid., p. 174.
24. For this and many of the details that follow, see Cordesman, Chapter 3, pp. 128ff.
25. Cremasco, Chapter 4, p. 182.
26. Cordesman, Chapter 3, pp. 131ff.
27. Quoted in Cremasco, Chapter 4, p. 184.
28. For example, 'major Soviet intervention in, or invasion of, Iran. . .', though certainly of enormous significance, and militarily demanding in the highest degree, was deemed very improbable. Moreover, it was, for these very reasons, judged likely to solidify Western policies and we felt that we could learn from an analysis of this situation little that would be relevant to lesser operations.
29. Cottam, Chapter 2, p. 67.
30. Cordesman, Chapter 3, pp. 125–6. See also Sherwood S. Cardin, *US Military Power and Rapid Deployment Requirements in the 1980s* (Boulder, Colo: Westview Press, 1983), pp. 60–1, where he estimates that two battalions of marines and a battalion from the 82nd Airborne Division could be deployed to Saudi Arabia within 36–48 hours and a full brigade of the 82nd within four days: if necessary, these could be supported by F-4 and F-5 fighter and F-111 strike squadrons operating from Turkish air bases or, should the fields be secure, from within Saudi Arabia itself.
31. Ibid., pp. 50–1.
32. Rummel, Chapter 5, pp. 208, 220.
33. Cottam, Chapter 2, p. 63.
34. Cordesman, Chapter 3, p. 124.
35. Stockholm International Peace Research Institute, *World Armaments and Disarmament, SIPRI Yearbook 1985*, London and Philadelphia: Taylor and Francis, 1985, appendix IIB, p. 400.
36. *The New York Times*, 15 December 1986, p. 1.
37. Cottam, Chapter 2, pp. 69–70. See also Cordesman, Chapter 3, pp. 119–21.
38. Ibid., p. 117.

Index